SURREY

The King's England

A New Domesday Book of 10,000 Towns
and Villages

Edited by Arthur Mee

Complete in 41 Volumes

Enchanted Land (Introductory volume)

*Bedfordshire and
   Huntingdonshire
Berkshire
Buckinghamshire
Cambridgeshire
Cheshire
Cornwall
Derbyshire
Devon
Dorset
Durham
Essex
Gloucestershire
Hampshire with the
   Isle of Wight
Herefordshire
Hertfordshire
Kent
Lake Counties
Lancashire
Leicestershire and Rutland*

*Lincolnshire
London
Middlesex
Monmouthshire
Norfolk
Northamptonshire
Northumberland
Nottinghamshire
Oxfordshire
Shropshire
Somerset
Staffordshire
Suffolk
Surrey
Sussex
Warwickshire
Wiltshire
Worcestershire
Yorkshire – East Riding
Yorkshire – North Riding
Yorkshire – West Riding*

NOTHING like these books has ever been presented to the English people. Every place has been visited. The Compilers have travelled half-a-million miles and have prepared a unique picture of our countryside as it has come down through the ages, a census of all that is enduring and worthy of record.

Guildford's Famous Guildhall
HEART OF THE CAPITAL OF SURREY

THE KING'S ENGLAND

SURREY
London's Southern Neighbour

EDITED BY
ARTHUR MEE

With Introduction by
DR GEORGE C. WILLIAMSON

With 164 Places
and 181 Pictures

THE KING'S ENGLAND PRESS
2001

First published 1938

This edition published 2001 by
The King's England Press,
Cambertown House, Commercial Road,
Goldthorpe, Rotherham,
South Yorkshire, S63 9BL.

© The Trustees of the Estate
of the late Arthur Mee

ISBN 1 872438 30 X

Printed and bound in Great Britain by
Woolnough Bookbinding, Irthlingborough, Northants.

PICTURES OF SURREY

Where the pictures are not on or facing the page given they are inside the set of pictures beginning on that page

		PAGE
Abinger Hammer	The Roadside Clock	16
Albury	The Silent Pool	288
Beddington	Brass of Nicholas Carew, 1432	53
	Carved Miserere	17
	The Medieval Church	32
Betchworth	Brass of William Wardysworth, 1533	53
Blechingley	Carved Corbel	17
	Old Manor Gatehouse	32
Box Hill	The Winding Road	33
	View Towards Leith Hill	33
Burstow	Medieval Chest	177
Byfleet	Brass of Thomas Teylar, 1489	53
Carshalton	Brass of Nicholas Gaynesford, 1498	53
	The Pond in the Town	16
Caterham	War Coppice Road	48
Chaldon	The Medieval Church	64
	Norman Wall Painting	17
	Thirteenth Century Bell	17
Charlwood	Village Street	64
Chilworth	Church of St Martha	65
Cobham	Church Stile House	69
	Norman Doorway of Church	77
	The Mill by the Mole	68
Coldharbour	Surrey's Highest Village	68
Compton	The Church and its Norman Work	76, 77
	The Watts Chapel	76
Cranleigh	The Famous School	49
Crowhurst	Brass of John Gaynesford	53
	Church and Ancient Yew	85
	Timbered Manor House	84
Croydon	Aerodrome Control Tower	93
	Airman's View	93

v

PICTURES OF SURREY

		PAGE
Croydon . . .	Brass of Gabriel Silvester, 1512	53
continued	Palace of the Archbishops	92
	Quadrangle of Whitgift Hospital . . .	92
Dorking . . .	The New Bypass Road	96
	Woodland Scene in Autumn	96
Eashing . . .	The 13th Century Bridge	97
East Horsley .	Brass of John Bowthe, 1478	53
Egham . . .	Brass of Anthony Bond and his family . .	123
	Royal Holloway College	49
	Runnymede by the Thames	113
Elstead . . .	Medieval Bridge	97
Epsom . . .	Carving on Font	17
	Grandstand on the Downs	112
	The Town Hall	112
Esher . . .	Claremont House	84
	The Old Church	128
	Tower of Esher Place	128
Ewell . . .	Brass of Jane Iwarby, 1519	53
	Nonsuch House	113
Farnham . .	Ancient Parish Church	129
	Brass of Sibil Jay, 1597	187
	Norman Castle	129
Frensham . .	The Great Pond	289
Friday Street .	Village Scenes 120,	121
Gatton . . .	Town Hall in the Park	257
Godalming . .	Brass of John Barker, 1595	123
	Charterhouse School and Chapel . . 49,	240
	Church Street	120
	The Old Church	120
Godstone . .	Winter Pastoral Scene	120
Gomshall . .	Beech Wood near Village	120
Great Bookham .	Brass of Robert Shiers, 1668	123
	Church and its Timbered Tower . . .	144
Guildford . .	Abbot's Hospital 160,	161
	Brass of Maurice Abbot, 1606	187
	Castle and Gateway	152
	Cathedral as Drawn by the Architect . .	153
	Doorway in Quarry Street	161
	Famous Guildhall . . . . . . Frontispiece	
	Grammar School	152

vi

PICTURES OF SURREY

		PAGE
Guildford	High Street	152
continued	Holy Trinity Church	153
	Loseley House	84
	Quaint Byway	161
	St Catherine's Chapel	152
	St Mary's Church	160, 161
Haslemere	Bracken on the Hills	176
	17th Century Almshouses	120
Hindhead	Devil's Punch Bowl	176
Holmbury St Mary	Village Scene	121
Horley	Brass of 15th Century Lady	123
Horsell	Brass of Thomas Sutton, 1603	123
Kew	Lovely Scenes in the Gardens	184, 185
Kingston	Coronation Stone	177
	Modern Guildhall	192
	Old Marketplace	192
Leatherhead	Bridge Across the Mole	193
	15th Century Font	17
	Old Church Above the Valley	193
Leith Hill	Magnificent Panorama	197
	Tower on Summit	197
Limpsfield	Norman Church	196
Lingfield	The Church and its Treasures	204, 205
	Brass of John Knoyll, 1503	123
Little Bookham	The Norman Church	144
Merstham	Brasses of Peter and Richard Best	325
Merton	Nelson's Church	225
	Norman Door	177
Mickleham	Brass of William Wyddowson, 1513	187
	Druids Grove, Norbury Park	48
	Norman Church Tower	225
Mitcham	Cricket on the Common	224
Mortlake	Old Parish Church	225
Oakwood	Brass of Edward de la Hale, 1431	187
Ockham	Brass of John Weston, 1525	187
	Church and its Famous East Window	85
Ockley	Cricket on the Green	224
	Windmill	145
Outwood	Windmills on the Common	145

vii

PICTURES OF SURREY

		PAGE
Oxted . . .	Brass of John Hoskins, 1613	187
	Church of the Peace of God	240
Pirbright . . .	H. M. Stanley's Tomb	177
Purley . . .	Promenade de Verdun	48
Pyrford . . .	Newark Mill and Priory	241
Reigate . . .	Colley Hill	256
	Medieval Church	257
	Mill Church	145
	Mill on Wray Common	145
	Scene on the Heath	256
Richmond . .	Barn Church at North Sheen	273
	Herd in the Park	320
	The Old Palace	273
	View from the Hill	272
	White Lodge	273
Shere	Brass of Robert Scarclyf, 1412	187
	The Village Street	288
Stoke D'Abernon	Church by the Mole	337
	Brass of Anne Norbury, 1464	187
	The D'Abernon Brasses	285
Thames Ditton .	Brass of Erasmus Forde, 1533	325
Virginia Water .	The Beauty of the Lake	289
Walton-on-Thames	Aerial View	304
	Brass of John Selwyn, 1587	325
	King's House at Burhill	113
Walton-on-the-Hill	Lead Font	177
Waverley . .	Ancient Bridge Across the Wey	305
	The Ruined Abbey	305
Weybridge . .	Brass of Thomas Inwood, 1586	325
Whiteley Village	The Octagon from the Air	304
Wimbledon . .	Silver Birches on the Common	320
Wisley . . .	Little Norman Church	321
	The Famous Pond	321
Witley . . .	The Ancient Church	336
	Iron Almsbox	177
Woking . . .	Mohammedan Mosque	336
Wonersh . .	Great Tangley Manor	69
Wotton . . .	The Ancient Church	337

The Editor is greatly indebted to
CONWAY WALKER
and
JOHN WILSON
for their valuable help with this book

For the pictures to
SIDNEY TURNER, ART EDITOR

and to the following photographers:
Messrs Aerofilms, E. Bastard, Edgar Bull, Central Aerophoto Company, Brian Clayton, Country Life, J. Dixon-Scott, G. C. Druce, Herbert Felton, F. Frith, Humphrey Joel, A. F. Kersting, Dorien Leigh, New Centurion Publishing Company, W. Suter, E. W. Tattersall, W. F. Taylor; the Director of the Royal Botanic Gardens, and the Controller of His Majesty's Stationery Office.

London's Southern Neighbour

SURREY is one of the smallest counties in the kingdom, but one of the most beautiful, and I think I may quite rightly say one of the best known, because there is, year by year, an increasing number of people who wander about its beautiful lanes and who visit its important places. It represents the green foliage of England unusually well, and is in many ways an exceedingly attractive county, London's near neighbour.

I have been much honoured, as Remembrancer for its county town, in being asked to write a preface to this volume that has been written concerning it, the pages of which I find full of entrancing interest, and I am anxious in this preface to draw attention to some of the special features that concern Surrey, and that will be of importance to those who read the book.

It is a well-watered county, its two chief rivers (excluding the Thames) being the Wey and the Mole, the Wey rising in the Hampshire hills and entering the Thames near Weybridge, the Mole rising in Sussex, breaking through the North Downs near Box Hill and joining the Thames at East Molesey. The presence of this amount of water is responsible, of course, for the greenness of Surrey.

Its great feature is its mass of gently sweeping hills known as the North Downs, delightful places for rambling and very attractive to the modern rambler. They are of some importance with regard to height, because Leith Hill reaches 965 feet, Holmbury 857, Pitch Hill rather less, and Hindhead 895, and when one speaks of Hindhead one thinks of the marvellous expanse of common land covered in places with gorse, heather, and fern, and offering extremely beautiful views in many directions. Hindhead, of course, includes what is known as the Devil's Punch Bowl, and (as a matter of incidental interest) that

THE KING'S ENGLAND

Punch Bowl contains two or three of the rarest of the Surrey plants, flowers the botanist seeks most eagerly.

Surrey is, of course, also noted for the possession of its Pilgrim's Way, although quite recently efforts have been made to disturb the name and to upset its attribution; but there is little question that the chief paths of the pilgrims to Canterbury had to traverse the central downs of the county, and the Pilgrim's Way was a national highway with tracks at different levels, and very likely was the site of far more remote ways by which the treasures of tin were brought from Cornwall.

One of the principal features of the downs is the part known as the Hog's Back, to which one ascends from Guildford; from it can be seen a great part of the county. From this point of vantage we see rising the only 20th century cathedral in the south of England, which in a few more years will crown with a new glory these famous heights of Surrey and its ancient capital. The view from the Hog's Back is a wonderful one, but apart from the downs the county is deservedly popular for its beautiful and extensive commons, its tree-clad hills, its delightful little winding lanes, its old hedgerows (many of which go back to a very remote period) and for the charming villages that are to be found by the rambler almost hidden away from ordinary sight, each delightfully self-centred with its old church, and in most cases with delightful old cottages.

It is not perhaps to be called a splendid county, but it is full of the greatest interest, and its two or three important towns are very old, and at the same time are rapidly becoming very modern, for all are increasing with considerable rapidity, and in every town efforts are being made to increase the popularity of the place, and to make it more and more attractive.

There can be few places more beautiful for situation than Surrey's county town of Guildford; in fact its High Street is one of the most lovely in England, and has been pronounced by Charles Dickens (no mean authority, because he travelled all over the country) to be the most beautiful High Street in England. It is perhaps permissible for me to add that I am old enough to remember seeing him in Guildford when he gave one of his celebrated readings there.

How old Guildford is no one can say, but we know that the place was mentioned in the will of King Alfred and left by him to his nephew, and we know that when its first charter was granted by Henry the Third in 1256 it alluded to a governing body then in existence and carrying on good work; in fact it is said that in three places only in England (Andover, Guildford, and Windsor) is it possible to trace in clear definite fashion step by step, the government of the town from that of the very early ages, through the Gilda Mercatoria and the unreformed Corporations down to the present day.

King Henry the Third placed the government of Guildford in the hands of a body called the Approved Men, but he did not create the body; he spoke of it as already existing and doing its work, and in the previous year the same king had granted a charter to Kingston-on-Thames (a place that is rather inclined sometimes to compete with Guildford for the honour of being the chief town in the county), but the Kingston charter says that the people may have their Gild Merchant "as our men of Gildeford have" and therefore Kingston in that respect is the daughter town of Guildford.

Guildford has nearly doubled itself in size since 1900, and is now not only climbing the Hog's Back, but climbing the hills in various directions, and even ascending close to St Martha's. Notable as it is, Guildford is not, of course, the biggest town in Surrey. Croydon is the biggest place, with nearly 250,000 people, almost entirely a new town, but possessing an extraordinarily great treasure in the Whitgift Hospital, which still stands as a haven of peace beside its noisy streets. Some of the Archbishops of Canterbury are buried in its old church.

Kingston was the ancient town of kings, and has one of the oldest historic stones in England, on which the Saxon kings were crowned, but it possesses also an unrivalled series of documents and archives, carefully arranged and displayed, such a series as exists in very few places indeed. Guildford cannot compete in that respect, but the town can compete with Croydon in the possession of its superb hospital; its wonderful buildings and towers fill a notable place in Guildford High Street, and are amazingly attractive. There are few squares surrounded by almshouses more eminently the abode of peace than the one enshrined in Holy Trinity Hospital, and there is perhaps no other chapel attached to a hospital possessing windows of such extraordinary rarity and beauty as those this hospital possesses. Many of its rooms are lovely, and furnished with the old furniture bestowed upon them by Archbishop Abbot who founded the hospital. He is the greatest notable of whom Guildford can boast, born a poor boy in the place, educated at its local grammar school, ascending through various dignities until he became Archbishop of Canterbury and crowned King Charles; and he had, moreover, two clever brothers, one of whom (Robert) became Bishop of Salisbury, and another (Maurice) Lord Mayor of London.

The allusion to Robert and Maurice Abbot leads one at once to think of the grammar school in the upper part of the town. There is hardly any grammar school in England that can boast of such a distinguished list of Old Boys, whose names are emblazoned on the great oak beams that cross the schoolroom.

In alluding to the towns of Surrey one must not on any account forget that a great part of Aldershot is in Surrey, although most of it is in Hampshire. It might almost be called the hub of the British Army, while Epsom, which is wholly in Surrey, may be called the hub of the sporting world, for all the world goes to Epsom to see the famous Derby.

Surrey is noted in quite another way for its trees. It is a tree county. At Pain's Hill, Cobham, is a cedar of Lebanon supposed to be the biggest in England; at Ranelagh is the biggest plane tree; at Addlestone is the well-known Crouch Oak, 24 feet round. But in yews Surrey is specially notable; there is one in Barnes churchyard that was planted in the time of Stephen Langton, and one at Crowhurst of unknown age, with a girth of eleven yards, and room in it for a dozen people to sit

SURREY

at a table. In Norbury Park, close to Mickleham, are some very remarkable yews of fantastic shape, and there is a grand old yew tree at Hambledon. Near to Guildford are yews that belong to the King's Warren, from which were made the bows that did such splendid service at Crecy and Agincourt. The State Papers refer in many places to sending down to the King's Warren at Merrow for yews for bows, and fortunately there still stand, close to the old racecourse that has not been used since the time of William the Fourth, certain old yews that go back to remote times, possibly to the ancient Britons.

The oldest tulip tree in England, planted in 1685, is still living in the grounds of Esher Place. There is a great oak tree at Tilford called the King's Oak, 26 feet round, a giant yew at Tandridge 32 feet round, and there are five splendid cedars at Compton and two or three very fine ones at Albury, the Albury ones planted from seeds from Lebanon, not perhaps of such great age as the other trees but of extreme beauty.

In referring to the Wey and the Mole the allusion was, of course, to them as distinctly Surrey rivers, for the Thames (which, after all, is *the* river in Surrey) is not a Surrey river. But part of it is in Surrey, and at the Boat Race every sportsman speaks about the Surrey side, and on the shore of the Thames three of Surrey's important towns are placed: Chertsey, with its monastic history going much farther back than that of Westminster; Kingston, crowning place of kings; and Richmond, unparalleled for its beauty.

Of Surrey's notable people the details will be found in the delightful pages that follow. Of the people of modern times it may suffice to refer to George Meredith living at Box Hill; to Gertrude Jekyll who lived at Munstead twenty years; to the wonderful author of Alice in Wonderland, who lived so long in Guildford; to Tennyson, George Eliot, Professor Tyndall, Grant Allen, George Macdonald, who all lived at Haslemere—the home, by the way, of Arnold Dolmetsch, whose unique work has so greatly revived the interest in the past of our English music.

Farnham, the famous and ancient town linked to Guildford

by the Hog's Back, will ever be associated with the presence of Sir William Temple, although he was not a Surrey-born man, for he and Stella and Swift are closely associated with that district. Cobbett is the notable Surrey man. He came from Farnham, and in his Rural Rides went all over the county and spoke very bluntly of what he saw, hating especially paper money and gunpowder, and entering into a long tirade when he found mills for paper-making and mills for making gunpowder in the delightful village of Albury. It is only within recent times that these mills have ceased to produce the things that so worried poor Cobbett. As a bluff outspoken man there have been few to equal him.

Among our eminent men we should include William Oughtred, the great 17th century mathematician, who lies in Albury Church, and near his grave is that of Henry Drummond, the founder, with strange Edward Irving, of the religious body calling itself the Catholic Apostolic Church. George Smith the publisher, who gave us the Dictionary of National Biography, lies in the churchyard at Byfleet, and near to him lies Joseph Spence, friend of Alexander Pope. The great G. F. Watts is buried at Compton, and there is a marvellous chapel to his memory, and a delightful gallery of his pictures. The American artist Copley lies in Croydon church. At Farncombe is a memorial recalling one of the greatest disasters of our own century, a cloister dedicated to the memory of the wireless operator on the Titanic. A pilot who won the Schneider Trophy lies buried at Bourne near Farnham, the great scientist Sir Richard Owen, at Ham. The first man to find a means of showing moving pictures, Eadweard Muybridge, was born and lies at Kingston. At Limpsfield sleep Professor Arthur Thomson and the composer Delius. At Mortlake, in an extraordinary tomb like an Arab tent, we find the burial place of Sir Richard Burton, and in the same church lie two old astrologers, John Dee and John Partridge. Vancouver, the great 18th century navigator, who gave his name to a vast piece of country, lies buried in the little churchyard of Petersham, and Stanley, who found Livingstone, lies at Pirbright.

SURREY

There are two links in Surrey with Sir Francis Drake, for at Esher is a monument to one of his kinsmen, Sir Richard Drake, who had charge of the Spanish grandees captured in those stirring days, and at Reigate was buried Lord Howard of Effingham, friend of Drake and Raleigh; his beautiful prayer-book is still preserved in Reigate church. The tradition is that Sir Walter Raleigh himself lies buried in the church at Beddington, though no one knows for certain whether this is the case; and there is also a tradition that Raleigh's head was buried by his son in the church at West Horsley.

Wotton is for ever associated with John Evelyn, for there he was born, there he wrote his diary and his wonderful Sylva, and there he lies with his family. In the family house are many treasures connected with him that the Evelyns have been wise enough to preserve with the greatest care.

One ought perhaps to mention that the gallant Australian Harry Hawker, first of all the Atlantic flying men, lies buried at Hook, and at Holmwood is a memorial to Vanderbilt, the American sportsman who went down with the Lusitania. The little churchyard at Kew has a wonderful array of names; Zoffany and Gainsborough are buried there, with Sir William Hooker, the great botanist, and others.

Suppose, however, one wants to go as far back as possible in Surrey notables, one would mention William of Ockham, known to his own generation in the 14th century as the Invincible Doctor, whose writings had the greatest possible repute, while in another period many people still associate Dorking with the residence of Malthus, whose treatises are so well known and still appreciated.

Surrey does not pretend to compete with some other counties in very special treasures, but it is notable still for fine glass, and specially notable for wonderful Norman woodwork, of which perhaps no county has more. Compton, a pleasant church full of architectural treasures of the deepest possible interest, has evidence of the visit of the Crusaders, and has the only Norman Gallery existing in England, fronting the upper chancel, the exact use of which is still to a certain extent in dispute. There are fine church chests, notably at Stoke D'Abernon, Betchworth, Oxted, and Newdigate. The oldest of all the brasses in England is at Stoke D'Abernon. There is still a fair amount of fine old glass (especially heraldic glass) to be seen at Ashtead, Buckland, Byfleet, Chiddingfold, the seat of an ancient glass industry, Crowhurst, Compton, Gatton, Ockham, Shere, Thorpe, West Horsley, Wimbledon, Walton-on-the-Hill, Worplesdon, and of course at Guildford. As regards architecture, Saxon work can be seen in at least 13 churches, and the work of Norman builders and craftsmen in over sixty churches.

There are fine old water mills at Shalford, Cobham, and Ripley, and fortunately it is the privilege of the National Trust to guard the finest of them, at Shalford. One ought to mention that, in addition to this mill and some cottages in Surrey, the National Trust owns 3400 acres in the county, which are therefore preserved for ever from desecration. Reigate still has three windmills, and there are two relics remaining of the old semaphore stations maintained by the Admiralty, through which came the news of Waterloo. The brick tower on Chatley Heath near Cobham is the most important, but part of Semaphore House at Guildford used to retain the old semaphore apparatus within living memory.

To run through these pages and pick out objects of interest will perhaps help the reader. Abinger Hammer still preserves the name of the Hammer Ponds, notable for the iron industry that has practically vanished. Albury has its unrivalled and much-visited Silent Pool. In the old church in Albury Park is an amazing door which certainly must go back seven hundred years. Ash and Cobham have both wooden fonts, very rare possessions, there being (I am told) only four or five in the country. Box Hill presents one of the finest view points in the whole of England. Bisley is the place where the Gordon Boys home has been established, and where General Gordon's walking stick can be seen. Busbridge has a fine bronze screen, designed by Sir Edward Lutyens, and beautiful ironwork by Mr Starkie Gardner.

SURREY

Chaldon has the oldest bell in Surrey, one of the oldest in England, and it has in its possession a 12th century painting of the Doom. There is not in all England a more complete example of Norman painting than this. Chiddingfold and Guildford both preserve memories of Edward the Sixth; he stayed at Somerset House in Guildford, and moved to the Crown Inn at Chiddingfold on his way down to Shillinglee. Eashing has an amazingly fine 13th century bridge, the oldest in Surrey, handed over by the Old Guildford Society to the National Trust, and in their safe keeping for ever. There is another fine old bridge at Elstead. Runnymede by the Thames is perhaps the most historic meadow in England. Epsom, is of course, noted for its downs, its beautiful old houses, and its admirable college. Esher possesses a historic tower, the only piece that remains of Wolsey's house called Esher Place, and in the same town is the fine mansion of Claremont, now a school for girls, a house of tragic interest. Gatton has its wonderful little town hall, and was one of the smallest places in England to send a representative to the House of Commons, the member being elected by perhaps about a dozen people in this extraordinary little building. In the church near by are greater treasures still, elaborate stalls of carved work from Belgium, carved doors from Rouen, an altar table from Nuremberg, and splendid Flemish glass from Louvain. Lingfield has a great church that has been called the Westminster Abbey of Surrey, with a rich array of the monuments of the Cobhams, three medieval oak screens, and some of the best carved stalls in the county. There is a peace memorial in this place crowned with a light that never goes out. Ockham has a lovely east window of seven lancets, unlike any other in England, Oxted a wonderful iron chest with 13 bolts turned by one key. At Walton-on-Thames is an ancient lead font, the only one in Surrey, and one of only 38 in all England, and there is another at Woking. Merton has a fine Norman door. Outwood Common has two good windmills side by side.

Notable among the county's modern buildings is the Mahommedan Mosque at Woking and the extraordinary Whiteley Village, an octagon with the biggest collection of almshouses in the country, hidden away near Weybridge. There is an interesting barn church at Richmond, a very unusual church at Lower Kingswood, and prominent on the hills round Godalming are the beautiful buildings that now enshrine Charterhouse School. On another hill is the dear little church of St Martha, known to every visitor in Surrey, as it was known to the Canterbury Pilgrims long ago.

With regard to civic plate Surrey holds a very high place; in fact, one of its treasures holds the highest position of all, for at Guildford is the biggest silver mace of the 15th century, and practically the only great mace of that period that has survived in silver, others being in iron or else small. Guildford also possesses a great mace of some considerable importance, and an Elizabethan mayor's staff, made of campeachy wood with a silver top, which is unique in England. The gift of Queen Elizabeth, it is dated 1563. It also has a wonderful gold badge worn by its mayor, which goes back to 1673, and an Elizabethan rosewater bason and ewer finer than anything else of its kind in the kingdom. Kingston has two silver-gilt maces, and also two delightful maces belonging to the sergeants, partly of the period of Charles the Second. This town and Guildford have wonderful old seals. Kingston has also an important silver tray fashioned from the Great Seal of Queen Caroline, and has another unusual piece, an oblong silver snuffbox. Godalming has an extraordinarily interesting old wooden staff with a silver cap, dated 1589, and also a very important seal.

Sufficient surely has been said to show what a fascinating county this is, and how many treasures it still possesses, but those who read these pages will find many more items of interest and will come to the conclusion that among English counties there are few that can compete in charm or delight with Surrey.

GEORGE C. WILLIAMSON
Remembrancer to the Corporation of Guildford

The Old Village Folk

ABINGER. It stands high in the beautiful Leith Hill country, a peaceful place. The church has a Norman nave with six Norman windows; the chancel and chapel are 13th century. The nave roof is 500 years old and is held up by beams probably a century older. The pulpit has good 16th century panels carved with the Annunciation, the Nativity, and the Resurrection; and near it is a beautiful Burne-Jones window of Faith, Hope, and Charity. There is a fine painting of the Entombment, after the 16th century artist Francia. The vestry wall is adorned with an unusual treasure, a carved bronze of the Crucifixion with vivid and expressive figures in the foreground and Jerusalem showing behind.

Two old parsons of Abinger sleep beneath the altar at which they served, with stones inscribed to their memory. One is Thomas Crawley, chaplain to Charles the Second, and the other Robert Offley, who died in 1743 after having been rector for over half a century. There is a tablet to Commodore William Robinson, telling how in 1774 he went to the Indian Ocean and explored a stretch of coast which had not been explored for 2000 years, since the Greek navigator Nearchus, a lifelong friend of Alexander, travelled thereabouts. William Robinson lived on into the 19th century and lies here.

In the garden of the manor house (behind the church) is the oldest thing in Abinger, going back as far beyond the Norman church as we are on this side of it. It is one of the ancient burial mounds of our British ancestors.

Two literary associations belong to Abinger. One is that the old stocks on the green are said to be those into which Riccabocca was put in Bulwer Lytton's novel; the other is that here lived John Hoole, famous for his translations and an actor at Covent Garden. He was a friend of Dr Johnson, and went to see him in his last illness, but Sir Walter Scott had a poor opinion of him, describing him as a noble transmuter of gold into lead.

The Lonely Memorial

ABINGER HAMMER. All who ride from Dorking to Guildford know the quaint clock projecting over the roadway here, with the figure of a smith striking the hours with his hammer to remind us of the iron industry that has vanished from this place. Those who are not in a hurry will have time to read its motto, By me you know how fast to go.

Across the road is the village green given by the friends and neighbours of 22 men who fell in the war; and a little way along the Dorking road is Crossways Farm, a 17th century house which comes into literature in George Meredith's Diana of the Crossways. It is delightful, with a trim walled garden and a gabled porch.

Not far away is a field where the remains of a Roman villa were unearthed last century, and, starting from the crossroads, is the lane leading to one of the loneliest memorials we have seen. Hard to find in its wild and deserted setting, it is the simple granite cross to Bishop Wilberforce, with his initials, his pastoral staff, and the date of that summer's day in 1873 when he lost his life at this very spot. He was out riding when his horse stumbled at a rabbit hole.

A son of the famous merchant friend of William Pitt, the William Wilberforce who helped to free the slaves, he won for himself high repute by his work as Bishop of Oxford for all but a quarter of a century; he became known as Remodeller of the Episcopate. He was rather unfairly given the popular nickname of Soapy Sam, and he did not deserve the deep personal suffering which came upon him with the abandonment of Protestantism by his two brothers and his only daughter.

He was one of the most popular bishops of his day and lies at Woolavington in Sussex, with a group of friends among whom is the wife of Cardinal Manning, whose sister-in-law he had married.

The Home of Archbishops

ADDINGTON. Less than a dozen miles from Charing Cross, it has kept much of its natural charm in a changing world, and is still a peaceful place of rest for the great leaders of the Church who sleep within the churchyard.

The old yew may well have been growing here when England broke from Rome. It was already a veteran of the ages when the Archbishops of Canterbury came to Addington, and it has seen five of them in succession laid to rest: Archbishop Manners-Sutton, who bought the great house for a palace; Archbishop Howley, who crowned Queen Victoria and has a monument in Canterbury Cathedral; Archbishop Sumner, who had been an Eton master; Archbishop Longley, who was headmaster of Harrow; and Archbishop Tait, who had succeeded the great Thomas Arnold at Rugby. Keeping the old yew company is a cross in memory of these five Primates put here by a sixth, Archbishop Davidson; not far from it is another, not of carved stone but of plain wood, so simple that its pathetic message is easily missed. These are the six words:

Bennie
Whom the Lord took up.

Parts of the church are 800 years old, and there are two good Tudor brasses, one showing John Leigh with his wife and five children, the other Thomas Hatteclyff, Henry the Eighth's Master of the Household. In the chancel is a big monument to three generations of Leighs. The pairs of kneeling figures on it are grandfather Nicholas (with charming curly hair) and his wife Anne, and father John with his wife Joan; the figures lying down are the son Sir Oliph of 1612 and his wife Jane. Sir Oliph fitted out a relief expedition for his younger brother Charles, one of the founders of British Guiana. He must also have taken care of the six hostages Charles Leigh sent home.

There is a memorial to Elizabeth Lovell and her daughter, both dying in 1691; a big urn in memory of Alderman Trecothick who was Lord Mayor of London in the 18th century; and a stone in the porch to a vicar's wife of 1633, with these words:

I believe with these my eyes,
to my comfort, shortly to see my
Redeemer in the Land of the Living.

The alabaster reredos is in memory of Edward Benson, who raised Wellington College to the first rank of public schools and was the last archbishop to live at Addington. He sleeps at Canterbury, but his figure is sculptured on this reredos with those of Theodore, Cranmer, and Laud.

Half a minute along the road we have a glimpse of Addington Park with the big white house (now a hotel) rebuilt by Alderman Trecothick before it became the archbishop's palace. It is an estate as old as Domesday, having been given by the Conqueror to his cook Tezelin. For 300 years the Leighs lived here, and the old chronicler Aubrey tells us how, at the coronation of Charles the Second, Thomas Leigh had to bring to the king's table a mess of pottage to justify his ancient right to the manor. The Lord High Chamberlain presented him to the king, who accepted the service but "did not eat of the pottage." A strange ceremony it must have been.

Here with his father, Archbishop Manners-Sutton, sleeps the first Viscount Canterbury, who was Speaker of the House of Commons when it was burned down but lived to see the noble Gothic group of Sir Charles Barry rise in its place by the Thames.

Queen Elizabeth's Picnic Tree

ADDLESTONE. Its two best possessions are close together, one of them new and the other old beyond memory.

One is the peace memorial, a beautiful garden and playing-field; the other is Crouch Oak, a fine bit of old England, 24 feet round. Gnarled and hollow with age, it is still very much alive in spite of one great limb fallen to the ground and another propped up. It is thought to have marked the eastern boundary of Windsor Forest, and must have seen many a sight in its long life. Beneath its branches Queen Elizabeth is said to have had a picnic when she was out hunting, and by it John Wycliffe once preached. Saved from the sawmill last century, it has seen this place grow up into something more than a village, and it must be by far the oldest thing in Addlestone.

The 19th century church is unattractive save for a handsome stone and iron screen and some good carved stalls. Its interest is in those who are remembered on the walls and in some who sleep in the churchyard.

One tablet tells of Vernon Lewis, a young Addlestone man who fell leading his men at the Relief of Ladysmith. Another tells of Francis de Visme, who joined the navy soon after Trafalgar, was twice shipwrecked, and went on to fight as a soldier in the Peninsular War. A third is to James Athol Wood, who went to sea at 16 and rose to be an admiral. He was in the navy for almost half a century, and one of his adventures was to be captured by the French and imprisoned in Paris by Robespierre.

There is a tablet to tell us that Samuel Carter Hall and his wife

Anna Maria are sleeping in the churchyard. Both were prolific writers last century, he founding magazines and editing books, and she writing novels about the people and places of her native Ireland. In his Art Journal he exposed the scandalous trade in what were called Old Masters, and told his readers how many of these pictures were manufactured in England. The result of his disclosures was that for a while people were afraid to buy even genuine pictures, and masterpieces by Raphael and Titian could be picked up for a few pounds. Anna Maria Hall was a benefactor as well as a writer; she befriended the down-and-out, and fought for temperance and women's rights.

Also buried here is Maria Theresa Kemble, who first appeared on an English stage at six and won fame in the Beggar's Opera before she married Charles Kemble.

At Anningsley, two miles away among the heaths, lived the eccentric and stoical Thomas Day, whose memory is kept green by his book Sandford and Merton. Here with his wife he settled on a farm, losing money at it but rejoicing at the employment he was giving to his men. His labourers were asked to his own house, and he used to teach them from the Bible.

The Strange Friend of Carlyle

ALBURY. In a scene of great tranquillity the old church stands near the great house in Albury Park. They are almost alone, for the village of today has developed from a hamlet half a mile away.

But there is nothing in Albury (unless it be the little gem of nature called the Silent Pool, where Tennyson saw the netted sunbeam dance) to compare with the charm of the park and the beauty of the gardens in it. Still here are the lovely terraces John Evelyn laid out for the Duke of Norfolk, the long tunnel he made through the sandstone of the hill, and the row of yew trees stretching in a straight line for a quarter of a mile. Often he mentions this garden in his diary, and William Cobbett, writing last century, said it was the prettiest garden he had seen.

The old church was opened again in 1922 after 80 years. Loving hands have cared for it, and, though the chancel is in ruin, it is a place not to be missed. The Norman tower is capped by a shingled dome, but it is not the oldest thing we see. The walls of the nave are

Saxon; and the Normans, wishing to build a tower, thickened the walls of the Saxon chancel to bear the weight of the new structure. In a strange way the wheel of time has made a turn, and with the later chancel fallen to ruin the altar stands again where it stood when the Conqueror came; the space under the tower that was the chancel 900 years ago is the chancel again today. Norman arches mark off this space at each end, and there are double Norman windows in the upper stages of the tower.

But there is more than the interest of age and architecture in this church. The Tudor porch is one of the best in Surrey, charming with its bricks and timbers and its beautifully carved bargeboard. The door within it is 700 years old and has long strap-hinges, a massive wooden lock, and a key about a foot long.

On the wall of the 13th century aisle is a remarkable painting 400 years old. Clearer than many such paintings, it shows St Christopher with the Child on his shoulder, between the cell in which he lived and a group of ships engaged in a fight. He has a beautiful face, and the Child is holding an orb. Traces of colour are also to be seen on a 14th century niche for a statue.

There is a massive Stuart chest, a coffin stone at least 500 years old, and in the ruined chancel is the gravestone of Henry Wickes, who served Queen Elizabeth, King James, and Charles Stuart. Very good and clear is the brass of John Weston, who died 15 years after Agincourt. He is standing in full armour with beautiful little spurs, flowers growing at his feet. His portrait is so like two others at Fladbury in Worcestershire and Arkesden in Essex that all three are thought to be by the same London craftsman.

On the wall is a memorial to Sir Robert Godschall, Lord Mayor of London in the 18th century, and a tablet describing a curious bequest of money for the rector to preach a sermon on May Day of every year. Thirty poor people may still have a shilling each if they go to hear him, and we were told that the legacy passes to another village if the rector defaults.

Somewhere in the ruined chancel sleeps a country parson who was one of the foremost mathematicians of his day, William Oughtred, who died here at the old rectory.

In the 13th century chapel sleeps a man who played a large part in the story of Albury last century. He was Henry Drummond, the

Abinger Hammer   **The Roadside Hammer Clock**

Carshalton   **The Pond in the Town**

Beddington Miserere   **Epsom** Carving on Font

Leatherhead
Fifteenth Century Font
    Blechingley
Carved Corbel
    Chaldon
Thirteenth Century Bell

Chaldon   Norman Wall Painting

RARE TREASURES IN SURREY CHURCHES

politician and banker who helped to found the Catholic Apostolic Church. The chapel, where he lies with his family, was decorated by Pugin, and is filled with bright paint and vivid glass out of keeping with an ancient village church. On the screen is the Drummond motto Gang Warily, monotonously repeated eight times.

It was at Henry Drummond's house that Edward Irving started what he called the Catholic Apostolic Church. Irving was nearing the end of his short life, during which he had created a great sensation in London by his preachings, his prophecies, his strange manifestations, and his unknown tongues. He had begun life in the same countryside as Carlyle, a tanner's son at Annan. Both were teachers, and became friends. Carlyle declared that but for Irving he had never known what the communion of man with man means. Both gave up their schools and went to Edinburgh, and soon afterwards Irving received an invitation to a little chapel in London. He came, having first introduced Carlyle to Jane Welsh. He crowded his chapel in Hatton Garden, gave London society a new sensation by his extravagance in the pulpit, started a new church in Regent Square, and drew to it every Sunday a thousand people who would sit and listen to him for three hours. He was tried for heresy, and though the prosecution failed he alienated much sympathy, and in the end came to hold meetings down at Albury, where Henry Drummond was one of his most enthusiastic friends.

Drummond built a church for him that cost him £16,000, and Albury became a stronghold of the Irvingites. Their church still stands, a spectacular structure built in 15th century style, a surprising sight among the trees as we turn the corner from the Dorking road. The interior is disappointing as a whole, but has some handsome woodcarving, much of which is the work of an Albury man, Anthony Browne. He fashioned the pinnacled sedilia, many of the poppy-heads, and, best of all, the carved and gilt tabernacle on the altar, looking very beautiful when the hidden light is turned on. It is made of cedar wood from the Holy Land. Two other notable pieces of woodwork are the rich canopy over the altar and the elaborate font cover. Joining on to the church is an octagonal Council Chamber built in the same rich medieval style.

Henry Drummond used his wealth to build two churches in Albury, the other being the new village church looking across to

St Martha's-on-the-Hill. It is copied from a church Mr Drummond admired in Normandy, and has in it an attractive peace memorial, showing in brass relief a kneeling soldier of the Great War.

The Genius at the Rectory

WILLIAM OUGHTRED, who sleeps here where he died, spent the last fifty years of his life as parson at Albury. Born at Eton in 1575, he passed from the college there to Cambridge University, where he revealed a genius for mathematics. While still an undergraduate he wrote his Easy Method of Mathematical Dialling, which Sir Christopher Wren, then at Oxford University, translated into Latin.

Ordained priest in 1603, he arrived here from Shalford in 1610, married, attended to his parish, and worked away at his problems, with an ink-horn fixed to his bed-head and a tinder-box and candle by his side, ready at a moment to record a solution of his difficulties. He would sit up night after night working out a problem. His most famous work embodied practically all that was known of algebra and arithmetic, and included Oughtred's invention, the × for multiplication, and the : : for proportion. Written in Latin, and added to from time to time, this book became the standard authority, and made its author a classic in his lifetime.

During the Civil War he was in danger from the Presbyterians, but on the day of his trial Lilly the astrologer took to his aid a body of friends who so impressed the Commissioners that by a majority vote the scholar escaped. His fame was European, and he had invitations to settle at practically every Court in Europe, but here he lived out his days, and here in 1660 he died.

Where Surrey Meets Sussex

ALFOLD. Down by the Sussex border, it has a delightful old church and an attractive black and white house with a carved bargeboard to its overhanging storey.

A charming paved way leads to the church, passing between the village stocks and an old house. We enter through one of the two 14th century porches, with its original door and decorated ironwork, and are struck by the quiet beauty of white walls and dark woodwork. The three arches on one side are Norman. Those on the other are a century younger, and rare and graceful in the way they vanish into the pillars that support them. Massive 16th century beams (with a quaint old iron weathercock come to roost on one of them) hold up the belfry, and slender 14th century beams hold up the nave roof.

The font was made within the lifetime of the Conqueror, and is one of the oldest and best in Surrey. It is decorated with a series of arches lightly cut, and a tall cross standing in each. By it on the floor someone has carved a little votive cross. There is old woodwork included in the pews and screen, and an oak chest made in 1687 with a slit for alms. The altar top is a fine piece of polished Sussex marble, found under the floor, where it may have been hidden at the Reformation. The Elizabethan pulpit is simple and beautiful and has a carved sounding-board. A few fragments of 17th century Flemish glass are in a corner of the east window, and there is a clearly cut consecration cross in the chancel.

Close to the peace memorial in the churchyard is an inscription marking what is thought to be the grave of an old local glassmaker. He was Jean Carré, who came from France and died in 1572 when the Surrey glass industry, with its headquarters a few miles away at Chiddingfold, was itself dying out; he may have worked here in Sidney Wood, where many pieces of old glass have been found.

Living here long before Jean Carré came, and living here still, is a great yew now breaking up with age. It is 25 feet round, and has probably been growing for 600 years.

Night Thoughts

ASH. A rather untidy mixture of country and town, it lies in that corner of Surrey with so many places which Aldershot counts as camp followers. Its big house is Henley Park, an 18th century mansion standing near a wood in which was captured long ago the Robert Holland who was sent by the Earl of Lancaster to raise troops against the powerful house of the Despensers. He was unfaithful to his trust, and the wrath of the Lancastrians descended upon him. They revenged themselves by sending his head to the brother of the earl he had betrayed.

In the dignified Georgian rectory Edward Young is believed to have written part of the long and almost forgotten poem which made his name famous in the 18th century, Night Thoughts; his brother-in-law was rector of Ash for 41 years and the poet would often stay with him.

The church has an imposing 15th century tower with a shingled spire, and in its 16th century timbered porch is the oldest possession of Ash, a Norman doorway with carved capitals. In the church are two unusual things, old and new. The new one is a pair of stone carvings on either side of the chancel arch, shaped as a toad and a toadstool; the old one is the 17th century font on nine legs, unusual because it is of wood, one of only two or three wood fonts in the country. Next door to the church is a handsome old college which was once an inn and may have been the church house.

In the neighbouring village of Wyke there lies in a cunningly carved tomb in the churchyard the first Jew who ever became a Privy Councillor in England. Known for many years as Baron de Worms, he lived through the whole of the Victorian Era and took an active part in public life. His father Solomon de Worms came over to England with two brothers in Waterloo year, married a sister of the first Rothschild to settle in England, and started banking. His son Henry sat in Parliament for Greenwich in succession to Gladstone, gave up the Jewish faith on his daughter marrying against the rules of his race, became a Privy Councillor, and died as Lord Pirbright, taking his name from the village near where he lies.

The Village of the Woods

ASHTEAD. Its woods are known to thousands of South London children, whose merry laughter rings through them every summer, when the children share the woods with the rabbits. It was a rabbit that gave us the oldest news of Ashtead, for it brought a Roman tile up from its burrow, and the tile led to the discovery of a Roman house of 19 centuries ago. It is thought it may have belonged to a maker of tiles, for scores had been laid in the sun to harden and many of them had footprints of dogs and cats.

Perhaps through nearly half of these long centuries the spreading yew has been growing by the church tower. It saw the building of the tower; it saw men hanging the oak door centuries ago, and today it is as high as the tower itself, one of the noblest trees for miles.

It is worth while climbing the winding steps of the tower for its fine view; we are looking down on historic ground, for where scholars now play Roman soldiers tramped down Stane Street; where these school playing-fields now are, the soldiers lighted their camp fires.

The great 19th century house is now a school, standing in the park in which John Evelyn stood admiring the chestnuts, oaks, and cedars of his day. We may walk through it as he did and see this lovely turf sloping to a lake of water lilies, and follow its avenue of cedars to the 16th century church. Old yew greets us at the door and Roman tiles peep out from the walls.

The treasure of the church is its east window, the work of a Flemish craftsman of 400 years ago. Its glass is from a vanished convent and has Calvary in the centre, our Lord in white with a green crown of thorns, with soldiers running in the background. Kneeling on one side is the Madonna with the Child stretching out his hands towards the aged St Anne, and in another panel is the Madonna in a blue cloak. Another scene shows St George fighting the dragon, with the terrified maiden standing by; and most charming of all is the kneeling nun in white with a little dog beside her and a saint protecting her.

The Wild Heath in Other Days

BAGSHOT. Its beauties are the beauties of nature, and its memories are of kings and queens and footpads. In Bagshot Park James the First and Charles Stuart would come to hunt; in it today is the great house of the Duke of Connaught.

The highway through the town was the old coaching road from London to Exeter, and as many as thirty horses would be changed here in a day. New inns have sprung up in place of the old coaching inns, yet there is something left to remind us vividly of those days when a journey was an adventure and a peril. It is Bagshot Heath, fifty squares miles, that were once a royal forest and a notorious haunt of highwaymen; it comes into The Beggar's Opera and into Smollett's novel Roderick Random.

Every coach must have dreaded its journey across this wild stretch in the old days, and many a tale was told when the shelter of the town was reached. The story goes that one highwayman would only rob passengers who were carrying gold. His efforts were successful until it was noticed that a certain farmer never paid his debts in anything but gold. Highwayman and farmer were discovered to be one and the same, and the wretched man was sent to the gibbet. The Jolly Farmer Inn at the top of Bagshot Hill was formerly named the Golden Farmer after this story.

The modern church has a graceful spire rising 140 feet, and contains several memorials to royalty given by the Duke of Connaught. The west window is in memory of Queen Victoria; the handsome east window of the Crucifixion is to her youngest son, the Duke of Albany, and was given by Edward the Seventh and his brothers and sisters; the attractive painted reredos is the Duke of Connaught's memorial to his brother Edward the Seventh; and the carved vestry door is the gift of many people in memory of the King. There are marble tablets to the Duchess of Connaught and her daughter. Brass inscriptions tell of the three wives of a soldier who died in 1927, two of the wives being charmingly portrayed in glass as angels. An attractive transept window is dedicated to Sir Howard Elphinstone, who won the VC in the Crimean War and was drowned at sea off Ushant in 1890. It shows Our Lord and two angels, and has these words: The sea gave up the dead which were in it.

Bagshot has many acres that are a feast of beauty at rhododendron time, and at Penny Hill, a mile away, there is a remarkable holly hedge growing in places to a height of 40 feet.

Here Died Hubert de Burgh

BANSTEAD. It was here in Saxon days, for the Saxon church is mentioned in Domesday Book; but long before that life was going on here, for the skeleton of a young man of the Bronze Age has been found in a garden, buried just deep enough to escape the plough of bygone days.

Within historic time its highest point, on Tumble Beacon 700 feet up, was a beacon for warning London when the Armada sailed up the Channel; but the chief historic event hereabouts was 350 years before that, when there lay dying in the manor house here (now gone but then standing by the church) the brave and famous Hubert de Burgh. Much has this stout soldier to his credit in our history, for he was a mighty man in the land, but when all else about him is forgotten the picture of Hubert by Shakespeare will live in the hearts of men. Shakespeare has given us no more moving scene than that in which Arthur, heir to the throne in King John's day, pleads with Hubert for his eyes, "These eyes that never did, nor never shall, so much as frown on you." It is as tender a scene as Shakespeare himself could give us.

It was next door to this church that Hubert died about seven centuries ago. The church comes from his time, but has 12th century pillars and arches in the nave. The font is 14th century. On the vestry wall is a flat sculpture of a child in a red robe with a ruff round its neck; he is Paul Tracy, who was in the world for a little while just after Shakespeare died. A brass tells us of a captain who fought for Charles Stuart by land and sea for 40 years, and a wall monument in the fashionable sculpture of the 18th century keeps alive the memory of Sir Daniel Lambert, a lord mayor who died from fever caught from the prisoners he was trying. Our prisons were beds of filth, and they killed those in the dock and those on the bench.

A tablet with a sculptured anchor is to a boy who went down on HMS Formidable in 1915; his name was George Stephenson.

In a fairyland of Banstead Wood the new buildings of Princess Elizabeth's Hospital for children were rising as this book went to press, a hospital translated into the country from London's Dockland, the patients coming by ambulance to a sunlight building, and resting when cured in a convalescent home close by.

Great Men and Great Trees

BARNES. It is one of London's suburbs by the Thames, and one of the greenest, for within its boundaries it has East Sheen Common with its 50 gorse-clad acres, Barnes Common of 120 acres, Palewell Common of 30 acres, and some acres of Richmond Park. It has also an attractive green with a pond, and a church consecrated by Stephen Langton in the year of Magna Carta.

The church has changed much under the restorer's hand and has little of its antiquity except three 13th century lancets and a 16th century tower, with a sundial reminding us that the night cometh. But in the churchyard is a yew planted in Stephen Langton's day, a veteran handsome in spite of the fact that its trunk has been preserved with three hundredweight of cement. The yew was centuries old when they laid a London citizen named Edward Rose to rest beside it in 1653, and it has been shading his grave ever since. One memorial to him is on the church wall, and another is the money the poor still receive from his will so long as they keep alive the name of Rose by growing three rose trees on his grave.

Several other memorials will attract the traveller who comes to see this church. There are quaint brass portraits of Edith and Elizabeth

Wylde, who died in 1508, standing at prayer on grassy mounds. There is a monument to the wife of Captain William Dawson which rests on the marble mouths of two cannon and shows the sorrowing husband in the naval costume of the eighteen-forties, and another of a woman leaning on an urn and holding a medallion of Sir Richard Hoare, an 18th century Lord Mayor of London.

Barnes has many links with famous names. In a house by the green Henry Fielding lived, and by the Common lived Douglas Jerrold for nine years, during that time writing Mrs Caudle's Lectures. Two years before the death of Queen Elizabeth there died here the man she sent to Fotheringay with the death warrant of Mary Queen of Scots, and who afterwards read the warrant on the scaffold. His name was Robert Beale.

But the town's associations with these names are now but shadowy memories, and Barnes has more tangible links with fame in the Ranelagh Club by the Thames. Ranelagh is the successor of the Old Manor House called Barn Elms which gave the town its name, and it is surrounded by many of the stately trees that gave the manor its name. With these elms is a giant plane 105 feet high, believed to be the biggest in England.

The story of this house goes back long before the spacious days of Elizabeth, but that was its Golden Age. It was the home of Elizabeth's Secretary of State, Sir Francis Walsingham, who kept an army of spies to protect the Queen and entertained her here three times before he brought himself to poverty. Later it was the home of Elizabeth's favourite, the Earl of Essex, and after the Restoration it became a place of public entertainment which often comes into Pepys's Diary. In the 18th century it was for a time the home of the witty and ugly John Heidegger, a Zurich pastor's son who made a fortune as George the Second's Master of Revels. Here he entertained his friend Handel. Early in the 19th century it belonged to Sir Lancelot Shadwell, the last Vice-Chancellor of England, who used to entertain the Varsity Crews here after the Boat Race. In 1884 the Ranelagh Club was founded, and today it is one of the most exclusive country clubs in the world, a great social centre and famous for polo, tennis, and golf.

In a smaller house on the Barn Elms Estate lived the poet Abraham Cowley, and here he was visited by John Evelyn. Ill-health drove him to Chertsey, but it was not long before he passed this way again, for when he died they brought his body down the river to the Abbey.

The Home of Old Sir Nicholas

BEDDINGTON. With its ancient church, the great house and its story, and the captivating possibility that here may be the body of Sir Walter Raleigh, Beddington remains a corner of Old Surrey, though it has grown up and linked itself with its neighbour Wallington. It shares with that thriving place a poignant Cross of Remembrance on the green. It shares the beautiful town hall at Wallington and the Library there, in which is one of the representative toys of English childhood, perhaps the finest Noah's Ark in England. But it is the old Beddington that we come to see.

The home of the Carews has suffered many changes since they left it. No longer does the River Wandle flow underneath in a culvert wide enough for a carriage and pair, coming out to be the central feature of the vista in the park: the river now goes another way. But the old house has kept its splendid 16th century hall, 61 feet long and 46 high, with its original stone floor and magnificent timbered roof. It has kept, too, the wall of the old orangery and the red brick pigeon-house with nesting-places for 1000 birds. The originals of the impressive iron gates are now in America, and the finely-wrought Tudor lock from the old gates has gone to South Kensington. The panelling of the hall was sold last century to a Mr Juggins, who made a living by turning it into snuff-boxes!

For 400 years the Carews were at Beddington, their direct line ending in 1762. Here Raleigh must often have come, for he married a niece of the Carews. After them came a miser who lined his coat with banknotes and hid money all over the house; a lady who gave away blankets at Christmas and had herself carried to church in a Sedan chair by four labourers in white smocks; an admiral who fought under Nelson; a young man who sold the estate to pay his debts; and an impostor who forced his way in and lived here until he was turned out. Finally the mansion was bought by the oldest orphanage for girls in the world (the Royal Female Orphanage), and it is now their attractive home. The orphanage was founded in London in 1758 by John Fielding, who, though blind from birth, became a celebrated lawyer and magistrate, and was knighted.

Ask to see the old hall if you come to Beddington, and ask to hold in your hand the tilting helmet of old Sir Nicholas, perhaps the greatest of all the Carews. He was a cousin of Anne Boleyn and a favourite of Henry the Eighth, going to the Field of the Cloth of Gold, and on one occasion entertaining Bluebeard in this very hall. But like many another he fell out of favour more than once, and lost his head on Tower Hill. One story says he quarrelled with the king over a game of bowls; but his execution was for treason in connection with a plot to put Cardinal Pole on the throne.

The church is a storehouse of Carew memories, and a museum of treasures old and new. For some of us its great interest will be that it was a familiar place to the wife of Sir Walter Raleigh, who was the daughter of Nicholas Throgmorton, lord of the manor and a kinsman of the Carews. The handsome tower is 15th century, with a big west window and a lofty arch into the nave. There is a Norman font with six arches, a Tudor bench with a poppyhead, a clock of 1718 from which the stage coaches may have taken their time, a coloured window to Bishop Wilberforce, and a fine modern painting (with over 20 panels) of the Last Judgment, probably copied from a German altarpiece. Nine miserere seats are 15th century, carved with heads and shields and leaves. The oldest treasure of all is in one of the two vestries, a Roman lead coffin dug up in the road outside, its top decorated with cockle shells, showing that it has held a pilgrim.

In the chancel are many brasses, some unfortunately hidden beneath the pews. One shows two sisters who died in 1507; another a man and a woman of about 1430; and a third Roger Elmebrygge in 15th century armour, his head on a cock and his feet on a very strange beast. There is a 19th century brass cross to John Ferrers, who was rector for 58 years. Two rectors before him met with strange fates, one being beheaded for treason in 1540, the other dying from smallpox caught at the coronation of George the Second.

Somewhere by these walls sleeps the first Nicholas Carew, founder of the family and Keeper of the Privy Seal in the 14th century. His grave is lost, but his memorial is in this very fabric, for he left a legacy toward its rebuilding. There are fine brass portraits of a second Nicholas and his wife Isabella, standing in 15th century costume under an ornamental canopy; another shows Philippa Carew and her 13 brothers and sisters. Four of the brothers were called John, and altogether they are a tragic group, for Philippa died in 1414 when only a girl, and the 13 seem to have died in infancy. A brass cross is the memorial of Margaret Oliver, who was a nurse in this sad family.

The Carew chapel and its screen probably come from the time of Richard Carew, who was Governor of Calais and died in 1520. His carved table tomb is here, with restored brasses of him and his wife let into the top. Next to it is perhaps the loveliest piece of carving in Beddington, the exquisite alabaster figure of Sir Francis Carew of 1611, lying here in his armour and skull-cap. It is a rich monument indeed, put up by his heir Sir Nicholas, who kneels on the front of it with his wife and children. This Sir Nicholas was the brother of Sir Walter Raleigh's wife. One of the children has put up a tablet to their mother, who fell asleep in 1633 after teaching them "heaven's great God to serve."

Sir Francis Carew who lies here was the son of the Sir Nicholas who died on Tower Hill, and he received back from the Queen some of the estates confiscated when his father was beheaded. He preferred a peaceful life at Beddington to the perils of being a Court favourite, and spent much time making his garden beautiful and famous. A walk he laid out is still called Queen Elizabeth's Walk. He planted an orangery with seed said to have been brought by Raleigh from Florida, and he grew the first orange trees grown in England. Evelyn tells us that they were 13 feet high, and that ten thousand oranges a year were gathered from them. The orangery wall still standing is a remarkable piece of workmanship a yard thick, pierced with flues to allow the trees to be kept warm. Sir Francis entertained Queen Elizabeth at his house and must have offered her his home-grown oranges with pride. He knew, too, that she was fond of cherries, and took steps to defeat nature that she might have them. One of his cherry trees he covered with canvas to keep the sun off until the queen's visit was due, when he removed the covering and allowed a few sunny days to ripen the fruit. The orange trees perished in a great frost, and the famous cherry tree fell in a gale which destroyed 300 trees in the park.

The fine pulpit with its linenfold carving was probably the gift of Sir Francis to the church in which he worshipped, and there is a brass inscription to Elizabeth Boys, one of his servants. Another memorial is to Thomas Greenhill, who was steward to the Sir Nicholas of his day. It was put here by his brother and sister, and tells how he was "born and bred in the famous University of Oxford." Very quaint is the epitaph about him, the last lines recalling the last lines written by Sir Walter Raleigh:

> *Under thy feet interred is here*
> *A native born in Oxfordshire.*
> *First life and learning Oxford gave,*
> *Surrey to him his death, his grave.*
> *He once a hill was, fresh and green,*
> *Now withered is not to be seen,*
> *Earth in Earth shoueld up is shut,*
> *A hill into a hole is put;*
> *But darksome earth by power divine*
> *Bright at last as the sun may shine.*

High up in the Carew chapel is a tablet to Sir Benjamin Hallowell-Carew, the admiral who inherited the estate and took the name.

He is remembered as the man who gave Nelson a reminder that he, too, was mortal. Born plain Benjamin Hallowell, a Canadian, who entered the navy as a boy, he came early under the influence of Nelson, with whom he fought not only at sea but in the trenches. A giant in stature as in courage, he quelled an incipient mutiny with his fist, fought wherever fighting was to be done, in fierce minor engagements and with distinction at the battle of St Vincent. But it is with the Battle of the Nile that his name is immortally associated.

As he drew into line to take the place of the disabled Bellerophon, his ship (the Swiftsure) was holed beneath the waterline by a shot from a land battery. He went into battle with pumps working, with four feet of water in the hold, let go his anchor, and in two minutes was discharging broadshots at the Franklin and the Orient. His was the bombardment that set fire to the deck on which Louis Casabianca and his little son were soon to die, the boy steadfastly refusing to leave the burning deck. In an hour and a half the great French ship blew up, and Hallowell was able to save only 11 men of all her crew. Seven years later Hallowell made Nelson a gift of wood and metal from the Orient, with a note saying, "My lord, herewith I send you a coffin, made of part of l'Orient's mainmast, that when you are tired of this life you may be buried in one of your own trophies; but may that period be far distant is the sincere wish of your obedient and much obliged servant, Benjamin Hallowell."

In that coffin Nelson lies under the dome of St Paul's, beneath the sarcophagus made for Cardinal Wolsey.

The Great Raleigh Mystery

IN spite of the fact that St Margaret's at Westminster claims the body of Raleigh, it is believed that it may be here at Beddington, his head being not far off at West Horsley.

It is certain that it was the wish and intention of Raleigh's wife that he should be buried here, as we know from the pathetic letter she wrote to her brother Nicholas Carew on the day of Raleigh's execution. Its 17th century spelling slightly altered, it runs:

I desire, good brother, that you will be pleased to let me bury the worthy body of my noble husband Sir Walter Raleigh in your church at Beddington where I desire to be buried. The lords have given me his dead body, though they denied me his life. This night he shall be brought to you with two or three of my men.
God hold me in my wits.

What, we may ask, happened to give rise to the tradition that the body was laid in St Margaret's? The execution was early in the morning, the body could not be kept lying in the street, Lady Raleigh had only the day before been granted possession of it, so she had no time to write to her brother at Beddington, for she did not leave her husband till midnight. It was imperative to seek the shelter of the church near by and put the body in a vault out of sight of prying eyes. This action was recorded in the register, as we know. But there was plenty of time to send the body later in the day to Beddington, and it may be that the letter came with the body.

There was no entry in the register of Beddington of the burial, but that might be accounted for by the need of secrecy and the wish of Sir Nicholas to avoid the risk of the king's disfavour. Raleigh's body would undoubtedly be placed in the Carew vault, but that cannot be searched because fifty years ago it was filled up with concrete.

So the mystery remains, but we are inclined to think with a descendant of Lady Raleigh that this brave woman was the last person to turn aside from her purpose. She who had her husband's head embalmed and carried it with her in a red leather bag almost to the day of her death would hardly have permitted the body to lie anywhere but Beddington where she hoped that her own body would lie when her time came.

THE KING'S ENGLAND

Brunel's Half-Sovereign

BETCHWORTH. It has all the atmosphere that makes our English villages what they are, a great house near an old church, a quaint inn sign, old cottages, a lovely bit of the Mole winding between high trees, and little memories leading us back into history. A quiet road leads to the church past an old house said to be the home of bygone priests; and we found the churchyard was delightful in the evening light, with the sun shining on the white tower and the old red roofs, and the breeze rustling in a ring of splendid trees.

The church has a roof of ancient Horsham tiles, and its interior has the dignity of 13th century arches lining the nave. The tower was moved last century from a central position to one side, and built into one of its windows is a stone capital carved by a Saxon craftsman. A Norman arch opens from the tower into an aisle.

The chancel has many things to see. There are three lancet windows 700 years old, a pair of old iron gates, probably made locally, a brass portrait of a vicar, William Wardysworth, who died in 1533, and a tablet to Henry Goulburn, laid here in 1856 after holding high positions in the Government under four sovereigns. The panelling was put in when James Richard Corbett had been churchwarden for 50 years. He lived at More Place, a fine house going back to the 15th century, and he gave the two rich candelabra in the sanctuary. His wife cared for this chancel for 40 years, carving the fine choir stalls and beautifying the sanctuary with her handiwork.

The village chest under the tower is one of the biggest we have seen. It is probably Norman, and the solid oak from which it is hewn may well have been growing 1000 years ago. It is seven feet long and nine round, with seven great iron bands and three keyholes. The ends are ten inches thick and the sides about half as much.

There is an elegant Flemish candelabra of the 17th century, and Tudor linenfold panels worked into the ends of the seats. Let into the floor is a brass plate with the names of seven of the Stables family, headed by one whose body lies near the field of Waterloo, where he fell.

The window of Our Lord knocking at the door was given by a doctor; and there are two other doctors we think of here. A little brass inscription to Thomas and Alianora Morsted brings the memory that their son Thomas, who died in 1450, was the surgeon of three

English kings, and left money for the repair of this chapel where his parents sleep; and a sculptured portrait is the memorial of the famous royal surgeon Sir Benjamin Brodie, who died in 1862 at Broome Park in the village.

Becoming President of the Royal Society and of the Royal College of Surgeons, he was one of the most distinguished men of his day. He attended Sir Robert Peel when he was thrown from his horse on Constitution Hill, and he counted Isambard Brunel one of the strangest cases of his long career. The famous engineer was amusing some children with conjuring tricks when he had the misfortune to swallow half a sovereign. He was put head downward in a revolving frame of his own design, and Brodie operated on his throat, tunnelling into Brunel! It was a very delicate task, but the coin that so nearly caused a tragedy was at last recovered.

One of 29 names on the churchyard cross is that of Major Noel Thornton, DSO, who rose from the ranks to command a battalion, at the head of which he was mortally wounded.

Gordon's Stick

BISLEY. It is known to riflemen all the world over for its annual rifle competition, promoted by the National Rifle Association. The shooting takes place on land hired from the War Office and the chief event is the shooting for the King's Prize of £250 for the highest score. But the village has an interest of its own, and has a stick more interesting than any of its rifles.

Its little 13th century church has several treasures: the bell given to Bisley by the monks of Chertsey Abbey 600 years ago, the Jacobean pulpit, a beautiful Elizabethan chalice, a silver cup engraved with leaves and flowers, and the charming 15th century porch said to be made from a single oak.

One would think a porch 500 years old would be lovingly cared for in a village which has almost lost its touch with the old world, but we found these fine old timbers disfigured and cut with the names of scribblers of two centuries.

Near by are several famous institutions doing fine work. The Bisley Schools educate poor boys and teach them a trade; Princess Christian's Homes and Workshops are for disabled soldiers and sailors; and the Gordon Boys Home, the nation's monument to

General Gordon, teaches and trains 250 poor boys. Here is kept the famous stick which was carried by General Gordon instead of a revolver and sword. It had the most inspiring effect on those who were on the verge of panic, and steadied others who were on the brink of disloyalty. If Gordon was not afraid, they would argue, there was nothing to be afraid of.

The Village of Great Delight

BLECHINGLEY. It has seen great days and lost a great castle. It is old enough to have been given away by the Conqueror, and its castle was lost and won again and again in the fight of the Barons against King John. Its famous folk include great lords who lost their heads on Tower Hill, Henry the Eighth's unwanted Anne of Cleves, and Howards of Effingham. But of all the glory of their great castle and their medieval manor nothing but a gatehouse and fragments of ivied walls remain.

We have only to run through it to see that it is a village of great delight, for it has one of those charming wide streets which climb up a hill between green banks and old houses, and at the bottom of the street is the white coaching inn at whose windows faces would be peering when Henry the Eighth passed by. There is a house built by Inigo Jones, and a charming gabled house called Pendhill Court. There are lanes not surpassed in beauty and character anywhere in England, bringing us to pleasant farms and captivating houses. One of the best of all is the narrow way that brings us to the church, little timbered houses clustering round with red roofs and red steps.

It has been the lovely corner of the village for 800 years, since the Normans came to build the church. They built the tower we see: its light still comes through their windows. Their arch into the nave has been pointed by our English builders, but the pillars with their capitals are as the Norman masons left them.

The church was refashioned in the 13th century and again in the 15th, and most of what we see has stood 500 years. The south porch has the old priest's room above it, and a delightful Madonna holding the Child with outstretched arms. The west doorway has heads of a bishop and a king, and in the south porch hangs the old panelled door with its knocker complete. It brings us into the spacious nave with four bays each side and with a great array of brass and stone. There are splendid stone corbels indoors and out, a 15th century

Beddington · The Medieval Church

Blechingley · The Old Manor Gatehouse

The Winding Road

The View Towards Leith Hill

THE FAMOUS HEIGHTS OF BOX HILL

font, and a fine Jacobean pulpit with the hourglass stand which kept it company and has missed it so long, for the pulpit was ending an adventure when we called, having been away for two generations. We found it home again. It was in this pulpit that Nathaniel Harris used to preach in the days of Cromwell, and one of his sermons brought him into trouble with the Parliament, so that he had to confess the fault on his knees and ask the pardon of the House.

There is a very attractive gallery of brass portraits of Tudor folk: an unknown girl of 1470 with long hair and a gown trimmed with fur, a priest of 1510 in his robes, Thomas Ward of 1541 with his wife in a butterfly headdress and a representation of the Trinity with the dove perched on the cross, and three stately groups of children who have lost their parents, all of about 1520, a group of six girls, another group of five, and a group of six boys.

Here lies near the altar, in a table tomb with richly carved panels, the owner of the castle in Elizabethan days, Sir Thomas Cawarden, master of the revels to Henry the Eighth, who entertained his royal master here. In a fashionable tomb which he himself designed and in his vanity set up to block the east window of an aisle, lies Lord Mayor of London Sir Robert Clayton and his wife Dame Martha, with urns and cherubs and painted shields about them. They stand under a canopy resting on fluted columns, he in his robes and his gold chain, she in a lace-trimmed gown, wearing gold earrings and bracelets. Below them is an appealing little figure of a child in a frilled bonnet resting on a cushion, and on each side of the parents is a weeping boy.

On another Clayton monument is a cherub by an urn, and there is a tablet to a General Clayton who served under Wellington. A wall monument to Sir William Bensley has the curious sort of sculpture fashionable in the early 19th century, with a woman weeping by a tomb, a ship on one side and an elephant's head on the other. Sir William served the East India Company.

In one of the west windows is David playing on his harp, and another window has fragments of heraldic glass from medieval days.

The White Track Up the Hill

BOX HILL. It is one of the natural glories of Surrey, the view from its summit so wonderful that no Englishman can see it without a thrill of pride.

Here is an ancient ford over the River Mole where Canterbury Pilgrims may have crossed centuries ago, though the 13 stepping-stones are new. At Burford Bridge, on one of the most famous roads in Surrey, is a green and white inn where Nelson spent some of his last hours before sailing to Trafalgar, and where he parted for the last time from Lady Hamilton.

Robert Louis Stevenson often looked up at Box Hill, and it was here that he heard the story of a rider by night who rattled on the shutters of the window, an idea he used in the short poem all children know, Windy Nights:

> *Whenever the moon and stars are set,*
> *Whenever the wind is high,*
> *All night long in the dark and wet,*
> *A man goes riding by.*
> *Late in the night when the fires are out,*
> *Why does he gallop and gallop about?*

West Humble, with a ruined chapel, is only a mile away, and Sheridan had a house near by at Polesden Lacey. It is said that Keats found his inspiration for the last 500 lines of Endymion on Box Hill, and in a letter to a friend he tells us how he went up the hill by moonlight and came down with some of these lines in his thoughts.

Who could count the thousands of pilgrims who have come up the white track bringing us to the top of this hill? They came centuries before Keats was here, and in our own day they come every day in summer, modern pilgrims from London and all the country round, everyone stirred by the wonder of the hill itself and the glory to be seen from the top. The winding track brings us 600 feet above the sea. In spring and summer the whitebeams show finely among the deeper green of oaks and yews and beeches. The box trees are perhaps the finest in England.

But even without its trees the hill would be famous for its view. It is not the most spacious in our Motherland, but where can we see more perfect loveliness, a more exquisite piece of countryside? The magic of the Weald is felt as well as seen, and from this view-point we look down on Burford Bridge, the valley of the Mole between Dorking and Leatherhead, the shining river winding to the Thames, and the spire of Brockham Green. There are the fair miles of Surrey stretching away to the South Downs and Sussex, all the glory of Ranmore Common, Leith Hill, and a peep of Hindhead.

George Meredith knew Box Hill and lived close by it for 40 years. He lived and died at Flint Cottage not far from Burford Bridge, and in all but the last few months of his life he loved nothing better than roaming about this countryside. No English novelist of his generation understood nature better, and in many of his books he has described the beauties of these woods and meadows round his home.

The Man Who Would Not Be Simple

HE was more famous then than now, and he may not be remembered. A strange man in many ways, George Meredith came to Flint Cottage in 1867. It was a house that had already become famous through Jane Austen's novel Emma. Here he wrote to his heart's content, lived like a little king, and did the strangest things to the astonishment of his neighbours. At the end of his garden he built a little summerhouse in which he hung a hammock, making for himself a retreat from the world. Here he would eat and sleep alone; he could often be heard talking to his own characters or breaking into singing.

He was never a popular novelist. He made it impossible that he should be, by the style he adopted and sedulously cultivated.

He was the only son of a Portsmouth tailor, and the father failed in the business his flamboyant grandfather had built up. Clever, sensitive, and lonely, the boy became acutely self-conscious, and he had no helpful home training. His mother died when he was a child and he was sent away to schools till he was 16, to grapple with life as best he could. His last years were spent at a good Moravian school in Germany, where he absorbed languages, liberal thought, and some philosophy.

At heart he was a poet. When he came home he was articled to a solicitor. He had been educated with money left him by his mother, and a little of it was unspent. He was poor, proud, ambitious, and above all sensitive, and he loathed the life represented by his Portsmouth childhood. It was natural that he should look towards journalism and literature as a way of escape into a wider life, and he began to send poems and articles to magazines.

He had the power of making friends, and among his earliest were Thomas Love Peacock, the novelist, and his family. Peacock had a widowed daughter with one child; Meredith fell in love with her and married her when he was 21 and she was 30. It was in every way an ill-assorted marriage, and eventually his wife deserted him, leaving him with a five-year-old son. When 36 he married again, happily.

The first ten years of Meredith's literary life were a period of hard and varied work in an atmosphere of uncertainty. He wrote for the papers, published novels and poems, but he did not grip public attention. His first success came when he was 31 with his novel Ordeal of Richard Feverel. Then he became an accepted novelist, but he would not be simple and his work declined in intelligibility.

He wrote his books with infinite pains, packing them with epigram and wit, for intellectual parade. But he does not get on with the story. He is afraid to be plain and simple, however much the tale may require it. He searches hard for unusual ways of saying anything. It is pleasing to those who learn how to play with him, but he could not find enough people to care for the game. He was one of the vain writers who let the vanity of authorship befog their commonsense, and he remains an oddity.

Two Brothers

BRAMLEY. Its chief attractions are to be found in the quiet lanes round about. Unstead Bridge, with its five stone arches, is one of a group of old bridges over the Wey. In Unstead Farm close by we see a delightful Elizabethan timbered house, in which 16th century wall paintings were discovered a few years ago. Another old house is Nurscombe Farm, not far from a lake and a mill prettily set among the trees.

Along one road we catch a glimpse of a Georgian house set in a park with a lake, a place all lovers of beauty will want to see, for it was the early home of Gertrude Jekyll, who sleeps not far away at Busbridge. Here as a little girl she came with her parents, and here she spent 20 delightful years, learning to love nature and a garden, learning to paint and to draw, and tasting in her father's workshop the joys of making things with her hands. Her fame is worldwide, though her life was chiefly lived hereabouts in Surrey. It was in this house at Bramley that the foundations of her career were laid.

Within a stone's throw of her old home is the delightful house called Millmead, which she built in partnership with Sir Edwin Lutyens in

1904. It is what she meant it to be, an object-lesson in designing a beautiful home on a narrow site built up on both sides.

Standing in a trim churchyard, the church has a 13th century tower with a shingled spire. The chancel is the same age and has eight lancet windows, three of them filled with good modern glass. Some of the moulding on the doorway is Norman.

Two brass tablets, side by side on the wall, are in memory of two brothers, Commanders in the Navy, who lost their lives as young men in the service of England. Henry Street was one of the 600 to go down in the Channel with the Formidable when she sank on New Year's Day in 1915, the first battleship of her class torpedoed by a submarine. George Street was killed at Jutland in the next year, his ship the Queen Mary going down after the battle had been in progress for only half an hour.

A Noble Avenue

BROCKHAM GREEN. Its name comes from the badgers on the banks of the Mole, and its charm from houses old and new standing round a wide green. Adding to the scene is a grey church built in memory of Henry Goulburn, Chancellor of the Exchequer under Wellington and Home Secretary under Peel.

The oak reredos is a fine carving of the Last Supper, and there is a memorial window to the diplomatist Sir George Hamilton Seymour, who died in 1880. Two much finer windows near it show Christ with the children.

Close to Brockham Green is Betchworth Park, where is one of the finest avenues in Surrey. It has about 150 tall limes in four straight lines, leading up to the ruins of Betchworth Castle. Two broken walls and arches and windows are almost hidden by trees growing in and round them, making rather a sorry relic of a structure going back to the 15th century.

A few years ago the village was mourning an old friend of the manor house who had in his will remembered apparently everyone and everything connected with Brockham Green. He had left three hundred pounds to the cricket club and enough more to make a better pitch; fifty pounds for billiard prizes; five hundred pounds for an annual holiday for the children; one hundred pounds for the carol singers; more than a thousand pounds for the Brockham Home to provide Christmas dinners, pocket money, outings, and so on, for the children; and a yet more substantial sum for church improvements; and beyond all this there was ten pounds for any girl in the village who became a servant and remained for five years in one place. Treasure on earth in this Surrey village Mr Sidney Michael Poland built up, as well as treasure in heaven for himself.

The Old Glass

BUCKLAND. The Reigate and Dorking road passes between its church and an old black barn. The church, with a little shingled spire and 14th century timbers in its roof, was restored in 1860. The barn, which has a running fox for a weathervane, looks rather like a church, and indeed was used as a church during the restoration work.

We come to Buckland for its natural charm and its treasured old glass. It is in the window facing us as we enter. Side by side under rich canopies are 14th century figures of Peter with his keys and Paul with his sword, unspoiled examples of the medieval glass that has vanished from ten thousand village windows. The figures are finely coloured; Paul, with his beard and curly hair, is very striking. In another nave window is a little 15th century picture of the Madonna, holding a small bird to amuse the Child. Very attractive in the chancel are two modern glass roundels of a kneeling monk in blue and a knight in red. They are made from a description given by old Aubrey of the glass he saw here two centuries ago on his travels in Surrey. Perhaps it is a wonder he saw anything at all, for in 1725 the rector was writing to the bishop that Buckland had "no chapel, no curate, no papist, no nonconformists, no school."

An inscription on the organ tells of one who was churchwarden for 55 years. He was a fine old squire, who lived at Buckland Court in the wooded grounds by the church.

First Chief of Greenwich Observatory

BURSTOW. A very secluded corner of the Weald, it has the memory of a great man lingering in the church. For 35 years he was its rector, and if his business in the wider world took him often away we can yet imagine him, old and infirm, stepping up from his rectory garden into the churchyard and walking through the little door into the chancel where he sleeps.

He was John Flamsteed, who saw the beginnings of Greenwich Observatory, bought its first instruments out of his own poor allowance, and laid the firm foundations of its great work. He was the first Astronomer Royal of England.

It is said that he built parts of his old rectory house himself. He must have loved its garden, which includes the moated site of a house older still. Nothing in the church marks his grave, but the east window of the Nativity is his belated memorial.

The church has Norman masonry in some of its walls, and was enlarged in the 15th century. Its most remarkable feature is the 15th century structure of immense beams supporting the tower and spire, both shingled. There are four quaint shingled pinnacles, and the entire western end of the church seems to be made of wood, with a wooden doorway and two little wooden windows. The parts covered with weather-boarding are not beautiful, but the whole structure is considered one of the finest of its kind in the country. The 15th century font is carved with quatrefoils, and there is a very old iron-bound chest.

Among the great timbers under the tower is a tablet telling of the very human bequests made by John Flamsteed and his wife Margaret. He left £25 for two coats to be given every year to two poor Christian people of good and honest report, and she in her widowhood left the same for two poor widows to have petticoats and gowns.

Belonging to Burstow, but a few minutes away, is Smallfield Place, the fine Jacobean great house of Edward Bysshe, a successful lawyer honest enough to admit that he built it with " woodcock's heads," meaning the fees of foolish clients. The house may be seen from the road, and is impressive with its mullioned bay windows and its porch with the Bysshe arms. There is another old home of the Bysshes near by, and Shelley was descended from one of the family.

Our First Astronomer Royal was born at Denby in Derbyshire in 1646, son of a maltster who, when illness caused the boy's withdrawal from school, taught him arithmetic with a view to a business career, sternly discouraging his bent for science.

But in spite of opposition Flamsteed studied astronomical works, sundials, and the quadrant; and by the end of his 20th year he had formed a catalogue of 70 fixed stars, and was calculating the distance of the sun from the earth and the positions of the planets, first gaining fame by predicting what was to happen in the heavens in 1670.

The young man's work created such surprise that he was invited to London, and came in touch with Sir Isaac Newton and other famous scientists. A year later Charles the Second read a statement by Flamsteed that the places of the fixed stars in the catalogue were false, "and said, with some vehemence, he must have them anew observed, examined, and corrected, for the use of his seamen."

The result was the setting up of Greenwich Observatory, with bricks from Tilbury Fort, wood, iron, and lead from a Tower gatehouse, and funds from the sale of spoilt gunpowder. In that ramshackle building, without expert help, and with instruments almost entirely provided by himself, this indomitable invalid founded modern astronomy, on a salary of £90 a year.

He studied the motion of the earth, the places and movements of the stars, made the first step towards forecasting the weather, and by his observations of the moon enabled Newton to work out his lunar theory for the Principia. He died here at Burstow in December 1719, and sleeps in the chancel.

The Lovely Windows

BUSBRIDGE. It stands a little apart from Godalming, and it has seen the uncovering of foundations thought to belong to a tiny church older than the one the Saxons built in the town, a little Christian temple probably on the site of a pagan shrine. The site is in a field beyond Busbridge Park, and the shrine may have been to the Saxon god Tiw, whose name gave us our Tuesday.

Busbridge church has a shingled tower and spire, and about it are many trees. It is one of the few churches in which the traveller will thankfully feel that every window is beautiful; but its interest does not end with stained glass, for here in the churchyard, not far from her home, sleeps Gertrude Jekyll, the grand old lady of English gardens. She lies beside her brother Sir Herbert Jekyll, the great civil administrator, who died a few weeks before her in 1932, and their very dignified memorial is fittingly crowned by a great bowl of growing flowers which were lovely when we called. We read on Gertrude Jekyll's grave that she was artist, gardener, and craftswoman, and of both these great lovers of natural things we read that

SURREY

*Their joy was in the work of their hands:
Their memorial is the beauty which lives after them.*

The church has a fine bronze screen designed by Sir Edwin Lutyens, who shared Miss Jekyll's workshop and was her partner in beautifying many English homes and gardens; it fills the upper part of the chancel arch and has figures of Our Lord and two kneeling angels. But finer still is the collection of lovely windows, those at the east and west and in the chancel being by Sir E. Burne-Jones, rich in colour and with many figures. The east window has St George, Elijah, Charlemagne, and three other saints; the side chancel windows have the Madonna, Mary Magdalene, and John; and the west window has Christ, John the Baptist, Elizabeth, Mary, and four New Testament scenes.

Very well drawn, though less rich in colour, are the windows of the nave, in which among other figures we see King Alfred holding a ship, Joan of Arc standing proudly in her armour, and the soldier and sailor saints Martin and Nicholas in memory of those who died in the war. One of the windows is a tribute to Charles Henry Tisdall who fell in gallantly rescuing one of his men at Ypres in 1916.

In the churchyard is a simple cross of great dignity by Sir Edwin Lutyens, a village peace memorial designed by the man who gave the Empire its Cenotaph in Whitehall.

Here, indeed, it is Lutyens everywhere, for our great architect built also Miss Jekyll's house at Munstead close by, Munstead Wood. It is a lovely place, the home of her creation and delight, in which she lived for 35 years and where she died.

The Lady of the Garden

GERTRUDE JEKYLL was born in London in 1843, daughter of a captain in the Grenadier Guards, who brought her into Surrey when she was still a child, but as she grew up allowed her to study art abroad, and gave her the advantage of the society of leading artists and musicians.

She became mistress of many arts, painting, silver-engraving, inlaying, woodcarving; embroidery, matching the dainty old church fabrics which she artistically restored; quilting with medieval fineness; banner-making, sign-painting for village inns. She made her own pot-pourri, her own omelettes, and her own gardening boots.

She became famous for her skill in furnishing and decorating houses, but still more as a gardener.

This work grew when, after the death of her mother in 1895, she established a home of her own at Munstead Wood, where she had 15 acres of land to beautify. Her garden attracted many distinguished horticulturists, one of whom, William Robinson, of Gravetye, encouraged her to depart from the formality of carpet-bedding and stereotyped schemes in favour of the informal, especially of herbaceous borders, with old and forgotten flowers brought again to perfection, with new hardy species and perennials sought from many lands.

We owe the modern garden, with its wonderful succession of floral splendours, mainly to her. A great prizewinner and a successful writer, she conducted an immense correspondence, teaching, guiding, and inspiring all whose love of gardens prompted them to write to her. Incomparable in her own sphere, she lived a beautiful and fruitful life of 89 years, and was laid to rest here beloved by all whose lives she had enriched.

Smith of the D.N.B.

BYFLEET. It has little chance to forget the Age of Power, with planes overhead and cars careering ten abreast round the three miles of Brooklands, not far off, but it has an ancient memory of a village of the Long Ago. In Dartnell Park has been found a polished axe of the Stone Age, and near the new church Roman pottery has been discovered. This fine flint-covered church of Byfleet West has a wealth of woodwork and a traceried reredos with 19 carved figures.

The old village is nearer the River Wey, and in the summer of 1937 there was found here evidence of a village far older than anything we see, for there was an Iron Age settlement in a sandpit by the river. There were people of the Belgic tribes living here when the Romans came, and the remains of their huts and their hearths and their rubbish pits have been found, with pieces of pottery and the curious pot-boiler pebbles used for warming water.

Long after this tribe had passed away the Saxons set up by the stream a manor house which was to have royal owners, starting with Edward the Second. It is one of the finest estates of the Black

Prince, and it is said that Chaucer himself helped to build the house. Here today stands its 17th century successor, with a golden gate flanked by fine pillars. It was the home of Anne of Denmark, queen of James the First, and it is thought the firs in the garden were planted to remind her of her native land.

The nave and the chancel of the church are 14th century, though the shingled bell turret is modern. Two fragments of the original decoration are preserved under glass on the wall, one a red consecration cross, the other a faded picture of a king, crossed by a pattern of red lions. There is a Jacobean pulpit, a 15th century font with four faces of angels, and a pathetic collection of wooden crosses from France as a permanent peace memorial. The chancel has been made attractive with modern woodwork, and the roof is gay with colour. The brass of a 15th century rector, Thomas Teylar, hangs on the chancel wall, showing him in the vestments of a cathedral canon, with a fur hood. Above him is a window of medieval glass, with an unknown saint giving blessing and girding his brown cloak about him, a strange beast showing among a medley of fragments, a lovely head of Christ, and a picture of Our Lord blessing the golden-crowned Madonna. In a three-cornered light above this old window is a picture in brown glass of a little house in Nazareth.

One of the rectors on the list here is Stephen Duck, the quaint parson poet who began life in the 18th century as a farm labourer in Wiltshire. Saving a little money, he bought books and pored over Paradise Lost with a dictionary. With the help of his friends he became something of a sensation at the Court of Queen Caroline, who liked his poems and made him her librarian at Richmond. He married Sarah Big, the Queen's housekeeper at Kew, and was afterwards rector here for four years, his life ending sadly when he drowned himself at Reading.

Stephen Duck owed his ministry here to the good offices of a Byfleet friend, who, like him, met his death by drowning. He was Joseph Spence, the Boswell of Pope and his circle. His marble monument is on the west wall of the church. Near it, in the churchyard, is the headstone of Elizabeth Ayres, a contemporary of his, who when she died had been "mother, grandmother, and great-grandmother of 125 children."

It is surprising to find at the entrance of a house, near the private zoo at Foxwarren, a totem pole covered with queer carvings. It is 41 feet high and came from the Queen Charlotte Islands, off British Columbia. The pole stood before the house of the Chief at a place called Masset, and the carvings on it represent the various clans into which his ancestors had married. At the bottom is carved the clan of the Killer Whale, in the middle the clan of the Grizzly Bear, and at the top are three little men in high hats keeping watch for strangers.

Under an oak in the churchyard, in a grave ever fresh with flowers, lies George Smith, the philanthropic publisher to whom English literature owes one of its noblest possessions, the Dictionary of National Biography.

He may be called a hero of the intellectual life of the English-speaking world, for with no hope of profit he issued the magnificent work which every English library must possess. The death of his father and the withdrawal of partners left him in control of a publishing business at 22, and gallantly he faced the task. One of the great romances of his career was his acceptance of the manuscript of Jane Eyre from an unknown author in the country, and the subsequent appearance at his office of Charlotte Brontë. He published for Ruskin, Thackeray, Matthew Arnold, George Eliot, and the Brownings. With Thackeray as editor he founded the Cornhill Magazine, and five years later, under the editorship of Frederick Greenwood, the Pall Mall Gazette.

It was in 1882, when he had deservedly amassed a fortune, that he launched his proudest work, the D.N.B., which he regarded as his gift to posterity. The completion of the first edition was marked by a dinner party attended by Edward the Seventh, and by an honorary degree from Oxford University, to whom his heirs presented the copyright of the great work.

The Notebook of Joseph Spence

JOSEPH SPENCE, who sleeps at Byfleet, remains immortal for two things, his friendships (of which he thought everything), and his notebook (of which he thought nothing). The first made the second possible, but he regarded it so little that he never published it. Booksellers paid him thousands of pounds for learned works now dead; the notebook, which is for all time, lay buried for fifty years and was then pirated on the same day by two rival firms.

The romance of it all began when the scholarly Spence wrote a review of Pope's Homer, so beginning a friendship with the fiery little poet which ended only with death. The young scholar came to know all the poet's friends; with his purse and his sympathy he was at the disposal of all who needed financial aid or the support of good comradeship.

He came to the help of James Thomson, author of The Seasons, when the poet had hardly a boot to his feet; of Stephen Duck, the Devonshire labourer-poet, who could not read a book without the help of a dictionary; of Thomas Blacklock, the blind Scottish poet; of Robert Hill, the Hertfordshire tailor and schoolmaster who taught himself Latin and Greek while labouring with the needle and mastered Hebrew while tramping the countryside. Spence's friends included all the luminaries of our Augustan Age of Literature, and he made notes of what they did, what they said of themselves, and what they thought of giants they had known. As Spence's Anecdotes, the little notebook is as precious to us in its way as Drummond's Conversations with Ben Jonson. Dr Johnson, who read it in manuscript, used many of the stories for his Lives of the Poets, and a host of others have had recourse to the same pages.

The notebook fills the blanks in many great lives with story and detail for which there is no substitute. We could not know the true Pope but for this volume. For the last 20 years of his life Spence lived here, and one morning in 1768 he was found drowned in a stream of water which ran at the bottom of his garden.

Bret Harte and Arthur Sullivan

CAMBERLEY. Till about the time of Waterloo the traveller would have found at Camberley little but heather and highwaymen. Then the Royal Military College came to Sandhurst across the Berkshire border, and this part of Surrey was changed from bare open common to wooded enclosures dotted with handsome houses and rows of shops. Wonderful Wellingtonias grew up forming an avenue a mile long at Heatherside Nursery, and today they are among the finest in England, over 80 feet high. The 40 feet of a tower still standing in a private garden is half an obelisk built 200 years ago by a man who devised this curious way of signalling to friends at West Wycombe 30 miles distant. The obelisk was burned by gypsies, but has given its name to the street in which St George's Church rises with its tall turret. Its east window has pictures of saints dedicated by Lord Ypres to the men who fell in the South African War. A church up the hill has an east window to a hero of the Great War, Admiral Sturdee, who sleeps at Frimley on the Surrey border. The church has uncommon columns of wood, and the east window has in it a compass and sextant with the sun and moon.

The Staff College at Camberley is older than either of these churches, though not yet very old, for it was while standing in the rain watching the workmen erecting this great brick block that Prince Albert caught the chill from which he died. The college, which was built at a cost of fifty thousand pounds, was founded by the Duke of Cambridge, after whom the district was called Cambridge Town. That name has disappeared, but today part of Camberley is still called York Town, after the Duke of York who founded the Royal Military College at Sandhurst. The Berkshire boundary runs through the college lake, a lovely stretch of water fringed with trees. It has a sad memory, for in York Town church, with a stone spire towering above the busy main road, is a window to a Major Francis Richard Taylor, professor of military surveying, who was drowned in the lake while trying to save the life of his child.

Camberley has a modest museum, including a collection of flint implements from the Stone Age found in excavating for the Guildford Bypass, and a stone hand of a Roman statue found at Bagshot. There are coins and a highwayman's pistol picked up on Bagshot Heath, and pottery from a Roman villa at Rapley Farm excavated in the 18th century. What many may think most interesting in this small collection, however, is the inkstand of Bret Harte, the American journalist and poet who made his home in Surrey, perhaps the very inkstand into which he dipped his pen to write those lines on the pen dropped by a beloved musician:

> *This is the reed the dead musician dropped,*
> *With tuneful magic in its sheath still hidden;*
> *The prompt allegro of its music stopped,*
> *Its melodies unbidden.*

SURREY

Long ago there was another musician hereabouts, Bandmaster Sullivan of Sandhurst Military College, and here lived his little son Arthur in Albany Terrace. He went to the National School at the back, and we may be sure he would often stand and look with wonder at his father's band. Many years after, when he was setting Longfellow's Golden Legend to music and wished to do it in the country, he asked some friends here to find him rooms to work in and they found him the very rooms in which he had lived as a boy. We read in his Life that in those early years he gained a knowledge of all the instruments of a band, "not a mere passing acquaintance, but a lifelong intimate friendship;" and we may look back to his days in this unromantic corner of the world as the beginning of one of the most romantic achievements in the annals of English music.

£20 a Year

CAPEL. It is close to the Sussex border; and its rickety old windmill two miles along the Horsham road is closer still, standing almost on the boundary line.

Its chief interest centres in the church, with a nave and chancel 700 years old. There are two good doorways, each carved with a pattern of crosses, and against a wall stands the base of a 13th century font. In the chancel are two small figures from the days of Drake, kneeling at prayer with a desk between them; they are John Cowper, a Serjeant-at-Law, and his wife Julyan.

There is a tablet to Rawson William Rawson, who was Governor of the Bahamas and the Windward Islands and was laid to rest here at the close of last century. He served England for 46 years.

On the list of vicars we come across Jacob Marchant, who served for 34 years in the 18th century, and would surely have agreed with Goldsmith that the Vicar of Wakefield was passing rich on £40 a year, for he had to manage with only half that sum.

Margaret's Well

CARSHALTON. It has in the very heart of it a lake of clear water, and near it a precious little pond fringed with trees. The pond was dry when we called, but on it was a stone which marks it as a place of pilgrimage for the disciples of John Ruskin, who had the pool cleared in memory of his mother and set up the stone with this inscription:

THE KING'S ENGLAND

In obedience to the Giver of Life, of the brooks and fruits that feed it, of the peace that ends it, may this well be kept sacred for the service of men's flocks and flowers and be by kindness called Margaret's Well.

In one of his books John Ruskin declares that there is no lovelier piece of lowland scenery in the south of England than that which borders the sources of the River Wandle. The lovely lake in the middle of Carshalton is one of the sources of the Wandle, and the main road runs between it and the church. The lake is crossed in the middle by a bridge, and on three sides is surrounded by trees, lawns, and shrubs. When we called the seagulls were on the water and were lining the clerestory cornice of the church.

The church walls, rising in flint, continuing in white stone, and crowned with a copper spire, are finely reflected in the lake. They are 700 years old and house an array of brasses in the south chapel. Above an altar tomb in the sanctuary kneels Nicholas Gaynesford of 1498 with his wife and their four sons. He kneels on a grass-covered mound with a drawn sword near him, she is wearing a butterfly headdress. It is one of the most important brasses in Surrey owing to the fact that the red enamel on the dress is still here. On the floor are brasses of a priest in his robes, probably Walter Gaynesford of 1493, and of Thomas Elymbrigge in armour, with his head on a helmet, under a double canopy. The brass was engraved in 1497 and a pedestal in the middle of the canopy has the Madonna with the crucified Christ in her lap. Joan Burton of 1524 is standing on a grassy mound in gown with a fur-trimmed cuffs.

A stone on the wall of the chapel near these brasses has a curious inscription about a vicar here and one of his successors; it tells us that under a stone guarding the ashes of a certain Fryer sometime vicar here is raked up the dust of W. Quelche, a minister since the Reformation "whose lot was through God's mercy to burn incense here about 30 years."

At the end of the aisle is a huge monument with the reclining figure of Sir William Scawen, an 18th century Governor of the Bank of England; he has long curly hair and is holding a skull. There is a modern iron chancel screen with fine foliage work at the top, 13th century pillars with beautifully carved capitals, and a small window panel of the Nativity by an 18th century artist. We noticed that an 18th century rector stayed 52 years.

Caterham War Coppice Road  **Purley** Promenade de Verdun

Mickleham The Druids Grove, Norbury Park

Charterhouse, near Godalming

Cranleigh School, near the Sussex Border

Royal Holloway College at Egham

THREE FAMOUS SURREY SCHOOLS

SURREY

In a nameless grave in the churchyard lies Sir Edward Whitaker, who captured Gibraltar for England one night with the loss of but one man; just outside the churchyard is Anne Boleyn's Well, where she stumbled one day in riding with her lord; and on a stone by the church are these lines to a Carshalton man of 200 years ago:

> *Tom Humphrys lies here, by death beguiled,*
> *Who never did harm to man, woman, or child;*
> *And, since without foe no man e'er was known,*
> *Poor Tom was nobody's foe but his own:*
> *Lay light on him earth, for none would than he,*
> *(Though heavy his bulk) trip it lighter on thee.*

Entrancing Landscape

CATERHAM. It is on the chalk hills of Surrey, 300 to 800 feet high, but no longer is it one of the quiet places, for it has developed with the railway and is a gateway to some of the finest countryside near London. What Nature made so beautiful has not been spoiled even in our Motor Age, for all about Caterham is entrancing landscape, and ramblers who love the treeclad hills and valleys find much to gladden their hearts. All who have walked along War Coppice Road, or climbed along the lovely Harestone Valley to View Point, with its glorious panorama reaching away to the South Downs, will bear witness to the beautiful scenery of this corner of Surrey.

In and about Caterham are many modern churches, but the church of St Lawrence, standing high above the busy Valley road, goes back 800 years, although it was refashioned in the 13th century. Its tiny nave of two bays has white walls, old timbers in the roof, a remnant of a Norman window peeping out by the porch, and fragments of the Norman mason's carving in the capitals of the massive piers. A worn face is looking out across the chancel among the foliage of one of the capitals (now set in the wall), and on the nave arcade, looking at all who come in, is a grinning head.

Kneeling at prayer on the chancel wall is the white figure of Elizabeth Legrew, a rector's wife laid to rest here in 1825. She kneels with an open book, her long hair falling on her shoulders. A rector of her time, Charles Hodgkin, was here for 55 years. The two bells in the little shingled turret were ringing here when Caterham was a hamlet, and when London was in the grip of Plague and Fire.

This is the mother church, a quaint, aged-looking place inside and out, and now used as a Sunday School, but across the way is the spacious and dignified daughter church of St Mary, a 19th century building with a tall and graceful spire. In the churchyard we noticed the graves of German flying men who perished in an aeroplane crash in 1929. The finest possession of the church is its beautiful reredos, richly carved and painted with 20 sculptured figures under golden canopies; in the central scene are the Wise Men bringing their gifts. In the south chapel is the stone figure of a schoolgirl by Matthew Noble; she is Alice Stewart Danvers, a lifelike figure with long hair and her hands clasped on her breast.

A tablet to Henry Sanders, who died for us in France, has these lines of Robert Louis Stevenson:

> *Glad did I live and gladly die*
> *And I laid me down with a will;*

and there is a tragic memory in the epitaph of Michael Bruce and his wife, who lost their lives in a wreck of 1910. A small brass tells us that William Brough who lies here was parish clerk for 62 years.

Down in the valley stands another modern church, St John, with winged gargoyles reaching out from the parapet of its fine tower. It has a window in the chancel beautiful with blue-winged angels, and another with glowing figures of Gabriel and Michael and St John.

The east window has 60 figures gathered about Our Lord in Majesty. There is a bronze figure of Christ on the cover of the 700-year-old font, and near it on the wall is a sculptured relief at which children growing up must look with much interest, for it shows a Caterham teacher with a book in her hand and the scholars about her.

The Monk's Ladder of Salvation

CHALDON. One famous thing draws the traveller to this beauty spot among the Surrey Downs, one of the finest ancient possessions of its kind in the land; but there are other treasures old and rare and quaint. They are gathered in the little church with more than 1000 years of history behind it, set quietly at home with nature, its companion an ancient farmhouse with a bargeboard 600 years old.

The church is high and short and wide, with a tower and shingled spire rising up from a corner by the porch. The outlines of the nave and chancel are as they were in the century of the Conqueror, and some of the masonry from that time is still here. From the next century come one of the aisles and the chapel. The other aisle was built on two centuries later.

One of the curious possessions of Chaldon is in the chancel, next to an arched tomb 600 years old, a remarkable tablet with a face in the form of a flaming sun. It does not seem to be anybody's memorial, yet it has a message for all from 1562, and says:

*Good Redar warne all men and women while they be here to be ever
  good to the poore and nedy.
The cry of the poore is extreme and very sore.
In thys worlde we rune oure rase:
God graunte us to be with Christ in tyme and space.*

It is possible that the initials on the tablet refer to John and Ellen Richardson, who were living here in Elizabeth's reign and may have wished to preach this little sermon.

From a century later comes the fine pulpit, one of the few known to have been made in the Commonwealth. It bears the name of Patience Lambert, who had seen her husband buried in the nave below.

In the porch hangs the oldest bell in Surrey, and one of the oldest in the country, its voice still heard. It was certainly made before 1250 and may be several decades earlier, and its tells us that it is Paul's bell. Its fellow, Peter's Bell, was here 400 years ago, but is now lost; the two may well have been ringing in the Norman church.

But the chief of all Chaldon's treasures is counted among the rare possessions of England, adorning the oldest wall of the church with a little Norman window above it. It is the great painting of the Ladder of Salvation, leading up to heaven and down to hell, an extraordinary achievement of Norman art thought to be the work of a monk 750 years ago. Preserved by a coat of whitewash (under which it was found in 1870), it is in wonderful condition, something to fascinate old and young today as it has been fascinating the people of Chaldon for centuries.

This great picture, 17 feet long and 11 feet high, is filled with astonishing figures and scenes. As old as the dream of Jacob, and perhaps much older, is the idea of the ladder of salvation with the ascending and descending figures. Halfway up the ladder is a band of cloud stretching the length of the picture. It is painted in the conventional manner of olden days and is the dividing line between the salvation of souls and the torments of hell. With the ladder it forms a great cross, cutting the picture into four parts.

At the right of the lower division is the tree of life. Its formal design is one of the clues that help us to guess the date of the picture, which was painted about 1170, the year Thomas Becket was murdered. A serpent is hiding among the branches. It is here that the story begins, for we are first reminded of the Fall of Man.

The remainder of the lower division shows the torments of hell. Next to the tree two huge demons hold up the bridge of spikes, over which cheating tradespeople, bearing symbols of their trades, are timidly walking. This punishment is another very old idea going back almost as far as thought can reach. The nightmare bridge over Gehenna was believed to be as narrow and sharp as a razor. A blacksmith is one of the unfortunate people in the act of crossing it. His hand is raised with a hammer, and he is ready to strike a red-hot horseshoe which he holds in pincers. Villagers of 700 years ago probably knew at once that he was the blacksmith of the well-known story who was condemned to forge a horseshoe without an anvil while crossing the bridge. The man who holds a bowl so carefully at the other end was probably a milkman who had given short measure to his customers, for the bowl is painted yellow and contains white fluid. He has been given the impossible task of carrying it across the bridge; and it looks as if he will soon be crying loudly over spilled milk in the awful abyss below, where a usurer sits among roaring flames on a fiery seat. A big purse of money hangs from his neck and three bags of gold are suspended from his waist.

Here again is a subject of countless stories familiar to the village people of medieval times. The usurer has no eyes, and gold coins, which he is forced to count, are pouring from his mouth. Two demons leap above him and prod at his head with their pitchforks. Fire is raging in the left division below the bar of clouds, where we see a great cauldron full of suffering souls. Two frightful demons are prodding them with pitchforks. The one on the left is holding a group of souls above a demon wolf gnawing at their feet, indicating that they are dancers, who were specially denounced by the monks of

Betchworth
William Wardysworth

Byfleet
Thomas Teylar

Beddington
Nicholas and Isabella Carew

Carshalton : Nicholas and Margaret Gaynesford with their four children

East Horsley
John Bowthe

Crowhurst
John Gaynesford

Croydon
Gabriel Silvester

Ewell
Jane Iwarby

OLD SURREY FOLK ENGRAVED ON BRASSES

those days. A dog is about to bite a lady's hand, the allusion being, no doubt, to the wealthy lady who pampered her dogs and fed them with the rich food she should have given in charity to the poor. Clinging frantically to the bottom of the ladder of life are more lost souls, most of them falling down, others being relentlessly picked off with a two-pronged fork by a monster demon showing his teeth. He is handing a victim over his shoulder to the demon of the cauldron.

It is a relief to look up to the top of the ladder, where angels help the good souls to reach the heaven of their aspirations. On the right, above the Tree of Life, is a dramatic rendering of the Descent into Hell. Satan lies bound, and Christ stands over him thrusting the staff of his banner into his mouth, while Adam and Eve and the souls of the patriarchs are set free.

The weighing of souls (on the left of the ladder) is one of the most interesting pictures in this old English Book of the Dead. Here is another idea found in ancient religions, particularly in that of the Egyptians. The Archangel Michael holds the scales. Another angel seems to be carrying a tablet with a record of good deeds. Satan, with his tongue out, is dragging along a group of souls by a rope, and slily tries to press down the scales on his side and thus secure another victim. One fortunate soul is being lifted up to heaven by an angel.

In all England there is not a more complete example of 12th century painting than this. It is one of the most precious of our national possessions; only fragments are missing.

In planning the picture the artist appears to have forestalled Dante, who used many of the same ideas in his Divine Comedy about sixty years after this Chaldon scene appeared. Here the artist has broken away from the Byzantine tradition of representing people conventionally. Although very few of the animated figures have faces they are full of expression and are painted in natural attitudes. The complicated subject is treated with great simplicity. The ease with which the painter has handled his brush, and the skill with which he has arranged the ideas he has taken from the legends and stories of his day, reveal him as an artist of no mean talent.

To the Chaldon people this painting must have been of tremendous interest. They could neither read nor write, but the picture's story was something they could understand.

SURREY

The Man of Desperate Adventures

CHARLWOOD. We walk along the stone causeway, passing a hollow yew 28 feet round, to find the best things of Charlwood in its church.

Built round a Norman tower and nave, it is one of the most interesting churches in Surrey. Its 13th century aisle was extended into a chapel in the 15th century, and this is now the chancel. The old chancel is 14th century, with a Norman arch at its entrance.

The 15th century screen is a great treasure. Above its tracery are two rows of carving delicately coloured, first a winding vine and then a band of lovely angels and quaint griffins, with shields and initials. The initials are those of Richard Sander, who died in 1480 and perhaps gave the screen. The shields belong to the Sanders and the Carews, who were connected by marriage.

On the wall of the aisle is a big group of old paintings. The clearest are 13th century scenes from the story of St Margaret (on the left), and the 15th century picture of the legend called the Three Living and the Three Dead Kings. The dark skeletons are contrasted with three kings enjoying the chase.

A 14th century window with beautiful tracery is by the side of a little Norman one in the nave. There are fragments of 14th century glass in three windows, including part of a white-robed angel. The Jacobean pulpit has texts in panels, and linenfold carving.

On the chancel wall are brass portraits of Nicholas Sander, his wife, and their ten children. He died in 1553 and is shown kneeling with his wife, the boys and girls standing behind them. The house of the Sanders was Charlwood Place, now a pretty timber-framed farmhouse; their family lived here for 300 years.

At this house there was born in 1530 another Nicholas Sander, one of the Roman Catholic conspirators against Elizabeth. He was famous in his day for his adventures and intrigues. A brilliant scholar and talker, he left England for Rome soon after Elizabeth's succession, and turned his talents to such good account that he was appointed member of a papal mission, and recommended for a cardinal's hat. He threw himself ardently into propaganda against Protestantism and, going to Madrid, found himself in high favour with Philip of Spain. He urged Philip to attack England from Ireland on behalf of Mary Queen of Scots, and promised him, on behalf of the Pope, a force of 5000 men. The expedition was fitted out and Sander, aided by Philip with men and money, went himself to Ireland to incite the chiefs to rise. This was the most astonishing period of his life. For nearly two years, in the face of continued failure, he maintained himself in Ireland, evading all Lord Burghley's attempts to capture him. He had hairbreadth escapes, his servant was caught and hanged, his belongings were seized, and at last, after wandering as a fugitive in the hills, he died of cold and want.

Proud Lord John

CHEAM. It has grown up in our time from a village into a town, and millions of red bricks and seas of red tiles now cover most of the fields which once separated it from its neighbours. Thousands of new houses, hundreds of new shops, and, of course, a kinema, are what the casual visitor sees of Cheam, although at its heart it has preserved something of its old village aspect; its past is revealed only to those who seek it diligently.

Most of its history is in a cottage in its Broadway, for it is thought to have been moved to make room for the marvellous palace of Nonsuch built by Henry the Eighth not far away. The palace has vanished but the cottage is here, and behind its sturdy oak frame are kept the witnesses of the village past, Roman coins and pots, and earthenware made here in the days of the Black Death.

Near this cottage are other timber dwellings with an old-world air, among them Whitehall, charming with its white boards and its room above the overhanging porch. Here Elizabeth held council when dispatches were brought to her in the hunting field.

In the mellow red brick rectory lived Lancelot Andrewes, the famous Elizabethan preacher. He was the first of four men who gave up the rectory for a bishopric, one after the other; the last was John Hacket, who was once ordered to stop the service here at the point of a Roundhead's pistol. He said he would do what became a priest, and bade the soldier do what became a soldier; and he was left alone. Opposite the rectory is a peace memorial garden with green lawns and grey stone seats, a place for meditation.

The church was made new in the 19th century and the 20th gave it a chantry in memory of its heroes in the war; in it we found the name of Commander Brock, the inventor of the smoke screen, who fell at Zeebrugge. The 16th century Lumley Chapel is all that is left of the old church. It stands apart in the churchyard, and has a fine plaster ceiling, sheltering the Lumley stones. A stone wall with marble pillars was put up in the lifetime of Lord Lumley, who was sent to the Tower for plotting to put Mary Queen of Scots on the throne, but died peacefully six years after Elizabeth. On the top are two popinjays with his beautifully carved arms. He was called Pedigree Proud Lord John, and the inscription traces his descent from the Saxons. He was an original member of the Society of Antiquaries, and his books, bought by James the First, became the foundation of the Royal Library in the British Museum.

His first wife was Lady Jane, here kneeling on a cushion in headdress, ruff, and gown. Her pomander hangs on her gown and her flowing skirts are arranged in a bunch behind. Her face shows character and intellect, and we can well believe she enjoyed translating the Iphigenia of Euripedes. Below kneel her three children, who all died young, the curly-headed heir in a manly cloak, and the girl in a mob cap and gown. The spirals above all these figures are their prayers ascending to heaven. In the background are arches, windows, and doors which may represent parts of their old home, and if so are the only indoor views we have of Nonsuch. The second Lady Lumley, full of vigour and health, lies in a ruff and fur-lined mantle, with wide-open eyes. Her sweet face is in a charming headdress, and the beauty of the whole figure recalls that of Mary Queen of Scots in Westminster Abbey. Engraved on brasses are the portraits of civilians of five centuries ago. We see John Compton, who died in 1450, with his wife, William Woodeward, the rector's brother, and John Yerde, his little brass showing him in armour, being less than seven inches high, one of the smallest adult figures we have seen. Set in a wooden frame is a brass made from seven earlier ones which were probably spoil from English monasteries. Its neat engraving shows Thomas Fromond, who died 500 years ago. He kneels in civil dress with six sons behind him, and facing him kneels his wife with four daughters. Above them all is a crowned figure of God the Father, a dove alighting on the crucifix before Him. On the back of this palimpsest brass we see the earlier work—St John the Evangelist, a kneeling lady, a long shrouded figure, and a heart between two hands.

It is only a short walk from the church to the gates of Nonsuch Park, with nearly 300 acres of country delight preserved as part of London's Green Belt. The Palace of Nonsuch is no more, but the grounds in which kings once walked belong to the people for ever.

CHELSHAM. It is one of a group of villages on the North Downs, with a church standing alone near the border of Kent. Beneath a tidy flint exterior it has Norman work, and the tower is 13th century.

The finest thing in the church is the low 16th century screen, but only a part of it remains. It is in 14 bays (including the two doors), all with carved shafts and tracery, and it is thought to be the work of a Flemish craftsman.

There is a striking 13th century piscina, and a 13th century marble font restored by "the cottagers" 600 years after it was made. One of the windows contains old glass brought back here from a builder's door at Bromley, and with them is a little pane scratched with the name of John Baker, who tells us that in 1791 he was glazier, painter, bricklayer, and stonemason.

Of great interest are the three fine yews in the churchyard, nine feet round; they were planted by the rector and the schoolmaster in 1746.

Fox Dying

CHERTSEY. One of the little towns by the Thames, it has the old world in its streets, a charming 18th century bridge of seven stone arches crossing the river into Middlesex, a church going back 600 years, and 12 centuries of history in the story of its lost abbey.

The poor fragments of the abbey still to be seen are a big brick tithe barn with a grey stone end, a blocked arch in a wall, and numerous stones scattered among other walls and buildings. Yet it goes back to the 7th century and was one of the greatest religious houses in the land. It was destroyed in the 9th century by the Danes, who killed the abbot and 90 monks, and it reached its prime under Abbot John de Rutherwyke, the great builder and road-maker who was called its second founder. He built the 14th century chancel of Great Bookham church, and may have built this at Chertsey. The foundations of the great Norman abbey church, 257 feet long, have been unearthed, as well as a collection of 13th century tiles said to be the best in the world. Some of them illustrate the legends of King

Arthur; many of them are scattered among museums and collectors, but there are a few rather plain ones here in the charming peace memorial chapel at the church.

The abbey comes into Shakespeare when he writes:

Come, now towards Chertsey with your holy load,
Taken from Paul's to be interred there.

He is speaking of Henry the Sixth, murdered in the Tower, whose body was brought by water to be buried at this place. Here the king lay until Richard the Third had him buried again at Windsor.

The church was much rebuilt last century, but the chancel is mostly as it was 600 years ago, with its original kingpost roof. The tower is partly medieval, and has in it six bells, four of them with a special interest. One, weighing half a ton, is older than the Reformation and probably came from the abbey; another lives in legend; the third is an Armada bell of 1588; and the biggest, weighing more than a ton, was recast last century by Baroness Burdett-Coutts, who devoted her father's vast fortune to a hundred generous purposes. Her bell rings the curfew for six months every year.

The oldest memorial is a tablet to Laurence Tomson of 1608, who sleeps in the chancel. He knew a dozen languages and made a translation of the New Testament. Other tablets are to Nathanael Rowe of 1778, who was the "one-and-thirtieth child of his father"; William Moir, a chorister for 76 years; and Admiral Sir Henry Hotham, a brave sailor in the wars against Napoleon. He captured a French squadron that escaped from Trafalgar; and on another occasion managed by brilliant seamanship to destroy two French frigates that were interfering with English shipping in the Atlantic. He became commander of the Mediterranean fleet, and he sleeps by the ocean at Malta. There is a beautiful sculptured relief by John Flaxman in the sanctuary. It is the Raising of Lazarus, put here in memory of a girl of 20 who died a few years after Waterloo.

The most famous name on these walls is that of the Whig statesman Charles James Fox, whose wife put a tablet to him here. She herself sleeps in the churchyard, while Fox rests in the Abbey at Westminster. He had a house on St Anne's Hill, near Chertsey, and loved it so much that he could hardly bring himself to leave it. Once, when a letter arrived summoning him to London, he wrote back:

THE KING'S ENGLAND

Never did a letter arrive at a worse time than yours this morning. A sweet westerly wind, a beautiful sun, all the thorns and elms just budding, and the nightingales just beginning to sing.

As he lay dying, Wordsworth was reading in his newspaper at Grasmere that the life of Fox was nearing its end, and it was then that the poet wrote those famous lines, Loud is the Vale:

> *Loud is the Vale; this inland depth*
> *In peace is roaring like the sea;*
> *Yon star upon the mountain-top*
> *Is listening quietly.*
>
> *And many thousands now are sad,*
> *Wait the fulfilment of their fear;*
> *For he must die who is their stay,*
> *Their glory disappear.*
>
> *A Power is passing from the earth*
> *To breathless Nature's dark abyss;*
> *But when the great and good depart*
> *What is it more than this—*
>
> *That Man, who is from God sent forth,*
> *Doth yet again to God return?*
> *Such ebb and flow must ever be,*
> *Then wherefore should we mourn?*

The house in which Fox lived has two stone eagles guarding the entrance, and the garden in which the nightingales were singing is beautiful with lawns and cedars, though its nightingales sing no more.

It was in a Chertsey house (now in Guildford Street, and changed beyond recognition) that the poet Abraham Cowley spent his last two years. A devoted Royalist, he had been arrested as a spy during the Commonwealth, but received a grant of land from the Crown after the Restoration. In all the stress of the Civil War it had been his ambition to settle down and live at peace, and in dedicating an essay and a poem to John Evelyn he wrote:

I have never had any desire so strong and so like to covetousness as that one which I have had always, that I might be master at last of a small house and a large garden, and there dedicate the remainder of my life only to the culture of them, and the study of nature.

We may wonder if he enjoyed his retirement here as much as he had hoped, for he wrote to another friend that his tenants would not pay their rent, and that his meadows were eaten up every night by cattle put there by his neighbours. His health declined, and at 49 he died, his body being put on a boat and carried down the Thames to London, where it was buried with great pomp. At Westminster he began his schooldays, and there they laid him to rest, within the walls of the Abbey he knew so well. One of the quietest little streets of Westminster, just behind the Abbey, is named after him; his name is still on the wall where it was put fifty years after his funeral passed.

In Chertsey's tower is a curfew bell which, according to old legend, was silenced one night when a girl clung to the clapper to save her lover.

Curfew Must Not Ring Tonight

IT is one of the best known of all our legends, the story of Blanche Heriot, whose lover was thrown into prison at Chertsey during the Wars of the Roses, and was sentenced to die at the sounding of the curfew bell.

She climbed the church tower, and silenced the bell with her own body as she clung to the clapper, gaining a few precious moments for the reprieve which arrived in time to save her lover.

The story crossed the Atlantic, and in 1867 Rose Hartwick, a schoolgirl of Litchfield in Michigan, wrote the poem we know so well, which usually appears under her married name of Mrs Rose Thorpe. She altered Blanche's name to Bessie, she changed the Wars of the Roses into the Civil War of Cromwell's time, and she did not even write good poetry, but because of the dramatic story it tells this schoolgirl's poem lives on, and children go on reciting how

> *OUT she swung—far out; the city seemed*
>   *a speck of light below,*
> *There twixt heaven and earth suspended,*
>   *as the bell swung to and fro.*
> *And the half dead sexton ringing (years he*
>   *had not heard the bell),*
> *Sadly thought that twilight curfew rang*
>   *young Basil's funeral knell.*
> *Still the maiden clung more firmly, and*
>   *with trembling lips so white*
> *Said to hush her heart's wild throbbing,*
>   *Curfew shall not ring tonight!*

*It was o'er; the bell ceased swaying; and
  the maiden stepped once more
Firmly on the damp old ladder, where for
  hundred years before
Human foot had not been planted. But
  the brave deed she had done
Should be told long ages after. As the
  rays of setting sun
Crimson all the sky with beauty, agèd
  sires, with heads of white,
Tell the children why the curfew did not
  ring that one sad night.*

The Forgotten Man

CHESSINGTON. It has fine views over the rolling Epsom Downs, a Zoo known to thousands, and a 13th century church with a short shingled spire and a timbered porch which was found covered with roses.

The real treasure of the village is far away at South Kensington; it is a tiny silver chalice fashioned by craftsmen before the Reformation, and is preserved in the Victoria and Albert Museum. The cup now used is a copy of a beautiful 13th century chalice.

A small alabaster sculpture 500 years old has a charming Annunciation scene with the Madonna in blue, blue curtains over the prayer desk, the angel Gabriel with the gold sceptre, and a dove flying in. The chancel has old roof beams, and the nave has rare pillars of timber.

Here lies a forgotten man much talked about in the 18th century, the patron and friend of Fanny Burney. He was Samuel Crisp, whose tragedy it was that he imagined himself a great dramatist and, on the rejection of his dramas, became, as Macaulay said, a cynic and a hater of mankind. But he loved Fanny Burney, whom he regarded as his daughter and called his Fannikin. The marble table there, written by Fanny Burney's father, tells us that his

> *Good humoured wit and wide benevolence
> Cheered and enlightened all this hamlet round.*

He lived and died at Chessington Hall where, wrote Macaulay, "no road, not even a sheepwalk, connected his lonely dwelling with the abodes of men." His retreat was kept secret from his old friends in the bitterness of his disappointment, but here Fanny Burney used to stay with him, and here, though the house has been made new, there was still growing when we called the mulberry tree round which Fanny danced (as she told Sir Walter Scott) when the news came of her first success. Here, too, she crept from Queen Charlotte's Court one day to stand by the grave of her Daddy Crisp.

The Men Who Made the Old Glass

CHIDDINGFOLD. It has known the time when its fame was European, and it has something still to remind us of those days. But for all who come it is a place of great delight, with a fine wide green, a church of much interest, and a wealth of old houses.

One or two of its houses by the green had their beginning 600 years ago and are charming still with newer fronts. Another a little way off, Old Pickhurst, is said to go back a century farther, and is chiefly Tudor as we see it.

The old thorn on Chiddingfold's green is famous among Surrey trees, mentioned as a landmark in a document 500 years ago; and famous among English inns is the Crown, lovely inside with old woodwork and remarkable for its kingpost roof. It comes into the records as far back as the 14th century and was one of the resting-places of the boy king Edward the Sixth on his way to Shillinglee. Here he came with a retinue of 4000, including high officers of state and many of the greatest in the land. Something like a little Field of the Cloth of Gold this village green must have looked on that day in 1552.

The chancel of the church was ancient even then, for it is 13th century and has five lancet windows now filled with beautiful scenes of the Annunciation and the Wise Men. The remarkably high pillars in the nave were a few decades old when the king came, and some of the oak benches of his time are here still. In one of the aisles are lovely modern windows showing Michael and Gabriel and two exquisite angel figures, and by the organ are four little panels of glass by 16th century Flemish or German craftsman, illustrating the story of the Prodigal Son and the anointing of the Blind Man. Near by is a 17th century font in which (as someone has calculated) at least 3600 babies must have been baptised before it fell out of use.

The tower, except for the top, is about 500 years old, and one of the bells is 15th century. The lychgate is one of the few in Surrey with an old coffin-rest; close to it, now hardly decipherable, is the gravestone of Arthur Stedman, an 18th century village blacksmith, with the quaint epitaph familiar in more than one churchyard:

> *My fire is out, my forge decayed,*
> *And in the dust my vice is laid,*
> *My coal is spent, my iron gone,*
> *My nail is drove, my work is done.*

Walking in this place we think specially of two of its old rectors, Dr Robert Tighe, one of the translators of the Authorised Version, who lies in the chancel, and Dr John Harris, rector for 55 years from Queen Anne's time. He gave the handsome flagon used at the altar, and for 50 years he had with him in this village the same parish clerk, Thomas Eede. In the churchyard lies the mother of Edward Young, the poet of Night Thoughts. Among the modern memorials is one to Commander Henry Halahan, who died at Zeebrugge having won the DSO and many foreign honours.

But almost more than to anything else we are drawn in Chiddingfold to a lancet window in the west wall, gay with vivid fragments of the ancient glass that brought fame to the village centuries ago. Here it was made, and here were some of the most famous glassmaking furnaces in the world. There are those who think that nearly all the glass made in England before the 16th century was made hereabouts.

Far back into history the names of the glassmaking families have been traced, and several of their actual furnaces have been unearthed. Not only was glass for windows made here, but vessel glass as well; yet it is the thought of the marvellous coloured windows made possible by these furnaces that thrills us. The record is an amazing one, for it begins with Lawrence the Glassmaker who comes into a Chiddingfold document 700 years ago and into a Westminster document of the same time. He was one of those who provided both white and coloured glass for the Abbey. After him are many other names and many other records, and altogether it is known that glass was sent from this corner of Surrey to beautify St Stephen's Chapel and the Chapter House at Westminster, St George's Chapel at Windsor, and probably New College, Oxford. From the 13th century to the 16th the glassmakers flourished, and then their industry seems to have declined. We are told by the chronicler Aubrey how in Elizabeth's

Chaldon — Church of Rare Possessions

Charlwood — A Village Highway

Chilworth   The Hilltop Church of St Martha

reign eleven factories were suppressed because the local people thought them a nuisance.

Those who look at the old glass in our village churches must often have gazed on the handiwork of the old Chiddingfold men, and, though there is nothing substantial of their work here, it is delightful to find this little window set apart as a tribute to them. It contains fragments representing every century and every colour, grouped so that we can see rich squares of red and blue and green. There are 427 pieces in all, the broken relics of a great and famous industry, dug up from the rubbish heaps beside the furnaces.

After the glassmakers came the ironworkers, with the clothmakers here all the time; and in our own day this place has still its distinctive industry, the making of walking sticks from little ash trees and chestnuts specially grown.

St Martha On the Hill

CHILWORTH. The famous little church of St Martha looks down on Chilworth from its high ridge against the sky; but there is little else here except a horde of modern bungalows, a simple cross to six men who never came back, and two houses, on opposite sides of the hill, with names that go back beyond the Norman Conquest, each a manor in Saxon Surrey. One is Tytings, a farmhouse with some parts Elizabethan or even older, and perhaps at one time the home of the priest who served in the church; the other is Chilworth Manor, with ancient fishponds and a Queen Anne walled garden.

It is St Martha's that we come to see, on the hilltop everybody in Surrey knows. It is hard to think that any village church in England stands so marvellously on a hill top as this. Proudly alone it is, keeping company with the trees and the grass and the winds, and a heavenly Surrey view. With a glorious countryside of woods and hills all round, St Martha's has the feeling of being above them all.

It stands in a place where, almost certainly, heathen worship was practised, and it is thought also to mark the place of a massacre of early Christian martyrs. But these are not the only memories it has for those who come here with imagination. Along these hills from Guildford ran the old road called the Pilgrim's Way, though it is far older than the time of the Canterbury Pilgrims; and it is impossible to think that St Martha's was not a landmark and a place of refuge for as motley a procession of people as England has ever seen. Yet long before Becket was murdered, and long before there was a church here, men were going this way, and some of their possessions have been found in the ground—prehistoric flints, Roman coins and burial urns, and a Saxon vase.

What we see today is a church made new last century, but there are Norman parts of it that the Canterbury Pilgrims would see. The nave stands on its original foundations, the tower rises up from old piers and arches, and there is old masonry in the chancel and the transepts. The font comes from another church, and the two coffin lids in the chancel are 15th century.

Much of the fascination of St Martha's comes from the way in which it stirs the imagination. We feel it is full of memories, yet we have only a bare outline of its actual story down the ages. We hear of it in the generation before Magna Carta, when its first known rector was appointed, and when it became one of the possessions of Newark Priory a few miles away. We have another glimpse of it in the next century when Edward the First and his queen were away in the Holy Land, and when candles were lit here while prayers were said for their little son Henry lying ill at Guildford castle. And we have here the only document actually known to connect St Martha's with the pilgrims, a 15th century letter of Bishop Waynflete granting 40 days Indulgence to any penitent who made a pilgrimage here or gave money for the upkeep of the church.

After the monasteries were dissolved St Martha's came again into the hands of a local squire, and gradually fell to ruin as the generations came and went. Roofless and neglected, but with services still being held, it had become a sorry sight when in 1848 a group of Surrey men rebuilt it for posterity. We may be thankful to them, for it is unthinkable that such a church in such a place should be allowed to disappear. Yet that is not quite the end of the story. St Martha's turned out to be in far too exposed a place to suit the years when men were flying over defenceless places and dropping death. It was set on a hill, and therefore it must come down or be hid. So it was that in the mad war years this church was not allowed to look like a church but was made to look like a clump of trees, with branches all over it and scaffolding to hold them up.

Odd it looks in the pictures of those days, but glad we are that St Martha's is itself again, looking out as in Sidney Allnutt's lines:

> *Safe sheltered by the encircling downs*
> *The chequered valleys show*
> *Their tapestry of greens and browns,*
> *Made rich by fields of golden grain,*
> *And threaded by a silver vein*
> *Where Wey's clear waters flow.*
>
> *And, oh, it must be good to sleep*
> *Within that churchyard bare,*
> *While turn by turn the seasons keep*
> *A bedside watch, and God may see*
> *Safe in St Martha's nursery*
> *His children pillowed there.*

In 1933 two pilgrim crosses were discovered, cut on a stone in the church, one a double cross indicating that the 14th century pilgrim was on the return journey from his holy place.

Modern pilgrims will be interested in two things on St Martha's walls. One is a pathetic crucifix picked up near a French village church after a heavy bombardment in 1915, and the other is a brass inscription to John St Loe Strachey of Newlands Corner, who lived in an old house with a tablet on it and died in the new house behind it. The inscription in the church has these words:

In his newspaper, The Spectator, he affected the thought of a whole generation. There and elsewhere, in speech and in writing, he used his great influence to unite in friendship the English-speaking peoples throughout the world.

Mr Strachey's ashes were laid somewhere in Somerset but he could not have wished to be remembered in a lovelier place than this hilltop, up which he would often come to look out upon England.

The Builder of London Bridge

CHIPSTEAD. In a rolling countryside of much delight its church and its peace memorial stand together among scattered houses.

Not much more than the doorway is left of the church the Normans built, but everything that matters is left of the cruciform 13th century church, and its interior looks as fine and new as on the day it was built. A modern aisle and transept match the old work perfectly, and it is hard to believe that most of these cool walls have seen seven centuries come and go.

Very impressive are the arches of the nave, the vaulting under the central tower, the fine symmetry of the building as a whole, and the 15th century screen. The pulpit and the reading-desk are 16th century, and the unusually good organ case is in keeping with them. The 14th century font is carved with tracery, and there are two coffin stones 600 years old.

The chancel has striking lancet windows, five in a row on one side and four on the other, and against the walls are stone benches with carved ends. Lucy Roper, who died at 24, is in brass on the sanctuary floor, dressed in the clothes of Shakespeare's last years; and we read that her father had the extraordinary Christian name of Lactansius. Close by sleeps a daughter of Richard Hooker, the famous Elizabethan theologian whose church and home and grave we come upon in Sussex. An old helmet and a tattered banner are hanging aloft, and there is a tablet to Christopher Shawe of 1618, a citizen and embroiderer of London.

On the wall we read of Peter Aubertin, a remarkable man who sleeps here after half a century as rector. Coming to Chipstead in 1809 he found the church dilapidated, and strange things are told of what this house of God had come to in those days. The parson before him had to come from Croydon, and the dead had to lie in the church till his visit was due. The next meet of hounds was announced from the pulpit, and when cricket was played outside on the green the players used the church as their pavilion, coming in for beer and bread and cheese, and even scoring the play in notches on the edge of the altar.

Peter Aubertin changed all that, and, acting as his own architect, he restored this chancel and rebuilt one of the transepts. It was his hobby to paint glass for the windows, and there is much of his work here. In the east window his borders and figures keep company with many little 15th century fragments, some of which he collected; and in a transept window are three rich panels of 13th century glass against backgrounds that he made. The old figures include Peter and Paul, and some of them have new faces. It is said that the old rector took a delight in deceiving the antiquarians, who found it hard to distinguish between the old glass and his clever copies.

Cobham   The Mill by the Mole

Coldharbour   Surrey's Highest Village

Cobham — Church Stile House

Wonersh — Great Tangley Manor

Looking out into the church he loved is the marble head of Sir Edward Banks, who began life as a humble labourer and ended as the head of a great firm of contractors. He built London Bridge, Waterloo Bridge, and Southwark Bridge; he made the naval works at Sheerness Dockyard; and he cut new channels for three rivers in Norfolk and Lincolnshire. In his early days he was a workman on the first public railway in England, the little goods line not far away at Merstham, and it was then that he fell in love with Chipstead and formed the resolve to sleep here when his labours were done. He died at his daughter's house in Sussex, and lies in a splendid tomb in this churchyard, near a magnificent yew (21 feet round) which shades a doorway 800 years old.

Nicholas Heath of the Tudor Age

CHOBHAM. For those who love the open country its great attraction is its common, a fine undulating stretch of gorse and heather with here and there a clump of pines. On high ground stands the monument put here by 400 parishioners in memory of the Victorian Era, recording the fact that on this common in 1853 the Queen reviewed 8129 of her troops. Here they were temporarily in camp, and within a year or two the military area of Aldershot sprang into being a few miles away, signing the death-warrant of much of the beauty of West Surrey.

Yet Chobham itself is in a district where many old cottages and fine old farms still preserve the spirit of the countryside, and it has its own attraction in a church which has grown up round a building raised by the Normans soon after the Conqueror came. Two little windows of this early building are still seen above the pointed arches made in later Norman times. The tower is 500 years old, and in one of the walls is an old stone which has been a sundial, pitiably disfigured by the louts who go about the country scribbling and cutting their initials everywhere.

The two treasures of the church are a fine chest 700 years old and a font which is almost unique in our experience, reminding us of the days of the very first fonts, which were probably in wood. The Chobham font has eight sides panelled in oak, the inside lined with lead, as most fonts are. Though there are only one or two other oak fonts in the country, it is odd that Surrey has another at Ash, which is, like this one, the work of the 15th or 16th century. Another is at Marks Tey in Essex.

Under a nameless stone in the chancel lies Nicholas Heath, a great man who saw his full share of religious turmoil under the Tudors. In the last years of Henry the Eighth he rose to be Bishop of Worcester after Hugh Latimer, only to be deprived of his see under Edward the Sixth, having announced that he would never consent to take down rich altars and set up tables in churches. When Mary Tudor came to the throne he was restored to his see, and John Hooper, who had been holding it, was burned alive at Gloucester. Two years later Heath became Archbishop of York and then Lord Chancellor, and on the death of the terrible queen he proclaimed the accession of Elizabeth in the House of Lords. But he found himself unable for conscience sake to take the oath under the Act of Supremacy, and once again was deprived of his office. He was sent to the Tower, and, being leniently treated there, was allowed to retire to Chobham Park, where he is said to have been allowed to celebrate mass in his private chapel. Here Elizabeth came to see him more than once before he died in 1579. On a tablet we read that he was an upright and brave man, firm in his convictions but tolerant of those of others.

Hereabouts every Sunday afternoon can be heard the ringing of 25 bells in Westcroft Park, one of the biggest carillons in England. It was built by Mr H. O. Serpell, who was one of the most cheerful young men of 80 when we called, and in this peal fulfilled a dream of his boyhood. As a lad at Plymouth he learned to love the sound of church bells and resolved that one day he would have a peal of his own, and he set up this carillon in his quiet park. The biggest bell weighs three-quarters of a ton.

The Last Home of Matthew Arnold

COBHAM. It is one of the most scattered of all Surrey villages. We have a view of a large part of it from the little grass-covered summit of Leigh Hill, the huddling red roofs half hidden among a wealth of trees. Up here in 1907 was found the earliest Cobham we know, about fifty pits dug in the dry gravel. In them villagers baked their pottery, ground their corn, and wove material for their simple clothes in the days when Christ was walking in Galilee.

SURREY

Near by is the great pit where have been found relics of an earlier people still, the roving men of the Bronze Age. Here was found the cremation urn of one of them, a brown vase a few inches high. Roman pottery has been found by the River Mole near the red brick bridge, which has an inscription on the parapet telling us that the old timber bridge which stood here was built by Queen Matilda, wife of Henry the First, because one of her ladies was drowned in crossing the ford.

Near the bridge is Pains Hill Cottage, the pleasant house where Matthew Arnold lived and died. He was here for 15 years, and from here many of his published letters were written. He wrote with nightingales singing all round him, and he was deeply interested in the natural life about him on the banks of the Mole. He wrote to a foreign friend that "If you come over to England the hermit and hermitesses of the Mole will be charmed to see you." It was here that he brought home a canary as a present for his little daughter, and set up a stone in the garden in memory of his little son's dachshund, Geist. Of the canary he wrote:

> *Here Matthias sang his fill,*
> *Saw the cedars of Pains Hill;*
> *Here he poured his little soul,*
> *Heard the murmur of the Mole.*

Of Geist he wrote the poem so familiar as Geist's Grave:

> *Only four years those winning ways*
> *Which make us for thy presence yearn*
> *Called us to pet thee or to praise,*
> *Dear little friend, at every turn.*
>
> *Yes, only four—and not the course*
> *Of all the centuries yet to come,*
> *And not the infinite resource*
> *Of Nature, with her countless sum*
>
> *Of figures, with her fulness vast*
> *Of new creation evermore,*
> *Can ever quite repeat the past*
> *Or just thy little self restore.*

Cobham is a village of glorious gardens, the most famous of them being the wooded domain of Pains Hill, with its beautiful lake fed from the Mole by a huge water-wheel. It is one of the best examples of natural landscape gardening in England, laid out on what was a barren heath when Mr Charles Hamilton bought it 200 years ago. He burned the heather, and, having obtained an excellent crop of turnips from the land, fed them to sheep. He then sowed fine grass, forerunner of the green carpets we walk on now. Then it was that Hamilton chose certain pictures of Old Masters and reproduced them in landscape, introducing temples and ruins as required.

His trees have grown more magnificent year by year. A huge Cedar of Lebanon is said to be the biggest in England. Horace Walpole came here and was greatly impressed by the trees; so was Charles van Linné, son of the famous Linnaeus, when he came here with Sir Joseph Banks. Another famous visitor was John Wesley, who wrote that he was able to walk round without an introduction, as we may sometimes do.

A smaller Cobham garden of which we have a glimpse is at Woodlands, the plot of ground Mrs Earle has told us of so delightfully in her books. Here came Burne-Jones and Henry James. Caroline Molesworth lived for half a century at Cobham Lodge, the house set in shrubs and great trees; we can just see it. Miss Molesworth's Cobham Journals were published in 1880, and summarise her observations of weather conditions and plant life for a period of 44 years. Her collection of dried plants was sent to Kew.

Far older than Cobham Lodge is the Church Style House, a timbered building at the corner of the churchyard. It has overhanging upper storeys and the date 1432, though most of what we see must be later.

And here is the church, its 12th century tower with a spire of oak shingles. The tower looks as if it were built of rubies when, after driving rain, it is lit by the level rays of the evening sun.

We enter the church by the 12th century doorway with three rows of zigzag, and find indoors a Norman tower arch, its strength and simplicity relieved by a few tiny scallops on each side. The nave has an old roof, and so has the north chapel, restored as a peace memorial. Here we walk on a most remarkable floor, made of Italian walnut from the waste wood of rifles during the war. An old brass candelabra hangs from the chancel roof by fine scrolled ironwork, and below is a beautifully carved chair nearly 300 years old.

SURREY

In the chancel is a tiny brass said to be the only one in England showing the Adoration of the Shepherds, and certainly unique in our experience. It was made about 1500. The Madonna lies in a low wooden bed with the Child at her side; two oxen thrust their heads into the stall, while at the foot of the bed are the Three Shepherds. Attached to a pillar in the south aisle is a revolving palimpsest brass, one side engraved with a 15th century priest holding a chalice, the other with a bearded layman in armour. On the south wall is a marble monument with a rhyming inscription to Ralph Coxe and his wife; he was a silkman of London in Charles Stuart's day. On one side is a marble figure of Time, and on the other a woman in a shroud; below is engraved a skeleton. Near by is another memorial with the figure of a pilgrim, by Westmacott.

West of the church is an old yew, and the evergreen shrubs and the grey stones give the churchyard a quiet dignity. There are Georgian houses near by.

In a corner of Cobham cemetery a broad concrete path leads to the concrete mausoleum built by Sir Robert McAlpine. Behind its bronze gates the old builder was laid to rest in 1934 after a life of persistent endeavour, success, and loss, followed by a second endeavour and a second and greater success. Pointing to the massive tomb is a bronze figure representing Life.

Cobham Mill stands astride the Mole, facing a meadow backed with trees. There has been a mill here since Domesday, but these walls and gables have stood for only a little more than a century. Cedar House across the road has been here for nearly 500 years, and thanks to Major Benton Fletcher and the National Trust is likely to stand for another 500. The front is Georgian, but at the back is an ancient hall with a mullioned window from another building. The fine front gate of ornamental ironwork is 17th century, and came from a house of Richard Brinsley Sheridan.

The road sweeps round by the river to Brook Farm, once owned by Admiral Graham Moore, and here is still growing an oak planted by his immortal brother John, before he set out on the campaign which was to end at Corunna, darkly, at dead of night.

Remote on Chatley Heath, in a distant corner of Cobham, stands a tall brick tower, the best preserved of the old semaphore stations linking Portsmouth with the Admiralty.

THE KING'S ENGLAND

Carrying the News Before the Electric Telegraph

THE tower is in itself a link with the days of Waterloo and the old wooden walls of England. Its master station was the signal tower in the dockyard at Portsmouth, which stood above where the Victory and the Implacable still fly their flags.

That station kept touch with ships in the harbour, and the signalling system was one of semaphore arms, in principle like the railway signals of today. A series of stations five to ten miles apart was built on points such as Portsdown, Pewley Down at Guildford, Chatley Heath, Hinchley Wood, Coombe Hill, Putney Heath, and Chelsea. The historic tower in Portsmouth dockyard was burnt in our own time, though its black twinkling arms continued to exchange signals with ships at Spithead till the last. Its signalman saw Queen Victoria's passing, when the royal yacht sailed from Cowes past the saluting battleships.

The old semaphore tower at Cobham had a shorter history, and its career ended when the electric telegraph took its place in 1847. But tidings of victory or disaster were flashed through it for more than a generation. The battle of Navarino was fought while it was in action, and, though a courier carried the despatches of the victory from Deal to London, its semaphore arms possibly confirmed the news. It may have told of the bombardment of Beyrout, the loss of troopships in Table Bay, and the wreck of a convict ship on Boulogne sands.

Watch was kept during six hours of daylight, and the naval men in the towers acquired extraordinary dexterity in transmitting signals swiftly. With a telescope fixed on the next station and a hand on the rope of the winch working the arms, a signal travelled from the coast to the capital in less than a minute. One of the minor uses of the system was to send Greenwich time. It could be sent back and forth (170 miles) in 45 seconds. The last of the signallers used to recall that in foggy weather, when Chelsea could not be seen from Putney, a man was sent to take the message on horseback.

The Camp Older than History

COLDHARBOUR. The highest village in Surrey, it lies 750 feet up on the side of Leith Hill not a mile from the summit, with a fine view looking out over the Weald.

The church is 19th century, but there is something in Coldharbour older than Christianity itself, something that was here before the Romans came to our shores. It is the fort of the ancient Britons known as Anstiebury Camp, a hilltop refuge where women and children and cattle were sent while men of the Stone Age were fighting their barbarian wars. It covers ten acres, and its double entrenchment can still be traced among the trees.

If Napoleon had come in the days when people expected him this old camp would have been used again as a place of refuge. The order was given that at the first news of his invasion the women and children of Dorking were to assemble in the ancient ring, as their ancestors had done centuries before.

Wonder of Wonders

COMPTON. There are 25 Comptons in England, but one of them is a wonder that takes us back to that year 1000 when the world was supposed to end, and brings us back to this age which is moving fast to the year 2000 when the world will be a marvellous place beyond our dreams. Even then men will be coming to see Compton.

It has something of the age-long beauty of Old England. It lies by one of our medieval towns. It is just off that great ridge which runs for miles at a height as straight as a hog's back. It has a tower the Saxons gave it and a church the Normans gave it, and we have only to open a door in one of its lanes to find ourselves with one of the spirits of the great Victorian Era, for we are in the heart of the little world, the great world, of G. F. Watts.

Here is his home. Here is the picture he left on his easel a generation since. Here he lies and here are his works, the pictures by which we know him, the great sculpture he built up inch by inch with his own fingers. If we would know what he said to the world, this great Victorian who knew Gladstone and Tennyson and Browning and all the rest, we have but to come to Compton and see the message in his pictures, hanging in the gallery he gave to his village, to be the nation's property for all time.

We run down off the Hog's Back, if we come from Guildford, or take the bypass road if we come from town, and a little lane brings us to the shrine the artist loved and that we must love, for it is like no other, and it goes back 900 years. These red fragments in the tower are Roman tiles put here by Saxon hands. These arches on great round pillars are Norman. The very timbers in the roof are Norman. This chancel like no other in the land is Norman. This little wooden screen with its nine simple arches is Norman, cut out of one piece by a Norman carpenter, unmatched in any other church this country has. This little stone chamber which leads us up the steps to the screen was the home of an anchorite, one of those hermits who lived immured in these small places day and night and year by year, with an altar for their eyes to rest on and an open grave at their feet.

So far back in the mists of Time we are at Compton, where the world of the Motor Age is rushing by. From this small church to the great highway is but a step or two in space, but in time it is a thousand years.

Time has changed the shape of the old Saxon shrine, and today it has dormer windows piercing its roof, and a 20th century porch sheltering its Norman doorway; but the stamp of the Saxon and the Norman are on it everywhere. The tower with its slit windows is Saxon, and the south wall by the door, and something of the chancel walls were all here when the Conqueror came in 1066. Long before then there had been another cell for an anchorite, now lost except for its little square peephole in the north chancel wall. Low down in this wall, facing the doorway into the anchorite's cell, is a small square opening through which an anchorite peeped at the altar before the Normans came. We have here a church with the story of two anchorite cells—a Saxon cell which has gone except for its little window, and a cell which remains for us to see. We shall not come upon this anywhere else. Outside we may find signs of the vanished cell with its deeply-splayed little window now glazed over; it is almost incredible that there should be two anchorite windows looking across the chancel.

It was the Normans who made this remarkable chancel, like no other in the world. It is one of the smallest we have seen, yet it has:

> *Two handsome Norman arches*
> *Two sanctuaries*
> *Two anchorite cell windows*
> *Two Norman aumbries*
> *Two east windows*
> *Two Norman timber structures*

The Watts Chapel    The Ancient Church

A Vista of Norman Architecture
COMPTON THE INCOMPARABLE

Compton

Compton Capital

Compton Soldier on Pillar and Chancel Screen

Compton South Doorway    Cobham South Doorway

THE WORK OF THE NORMANS

SURREY

The Normans timbered the roofs of the chancel and the nave, made the font and the upper chancel screen, set a piscina and three aumbries in the walls, and put in the windows and the north and south doorways. They scratched the dial on the south wall outside and the Norman knight and his cross on the chancel pier inside. They built the arches of the nave, placing their pillars where the Saxons had placed theirs, and they gave their round arches the smallest suggestion of a point, marking the beginning of the change which was coming about between the years 1165 and 1185, when they were set up. When the change had really come about, and English Gothic was beginning, our builders gave the church some lancet windows and a canopied tomb.

The 14th century gave it another window and another doorway, and the shingled spire above its Saxon tower, and the 15th century put a window in the Saxon wall of the baptistry. The 16th century left us a brass in the nave, the 17th gave the splendid pulpit, the altar rails, the oak screen in the tower, and the clock which has been beating out the hours for nearly 300 years. It is a church of all our ages.

The eye is drawn at once to these impressive arches and to this chancel twice unique. The arches rest on round columns bedded in circular bases on square plinths; the columns are entirely chalk, so hard that they have stood eight centuries without flinching. The capitals are carved in chalk and are very beautiful, with various kinds of carving which lead the eye up to the insides of the arches, where our gaze is arrested by something not found anywhere in England out of Surrey, except once in a crypt in London. The coating of the Norman plaster inside the arches is cut into neat patches at the edge, and we believe the only other examples known of this kind of decoration are in the church at Godalming not far away, and in the crypt of St James's church at Clerkenwell.

The Normans were busy in this church many times in the hundred years while they were building churches in this country. They built the chancel soon after they began, and their first chancel arch was built about 1080. It was in another 100 years, when their style was changing into English, that they gave this chancel its remarkable upper storey. It is these two arches, both built by the Normans with a century between them, one set back inside the other with an upper sanctuary over it, which made Compton unlike any other church in England.

We suppose there is not anywhere a small place like this more packed with architectural interest. Just inside the greater chancel arch is the small square window of the Saxon cell on the left and the quatrefoil window of the medieval cell on the right. We come into the Norman cell through a doorway now made into it, and we are on the spot where lived a hermit long ago. The window has the thin piece of wood on which the hermit would lean when at prayer, and the wood is worn where the hands have rested. The window of the cell is in the shape of a cross with four leaves at the four ends. Out of the cell today rises a flight of steps replacing a wooden ladder of medieval times, and the steps bring us to the upper room of the sanctuary, the only place of its kind in our ten thousand churches.

We try not to see the pitiful glass that spoils the upper east window, and the window itself is not original, but there are two things here of remarkable interest—the timbers of the roof and the simple screen which protects us as we stand looking down. Both are Norman, and this is the oldest screen known in England. It is either oak or chestnut, and is made in one piece from an inch plank, pierced with nine round arches of the simplest kind. The columns that have stood where they are for 750 years are slender enough for a child to break, and their capitals are rough and crude. This simple screen was made from a tree that must have been growing in Alfred's England, as were all the timbers in these nave and chancel roofs; there are no older roofs in this country, and it is believed they belong to about the year 1165.

The lower sanctuary, facing us as we come into the chancel through a Jacobean gateway, has a 12th century aumbry and piscina, but its chief possession is the little east window beyond the little round arch. The window, like the arch, is Norman, and in it is a very precious piece of glass. There are those who believe it Norman (in which case it would be one of the only two Norman windows in England) but it is more likely to belong to the end of the 12th century or the beginning of the next. It shows a Madonna crowned. She has in her right hand a flower sceptre, and with her is the Holy Child holding up the right hand in the act of blessing, while in the other He holds a book. It is believed that this fragment was part of a big window and its preservation is a very great blessing, for it is one of the oldest Madonnas in the country and is still rich in ruby colour.

But not even yet is the interest of this chancel exhausted, for on the face of the arch, close by the steps to the pulpit, is the figure of a Norman knight cut in the chalk, an almost comical figure such as a schoolboy might draw, all straight lines yet with a vivid suggestion of movement, showing a soldier in a close-fitting helmet with a nose protection, and at his side an eight-armed cross. The knight is standing akimbo, and is an engaging little figure. Close by is what we can only interpret as the signature of the mason who put him here, a mason's mark with five linked circles drawn with compasses. The carving on both the chancel arches is a great enrichment to this small place, and happily there stands at the entrance to the chancel a splendid Jacobean pulpit, with richly carved panels and a handsome canopy. In this pulpit John Fulham preached for 55 years in the 18th century, and George Molyneux 49 years in the 19th. The pulpit matches the beautiful oak rail and gates at the chancel arch, all early 17th century craftsmanship. On the other side of the chancel arch are the old roodloft steps in the wall, remarkable for being made of wood.

In the floor of the nave is a brass of 1508 with the portraits of Thomas Jenyn and his two boys. The font at which Compton children are christened is as old as anything inside the church, and the light falls on it through a window made when it was new, and now filled with a crude picture of the Baptism in Jordan, probably the work of a foreign artist 300 years ago. The font has holes where the staples used to be in the days when it was locked against witches. A door in the Jacobean oak screen brings us into the Saxon tower, and an ancient ladder leads to the belfry and the 17th century clock. Preserved in the safe is a churchwarden's book bound with a parchment page from an old processional service book belonging to the monks at Hyde Abbey, Winchester, in whose ruins King Alfred lies.

Looking down on this old shrine are five magnificent cedars of Lebanon in the garden next door; one is about 17 feet round, one of the biggest known in England, and one throws its branches 15 yards from its trunk.

A little walk through the lanes brings us to the hillside garden in which the great artist friend of Compton lies among the village folk. It was he who helped to lay out the ground, and Mrs Watts who planned the terracotta chapel that rises in the midst of it. It was built from local materials by local men, and in the procession at the unveiling was the Archbishop of Canterbury in his stately robes and Mr Watts in his Oxford scarlet gown.

Indoors and out the burial chapel is covered with mystic symbols. The great frieze running round the outside walls suggests in symbolical ways the idea of the Way, the Truth, and the Life. Scenes of angel faces look down, and there is a charming band of faces in the triple arch of the doorway. In the door itself is a wrought-iron cross copied from a gravestone at Iona. The remarkable interior with walls of plaster has silver roots of the Tree of Life round the walls below, and in the roof the Circle of Eternity. On the walls are four great groups of angels, all carrying symbols of such things as night and day, ebb and flow, growth and decay, life and death, good and evil, joy and sorrow, labour and rest, stability and change, the real and the ideal. The walls are covered with mystical work in ruby plaster and gilded; there are over 100 medallions and winged cherubs. There is a picture of Mr Watts painted to express the idea of the All-Pervading, with suns and rolling systems in the lap of a great enfolding figure encompassed by the hands of Love.

To all pilgrims the sacred corner of this burial ground will be the cloister along the top of the hillside in which Mr Watts lies. In the centre is a classical wall monument with two relief panels from well-known pictures by the artist, Destiny representing the beginning of life, and the Messenger calling the weary one to the life beyond. Between these two panels is the loveliest thing in all this burial garden, a small figure of Mr Watts as he lay when they brought him to rest in this place. Below are six laurel wreaths with designs representing honours held by Mr Watts.

Another little walk and we are in the shade of the trees growing in the artist's garden, and at the entrance to the Potter's Guild he founded here, by the walls of his Art Gallery. Here hang his pictures, about 100 of those great conceptions through which he still speaks to the world his message of Life and Truth and Love. It is open to all on every day but Thursday, and is perhaps the most surprising gallery we come upon in any English lane.

SURREY

Across the road the flowers in his garden were blooming when we called, and the gracious lady who shared his life so long took us round his studio, gave us tea, and talked of those Victorian days when Cecil Rhodes came here and saw the great white horse which all unknown to him was to be his monument in South Africa. She talked of the days when G. F. Watts stayed in the house of two young people who loved each other, who had wealth and friends and a beautiful home and only one sad thing between them, for the rich young man was dying and could not be saved. It was the thought of the shadow across this home, Mrs Watts told us, that led him to paint his picture of Love and Death.

We left this fine lady of the Victorian Era filled with the thought of Love and Life, alert and talking of affairs with the memory of the great artist all around her, hardly realising that a generation had gone since he went, and that she herself was on the way to ninety.

Wilson of Antarctica

COPTHORNE. It has little for the traveller to see except its new church, which has a chime of six bells in memory of the men who did not come back from the war; but those who ask to see the chapel of Copthorne School will be well rewarded, for in it is enshrined the memory of one of the noblest Englishmen who ever lived, Captain Scott's friend Wilson.

Dr Wilson loved this school, and stayed at it with his wife through the Easter term of 1910. His sister was the wife of the headmaster, Mr Bernard Rendall, and great interest had naturally been aroused there in the Expedition which was then being prepared for the South Pole. The boys of Copthorne provided a sledge for the expedition and contributed to the scientific instrument fund. Dr Wilson, much moved by this generosity, came on a second visit to thank them for it. As Scott found time to visit his brother-in-law at the Warwickshire village of Binton just before he went away, so Edward Wilson found time to visit his brother-in-law at Copthorne before they left England for the South Pole.

When the tragic news came home from Antarctica it was nowhere received with deeper sorrow than in this Surrey school, and it was resolved to set a window in the chapel in memory of Dr Wilson. It is a small lancet bordered with the rose of England and the cross of

St George suspended from the apex, and in the centre of the device is a singularly beautiful reproduction of one of Wilson's own sketches of Mount Erebus, with two small figures marching. The sketch is enclosed in a wreath held by two saints. With it is the motto he had adopted for himself and to which he was so true, "Deeds not Words," and below is Wilson kneeling in prayer, a passage from the 148th Psalm on a scroll before him, saying,"Snow and vapour, stormy wind, fulfilling His word." We read in the inscription that "his body lies far away in the Antarctic, but his name shall live for ever."

COULSDON. It knows the hubbub of the Brighton road; it knows the fine expanse of Farthing Down where our Saxon ancestors laid their dead; and it knows a quiet village corner with an old church among the trees.

The chancel of the church is longer than the nave, and was built 700 years ago probably by the abbots of Chertsey, who owned property here. In the walls are the blind arches found in several Surrey chancels, all having been built within a few decades of each other. The piscina and sedilia make a little row of four trefoiled arches deeply and beautifully moulded.

Under the 15th century tower lies an old coffin stone with a raised cross, and here on the wall is an inscription in brass to Anthonie Bois, rector for 22 years from the year of the Spanish Armada. His father, we read, was a man of arms in Calais and Captain of Dele Castell. On an aisle wall 700 years old is the monument to a lady of 1633, with a small woman's figure carved in alabaster. It is written with texts and philosophy, and the first letters of the lines of the rhyme make up the lady's name Grace Rowed. On the other side the letters make up the name Thomas Wood, though why he is here no one seems to know. Perhaps he is the churchwarden Thomas Wood, whose name is on the five 17th century bells.

Still flourishing in the grounds of Garston Hall, at Kenley near by, is a cedar planted in the Tudor days when the house was built.

A School's Achievement

CRANLEIGH. Something between a village and a little town, it is alive and interesting, with character in some of its new possessions as well as in its old church and houses.

Cranleigh School, founded in 1865, has a handsome chapel full of its own memories, and a fine new Speech Hall. The spacious village hall, built in 1933, blends well with old and new in this attractive main street. The Village Hospital goes back to 1859 and has the distinction of being the first of its kind in England.

Set back among old houses, the 14th century tower looks a picture of age and is rivalled in height by a splendid cedar brought from Lebanon. Eight bells ring out from the tower, the oldest 16th century, and the heaviest weighing a ton.

Most of the church is as old as the tower, with lofty arches and a feeling of size. The pillars of the nave are Norman, and built into a pier is a quaint Norman cat's head, with holes for eyes. Someone has suggested that Lewis Carroll may have got his idea of the Cheshire Cat from this quaint creature. The nave is guarded by dignified sculptures of St Nicholas and St John, given in memory of John Henry Sapte, who came to be rector in 1846 and ministered for 60 years.

In the chancel are brasses from the tomb of Robert Harding, a London alderman and goldsmith who died in 1503. The best of them shows Our Lord stepping from the empty tomb, amid a group of soldiers in armour. On the floor is a half-length brass of a 16th century priest who was probably rector, and under the tower is a tablet to Lord Alverstone, who was Lord Chief Justice for the first 13 years of this century and worshipped here.

The font is 14th century and has eight pillars linked by a rope carved in stone. A 15th century screen marks off a chapel, and the pulpit is decorated with tracery from another screen of the same age. There is a finely carved table in the sanctuary. A little 14th century glass is left at the top of the east window, showing Christ in Glory and two angels.

An unusual memorial is crumbling outside in the wall by the porch. Almost illegible, it is in memory of an unknown man who 300 years ago discovered the use of lime in agriculture, a discovery which would be specially valuable at Cranleigh, where the soil is heavy.

The tall churchyard cross under a fine yew was set up by George Edmund Street, the famous architect of the Law Courts, and tells a sad little story. It is to his first wife, who died before they had been married two months.

Two miles away towards the Sussex border we have a glimpse

through the trees of Baynards Park, one of the big Tudor houses of Surrey. It was rebuilt by Sir George More of Loseley, whose memorial is in St Nicolas Church at Guildford, and the house has belonged in turn to four great families.

While this book was being written a group of excavators from Cranleigh School (following up a suggestion of Mr S. E. Winbolt, who had found Roman fragments in a field) were excavating in a pasture between Ewhurst and High Wykehurst and had brought to light evidence of Roman brickworks. About 60 feet of pavement 30 feet wide was found paved with Roman bricks and tiles and roofing tiles, and a brick kiln with the furnace well preserved was found, with an arched flue eight feet long. The road on which it lies was part of a Roman road running for nine miles through fields and woods. So far as is known this pavement discovered by the boys of Cranleigh School is the only sign of a Roman building on this road, and it helps to determine the position of the road.

Old Yew

CROWHURST. How many villages, we wonder, have a living inhabitant twice as old as their ancient church? The pride of Crowhurst, like the pride of Crowhurst in Sussex, is its ancient yew, both growing by churches dedicated to our patron saint.

We do not know how old this giant is, but nothing is too old for Crowhurst; if we call it 1400 years they will not contradict. They say it was old when the Conqueror came, and certainly we know that people were astonished at its size when old John Aubrey was going about England writing things down. What we do know is that it is growing still, though it was hollowed out a few years after Waterloo, when they found a thrilling thing inside it which we have seen—a cannon ball fired in the Civil War.

This famous tree, throwing its shade over the east window of Crowhurst church, is about 11 yards round its trunk, and there is room inside the hollow for 12 people to sit at a table. We must believe that at least it was here when the Conqueror came, and that, if a tree remembers, this most ancient yew may remember as far back in the annals of our land as anything now alive. It looks out from the crest of a hill with fine wide views across a delightful landscape, and in all the years of its long life there have been few memories more

Guildford — Loseley House

Crowhurst — Timbered Manor House

Esher — Claremont

THREE OF SURREY'S MAGNIFICENT OLD HOUSES

Crowhurst — The Church and the Age-Old Yew

Ockham — The Church with its Famous East Window

poignant hereabouts than that which comes to mind at the oak crucifix by the gate, with the words:

The men were very good unto us,
and we were not hurt.

It is good that in this old place there is a little Norman work still in the walls, and a south door still swinging on its 13th century hinges. All these 700 years Crowhurst people have been christened at the massive font.

We found its chief beauty in its windows, for it has 15th century glass. The tracery has Gabriel and the Madonna with modern faces, and below them feathered angels in old glass. In the middle of the window is a modern Crucifixion with 15th century fragments round, including a shield supported by two fine eagles and another with three greyhounds. Below are 20 little maidens with long golden hair carrying garlands. They are nearly all modern. A nave window has the kings bringing their gifts and another St George on horseback.

In the sanctuary lies a father with his son, both in fine tombs and both with their brass portraits. They are both John Gaynesfords, and died within ten years of each other in the 15th century. The father is armoured, and has his feet on a lion; the son has with him his faithful hound.

They lived at Crowhurst Place, a mile away, one of the best timbered homes in Surrey, still in the moat which has surrounded it about 500 years. Set with many gables among great barns, with a wooden bridge across the moat and stone walls covered with creeping plants, the house is a splendid spectacle. Its great hall rises from floor to roof with grandly moulded timbers, and we may well believe that here came Henry the Eighth on his way to visit Anne Boleyn at Hever. He is said to have planted a yew hedge still flourishing.

The Gaynesfords are one of the first families we hear of in Surrey. One is said to have had six wives (which would at least have pleased the lover on his way to Anne Boleyn), and one is said to have made a paved way over the fields because he disliked wet shoes. We were told that these stones still turn up in the fields.

In the floor by the altar is what is said to be the only Sussex iron tombstone in Surrey. Under it a Gaynesford has slept since 1591, and on it are raised figures of two boys and two girls at prayer, with a shrouded figure between them. They were five of the mother's 16 children. Not far away is a brass inscription in memory of the butler of our two first Stuart kings.

It was good news, when we called, to find that a great effort to save this fine old place had just succeeded. It was threatened by the death-watch beetle, which was making its way about the tower. The repairs involved the underpinning of the tower, the strengthening of the foundations, and the reconstruction of the floor, and a beam weighing about a ton had to be replaced. It was all well and truly done with English oak, so that the belfry has now 15th and 20th century timbers side by side, and a graceful shingled spire over all.

There is an ancient chest, and a pulpit old and new, with linenfold. Hanging on the chancel wall, above a 15th century tomb of somebody unknown, is a little modern carving above of the Descent from the Cross. It is splendid.

The Charing Cross of the Flying World

CROYDON. It is the Charing Cross of the Flying Age, famous all the world over, but long before men began to fly it was famous to travellers about our little land, for its High Street is on the road from London to Brighton. It has become the busiest town in Surrey, with a host of industries, and at least some of the things it makes (its bells) known as far as its planes can go; and it has become the biggest town, for the last century has seen it grow from a market town with about 12,000 people into a county borough with almost a quarter of a million, its boundaries extending 45 miles and embracing the villages of Addington and Shirley, and the residential districts of Upper Norwood, South Norwood, Addiscombe, Woodside, Thornton Heath, Norbury, and Waddon (where the aerodrome is). Croydon has a church like a small cathedral. It has been the home of many Archbishops of Canterbury and has a famous hospital founded by one of them. Its story goes far back through the Tudors and Saxons to the days before our history began.

We find nothing here to remind us of its Tudor charcoal-burners, who were called colliers and supplied London with charcoal, but they were celebrated in their day, and one of our early English dramas is called Grim, the Collier of Croydon. There are a few little things older than Grim kept in the town hall—Saxon wooden brackets,

SURREY

a Saxon sword, many spearheads, and bosses from shields, but by far the most ancient relics of Croydon's past are a group of depressions in the ground known as hut circles, and thought to mark the sites of the homes of prehistoric men. They are to be seen on Croham Hurst, a delightful wooded hill 475 feet high, which is among the 780 green acres Croydon has preserved for ever.

It is dramatic to pass from these to the great place for which Croydon is famous today, the Flying Centre of the Empire. It was soon after the war that Croydon succeeded Hounslow as the Airport of London and the chief Customs Aerodrome in the country; and after twenty years it may be succeeded by the new aerodrome at Lullingstone in Kent, within sight of the valley which so narrowly missed being the birthplace of flight. But Croydon's connection with flying dates back to 1915, when a section of the present flying ground was used as part of the Air Defence of London. The aerodrome covers 330 acres, including 34 acres of building. The great Administration Building has a booking hall with waiting rooms, buffet, and post office, goods warehouses, and numerous offices for air transport companies, customs and immigration staffs, and meteorological and wireless services. There is also a residential hotel, first-aid and police headquarters, and sheds with nearly 200,000 square feet of floor space for aeroplanes and half as much for workshops.

The nerve-centre of the aerodrome is, of course, the Control Tower, where, high above all obstructions sits the Aerodrome Officer, rather like an admiral, with the aerodrome as his flagship and liners of the air as his fleet. The officer's permission for pilots to take off is indicated with a signalling lamp. Conical streamers indicate the direction of the wind by day, but at night incoming pilots see on the aerodrome a great neon light shaped like a T, which is mounted so that it can swing in the wind. The boundary of the safe landing area is indicated by red lights.

Night-flying aircraft can recognise Croydon 45 miles away (in favourable conditions even 80) by the distinctive flashing of the red light of a 6080 candle-power beacon. Situated at various points round the aerodrome are eight banks of floodlights, each of half-a-million candle-power, and the aerodrome has also a portable floodlight which gives a diffused light through an angle of 180 degrees or can project a beam of a million candle-power. The aerodrome has also the Lorenz short-wave approach equipment, which enables planes to make safe landings in fog.

The wireless masts for the Croydon transmitters are two and a half miles away at Mitcham, but the plant is worked by remote control. The man in the tower keeps in touch with all aircraft on cross-channel routes and marks their positions with flags on a map.

Croydon has a direction-finding apparatus, and in conjunction with Lympne and Pulham pilots flying far away in fog or cloud can be given their positions within two minutes of asking. There is also a beacon which transmits signals one minute in every three, so that planes having direction-finding apparatus can work out their own positions in conjunction with signals from similar beacons operating at Le Bourget and Amsterdam. Besides possessing its own meteorological station, the Airport collects reports from stations along the routes and gives news to aircraft in flight, so that a plane is often enabled to fly round a bad-weather area instead of through it. An important part of the Croydon equipment is a huge turn-table on which planes weighing up to 20 tons can be placed for the purpose of compass-swinging.

An enclosure from which excellent views of arriving and departing planes can be had is set aside for the public.

Croydon has over 120 churches and chapels and mission halls, but the only one of historic interest is the mother church of St John the Baptist. It is one of the biggest and finest in the county. We see it as Sir Gilbert Scott refashioned it after a terrible fire in the eighteen-sixties, when little but the pinnacled tower (124 feet high) and the two-storeyed south porch were saved. Both are 15th century, but the tower has much new masonry. The porch is vaulted and has bosses carved as faces. The nave and the aisles have a forest of pinnacles springing from their battlements.

We may be thankful that some of the best possessions escaped the fire. In the chancel is a tall arch with two quaint heads probably more than 500 years old; inside the tower are two 17th century tilting helmets; and in the nave is one of the greatest treasures of Croydon, a 15th century eagle lectern with three leopards sitting round the pedestal. England has only about 50 of these old brass lecterns.

SURREY

The modern glass in the big windows has a pleasing effect, but it is the collection of monuments that we come to see in the church, the old brasses and the fine tombs. One brass portrait shows the master of a Cambridge college, Gabriel Silvester of 1512, in his robes, another a group of seven sisters from Henry the Eighth's time, and a third William Heron of 1562 in his armour, with part of his wife's portrait still beside him.

There is a beautifully decorated altar tomb of one of the Warham family in the 16th century, but the finest monument of all is the magnificent classical tomb of the man who gave Croydon its most famous building. Here lies John Whitgift in his robes, his head resting on two embroidered cushions. For 20 years he was Queen Elizabeth's Archbishop of Canterbury, living just long enough to celebrate the coronation of King James.

Whitgift, a merchant's son educated at Cambridge University, became Master of Trinity at 37. An earnest advocate of the Reformation, he was sheltered from Mary Tudor, and after the accession of Elizabeth he became Dean of Lincoln, Bishop of Worcester, and Archbishop of Canterbury all in twelve years. He sympathised with Puritan doctrine but not with Puritan practice, and, believing that salvation and the safety of the kingdom depended on strict conformity with the Prayer Book, he relentlessly persecuted the Puritans, and drew up new articles worthy (as Burghley told him) of the Spanish Inquisition. They compelled ministers and worshippers to give evidence against themselves and to procure their own conviction. He followed this by gagging the Press, forbidding the publication of any book or pamphlet not licensed by himself or the Bishop of London, and restricting the number of printers. Yet, though narrow and bigoted in religion, he was entirely unselfish, and refused the Lord Chancellorship. While condemning Puritans to exile and death, and crippling the Press, he made partial atonement by building here his grammar school and hospital, spending on it the fortune left him by his father. Here was his country home, and here he lived when he could absent himself from Lambeth Palace.

On another tomb, much damaged, lies Gilbert Sheldon in robes and mitre, with a fearful array of bones and skulls carved below. He became archbishop soon after the Restoration, and is remembered for the part he played in the rebuilding of St Paul's and for the

Sheldonian Theatre he gave to Oxford. Among four archbishops who lie here without any memorial is Edmund Grindal, the Lakeland farmer's son who rose to be Primate and asked to be buried "without any solemn herse or funeral pomp"; he was one of the few men bold enough to speak plainly to Queen Elizabeth.

One other famous man lies here and is remembered by a sculptured portrait, John Singleton Copley, who as a youth painted George Washington's portrait and grew up to paint a fine series of historical scenes. The English-speaking peoples in both the Old World and the New recall his work and memory with pride. He was born at Boston, USA, in 1737, the son of parents who had emigrated from Ireland. His father died when he was a child, and John was educated by an artist and a lover of books. Though in those days artists were rare in the British colony, young Copley taught himself to paint so well that men and women vied with one another to sit for their portraits in his studio, George Washington (then a British colonel) being one of them. A Copley portrait is a treasured heirloom in many American homes.

One of these portraits made its way to England, where Benjamin West persuaded the Society of Artists to include it in their exhibition. Copley wished to come too, but his marriage and the birth of three children (one of whom became Lord Chancellor of England), delayed his journey till 1774. Reynolds hastened to make his aquaintance, and he was introduced to George the Third and the queen, who sat to him for portraits to be sent to Governor Wentworth in New Hampshire. It may be that he told his royal sitter, as he told others, that war would come from the attempt to tax the American Colonies; certainly he would think so, for his wife's father, Richard Clarke, was actually the merchant whose tea was thrown overboard in Boston Harbour.

War did break out in the following year while Copley was studying art in Italy, and his family left Boston just in time, all settling in London, where Copley began those great canvasses on which he has dramatised some of the most stirring scenes in English history. The first was the Death of Chatham, painted a few months after the event, every face a portrait from life. Bartolozzi engraved it, and 2500 copies were quickly sold, many in Copley's native town of Boston, where his mother gazed on it with pride.

Next came the Death of Major Peirson, which is in our National Gallery, together with the sketch for the Siege and Relief of Gibraltar, which fills a wall of the Guildhall Art Gallery. Charles Stuart and his adversaries appealed to his dramatic instinct, and among the series are the well-known canvases of Charles signing Strafford's death-warrant and ordering the arrest of the Five Members, and another of the triumphant return of the Five to Westminster. Many religious paintings came from Copley's brush, but portrait painting remained his chief love, many Americans coming to London to sit to him, proudly taking back home a portrait painted by this self-taught Boston boy. He died in Waterloo year, leaving 269 oil paintings, 35 crayons, and 14 miniatures among his known collection. His last picture was of the Resurrection and his last portrait was of his son.

But among all the modern memorials the pilgrim to Croydon will surely be drawn to the simple brass telling of John Corbet Anderson, who died an old man in 1907. He could remember the fire which destroyed the church, and the appearance of the church before it, and from his books and sketches it was possible to restore the fine tomb of Archbishop Whitgift precisely as it was.

Whitgift's Hospital stands like an oasis of quiet beside the noisy street. Its charming homes for aged folk lie round a courtyard, with a lawn for the old men to play bowls and another for the old women to play croquet. As well as the rooms in which they live there is a hall, a little chapel with 17th century wainscoting, and a room called the audience chamber which has the greatest interest of all. It is panelled, and has a rich overmantel with John Whitgift's arms, and it is one of the rooms the archbishop himself often used. Here we see his table and stool, a picture of the hospital as it was in the 18th century, an old inn sign, some wooden salt-cellars, and a copy of what is called the Treacle Bible, in which the Elizabethan printer put treacle instead of balm in the eighth chapter of Jeremiah. Here, too, is a table with a rim to stop the old people's money from rolling off when they were paid, and here is the fine Armada chest in which the money was kept, its interior still lined with sail-cloth. A document once in the chest and now in the safe brings to mind one of the darkest deeds in our history. It is a deed of 1600, by which Susan Tracy gave money to the hospital to expiate the crime of her ancestor Sir William Tracy, one of the murderers of Thomas Becket.

John Whitgift's Hospital, built at the very end of the Elizabethan Era, is important for the influence it had on other charitable houses founded after the Reformation. Its plan and its statutes were directly copied in another famous Surrey almshouse, Abbot's Hospital at Guildford.

Centuries ago, when Croydon was a country town and no one had dreamt that the houses of a Greater London would grow out to meet it, the archbishops would spend part of each year here in a palace that has seen many changes and adventures. It was the manor house round which the town grew up, and no one knows when it was built or who first lived in it. Among the masonry is a 12th century arch, and among the records is a document signed here by an archbishop as long ago as 1273. The last archbishop came in the 18th century, and since his day the palace has been used as a factory and as a laundry. Now it is a school, and though some of the old parts have been destroyed there are still standing by the churchyard the Great Hall, the Chapel, Arundel's Hall, and the Long Gallery.

The Great Hall is chiefly 15th century, though it has a vaulted porch a century older. It is a noble room 56 feet by 38, with arms of the archbishops carved on the corbels of its fine open roof of chestnut. Here it was that Cranmer examined John Frith, the martyr of Westerham, brought before him on a charge of heresy. Frith had helped William Tyndale to translate the Bible, and it was Tyndale who wrote to him these brave words in a letter of consolation:

Sir, your wife is well content with the will of God, and would not for her sake have the glory of God hindered.

He was only 30 when the fires of Smithfield claimed him, and Cranmer a generation later was to die the same death. In this hall, too, Queen Elizabeth was entertained by more than one of the archbishops, including Whitgift himself, whom she called her " little black husband." He was afterwards to stand at her deathbed, and to walk with her coffin as chief mourner.

Arundel's Hall has a roof with corbels boldly carved as angels, but it has been much altered since Thomas Arundel built it early in the 15th century. He was the brother of the Earl of Arundel executed by Richard the Second, and as archbishop he held here in custody the boy who was to become the first King James of Scotland.

The Palace of the Archbishops

The Quadrangle of Whitgift Hospital
OLD CROYDON

The Control Tower of the Aerodrome

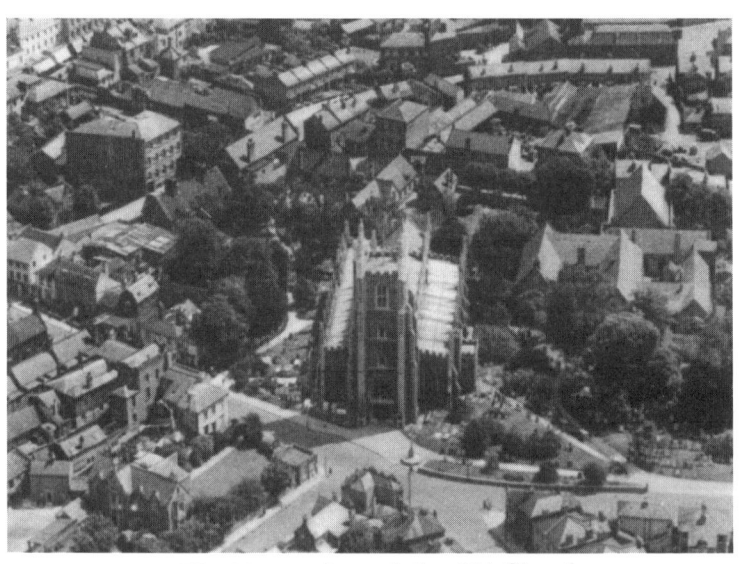

The Houses Around the Old Church
CROYDON AS THE FLYING MAN SEES IT

SURREY

The Long Parlour was probably first built by Archbishop Bourchier, who crowned two Plantagenet kings and lived on to start the Tudor Age by crowning Henry the Seventh. Most of the chapel as we see it was also built by him, and it has much that is delightful. Round three sides there are benches and panelling, some of the poppyheads having 15th century carving of foliage, while others have the arms of Archbishop Laud who restored them. Two of the bench-ends are carved with little heads of a man and a boy, thought to be Edward the Fourth and his son. At the east of the chapel is a very wide window of seven lancets, filled with attractive modern glass of the Madonna and saints. At the west is a gallery-pew beautifully panelled, probably also an addition made by Laud. The old font has come from a church in Southwark.

Of Croydon's many modern buildings the most notable are the Whitgift School at Haling Park, built round a quadrangle and possessing 60 acres of woods and playing-fields; the Whitgift Middle School with its fine clock tower built in 1871 by Sir Arthur Blomfield, at North End, in the heart of the town; and the town hall, with a clock tower 176 feet high, looking, with other municipal buildings, on to a delightful little garden in Katharine Street. This fine red brick building, the third town hall Croydon has had since the 16th century, must in time give way to a fourth, for it is already proving too small for its duties. Outside is Croydon's peace memorial, by Paul Montfort, a stone pylon with a bronze cross and bronze figures of a wounded soldier, and a woman with a child. In one of the wings of the town hall is the public library, which with its branches in other parts of the town possesses 200,000 books. On the walls of the reference library are medallions symbolical of Knowledge, and others with portraits of writers and thinkers; in front of it is a bronze statue of Queen Victoria, and near it a seated stone figure of Archbishop Whitgift.

With its long line of archbishops Croydon has had some of the greatest figures in our history living in its palace; and it has had some smaller figures who are not forgotten. We think here of Michael Murgatroid the scholar, Whitgift's faithful secretary, who was laid to rest in Croydon church as close as possible to his master. We think also of Daniel Quare the clockmaker, who died at his house here in 1724 after being persecuted for years as a Quaker; he invented repeater watches, and made for Hampton Court a fine clock which needed winding only once a year. And we think of Samuel Coleridge-Taylor, the son of a Negro doctor and an English mother, who loved and studied the music of native Africa, and whose setting of Hiawatha is sung everywhere. Here he lived and worked and died, and he was laid to rest in Bandon Hill cemetery close by.

One more memory the town has, not of a man but of a railway, the very first public line to be opened in England, in the earliest years of last century. It was the Surrey Iron Railway, running from Wandsworth to Croydon, with goods trucks drawn over stone sleepers by horses; and it was killed by the coming of steam. Its builders hoped to carry it from London to Portsmouth, but it never got farther from Croydon than Merstham, where the cutting made for it can still be seen.

A Famous Old Street

DORKING. All the world knows its famous street and the lovely country round it. It is the great centre for Box Hill and Leith Hill and Ranmore Common; we must think of it, set in all this natural beauty, as one of Surrey's luckiest towns. One of its commons, Cotmandene, is famous in cricket history as the ground on which Caffyn learned the game, he who was the first to teach Australia to play cricket. Henry Jupp, another old county cricketer, was born at Dorking. Glory Woods belong to the town, given to it by the Duke of Newcastle, as rich a gift as any duke could give; and those who love a noble view may climb to the summerhouse at the top of the wooded parkland called the Nower.

But we need not climb so high for the entrancing interest of this place; we have only to stand in the High Street and see the world go by. Everybody passes or bypasses the town sometime or other, and everybody passing through looks up at the gabled White Horse Inn, and at the quaint houses and shops. The White Horse was a great place in the coaching days; its front is 18th century and some parts of it are 400 years old. A 17th century house in another street is believed to have been the original of the Markis of Granby, "just large enough to be convenient and small enough to be snug", the place where the immortal Sam Weller met his mother-in-law.

The town is also memorable as the scene of the fictitious Battle of

SURREY

Dorking, Sir George Chesney's account of which first appeared in Blackwood's Magazine in 1871, portending the invasion of our shores by Germany after our fleet had been wiped out by torpedoes, and the final overthrow of our armies on a ridge north of this town.

The Independent Chapel in West Street is on the site of the oldest Nonconformist church in Surrey, and has an old organ from the Pavilion at Brighton; but Dorking's spacious church has little of the age of the town about it, its foundation stone having been laid by Bishop Wilberforce not long before he fell from his horse and was killed. The tall and graceful spire is in his memory. A tablet in the church is to Canon Chichester who ministered here for a quarter of a century, and its walls are decorated with marble and beautiful mosaics of the Wise Men, the Flight into Egypt, and adoring Angels.

The town is rich in memories of scholars and writers, some with memorials on these walls, and others buried in this churchyard, where many coins have been found from the Roman Stane Street which runs close by. We come upon Abraham Tucker, the 18th century philosopher who wrote his philosophy in seven volumes at Betchworth Castle close by, and died there; upon John Hoole, the dramatist and translator of Tasso and Ariosto, of whom Sir Walter Scott said so unkindly that he was a noble transmutor of gold into lead; upon Jeremiah Markland, translator of Euripides, who died at the fine Jacobean house, Milton Court, with its ruined gables, noble rooms and massive staircase. We remember also among the humbler memorials one to a faithful servant in a Dorking family for half a century.

It was a few months after Waterloo when they laid to rest here a Duke of Norfolk, buried with the pomp and pageantry of a royal prince. He was lord of the great house called Deepdene, now open to all as a hotel, and still surrounded with some of the noble trees the duke would know. To this house came Benjamin Disraeli, and here he is said to have written much of his novel Coningsby. Here also came the famous chronicler John Aubrey the antiquary, who lived through the last three-quarters of the 17th century. He lived in constant trouble through law suits which drove him to part with estate after estate, and was in frequent danger of arrest in spite of influential protectors; but he accumulated immense masses of material, much of it about Surrey, and of Deepdene he said that he found the pleasures of the garden so entrancing that he never expected any enjoyment beyond them except the kingdom of heaven.

A Benefactor of India

In the cemetery at Dorking sleeps a great benefactor of India who spent his last years here, Sir Arthur Cotton.

ONE of the regenerators of the Indian Empire, he was born at Woodcote in Oxfordshire just before Trafalgar, was trained at the East India Company's military college, and went out to Madras in his youth. During the Burma War he showed great gallantry as a soldier, but it is as a saviour of life that he lives, a shining name in the annals of the eastern empire.

The great Cauvery delta, of which the northern arm is known as the Coleroon, had been used imperfectly for irrigation for 1600 years, but the water tended more and more to follow the course of the Coleroon, leaving arid the lands along the southern section of the delta and exposing a great population to recurrent famine. Sir Arthur Cotton dammed the Coleroon at two points 70 miles apart, bringing abundant water to the stricken area without depriving the southern lands of their supplies; and the result was that the irrigated area produced abundant crops, not only for its own people but for the relief of areas later stricken by famine.

His next achievement was to dam the great Godavery river below Rajahmundry. Cotton chose a point where the river is over three miles wide, and although he utilised two islands he still had to build two miles of masonry to form his dam, a work of five years, fruitful of immense gain to a teeming population.

His work well done, he settled down at Dorking and became deeply interested in agricultural improvements to the close of his long life. He died in 1899, only four years short of his century.

Some of the Oldest Pews in England

DUNSFOLD. A village attractively open, with a strip of green common separating its line of houses from the road. At one end is a magnificent oak 20 feet round, and on the banks of the Arun is a holy well with a fine shingled canopy over it, and a carving of the Madonna. The lid of the well has the ancient hinges.

But it is to the church that all who come here must go, for the treasures of Dunsfold have been gathering in it since the century that saw Magna Carta.

On the New Bypass Road

A Woodland Scene in Autumn
DORKING'S BEAUTIFUL COUNTRYSIDE

Eashing   **700-Year-Old Bridge**

Elstead   **The Medieval Bridge**

Little has it changed in 650 years. The porch by which we enter has its original bargeboard and its original red patterns in the roof, and was made new in Tudor times. The door we open was opening to worshippers in Chaucer's day, and has its original ironwork and its great key a foot long. The graceful 13th century font has a 17th century cover. Most fascinating of all, we can sit down in pews that were put in this church when it was first built. They are still in use and are among the oldest in England. Roughly hewn, the shape of their ends is said to be unique, with tops that curve round and rise up to knobs worn smooth with age.

Many of the windows show the beginnings of decorated tracery, and in one or two of them are fragments of old glass. There is a hazy wall-painting, a chalice made in 1566 by a London craftsman, and a 15th century bell turret rising up from beams in the nave.

The churchyard is approached through a modern lychgate and a trimmed yew tunnel, and is shaded by a crippled yew 23 feet round. Trodden under foot in the path is a stone altar probably turned out of the church at the Reformation.

Among the rectors here was Erskine William Holland, who served for half of the 19th century, and Nicholas Wildear, who died in 1633 and must have been something of a litter lout in his day. He has left his initials carved on the slender columns of the sedilia, and his name Nick written in black letters under the Elizabethan communion table in the vestry.

Born here at the old rectory was Dr Joseph Warton, schoolmaster and critic and friend of Dr Johnson. Once they quarrelled at Sir Joshua Reynold's house, Johnson telling Warton he was not used to contradiction and Warton replying that it would be better if he were. At one time Warton went with Johnson to the old College at Oxford, where, as a student, he had been so poor that somebody offered him a pair of boots (which he threw out of the window); and his friend records that the master of Pembroke received him coldly, did not mention the Dictionary (which was then being published), and did not invite him to dinner.

A Hairpin and a Tragedy

EASHING. Before reaching Peper Harow Park the Wey flows under Somerset Bridge, with a middle arch 700 years old. After crossing the park it reaches the beautiful 13th century bridge at Eashing, belonging to the National Trust and the finest old bridge in Surrey. Its seven stone arches stand with several old cottages only a few yards from a factory, and we may be thankful that a fire which broke out in the factory not long ago was mastered before it reached the bridge.

Yet, old as this fine structure is, Eashing has a still older tale to tell; it was brought to light, oddly enough, by a very modern thing, the making of the bypass road close by. The workmen were digging in a cutting about a quarter of a mile above Eashing Bridge when they came upon a company of skeletons, with a Roman hairpin lying near the head of one of them. Experts decided that they were not buried in times of peace, for with them were no weapons, ornaments, or pottery such as our forefathers laid in graves. It seemed as if they were killed and buried in haste, and this, it is thought, may have been their story.

They were Romanised Britons, short dark folk, who might have lived happily if they could only have been born a little earlier; but the strong shield of Rome was withdrawn, and fierce invaders were raiding and conquering Britain.

This little family probably took fright, and decided to leave their home in the Weald and go to the south-west. Behind Wansdyke, the great defensive earthwork stretching from east of Savernake almost to the Bristol Channel, they would be safer from the Saxons. There they would be among other Britons. There, if they could only reach it, were peace and safety. So they packed up their possessions and set off, hoping to gain the east-west route along the Hog's Back at Seale or Farnham. They were going to ford the Wey at the place where men have crossed for centuries when out of the woods burst the Saxons. Those invaders had come up the river and founded a settlement at Eashing. The luckless Britons had blundered straight into the people from whom they fled.

It was all over in a minute. The Britons were killed and their possessions shared among the conquerors. Nothing was left to the dead except one hairpin, and on that solitary clue our tale is founded. Some days later the Saxons came back and buried their victims, just as they happened to lie, the woman on her face. That, they thought, was the end of it, but murder will out even after 15 centuries, and the fate of those six people is revealed to us, though their kinsmen probably did not know it.

Here the Saxons conquered, but they did not conquer everywhere. Many of the little dark people escaped. You come upon clans of them today in country places. The poor bones of Eashing tell us of an adventure that ended in tragedy, but there were other fights which ended happily for them on the right side of Wansdyke.

Old Dreadnought

EAST CLANDON. It has the quiet serenity and charm of timbered cottages and old barns gathered about a church with an attractive shingled spire. By the porch stand two big iron-bound stones that were once the weights of a clock. The chancel is 13th century. There is a Norman wall-painting almost faded away, a bell that was ringing when the English were fighting Joan of Arc, an Elizabethan chalice, and good modern glass in several windows.

There are several memorials to the people of the great Georgian house called Hatchlands, built by Admiral Boscawen, who defeated the French at Lagos Bay in the 18th century. It was to be the home of his old age, and East Clandon might have seen him for many a year, walking (as he would) with his head on one side. But the house was scarcely built before fever struck him down, and the man, who was called Old Dreadnought by his sailors, passed away. He sleeps at Saint Michael Penkevil in Cornwall, and his epitaph there tells how Hatchlands was built by him "at the expense of the enemies of his country," and how this gallant and profitable servant of his country was laid to rest in Cornwall "amid the groans and tears of his beloved Cornishmen."

Portrait of a Bishop

EAST HORSLEY. Its tower has been standing for 900 years. Beneath its unbeautiful face it is partly the work of Saxon builders, and those who look inside it will see a Saxon window above the western doorway. Those who seek will also find the remains of a flue made by the Saxons to serve as an outlet for an oven, perhaps for a priest who had his home in the tower, perhaps even for baking the sacrificial wafers.

But there is more than age to attract us to this church. There are the beautiful sleeping figures of Thomas and Catherine Cornwallis, he in plate armour and she in the costume of the early Stuart period. Watching over them is a little angel head with golden wings, and by them kneel their two sons, Robert, who died as a young man in France, and "young Henry," whose head is lost and who died at only three. Thomas Cornwallis was Groom Porter to Queen Elizabeth; Catherine was the daughter of Sir Thomas Wriothesley, Lord Chancellor, and the aunt of Henry Wriothesley, friend and patron of Shakespeare.

On a wall are brass portraits, preserved under glass. The oldest is a fine old figure, Robert de Brantyngham of the 14th century. He was a brother of the bishop who finished the fine west front of Exeter cathedral, and he sleeps here because the bishops of Exeter had a manor house at East Horsley. It is thought that Robert died here while on a visit to his brother. There is a remarkable portrait of John Bowthe, Bishop of Exeter in the next century, who was buried in this chancel after governing his church "wondrous well." It is of a rare kind that shows him in profile, a dignified kneeling figure with his hands raised in prayer. He wears a mitre above which his pastoral staff is showing, and it is said that in only two other brasses in England can we see so much of the back of a figure as we see of this old bishop in his vestments. Below him is a Latin inscription with these stern words:

Whosoever thou mayest be that shall pass by, stand, read carefully, and weep. I am what thou shalt be; I had been what thou art: for me, I beg thee, pray. Here lies John Bowthe, formerly Bishop of Exeter.

John and Alice Snelling of the 15th century are shown with six sons and five daughters, and there are portraits of the 13 children of Thomas Snelling, a blacksmith 400 years ago.

The communion plate of East Horsley shows exceptionally fine workmanship of Charles Stuart's time; some of it has been shown at South Kensington. From the same period come the two chairs in the sanctuary. The list of rectors includes Joseph Greenhill, who served for 61 years in the 18th century, and Freeman Wilson who, after 31 years service, died suddenly one Sunday in the vestry of the church he had restored.

On the peace memorial cross by the tower is the name of Colonel Courtenay, who won the DSO by conspicuous gallantry and resource in action. While directing the advance of his battalion one company became disorganised under heavy fire. He rushed forward and led the men on. He then went to the left of the attack, where it was held up by wire, and encouraged short rushes, himself setting the example, until the last objective was reached.

Lord Darnley's Cupbearer

EAST MOLESEY. Here the River Mole ends its journey from Sussex to the Thames. It has come 42 miles, first across the Weald, then in its lovely valley through the North Downs, where it plays hide and seek with itself above and below the ground.

The old church of East Molesey suffered badly in a fire last century, but some of the old memorials were saved and are now in the porch of the new one. Among them is a brass inscription to Anthonie Standen, who must have seen something of the tragic life of Mary Queen of Scots, for he was the cupbearer of Lord Darnley. A tablet to Sir Edmund Nagle reminds us that he joined the navy at 13 and was knighted for his part in capturing a crack frigate of the French fleet. He married a rich lady, and with his Irish humour became a favourite of the future King George the Fourth, who made him groom of the bedchamber. In the chancel are a tablet and an attractive east window in memory of a soldier who marched with Sir Henry Havelock to the Relief of Lucknow.

A quaint weathervane on the Bell Inn is in the shape of a man in a high hat, standing on one leg and looking through a telescope. Equally quaint is the inn itself, parts of it going back to Tudor times. Every line of its gables and windows is askew, reminding us of a famous Crooked Inn we saw in Staffordshire.

The Wonderful Chain of Vicars

EFFINGHAM. Its name is known to every schoolboy from the famous Howards who had a manor here, the father who crushed Wyatt's rebellion, and the son who shared in the defeat of the Armada; but Effingham has little beyond its name to remind us of them.

Save for its 18th century tower the flint church has preserved its outlines since their day. The chancel has 14th century windows, probably dating from the time William of Wykeham gave an order for its repair. The transept is a century older, with two kingposts in its roof, a few fragments of 15th century glass in its windows, and an old bench-end with a poppyhead standing in the corner. Near the pulpit is the tombstone of Walter de Geddyng, lord of the manor 600 years ago; and there are brass inscriptions to John Aley of 1507 and to John Cooke and his wife Frances, who were buried on the same day in 1629.

Looking round these walls we come upon tablets to a group of distinguished men, among them Andrew Bogle, a Highland soldier who won the VC by leading his men into a fortified house at Oonao during the Indian Mutiny; a man who traced his lineage back to the Prince of Wales of 1202; and Sir George Frederic Edmonstone, who, following the profession of his father as a civil servant in India, became Governor of the North-Western Provinces. He died at Effingham in 1864 and sleeps in the churchyard. A more unusual memorial is the row of tiles inscribed to the three young children of William Walker, vicar here in the 17th century.

There is a tablet to William Farley, who came to be vicar in 1793 and stayed 44 years. He was the first of a remarkable chain of three vicars of long service, the other two being Henry Malthus, a son of the famous political economist, and Ernest Bayly. Between them these three covered a span of 137 years, the first preaching to congregations who had never heard of Napoleon, and the last living among boys and girls too young to remember the Great War.

A few minutes along the road to Effingham Junction is Norwood Farm, a red brick house with a tithe barn 103 feet long. It is thought to have been built about 600 years ago by a Bishop of Winchester as the residence of a bailiff.

Down in the Catacombs

EGHAM. We can hardly call it famous as Egham, but it has a name that is known to the end of the English-speaking world, for here is Runnymede. Here in the year 1215 were sown the seeds of English liberty. Here the worst king who ever sat on the English throne sealed the landmark of freedom which the world knows as Magna Carta.

Nothing else has Egham to match the fame and beauty of the Thames flowing through these meadows; no memory has she to compare with this. We may still see these 160 acres as they must have looked on that historic day when John sealed Magna Carta in his rage, biting twigs and straw, we are told, as the Barons pressed about him. In our own time the meadows have been given to the nation, and a fitting and impressive gateway to them has been designed by Sir Edwin Lutyens. Three walnut trees were planted in them for the Coronation of George the Sixth, and in the church is a company of painted shields deposited by descendants of the Barons who stood as Sureties for the Charter. There is also on the wall of the church a thing we have not come upon in any other church in England, the head of a buffalo; it was given to the church by Canadian members of the Royal Order of Buffaloes, who have always believed that there were Buffalo knights at the sealing of Magna Carta and wished to commemorate the fact in this way.

The church was built last century at a dark period in English architecture, and is not attractive, but its memorials are full of interest and its weird catacombs are eerie and unusual. We go down into them among the church's very foundations, peering by the light of a taper into family vaults and little chambers where coffins have lain for generations. At one place the foundations of the medieval church are revealed, and down in the crypt we found a 17th century bust of Sir Robert Foster, who was made Lord Chief Justice at the Restoration for his zeal in trying the judges of the King. Sir Robert was one of those who were more royal than the king himself, inciting Charles to press on in courses which were bringing him to destruction. He sought to set at defiance Magna Carta itself by following the King to Oxford and holding a Court of Law there. The chief stain on his name, however, is his browbeating of Sir Harry Vane. Both Houses had petitioned the King to spare his life, but Foster, presiding over the trial, secured his conviction in spite of a noble defence, and personally persuaded Charles to sign a warrant for his execution.

The oldest tablet in the church has a beautiful inscription stone which has for six centuries recorded the fact that Abbot Rutherwyke of Chertsey Abbey built the chancel of the old church. Above this stone is a brass portrait of Anthony Bond with his two wives and a son; he died in 1576, and is described as the writer of the Court Letter, a post once held by the father of John Milton. There is also on the walls a tablet to Richard Kellefet, Groom of Queen Elizabeth's Wardrobe; another to old John Sleep who was 65 years a chorister, clerk and sexton here; and one to Sir Felton Hervey, the Duke of Wellington's secretary, who lost an arm with him in the Peninsula and stood by him at Waterloo.

Here in 1895 was buried a famous soldier wounded at the Siege of Delhi, Sir George Chesney. He started an engineering college on Cooper's Hill, but is best remembered for the clever skit he wrote imagining the invasion and conquest of England. It was meant to encourage national defence far back in the eighteen-seventies, and under the title of The Battle of Dorking his book ran through many editions in England and on the Continent.

Looking almost as grisly as the catacombs in which he lies, is Sir John Denham, sculptured with skulls and bones and shrouds about him, an odd-looking figure. He was a judge, and caught his last illness while on circuit at Winchester; it was the time when John Hampden's case came up for trial, and Denham was too ill to do anything but write a few words in Hampden's favour. On another monument are the two wives of Sir John Denham and a little red figure of his son, the boy who became the second John Denham, and won some renown as a poet. His poem on Cooper's Hill describes the scenery round Egham and was highly praised by Herrick, Dryden, and Pope; it has been called the earliest example of strictly descriptive poetry in the English language. In it Denham imagines himself on the hill he must have learned to love as a boy, and lets his imagination roam over the landscape spread before him. He dwells on old Saint Paul's (little thinking, we may be sure, that he would live to see its destruction), on the strength and beauty of Windsor Castle, and on the river itself, "most loved of all the Ocean's sons." Sir John was captured at Farnham Castle which he was defending for the king, and was sent up to London, where his life ended in misery and poverty.

One other literary memory comes to us in the church, for among its 19th century vicars was the famous hymn-writer J. S. B. Monsell; he left the rectory here for Guildford and met a tragic fate in his new church, for he fell from the scaffolding of St Nicolas and was killed.

At Egham also there lived (though she sleeps two miles away at Old Windsor) a well-known literary figure of the 18th century, Mary Robinson, known as Perdita. She was educated at a school kept by Hannah More's sisters. She lived a fashionable life, managed to get imprisoned for debt, wrote poems in gaol, became a popular actress, and was the centre of one of the scandals of the Prince of Wales who became George the Fourth. After he tired of her she would ride about daily in a ridiculous chariot looking rather like a coronet. One day she would be like the Belle of Hyde Park, painted and patched; another day she would ride her horse in the Row, but always "the hats of the fashionable swept the ground as she passed." She was painted by Reynolds and Romney and Gainsborough, and Zoffany portrayed her as Rosalind.

The High Street of Egham leads (past the almshouses founded by Judge Denham) to Englefield Green half a mile away, where stands the spectacular Royal Holloway College, an immense pile of red and white buildings which have now become part of London University. It is a remarkable place.

A mile away from Egham is Great Fosters, a fine Elizabethan brick house with gables topped by little pinnacles; it is now a hotel. Near by on the same road an inscribed stone marks the position of the Roman road from Silchester to London, the stone being, it is said, more than 17 centuries old. At Egham Hythe is a delightful new church with an attractive tower, windows in 15th century style, and a charming interior both light and cool. The pulpit is carved with a fine frieze and the font was given by the children, some of whom we heard singing Blake's Jerusalem in the school across the road.

Thomas Holloway and His College

THOMAS HOLLOWAY will be remembered by some for his box of pills, and by others for his casket of learning. The one was a small thing that went round the world for years from the middle of last century, the other is the astounding spectacle at Egham, one of the most curious contributions to 19th century architecture, characteristic of the artistic ideas of Thomas Holloway who built it and of Queen Victoria who opened it.

This remarkable man was born in the closing weeks of the 18th century, and lived through all but 16 years of the 19th. He helped his widowed mother in a little shop in Penzance, but came to London to seek his fortune in 1828. He found his fortune in a pill-box, and his box of pills and his pot of ointment became known throughout the world. He would go down to the docks himself and persuade the sailors to believe in them. He would tour the countryside in a little buggy selling his remedies. He was one of the first men to spend a fortune on publicity, and he started his own almanac. He became so rich that at the time of the Franco-German War he was one of the very few men in England who could let France have a great loan.

He became much interested in education, and resolved to set up a college for women on a more magnificent scale than had ever been known in England; he hoped it would grow into the first women's university, granting its own degrees. Though over 70 when the idea came to him, he went through Europe looking at great buildings, and fell in love with the palatial splendour of the Chateau de Chambord. There were those who wanted him to build in the style of Oxford or Cambridge, but Mr Holloway had a mind of his own and he set to work an architect (Mr W. H. Crossland) working with assistants for more than two years in getting out the plans, elevations, and details of the French Chateau. He would have his own way. When the residents of Englefield Green wrote to him hoping he would not put the ugly brick wall but would surround the college with elegant railings, Mr Holloway said: "Put the brick wall." It was the spirit that had sent his pill-box everywhere, and was now to put up his casket of learning.

He built his architect a bungalow so that he could live on the spot for six years, and he drove round the work almost daily and watched its progress. He spent £600,000 on the building and endowed it with £200,000 more. It is 550 feet long and 376 feet wide, a third of a mile round. It is covered with ornament in the style of the Albert Memorial, and has a mass of sculpture outside designed and modelled by the Italian Signor Fucigna. The chief statues are under four pediments forming the centres in the two quadrangles over the main staircases; they represent Commerce and Medicine, Poetry and Science, Charity and Education, and the portrait bust of the Founder supported by allegorical figures of Surrey and Agriculture. The keystones of the chapel and the picture gallery windows, and of the arches in the main gateway, form a series of heads, the last on the outside being Minerva, and on the inside Hope. On each side are the three prophets, Moses, Ezekiel, and Elijah facing the three kings, Joshua, Saul, and Solomon. On the gateway towards the quadrangle are Faith on the inside and Homer on the outside. On the keystones of the chapel windows are Christ with Paul, Peter, and John on the outside, and Mahommed, Confucius, Savonarola, and Pope Julius the Second on the quadrangle side. Flanking these are symbolical heads of the elements, Fire, Earth, Air, and Water. On the quadrangle side of the picture gallery are Dante, Aeschylus, Molière, and Shakespeare. On the outside are Handel, Rossini, Schiller, and Machiavelli. In the upper quadrangle is Queen Victoria, and in the lower quadrangle a group of Mr and Mrs Holloway, both the work of Count Gleichen. There is another sculpture which is described as Erinna, by H. S. Leifchild.

The ceiling of the chapel is modelled in bold relief in the style of much of the work at Fontainebleau, the figures representing the Prophets and the Evangelists. In the half-domed apse the relief represents the creation of Eve. The chapel is treated with decoration in colour and gold, and in the vault and the ceiling are medallions representing the six archangels. The two stained windows of the chapel have in them the head of St Augustine and a portrait of Archbishop Benson, with the figure of St Alban and portraits also of St Helena and St Hilda.

The picture gallery has a collection of paintings for which Mr Holloway paid huge sums. He offered 10,000 guineas each for two paintings by Rosa Bonheur, but failed to get them. He bought on one day five pictures at Christie's for nearly £20,000, and was continually buying in these famous auction rooms in the name of Thomas, a bidder who was supposed to be an American millionaire, so that The Times was much concerned about the departure of these pictures across the Atlantic.

This vast place is today one of the most efficient parts of London University, and would be a noble monument to any man. Its benefactor was a man with a mind a little closed to himself, but with a pocket wide open to the world. When he died his staff were assembled in Oxford Street and told that every head of a department was to have a cheque for a hundred pounds and a rise of £30 a year, and that all others were to have gifts and advances according to their length of service. He lies in the churchyard at Sunninghill.

The Great Charter of Runnymede

THE flat grazing ground of Runnymede, in Surrey, at the foot of Cooper's Hill between Egham and the Thames, is not in itself romantic, but it was the scene of doings that have been reverberating through the history of our country since 1215.

Round it in May that year was gathered a concourse representative of the Church in England, of the English barons, or noblemen, of the City of London, and of the mass of the English people, though these last had no organised power at that period. They were united in distrust of King John, and were determined that he should pledge his word to cease his oppressive ways of governing the land.

The leader of the king's opponents was Stephen Langton, Archbishop of Canterbury. John had done his utmost to prevent his becoming archbishop, and had failed. Langton was not acting as his enemy, but was trying to mediate between him and the barons, and to persuade him to be sensible and do what clearly was right. He it was who took to the king the 48 demands drawn up by the barons and their supporters, Articles to which John attached his seal, and which were re-written four days later and sealed again as Magna Carta, the Great Charter of English law and liberty.

That is what Magna Carta has been said to be and felt to be for seven hundred years, and there are some stirring clauses in it which seem to justify that view. These, for instance:

No freeman shall be seized, or imprisoned, or disseised, or outlawed, or any way destroyed, nor will we go upon him, nor will we send upon him, except by the lawful judgment of his peers, or by the law of the land. To none will we sell, to none will we deny, to none will we delay right or justice.

But when the Great Charter is examined in its entirety it is seen to be almost wholly composed of regulations dealing with matters that were important, or in dispute, at that particular time, but have long since become obsolete. The framers of the Charter had no broad idea of a balanced and controlled Government. They saw a few great and many comparatively small evils, and they put a check on the uncontrolled power of selfish kings, and began to lay the first stones of a foundation for constitutional government. Most of the clauses of the Charter, however, dealt with practical everyday affairs as they cropped up in the life of that day.

A most definite and outspoken part of the Charter was that which sought to guard against unjust exactions and damage by the king or his agents. In fact they claimed the right to make war upon him till they had righted any wrong committed on his behalf. In signing the Charter John agreed that the barons should elect 25 of their number, and commit to them the duty of forcibly taking back from the king anything he had gained by extortion :

If we [that is the King] or our justitiary, or our bailiff, or any of our officers, shall have injured anyone in anything, or have violated any article of the peace, these barons shall come to us (or to our justiciary if we are out of the Kingdom) and, making known to us the excess committed, shall require that we cause that excess to be redressed without delay; and if we have not redressed the excess within forty days the foresaid barons, with the community of the whole land shall distress and harass us by all the ways in which they can, that is to say, by the taking of our castles, lands, and possessions, and by other means in their power until the excess shall be redressed according to their verdict, and when it hath been redressed they shall behave to us as they had done before.

Of course King John did not agree in his mind with these naïve conditions and though he had sealed the Charter he at once began war on the barons, helped by the Pope, who declared the Charter null and void, and the war was going on when the king died in 1216.

The man who won most honour from the Charter was Stephen Langton. He had been forced into the see of Canterbury against John's stubborn resistance. When John submitted to Rome, Pope Innocent the Third governed England through his Legate, though John was the titular king. The Charter was cursed by the Pope, and Langton was suspended from his office for supporting it. Convinced that Pope Innocent had been misled, Langton went to Rome to give his view of the position in England, and presently was reinstated at Canterbury. Not only did Langton establish the Charter but he gave it such a send-off that it has come down the centuries with a resounding fame that somewhat exaggerates its intrinsic value.

Made up largely from old Charters, it was boldly presented in defiance of tyranny, and as a gesture made a fine impression. The spirit of freedom has often rallied round it, and it remains a most fascinating survey of 13th century conditions of life and government, but it does not reach through the centuries in any practical way to the life of today. It is a historical fragment.

A Stairway From a Tree

ELSTEAD. It lies round the green, and along the road is a delightful bridge and a rambling mill. The five stone arches of the bridge are 500 years old; parts of them may be 200 years older still. The brick parapets were added a century ago.

The church is chiefly remarkable for its timber work. The beams of the porch are 14th century, and the unusual oak doorway is 15th. There are five fine old tie-beams with kingposts in the roof, and a remarkable belfry stairway cut from a solid tree. Two of the windows are 13th century lancets, and another in the nave has fragments of old glass. The chancel is tiny, and has stalls, desk, and communion table in memory of J. R. Charlesworth, rector for fifty years. The peace memorial tablet of wood is beautifully carved with flowers, and tells of 38 villagers who fell. There is an Elizabethan chest.

Across the River Wey from Elstead is Cutmill Common, a gracious piece of unspoiled Surrey countryside with two lakes and a wealth of silver birches.

The Most Famous Race in the World

EPSOM. It is famed for a horse race that is on everybody's lips once a year, but not for that alone do we remember it. We think of the old houses and inns belonging to its fashionable days, and the rolling Downs, and of the common where we may look over a garden hedge at a famous well which, as Pepys tells us, drew Charles the Second and all his Court. We think, too, of the church with its medieval tower, its wealth of monuments, and its beauty of newer things; and, among Epsom's modern buildings, of the dignified town hall, and the College with its fine playing-fields and iron gates.

Epsom is a borough now, sharing this distinction with its neighbour Ewell, and bearing the proud motto of None Such. It has grown rapidly in the last few years and has had to widen its old-fashioned High Street to meet the ever-growing demands of the motor age, yet it remains a blend of country town and an outer suburb of London, and still has houses taking us back to the days when it lay with green fields all about it. Still in the broad market-place is a house fronted by a splendid yew hedge, and here also is a tall red brick house, with a great gable and dormer windows. This was the New Inn of the Restoration period, said to have been the biggest English inn of its day, built for the visitors who came flocking to the wells. Nearly a century younger is the great house of Durdans in a park by the Downs, which we see through a fine pair of iron gates looking down a vista of limes. The house is of brick covered with ivy, and has a stone balustrade on the roof. It was the home of a Prime Minister, Lord Rosebery, one of the most brilliant failures in the politics of the last generation. Tucked away in quiet corners near the Durdans are several other 18th century houses, all delightful.

We come to the church by a wide flight of steps from an open space. The tower is 500 years old and has a very slender shingled spire, but the rest of the building is modern. Among its treasures, however, are some old things not to be missed. There are three old carved chairs, one with winged monsters on the back, and another an armchair adorned with flowers and foliage. There is a 15th century font with flowers and leaves in quatrefoils round the bowl, and with more flowers and faces and a fish down below. There is a glazed case containing a Vinegar Bible, open at the page where the old printer has put the Parable of the Vinegar instead of Parable of the Vineyard. Best of all is a huge and wonderful 18th century chest, made of Spanish mahogany and ornamented with raised figures drawn in sepia.

They are blurred with age, but clear enough for us to see an Elizabethan horseman with a woman following, a domestic scene of a woman brandishing a broom at a man while someone pours water on him and others watch, and a picture of Adam and Eve with a scaly figure picking the fruit above them. On the right is a queen, and on the left are Roman figures with an emperor on his throne. The chest is said to have been saved from the Great Armada, and to have found its way into Nonsuch Palace at Ewell. It is not the only thing Epsom has from Nonsuch, for, sitting on the gateposts of Pit Place near the church, are two stone lions also said to have been brought from the palace.

Worthy company for the old things in the church is the modern pulpit, rising on a slender stem. The sides have linenfold panels with bands of vines, and below are squares of leaves and flowers.

The memorials on these walls take us back to the time of John Evelyn, for here is a tablet to his brother Richard who died in 1669. Richard comes into the famous diary, where we read how the carriage bringing him home from his wedding was overturned, but "no harm was done." His beautiful Woodcote Park near the Downs is now a golf course, and there John Evelyn came in 1655 to spend Christmas with him. Another tablet, elaborately made of white marble, shows the head of Robert Coke in his wig and cravat, and his wife and child in their hoods. He was the son of the famous judge and law writer Sir Edward Coke, prominent in the legal history of the first two Stuart kings.

Among the many monuments we come upon the work by three of the most famous sculptors of the early years of last century. One by the great Chantrey is a beautiful and pathetic tribute to a young mother and her babe, who died within a few months of each other. It shows a kneeling woman looking upward with an infant in her arms. Near by is the work of the younger John Bacon, a monument with two draped figures to Jane Rowe.

There are three examples here of the art of John Flaxman, two of them with figures of women resting on urns, and the third a marble tablet with little symbolic figures at each end. It is to John Parkhurst of 1797, who is remembered for his lexicons to the Bible. A bust on the wall shows us the determined face of a man whom John Parkhurst brought here as vicar, Jonathan Boucher. He was of the time of the American War of Independence, and we read how his loyalty to the king remained unshaken, even when the madness of the people raged furiously against him, and how he resigned ease and affluence in America to endure hardship and poverty at home. Though a friend of George Washington, he denounced the rebels when war broke out, and preached his last American sermon with pistols on the cushion in his pulpit.

One of the loveliest things in Epsom is here by the peace memorial and the two wooden crosses from a foreign field. It is a beautiful window dedicated to two of the fallen, showing figures of Air and Water, Fire and Earth, Wind, Summer, and Winter, as well as the Madonna holding up her Child, angels, and four saints representing Holy and Humble Men of Heart. Very charming it all is, with Summer as a golden-haired figure in red, Winter crouching among the snow, the purple and blue Wind blowing his own trumpets, and a man in yellow and red holding up his arm in praise. Earth is shown in this gallery of the elements as a girl in scarlet and grey, with corn and poppies against her dress, giraffes and grapes behind her, and a little rabbit nibbling in the foreground. Air is another girl in lovely blue, and Water is a sea-green figure among the fish.

In the churchyard is one of those pathetic epitaphs we have come

Epsom — The Grandstand on the Downs

Epsom — The Town Hall

Egham   Runnymede by the Thames

Ewell   Nonsuch House

Walton-on-Thames   The King's House at Burhill

upon to little ones who came into the world and went swiftly out again. It is to four Langlands, and runs:

> *The cup of life just with their lips they pressed,*
> *Found the taste bitter, and declined the rest.*

In its vast and rapid growth Epsom has not been unmindful of the need for preserving parks and open spaces, and of the borough's total area of nearly 14 square miles approximately one sixth is downland, or common, or parkland, belonging to the people. It has a proud list of parks and recreation grounds, chief among them being Rosebery Park of 11 acres, named after the Prime Minister who gave it, the 400 acres of Epsom Common, and the historic park of Nonsuch.

Most of the Downs are outside the borough boundary but they are there at its portals for all who would roam them. They would be celebrated were there no such thing as racing. Here we can hear the lark, and may stand with a far-spread landscape before us. The hills of Berkshire and Hertfordshire can be seen, the towers of the Crystal Palace and Windsor Castle, and, if we climb the grandstand, the dome of St Paul's. The grandstand was built in 1927, and has an interest apart from the view it gives, for it was the first stand of its kind to be made of reinforced concrete.

It was the racing that brought Epsom a second fame when the great days of the wells were over, the days when this place rivalled Bath as a spa. It is said that under Cromwell the Royalists would hold race-meetings here as an excuse for a gathering, but the story really begins toward the end of the 18th century when the Earl of Derby founded his famous race. Lord Rosebery once described its origin: "Though the waters failed us, a miracle yet remained to be wrought on behalf of Epsom. In the last quarter of the 18th century a roystering party at a neighbouring country-house founded two races, in two successive years, one for three-year-old colts and fillies, the other for three-year-old fillies, and named them gratefully after their host and his house—the Derby and the Oaks. Seldom has a carouse had a more permanent effect. Up to that time Epsom had enjoyed little more than the ordinary races of a market-town."

There is no spectacle quite like the scene on Derby Day anywhere else in the world. It is the world's most famous race, and is witnessed by a crowd of hundreds of thousands of people. Millions wait for the result, and more money changes hands over the Derby than over any other single event. Even Parliament used to adjourn for the race until the eve of our own time. It is one of the richest prizes in the world of racing and the winning horse also adds thousands of pounds to its value. In the whole world of sport this is the victory most sought-for, and it is also the most elusive, so that even a millionaire cannot make sure of winning it.

Cardinal Wolsey Passes By

ESHER. Like so many places near London, it has the builders in, but it keeps its sloping village green and glorious commons where all may wander in the shade of pines and silver birches. Thousands know the wooded hill of Sandown Park by the famous racecourse. The property is on the site of a small hospital founded in Norman times and absorbed by a London hospital 500 years ago.

Set on wooded slopes fast becoming covered with houses is the tragic mansion of Claremont. It was about 1700 that Sir John Vanbrugh, the architect of Blenheim Palace, here built himself a low brick house at the bottom of the hill. Some years later he sold it to the Duke of Newcastle, Prime Minister. Vanbrugh's house has vanished but one part of it, a tall ornamental tower with deeply arched windows, remains, and so does the long garden wall, its many bastions lovely in blossom time. After the Duke's death in 1768 Lord Clive bought the estate and built the present house, said to be the only house designed by Capability Brown which is still complete. It is square-looking but stately, with a balustraded parapet and a grand pillared entrance, a majestic cedar growing close by. "General Clive has arrived, all over estates and diamonds," Horace Walpole wrote; and rich indeed he was, spending, it is said, over £100,000 on his new home. But the conqueror of Plassey was never to live in this lovely place; he died in his London house embittered by the accusations of his enemies.

In 1816 Claremont became the home of Prince Leopold, who was afterwards to become first King of the Belgians, and his bride Princess Charlotte, daughter of George the Fourth. Their happiness was shortlived, for in the gloomy November of the following year the princess, a girl of 21, died with her baby. During the next few years the little Princess Victoria was often here, staying with Uncle Leopold, and for the first ten years of her reign she spent her birthday at

Claremont. After the revolution of 1848 the house became the home of the exiled royal family of France, and in it Louis Philippe died. Now it is a fine school for girls, and the tall boots of the French king's postillion hang in the dining-room of Esher's coaching inn.

Two stone bears sit on the roof of this inn watching the neverending stream of traffic go by between London and Portsmouth. Tucked away behind the inn is the 400-year-old church, little used. The walls are built of chequered stone, and perched on the roof at the west end is an old shingled bell turret of wood. The roof beams are original, and so is the south doorway, though now covered by the vestry. Set into the wall near this door is a scratch-dial facing inwards, a relic of an earlier church. At the west end lies the vaulting stone of a Norman doorway, found under the floor. The curious clock may be of Tudor date; its weights are cannon balls, and are raised by a little capstan. The altar rails are 300 years old, and beside them is a remarkable 17th century painting on wood. It imitates a stone monument, and shows a widow kneeling at a desk. She is mourning Sir Thomas Lynch, Governor of Jamaica, who is said to have sent home the first consignment of sugar from the West Indies. The royal arms high above the chancel are those of George the Second, and the three-decker pulpit is a relic of his century. Wadham Diggle preached from it for over 50 years, for he was rector here from 1777 to 1828. The old church chest has a slit so small that it would take only the silver coins which Edward the Sixth ordered to be collected for the poor.

The most remarkable feature of the church is the chamber pew built in 1725 by the Duke of Newcastle. The only entrance to it is outside the church, and the front looks into the chancel. The Duke divided the pew so that his brother of Esher Place might share it, and each part still has its own fireplace, with high box pews at the back for the servants.

The north aisle was built in 1812, but its gallery has gone, though the teak front still stands on the oak pillars. The front beam of the lower west gallery is 500 years old; the upper gallery belongs to last century. The old altar picture of Christ is by Sir Robert Ker Porter, known for his big battle scenes. His sisters Jane and Anna Maria Porter were well-known novelists; they lie in the churchyard; a picture on the west wall, by Arthur William Devis, shows Princess

Charlotte being received into Heaven, and below is a remarkable white marble memorial of her by the Esher sculptor, Francis John Williamson. Queen Victoria had it put on the staircase of Claremont, and a later tenant, the Duchess of Albany, gave it to this church. It consists of three reliefs, the middle one showing the Princess and her husband walking with a dog. On the right is Prince Leopold receiving the crown of Belgium with the approval of Britannia, and on the left appears the death of his wife at Claremont. In a glass case is a locket containing locks of Princess Charlotte's hair, around it being little books published on the occasion of her death. There is a marble wall monument by Flaxman with lions and lilies, in memory of Catherine Caroline Ellis who died at Nice. In the vestry are displayed some old parish papers, and the church has a fine collection of pictures of bygone Esher.

In the churchyard is a brick tomb with an inscription to William Duckett who died at the Cape, "to which settlement he was sent with a large establishment by George the Third to introduce his father's system and implements of agriculture."

The impressive modern church, with its tall stone spire, was built in the middle of last century on the other side of the main road, from which it is now hidden by houses. King Leopold gave £1000 to the building fund, and in the tower is his grandiose monument, set up by Queen Victoria "in memory of the uncle who held a father's place in her affection." It is by Susan Durant, and shows the king lying on a couch wearing the Order of the Golden Fleece, two guardian angels above, and a lion below.

An elaborate niche in the north wall has a marble bust of the Duke of Albany, Queen Victoria's youngest son, a soldierly figure wearing many medals. His faded banner and his wooden coronet hang above. Opening into the chancel is his private pew, later used by the owners of Esher Place.

The figure of an earlier owner of Esher Place kneels at prayer in the nave, wearing armour, ruff, and sword. He was Sir Richard Drake, equerry to Queen Elizabeth and kinsman of Sir Francis, whom he accompanied on a voyage to the East Indies. Here at Esher he had charge of the Spanish grandees captured in the stirring days of the Armada, including Don Pedro de Valdez, the second-in-command. Near by is a bronze relief of a shepherd and his sheep

SURREY

in memory of Francis John Williamson, the sculptor, who lived here for 60 years of last century.

High on the chancel wall hangs a beautiful altar frontal, probably 18th century Italian work. In the vestry is a 200-year-old chest, a pair of fine old chairs, and a table apparently made from the sounding-board of a pulpit. On the walls are pictures of the church when it was new, one with a man cutting corn in a field where shops now stand. On the list of rectors by the door is a picture of the ash tree from which Esher gets its name.

In the churchyard is a canopied tomb on which lie figures of a 19th century Master of the Rolls, the first Lord Esher, and his wife. He wears a wig, a rich robe, and buckled shoes; his lady is in a tight-waisted dress falling to her feet. Near by another canopy shelters a seated statue of Edith Amy Clarke with a harp, gazing pensively downwards.

The entrance to Esher Place is across the Upper Green, small houses now lining the drive to the Georgian mansion. It stands on a historic site, but today, with its raked roofs and wide windows, it rather resembles a French chateau. It has in its grounds a wonderful tulip tree with a trunk so great that it takes five men to reach round it with their outstretched arms. It was planted in 1685 and is the oldest tulip tree in England, the pride of Esher Place.

Here stood that earlier Esher Place built in the 15th century by Bishop Waynflete to form a halting-house for pilgrims on the road to London. A red brick tower is all that remains of it, standing forlorn and neglected on the banks of the River Mole. The poor porch was added by William Kent 200 years ago. William Howitt, who had a cottage at Esher for three years, described the tower in his Visits to Remarkable Places, which he wrote here, and James Thomson in his Seasons wrote of

> *Esher's groves, in the sweetest solitude embraced,*
> *By the soft windings of the gentle Mole.*

The house and grounds now belong to a philanthropic society which is not unconscious of their historic past, the Shaftesbury Homes. The seven Homes under this name, together with the training ship Arethusa on the Medway, exist to give poor boys and girls a chance in life in the name of Lord Shaftesbury. Esher Place, where

175 girls are trained, has a long history, but has been in the hands of the Shaftesbury Homes since 1930 only. Its character has been changed as little as possible and about it still lingers the grace of a day that is dead. Carved into the stone front of the house are pathetic words which bring up the saddest day of its long past.

I have found a haven. Farewell Hope and Fortune. You have made enough sport of me; now make sport of others.

They are meant to express the bitter spirit in which Wolsey came to Esher Place in that desperate hour when Shakespeare makes him say:

> *I have touched the highest point of all my greatness;*
> *And, from that full meridian of my glory,*
> *I haste now to my setting. . . . O Cromwell, Cromwell,*
> *Had I but served my God with half the zeal*
> *I served my king, he would not in mine age*
> *Have left me naked to mine enemies.*

It was in this mood the fallen cardinal came here, but not for long. He went to Richmond, and in the end knocked at the door of an old abbey in Leicester and begged a little earth for charity to lay his bones there.

The Mole flows gently by as it has flowed for centuries, silent witness of this earthly glory and the passing of cardinals and kings.

Tragedy of an Inventor

EWELL. It has a past as old as Rome, as we know from the frequent digging up of Roman relics here; but today it is houses, houses all the way, and is part of the great new borough of Epsom, but in spite of the transformation of so many of its fields into villas and back gardens it has not quite surrendered its village air, and keeps much of its old rural charm. Some quaint houses still overhang the High Street, its horse-pond close by remains a charming old-world sight, and there are still delightful scenes by the Hogsmill river with its mills and old packhorse bridge. Here it was that Sir John Millais painted the weeping willow in his picture of the Death of Ophelia, and Holman Hunt painted the stream in his Light of the World.

Ewell has lost its medieval church, but the 15th century tower still stands, a lonely sentinel near the garden of remembrance to 82 men who never came back. Their names are at the end of a rock garden with a turf cross in the middle.

SURREY

The new church keeps from the old a Tudor font, a Jacobean altar table, and something of the 15th century screen. On a tomb lies Sir William Lewen, in the wig he may have worn in the days of Queen Anne.

There are three brasses of women of the 16th century. Lady Jane Iwarby wears a mantle embroidered with a lion, three boars, and a bird; Margery Treghstin has what is called a kennel-shaped headdress; and Lady Dorothy Taylare wears a French hood, as do the five daughters beside her. On the other side are her five sons, of whom Edmond appears again below in all the grown-up dignity of a beard, with his wife, three sons, and three daughters.

In a grave in the churchyard lies James Lowe, of whom we are told that he invented the segments of the screw propeller. As a lad he was apprenticed to Edward Shorter, a mechanic who had invented a perpetual sculling machine. But for a short period when he ran away to serve on a whaler he remained with this man, gaining valuable experience, until he was able to set up in business. From this time he spent all his leisure experimenting with screw propellers, and in 1838 patented one with curved blades fixed to a revolving shaft. The invention was used on a few steamships, but he gained no reward, although he had spent his wife's fortune and made himself poor. In 1866 he came to a tragic end, run over by a waggon in a London street. His daughter, Henrietta Vansittart, went on with his experiments, and only two years after her father's death she patented the Lowe-Vansittart propeller, which was used on many boats.

Although Sir Francis Pettit-Smith was the inventor of the first practical screw propeller, James Lowe, now almost forgotten, deserves a place in the annals of steam navigation. A better known Ewell man was Richard Corbet, a gardener's son who rose to be Bishop of Oxford and of Norwich, and was also famous as a poet and a wit.

Ewell, of course, has its rightful share in all the parks of Epsom and a special interest in those within its own confines. There are many acres of them, including the 15 acres of Auriol Park, and the 12 acres of delightful grounds round Ewell Court. But by far the most important, most extensive, and most beautiful is Nonsuch Park, nearly 300 acres of parkland with glorious trees and lovely gardens surrounding the castle-like mansion built last century by

Sir Jeffry Wyatville. The house is a delightful sight in autumn when its creeper covering has become a crimson mantle, and the park is a joy all the year round. The palace of Nonsuch stood at the other end of the park, and all that remains of it are a few bricks of the Banqueting Hall still visible close to the Ewell Bypass Road.

EWHURST. Its crown is a church going back to Norman times, and made new a few generations later. A Norman doorway has been uncovered this century, and there is a square Norman font bowl. The modern tower rises from four rugged 13th century arches in the centre of the church.

The charming timber porch and the kingpost roof in the nave are Tudor work, and the lightly carved pulpit is Jacobean. The 18th century altar rails were once in the Tudor great house Baynards Park, three miles away.

Two faithful rectors are remembered by tablets in the chancel. One was Edward Bickerton, who died in 1810 after serving Ewhurst for 55 of his 78 years; the other was John Barlow, rector for 47 years last century. There is a good modern window of Mary and Martha, given by the friends and pupils of Helen Madeline Topham in gratitude for her life of beauty and service. Some old possessions of Ewhurst are kept in a case, including three pewter plates and a flagon.

A mile along the road is Coneyhurst Hill, 844 feet high. It is a glorious place from which to look out over the Weald, and has much the same view as its bigger brother Leith Hill.

The Pastor and the Poulterer

FARLEY. Ringed in by trees high on the North Downs, its little church is very much as the Normans built it; we come into it through their doorway.

The chancel was made a little longer in the 13th century, and in it is a brass portrait of John Brock, a 15th century London poulterer who lived long enough to hear that Columbus had discovered America. With him is his wife, who has a very long face, and five children, and they are looking across the chancel at the memorial of another old couple. It is the tablet on which we read that Dr Samuel Bernard was "a faithful pastor, and a man stained by no covenant." He was turned out of Croydon vicarage in the Civil War, and would

Friday Street   Hamlet Enchanting

Godstone   A Winter Pastoral

Gomshall   Beech Wood near the Village

Godalming Church Street **Godalming** The Old Church

Haslemere Seventeenth Century Almshouses

Friday Street

Holmbury St Mary
TWO ENCHANTING SURREY HAMLETS

have nothing to do with the Puritans. His wife lived to be 96, and spent her last 48 years without him.

The big yew in the churchyard may well have been a sapling when they buried old John Brock five hundred years ago.

The Hero of the Titanic

FARNCOMBE. It has been almost enfolded by Godalming, but it keeps in its church the proud memory of a brave son, and it has by the Portsmouth road a touch of ancient charm in its line of almshouses.

These homes for ten poor men were given in 1622, we read over the door, by Mr Richard Wyatt of London, with sufficient lands to maintain them for ever. In the centre of the building is a simple chapel with brass portraits of the founder and his wife kneeling at a table, their three sons and three daughters behind them.

The church is modern, and has a peace memorial chapel enclosed by handsome carved screens and panelling, with St George and St Margaret looking down from lancet windows. Beautiful and expressive also is the glass in three of the aisle windows, one showing Peter and Paul and a ship in full sail, another Luke and John and the Holy Dove, and the third James and Jude with a proud lion.

One of the brass inscriptions tells of a rector who in his boyhood had been an ensign and was wounded at Quatre Bras; for 25 years he ministered to a Hampshire flock, and then for 21 years to this one. But it is another brass that moves us more than anything else in this place, the simple tribute of Farncombe to a young man whose home was here, who sang in this choir, and who is remembered also at Godalming in the delightful cloister close to the church. He was John George Phillips, wireless operator of the Titanic, who perished in the most terrible peace-time sea disaster in modern history.

In the middle of an April night, crossing the Atlantic on her maiden voyage at full steam, the Titanic struck an iceberg, and, though believed to be unsinkable, sank in less than three hours with a loss of 1513 of the 2224 souls on board. Over 700 were saved, thanks largely to Phillips.

After a light-hearted preliminary signal, sent out when the ship seemed safe, his captain hurried to him saying, "Send SOS; it may be your last chance." Eight miles away lay the California, but her wireless operator had gone to bed, and, although from her deck the distress signals of the Titanic were seen, they were misunderstood and unheeded. Phillips got in touch with the Carpathia, 70 miles away, and exchanged messages with her as she steamed to the rescue. Water reached the engine rooms, the dynamos began to fail and his signals to weaken, but he sent the captain a cheering message of coming help; and his assistant strapped a lifebelt round Phillips as he went on with his work.

The captain appeared again at the door, bidding Phillips save himself, but he stayed at his post. A frenzied stranger rushed in and sought to tear the lifebelt from him, but Phillips went on tapping at his instrument. Not until the wireless room was flooded did he leave it. All was terror and confusion when he reached the deck. A great wave washed him from the sinking ship, and he was seen no more.

So passed out of the world one of the first immortal heroes of the Wireless Age, a chorister of Farncombe church.

History Round a Norman Castle

FARNHAM. We come to it by one of the finest rides in England, along the ridge of the North Downs which we know as the Hog's Back because it is so narrow and so straight. It rises 500 feet above the sea, dividing the Thames Valley from the Great Weald. At one end of the Hog's Back is the most characteristic town of Surrey, the ancient capital town of Guildford, and outspread from the ridge as we ride along is England north and south, hundreds of square miles of green fields and villages and towns, with heights like Hindhead and Leith Hill standing out like bits of Switzerland.

Farnham lies in a dip carved out by the River Wey, which flows south of the ridge to break through at Guildford on its way to the Thames. Even if Farnham were not in itself a spectacular and historic place it would be captivating for its setting, for the magnificent natural country at its doors, the sea not far away, Gilbert White's Selborne near at hand, and within a little run by car or bus the incomparable city of Winchester.

But Farnham indeed is in itself a fascinating place. It has the inn at which William Cobbett was born and the grave in which he sleeps. It has the castle in which the bishops of Winchester have lived for a

Egham: Anthony Bond with his two wives and his son, 1576

Godalming
John Barker, 1595

Great Bookham
Robert Shiers, 1668

Lingfield
John Knoyll, 1503

Horley
Unknown lady of the 15th century

Horsell
Thomas Sutton, 1603

ENGRAVED BRASS PORTRAITS OF SURREY PEOPLE

thousand years. It has the memory of King Alfred and King Charles. It is linked with the very distant past, for here men found a mammoth tusk which was one of the biggest ever discovered in this country, ten feet long. Its church has come down through time with its castle, and gathered about this fine wide street is a wealth of old houses, some of them Tudor, and more of them with a quiet dignity of the 18th century. Everywhere in Farnham we come upon the fine front doors of the Adam period, with a charm unsurpassed since their day.

The inn at which Farnham's greatest son was born is the Jolly Farmer; it stands in company with timbered gables which were old when William Cobbett opened his eyes in 1762. One of the houses in the heart of the town, called the Spinning Wheel, is delightful with overhanging gables and decorative timbers, and farther along the street stands Vernon House, where Charles Stuart stayed for a night with Harry Vernon, coming as a prisoner on his way to trial. He sat chatting here with the Roundhead general Thomas Harrison, who was soon to sign his death-warrant, and on the next bleak December morning he bade a sad farewell to his friendly host and gave him in parting the only little keepsake he could spare, a padded silk cap, which was long kept in this house. The house was built in Tudor England and has since been refashioned with a classic doorway, lovely with creeper in the autumn.

The oldest memories of the town are gathered about the castle. Some of its lands were given by the Saxon King Ethelbald to Saint Swithun. Within the walls still standing bishops have lived 800 years, and in our own day this ancient place has renewed its youth and become the home of the first Bishop of Guildford. Surrey has a remarkable lady, Mrs Rupert Anderson of Waverley Abbey, to thank for the castle's preservation. So costly had it become to maintain that one of the bishops was called upon to lay a mile of stair carpet and repair an acre of roof, and it was Mrs Anderson whose enthusiasm raised £18,000 to save the castle for the Church.

The great Norman keep, built by King Stephen's brother Henry of Blois, is now in the safe hands of our Office of Works, and all may see this mighty monument. It stands proudly on its hill, approached by a flight of steps leading from a gateway with the grooves of the portcullis still in the walls, and those who climb to the top are rewarded with wide views of Farnham Park, Hindhead, and the sweeping Downs.

From the same Norman days as the keep is the core of the triangular group of domestic buildings joining on to it, much transformed as the castle grew in magnificence down the centuries. Some of these buildings form the bishop's house, some are places of quiet and retreat belonging to the Church.

The castle stands roughly as the Normans left it, but its noble entrance tower was built by Bishop Fox early in the 16th century. Looking out over the terrace and the town, it stands as uncompromising as the old bishop himself—for it was Richard Fox who, in his last years, refused to give up office at the bidding of Cardinal Wolsey, retorting that even if he was too blind to see white from black he could still see the difference between right and wrong. In the end the ambitious Wolsey had his way; to all his other offices he added the bishopric of Winchester.

Through this red brick tower, with its turrets and its cornice of little arches, we pass to see the chief rooms of the castle. On one side is the Norman kitchen with five deep little windows and a colossal fireplace. On the other side is the great hall, a splendid room with Norman walls refashioned in the 17th century. It has a minstrel gallery, a carved fireplace, and three windows in which a bishop set the arms of nine of his predecessors who had all been Chancellors of England.

But most rare and thrilling of all the possessions of this great hall is something still visible in one of the walls, a wooden pillar with scalloped capitals shaped by a Norman carpenter. It is one of the original pillars from the time of Henry of Blois. Very little Norman timber have we still left in England, and Surrey has a remarkable share of it. There are two Norman doors still swinging on their hinges in Surrey churches, and at Compton, a few miles away along the Hog's Back, is a Norman roof and a Norman screen, among the oldest timbers in the land.

The castle has two chapels. One is of the 17th century near the old dungeons which have now become kitchens, the chapel of the bishop, with carving by the school of Grinling Gibbons. It is a rich little place, carved and panelled all round, has an attractive east window with a Crucifixion, a quaint pulpit approached through something like a trap-door, and a plaque to Gilbert Talbot, inspirer of Toc H, who used to worship here. The other is the original Norman chapel beautifully restored, still with the doorways, windows, and sanctuary arch of the Normans, and in one of its walls are two built-up 13th century arches. The buildings about the castle are of various periods, but all have their charm. The gate house guarding the entrance to the terrace has much 14th century masonry under its plaster; the attractive stables are about 200 years old and the boundary wall of the grounds is chiefly 15th century.

To this episcopal palace came the greatest churchmen in the land. Here lived William of Wykeham, builder of Winchester; William of Waynflete, Lord Chancellor and founder of Magdalen; Cardinal Beaufort, who saw Joan of Arc burned in the marketplace at Rouen, and Cardinal Wolsey in his pride. Here came the Cardinal's master, Henry the Eighth, followed by the terrible Mary Tudor, who was entertained here by Bishop Gardiner on her way to marry Philip of Spain at Winchester (we may see in the cathedral the chair in which she sat). Here Queen Elizabeth delivered her famous warning to the Duke of Norfolk (then planning to marry Mary Queen of Scots) to beware on what pillow he laid his head. Here, after Elizabeth, came James the First; and there are visits recorded by George the Third and by Queen Victoria, who came riding one day from Aldershot and was interested in looking at the Bible on which she had taken her coronation oath.

The history of the castle tells how the French Dauphin, crossing England in pursuit of King John, captured Guildford and Farnham castles on one day, but it was in the Civil War that Farnham witnessed its most stirring scenes. For the first few weeks of the war the castle had for its governor not a soldier but a poet, George Wither. A fiery Puritan, he had sold his estate to raise a troop of horse for the Parliament, and Cromwell made him major-general in Surrey. A cynic has said that his most distinguished act at Farnham was to ride out alone to collect horses and carts for his garrison's evacuation. His successor, curiously enough, was another poet, the Royalist Sir John Denham, high sheriff of Surrey at the outbreak of the war. He fell into the hands of Sir William Waller when that general captured the castle, and was sent to London. Wither was eventually captured by the Royalists, and the little tale comes to an end with

SURREY

Denham begging that Wither's life might be saved, because it was only Wither who saved Denham from being the worst poet alive!

Sir William Waller ordered the keep to be blown up so that it might never be a fortress again, but fortunately it was only partly damaged, the breach being where a line of little steps still goes up the mound. One day in 1648 Cromwell himself came this way, and soon afterwards Parliament ordered the castle to be finally dismantled. Never since has it had any military glory, but it has a little memory of Restoration literature, when Bishop Morley, who preached the coronation sermon of Charles the Second, gave up one of his rooms to the famous Izaak Walton. Here, it is thought, Walton wrote one or two of his biographies, while the bishop chose to live an austere life in a little cell only eight feet square, still to be seen under Fox's tower.

The church is worthy of the castle, for it is one of the biggest in Surrey and has much that is ancient as well as much that has been refashioned. Very long, with a narrow nave and chancel, it is filled out with wide aisles, deep transepts, and spacious chapels. The 16th century tower has a 19th century top and looks like a fortress.

The church has grown up from a Norman cross-shaped building, and still in the chancel are two high Norman arches with two a little younger, dividing the chancel from the chapels. The sanctuary is 15th century, and so are the three handsome stone seats grouped with a piscina in the wall. A great 15th century arch built up in one of the aisle walls once led into a chapel used as a school. Each aisle has a Tudor roof, and each chapel is entered through a 15th century screen. The fine solid altar rails were carved in the 17th century.

All about the church we come upon beautiful and interesting tributes to Farnham people. There is a charming little modern window to Mary Falkner, with figures of children and angels. There is a stone engraved with the portrait of Andrew Windsor, who lived in Shakespeare's day and gave the little line of almshouses in Castle Street for "eight poor honest impotent old persons;" and a tablet to 20 men who fell in South Africa, has these brave words:

> *They seemed to die before their day:*
> *but they were soldiers: they died for their country.*

Next to it, so heroic that it bears no name, is a little brass inscription "in thankful memory of a dear son who died for England."

The grave of William Cobbett is outside by the porch, but there is a tribute to him set up on these walls by his fellow-reformer John Fielden, with his portrait carved in relief by the sculptor John Henry Foley.

But it is in the south chapel that the pilgrim will want to stay, for it is packed with memorials fascinating, old, and quaint. There are stone inscriptions to Robert Quynbye who died a few years before the Great Armada, and to the brothers Marson in the next century, who were both locksmiths and left money for the poor to have bread "on Matthias day." There are portraits on brass of an Elizabethan lady, Sibil Jay, with her six children, all kneeling on a chessboard floor; and of Benedict Jay kneeling with his wife and six children. He was Sergeant of the Woodyard to Queen Elizabeth and lived at Waverley Abbey, and his epitaph begins almost jovially:

Who lies here? Here lies Benedict Jay and his wife Elizabeth.

The chapel also has a monument to Sir Nelson Rycroft with the figure of a resting pilgrim sculptured by Westmacott; and there is a tablet to an 18th century vicar telling us quaintly that if primitive simplicity, an open and ingenuous disposition, and a heart overflowing with the milk of human kindness can preserve the memory of the Reverend Mr John Wigmore, then he will be long remembered. A brass inscription close by tells of another 18th century parson who was born in the town (at a house now pulled down) Augustus Montague Toplady. The world has forgotten his bitter writings on Calvinism and remembers only that he wrote Rock of Ages.

One of the newest delights of Farnham is its Roman Catholic church of St Joan, a brick building with the Stainless Maid standing proudly above the doorway. Very attractive for its modern simplicity, it is also the home of several ancient and beautiful treasures. Its gilt reredos is 17th century and has a most expressive crucifix a century older; its chapel of St Margaret and St Catherine has delightful statues of these saints, and a crucifix of the 17th century; its lady chapel has a charming Madonna and Child; and its beautiful little baptistry cherishes some old carved stones from Waverley Abbey and from a lost chapel of the parish church. We were shown all these things by the priest who collected them from far and wide to adorn this church built under his care; and we were shown, too, the little

Esher   The Old Church

Esher   Fifteenth Century Tower of Esher Place

The Ancient Parish Church  · Tudor Tower of the Castle

The Norman Castle Above the Street
THE OLD-WORLD TOWN OF FARNHAM

shrine by the lady chapel on which he has set the greatest treasure of all, a vivid sculpture in ivory of the Annunciation, with an eloquent Gabriel and an awe-stricken Mary carved somewhere in Europe about 600 years ago.

A mile away from Farnham, in the graveyard of the modern church of Bourne, a sculptured eagle outspreads its wings over the grave of one of our heroes. He is Henry Danvers Waghorn, a Schneider Trophy pilot who came safely through the hazards of flying at 329 miles an hour, the highest speed at which any man had then flown, and in a few more months was one more victim of our roads, killed by a car.

The Man Who Rode Through England

WILLIAM COBBETT, born at Farnham and here laid to rest after a remarkable life of 73 years, was the son of a small farmer. He was crow-scarer and ploughboy in his youth, yet a reader who, on enlisting at 20, became a devoted student, mastering the elements of rhetoric, geometry, logic, fortifications, and French, so that during his six years' service in America he had charge of the regimental accounts and registers.

Returning to England, he married a soldier's daughter, spent some time in France followed by two years more in America, where he wrote fiery pamphlets, involving him in lawsuits which became so serious that he left America and, returning home, entered on his long career as publicist and reformer. In 1802 he founded his weekly Political Register which, beginning as a Tory, gradually became Radical, and so remained to the end of his life. He published the Parliamentary Debates which were afterwards taken over by Hansard, and issued books and pamphlets on current political issues.

In 1810 he was sentenced to two years' imprisonment for denouncing flogging in the Army, but he managed to continue his Register in gaol. After his release his political opinions drove him once more to America, but he was back in 1819, farming, writing, fighting elections, and finally winning his way into Parliament.

Four years later he died at Normandy farm near Guildford, leaving in his writings a rich heritage of fine thought finely expressed. Of these his Rural Rides, collected from the Register, are the most famous. Like John Wesley, he had travelled through England on his horse, not preaching to them the gospel of salvation but studying their lives and ways. His Rural Rides describe the English scene, the people, the land, the rivers, the problems of home and farm, of estate and kingdom, and the work is his chief legacy to his country.

John Evelyn's Chestnuts

FELBRIDGE. It has a fine line of 37 chestnuts planted by John Evelyn to mark the coming back of Charles the Second. One of the joyous events of his life, he marked it in the way he chose to celebrate good things—by planting trees. He saw the king, after a splendid cavalcade, create six barons and six earls; he saw him crowned; he saw the fountains running wine, the banners waving with loud music, the street strewn with flowers, the horses hung with tapestry, the balconies full of ladies; and one day soon after, being hereabouts, he was greatly struck with the "extravagant turnings, insinuations, and growth of certain birches." He planted a line of 55 chestnuts here and 37 are flourishing still. We picked up some of their chestnuts and found them rich and sweet.

The Saxon Builders and the Roman Bricks

FETCHAM. It lies across the Mole from Leatherhead, a place where the Saxons buried their dead and where people lived before the Romans came.

In Fetcham Park many new houses are springing up round the ancient church and the great red house. The park was planted by a man of Queen Anne's time who sleeps at Fetcham, Arthur Moore, who rose from footman to politician, drawing up important trade treaties and moving among the great folk of his day. A director of the South Sea Company, he was living in the great house here when the famous Bubble burst.

The church impresses us most with its great age and its striking contrast of architecture. It is hard to believe that in a single century the style could change from the fine sturdy Norman arches (with scalloped capitals) on one side of the nave to the tall and graceful English ones on the other. The oldest things we see are the Roman bricks used by Saxon builders in the walls and placed by them round the window we now see above the Norman arches. There is a 13th century doorway, a 15th century stairway winding up by the pulpit, and a bell made in the year of the Armada.

SURREY

In the 13th century chancel Henry Vincent looks down at us from the wall, his hands folded above an open book. He lived to be 80 and died in 1631. There is a tablet to Admiral Sir George Richards, who was laid to rest in the churchyard after a life devoted to hydrography and the development of submarine telegraphy. He went with more than one of the sad expeditions to search for Sir John Franklin.

Also sleeping in the churchyard is Sir Francis Graham Moon, printseller, publisher, and Lord Mayor of London in 1854, who brought out prints of pictures by the greatest artists of his day. His son was rector here for half a century and sleeps by the porch.

The Great Copper Cauldron

FRENSHAM. Fine it is to stand here by the most attractive peace memorial cross, looking over the gorse and heather of Frensham Common, and then to go down the road and stand by the glittering expanse of Frensham Great Pond. The water stretches over 108 acres, seven of them being across the Hampshire border. Across the Wey is Pierrepont House, the seat of the Duke of Kingston in George the Third's time.

A few minutes away is Little Pond, beautiful in summer with water lilies, and farther on towards Churt are the three curiously abrupt hills known as the Devil's Jumps.

The church has a 14th century tower with massive buttresses. It has a lancet window, a piscina, and a doorway which were part of the first building raised on this site, a generation after Magna Carta. Below the lancet is a 14th century tomb with a cross on it, lying between two tall ornamental pinnacles.

The porch has timbers 600 years old, two of them carved with odd faces; and very weird and grim are some other heads looking out in stone from the windows of the nave. The font is Norman and lay neglected in the churchyard for many years.

Perhaps we may think the most remarkable possession of Frensham is something lying under the tower, a great copper cauldron standing on a tripod, 400 years old. It is nearly nine feet round the bowl and a foot deep. What its use was and where it came from we can only guess. Some say it belonged to Mother Ludlam in her witch's cave at Moor Park near Farnham, but who is Mother Ludlam? John Aubrey, the antiquary of Stuart times, wrote that the cauldron was brought here by the fairies and used for their feasts; and an 18th century writer tells us that it was filled with ale to entertain the village "at the wedding of poor maids." So we may think as we will of this queer thing, the copper cauldron of Mother Ludlam, the fairies, or the poor wedding maids.

Why Friday?

FRIDAY STREET. It has the sound of falling water and the sight of Nature at her best, all in a far-away corner of England at the end of a long, long lane. That is all.

It lies off the busy road which takes us past John Evelyn's home at Wotton, not far from the height of Leith Hill which gives us on a magnificent scale the beauty Friday Street gives us in miniature. A few cottages with gay gardens run along the single street, and were they built of timber like Swiss chalets we might easily imagine ourselves transported to that enchanting land. They lead us to a pond with great trees rising all about it, tall pines and sturdy oaks reflected in the shimmering water. We do not know why it is Friday Street, for in truth it is a lovely street to visit any day.

A Churchyard of Surprises

FRIMLEY. It has a churchyard of surprises, with a fine old yew throwing its shadow over the graves of a remarkable group of men. Very attractive when we called was the nursery garden, with its splendid avenue of pines climbing towards the sky and stretching for more than a mile, and in the church we loved the beautiful Elizabethan chalice; but it is chiefly by its memories that Frimley comes into fame.

Yet it has also within its boundaries an institution which has made for it a great name among those who heal disease, for here the National Association for the Prevention of Tuberculosis founded the first colony in England where boys in their teens are cured of this disease and educated as if they were at school. The Sanatorium Colony is on Burrow Hill, and its record has been wonderfully encouraging.

In this part of Surrey, associated with the army, many of its memories are of officers and colonial administrators sleeping in the churchyard; yet they are not the only sleepers here who have won renown and fame. Walking round among these graves we wonder if any village in Surrey has a more notable array of names.

SURREY

We come upon the surprising name of Bret Harte, the American humorist who tried his hand at mining and teaching as well as writing, and there is William George Cubitt, who, in the Indian Mutiny, won the VC for saving three men's lives at the risk of his own during the retreat from Chinhut. There is John Frederick Lewis, an artist of last century who loved to draw animals and scenes of Spanish and Oriental life. His pictures won him much distinction, being highly praised by Ruskin, and some of his water-colours are at South Kensington. There is Charles Wellington Furse, who spent the last years of his short life, when he was dying, at his house near Camberley, making a beautiful garden of a sandy waste and painting the pictures by which he is best remembered. His Diana of the Uplands and the Return from the Ride are in the Tate Gallery. Diana is his wife. Daughter of one famous man and wife of another, Dame Katharine Furse is known to fame on her own account for her achievements as founder and director of the VAD in France during the war, and for her work among the Girl Guides. Furse was a masterly painter of horses and an excellent portrait-painter, and his early death was a tragic loss to English art.

And there is Sir Doveton Sturdee lying here, the gallant sailor who was a lieutenant in the Egyptian Wars of Gordon's day and an admiral at Jutland in our day. He won his chief fame in the early months of the Great War by his victory at the Falkland Islands, and became popular in peace by securing the restoration of Nelson's Victory at Portsmouth. He died in 1925, and his memory is kept green here by a wooden cross set in an arch of stone, a cross made from a beam of Nelson's flagship.

It is fitting that Admiral Sturdee's grave should be marked by a cross of wood from the timbers of the Victory, for, quite apart from his share in restoring Nelson's ship, he had himself what we call the Nelson Touch. Nowhere was this better displayed than at the Battle of the Falkland Islands in December 1914, when he defeated a German squadron.

The admiral was never tired of telling the story of the three women who sent the news which gave him the chance of his great victory.

The British Fleet did not expect the German Fleet at the Falklands, and the Germans had no idea of finding our ships there. But Mrs

Felton, the wife of a sheep farmer, hearing that strange ships were about, sent two of her maids to a headland overlooking Stanley Harbour and received news that a German cruiser and two supply steamers were in sight. Our ships were coaling at the time, and the Germans were hidden from them. Mrs Felton telephoned to the naval authorities, and sent back her maids with a notebook and pencil. While one maid remained as observer and wrote notes of all she saw, the other ran with messages back to the house, where they were telephoned to Admiral Sturdee. A woman had seen what no look-out had discovered, and the result was that a German squadron soon lay at the bottom of the sea. The Admiralty recognised the great importance of Mrs Felton's conduct, and sent her a letter of thanks and a massive silver salver. Her lieutenants, the two nimble-witted maids, were also remembered and the Admiralty presented each with a handsome start for her bottom drawer, a silver teapot. But for their presence of mind the German Fleet might have escaped.

Bret Harte

FRANCIS BRET HARTE, whose name is so unexpected at Frimley, was the poet and story-writer of the Californian mining region, who became widely known and appreciated in England in the seventies of last century, and deserves lasting fame. He was born in 1839 at Albany, in the State of New York. His father was professor of Greek at the local college, dying when the boy was quite young. As was customary in the States at that time, Bret Harte went west to find a career, and at 17 began to sample a number of occupations in California; he became in turn messenger, miner, printer, teacher, secretary, and editor.

His stories described vividly the romance in the rude life of the mining camps, and the sketches were accompanied by equally original short poems, picturesque, humorous, pathetic, and idyllic. For a short time Bret Harte held a professorship in the University of California, but in 1871 he left the West and lived in New York. His poems had now been collected, and he was admired throughout the English-speaking world. His writing activity continued, and he also made repeated lecturing tours through the States. In 1878 he was appointed United States Consul in Germany, and on his journey there he lectured in London on the emigrant movement which linked the Eastern and Western shores of America across the central barren lands. After two years in Germany he served in Glasgow in the same capacity, and at last retired and made his home in or near London till his death.

Though he lived most of the last 17 years of his life in England, he remained to the end a 100-per-cent American. Almost to the last he continued writing, and wrote more than forty books. His distinctive work, however, was done in the first half of his writing-life. It depicts types of character much rarer now than then, rough in the extreme, though he interpreted it with a sensitive spirit, and with a literary flavour unrepresented elsewhere. The man who could produce such wares as The Luck of Roaring Camp, The Heathen Chinee, and the lovely verses on Dickens in Camp, will never be forgotten.

Treasures From All Europe

GATTON. Its name is known to all who use the Brighton road, and in other days its great house was known far and wide for its wonderful marble hall. The house and the church stood together in the 558 acres of Gatton Park, the lovely estate of Sir Jeremiah Colman, a friend of this place for half a century. It was a bitter thing to find the house in ashes, for it was burned down in 1934, leaving the outer walls standing but the marvellous marble hall a memory. Those who asked could go and see this wonderful place, built by Lord Monson last century. As a notable example of its style it took the breath away, for everything in it seemed to be marble, from the floor to the ceiling 90 feet up, rich in colour and marvellously inlaid. Sir Edwin Cooper has done wonders with the ruins, building a new house on the same site, with stone from the old building treated and refaced so that it looks as if it had been quarried yesterday. The old walls are inside the new ones, and the great portico was saved from the fire and has been joined to the new building. One of the art treasures of the marble hall has happily been preserved. It is the statue of an Athlete in Repose, saved by a miracle, for a five-ton iron girder crashed near it in the fire. The great bronze gates to the marble hall have also been preserved and are in the new house.

A remarkable fact about the new house is that one of its rooms has been panelled in walnut from a tree blown down on the estate.

THE KING'S ENGLAND

This huge tree was about 100 feet high, and it gave sufficient panelling (¾ of an inch thick) to cover the walls of a room 29 feet by 24 by 12. It was one of the noblest trees in Surrey, and one of the finest walnuts in the country.

One of the outdoor sights of this fine estate is the rock garden, which looks out across a lake, and a marvellous indoor spectacle are the great orchid houses, having been untouched by the fire.

In his short life of 32 years Lord Monson spent a small fortune on the little church, collecting old treasures for it from all over Europe. The effect is one of great richness, more suited to the choir of a cathedral than the interior of a village church. Elaborate stalls from Belgium face inwards in the nave, many of them having misereres carved with faces. Looking down on them from a height is a rich pulpit which came with the altar table from Nuremburg. There are carved doors from Rouen and altar rails from Tongres, and the windows have 16th century Flemish glass from a church near Louvain. All round the nave are delicate traceried panels, leading up to a beautiful old screen beneath the gallery.

It is something of a relief to see a 13th century English piscina peeping through the chancel panelling. That and the 13th century carving on the font are among the few things that would be remembered by a certain rector if he came back after 300 years. He was Edmund Shove, whose son died at sea going out to New England, and he must be mentioned because one of his descendants has given a new chapel to Colorado College in America, and the college asked for an old stone from Gatton Church to build into its new fabric. There is a tablet in the chancel to one of the four Gatton men who died in the Great War; he was Major Rogers, a rector's son, who fell at Arras and won the DSO.

A lovely little building in classical style stands under a group of fine chestnuts in the park. It is still fondly known as the town hall. That is to say, it was in the 17th century the place where they elected Members of Parliament in the days when two men went from here to Westminster. Gatton was one of the rottenest of the rotten boroughs swept away by the Reform Act. It had returned two members since 1450, and in one year both were elected by one man. Perhaps we may think of the urn in this little town hall as a monument to the memory of a dead borough.

SURREY

Ancient Street and Famous School

GODALMING. Its busy street has something of the charm of Surrey's capital not far along the Portsmouth Road, and its church tells a story of building through nearly a thousand years. All about the town are old houses, some with Tudor timbering, some with overhanging storeys, some with fine ornamental brickwork of the 17th century, and some with their beauty still preserved as shops. At the head of the High Street is the quaint little building set up in 1814 as a town hall. Long outgrown by the town, it is now a museum, with many curious and interesting relics of Godalming's old days. It has pictures of the streets and the church as they were long ago, Roman coins, prehistoric flints found hereabouts, and farming implements of the days before machinery.

One of the inns has a memory of Peter the Great coming to dine, his menu being still in the Bodleian library at Oxford. It has a record, too, of a visit from a Russian Tsar and a Prussian king not long before Waterloo. Less romantic but more vital is Godalming's boast that its streets were the first in the land to be lit with electric light, the earliest lamps being set up here in 1881.

A fine picture the town makes in the sunlight for those who climb Frith Hill. It has the River Wey winding through green meadows, hills and woods for a background, and a splendid church watched over by a 14th century spire, one of the few spires in England covered with lead, and (like most of those few) a little crooked and twisted.

We must think of the church as having grown up through all our great building centuries, starting with the Saxons just before the Conquest and ending with the 19th century builders of some of its outer walls. From a simple nave and chancel 900 years ago it has grown in every direction, and we see it with aisles and transepts and chapels, and a steeple rising up in the centre of all.

The core of the structure is Saxon still, and the Norman tower rises from what was the Saxon chancel. The Normans fashioned the church into the shape of a cross, as they loved to do, building a new chancel beyond the Saxon one and adding these transepts beside their central tower. The chancel walls, though pierced with 13th century arches, have still the remains of their Norman windows, three on each side, and some of the splays have still their reddish patterns, painted about 800 years ago. The eastern end of the chancel is as the 14th century builders altered it, with their handsome stone seats in the wall.

The south chapel has kept much character from the 13th century builders, who added it to the Norman church. It has a threefold lancet window with slender marble columns, a big east window with some of the earliest simple tracery, and a built-up window-splay still showing a clear picture painted 700 years ago of John the Baptist holding a lamb. In the chapel we found fragments of Saxon carving, and a medieval font no longer used.

Some of the lofty nave arches are 13th century, others are 15th, and others 19th. The roof has many painted shields going back to the 16th century, and the richly patterned pulpit is probably the work of Elizabethan carvers. There is a fine oak chest 700 years old, a splendid 18th century candelabra, a medieval tomb without a name, and a tiny shield of ancient glass.

On the chancel wall kneels Judeth Eliot of 1615, and on the floor are brass portraits of three Tudor folk—Thomas Purvoche with his wife, and John Barker in his rich armour and ruff. Among the tablets we noticed one to Nathaniel Godbold, an 18th century gentleman as quaint as his name, for his epitaph tells us he was the inventor and proprietor of that excellent medicine the Vegetable Balsam, " for the cure of consumption and asthmas." Sleeping in one of the transepts is John Coston, also of the 18th century, whose stone says he was made sexton at 14 and held the office for 59 years. He was the King of Humours, we read, and the best of husbands to his well-beloved wife Jane, " who now is in great sorrow and grief for her loss of him."

The north chapel has a tablet to one of the town's famous vicars, Owen Manning, who was laid to rest in the churchyard in 1801 after ministering here 37 years. He wrote a Saxon dictionary and a book on King Alfred, and was one of the authors of a celebrated history of Surrey which blindness prevented him from finishing. It is said that in his days at Cambridge he was so ill from smallpox that they took him for dead and were on the point of burying him when his father lifted him in his arms and said "I will give him another chance." The movement seemed to revive him, and he recovered after all. Among his predecessors on the roll of vicars are Nicholas Andrews,

SURREY

turned out in the Civil War and sent from gaol to gaol until he died in captivity, and Samuel Speed, who is said to have been a valiant sea-chaplain and a sailor. He was a grandson of John Speed the chronicler, and is remembered in a stirring story written by the royalist author, Sir John Birkenhead, after a sea-fight with the Dutch:

> *The chaplain, he plied his wonted work,*
> *He prayed like a Christian, he fought like a Turk,*
> *Crying, Now for the King and the Duke of York!*
> *With a thump, thump, thump.*

It is not the only little tale Godalming has to remind us of the difficult days of the English throne, for at Westbrook Place lived Sir Theophilus Oglethorpe, who led the charge against Monmouth's rebels at Sedgemoor and was equerry to James the Second. The extraordinary tale is told that the Old Pretender of our history books was in reality not James the Second's son but a son of Sir Theophilus, substituted when the real prince died in convulsions as a child. We do not know how true it is, but there is more than a little evidence for it. What is certain is that Westbrook was inherited by Sir Theophilus Oglethorpe's son James Edward, the famous founder of Georgia known to history as General Oglethorpe.

Almost in the shadow of its ancient spire Godalming has a public garden of great charm, made still more beautiful by the cloister and lilypond set up as a tribute to a hero who perished in one of the darkest sea tragedies of modern times. He was John George Phillips, who, faithful to his post of chief wireless operator, went down with the Titanic. We come upon him a mile away at Farncombe, where he lived and sang in the choir.

The Roman Catholic Church of St Edmund has a notable reredos in its lady chapel, with graceful carvings of the Madonna, the Wise Men and the Shepherds; the chancel has another handsome reredos with six carved figures in niches.

Widely seen in this part of Surrey are the spires of Charterhouse School, standing finely on a hill above the town. Not until 1872 did the school move here from its ancient buildings in the heart of London, but with it have come many memories of its past and of its famous old boys. The grounds are watched over by fine statues of Thomas Sutton, the founder, and of William Haig-Brown, the headmaster who may be said to have brought Charterhouse into Surrey.

Charterhouse was founded by Thomas Sutton, a Lincolnshire man who discovered the riches hidden in the Durham coalfields. Licensed to work the coal, he built up a great trade, married a wealthy wife, and was reputed to be the richest commoner in England. He paid £13,000 for a site in Smithfield, and there founded a school for 44 poor boys and a hospital for 80 pensioners, who were to be impoverished gentlemen, men who had borne arms by land or sea, servants of the royal household, or merchants ruined by piracy or shipwreck. He left ample funds for teaching the boys and lodging, clothing, and feeding the pensioners. When he died, in 1611, his body was embalmed at his house in Hackney for five months, was kept in a London church for two years, and was then carried by the first of his pensioners to Charterhouse Chapel in London, where it now lies under a sumptuous monument by Nicholas Stone. Only the school was removed to Godalming; the rest remains as Sutton devised it in the heart of London, and there he sleeps in the midst of it.

In the windows of the library are coats-of-arms of 60 old Carthusians, including Richard Crashaw, Sir Richard Lovelace, Joseph Addison, Richard Steel, John Wesley, John Leech, and William Makepeace Thackeray. There is a collection of John Leech's inimitable drawings, some done for his Comic History of England and some rescued from his wastepaper basket by his sister; and there is a case of Thackeray's belongings, including a book he used at school, part of his manuscript of The Newcomes, and a fascinating tray of oddments found on his desk when he died. In it we see his spectacles, his pen, his cumbrous paper-clips, and his gloves. A bronze bust by Epstein, strong and rugged, of Sir Frank Fletcher watches over the room, a tribute to his 24 years as headmaster; and in another room are shown autograph letters of Thomas Sutton, Steele and Addison, and Richard Lovelace. Here too is a book by the poet Richard Crashaw, his Epigrammata Sacra, which came out in 1634 soon after the school was founded, and is thought to be the first book published by an Old Carthusian.

The school museum has a splendid collection of Surrey birds made by a Godalming man, and among its treasures are a lock and

SURREY

a fire-basket from the house where Shakespeare was born, and a chair belonging to John Wesley.

Two memorials there are to old boys fallen in war since Charterhouse moved to Godalming. One is the cloister in memory of those who died in South Africa, with a foundation stone laid by one of the greatest Carthusians of modern times, the Chief Scout. The other, dominating this hilltop, is the fine chapel in memory of nearly 700 who fell in the Great War, a spacious building designed with great dignity by Sir Giles Scott. It has tall lancet windows, beautiful oak panelling hand-carved with much variety, and a stained east window by Powell in which we see a knight dedicating his sword at the altar and receiving his crown of glory from an angel when the strife is done.

Among the names that will live for evermore in this chapel is that of Eric McNair, who was head of the school in his day and went on to win the VC. When a mine exploded, throwing him and those around into the air and burying many, Lieutenant McNair rallied the survivors to prevent the advancing enemy from breaking through. The first onslaught was repelled, and then, as the communication trench was blocked, he crossed in the open under heavy fire to summon reinforcements. His coolness and courage in nerve-racking circumstances saved the position.

In the hillside cemetery halfway between Godalming and Farncombe sleeps Arthur Clutton-Brock, poet and critic. On his gravestone is a charming little verse he wrote on Christmas Day in 1923, only a few days before he passed away:

> *I am a man by sickness worn*
> *On this day that Christ was born.*
> *Turn again to this strange story,*
> *All humility mixed with glory.*

Six years later they brought to this graveyard Philip Heseltine, the turbulent and eccentric figure who as a musician called himself Peter Warlock. He was a musical scholar of rare distinction who did much to make known the works of our incomparable Elizabethan masters, and himself composed many delightful songs and carols which carry on the spirit of those old times. Something of an Elizabethan, he died tragically when he was only 36, leaving the pathetic memory of a strange dual personality more than a little touched with genius.

THE KING'S ENGLAND

The White Lady

GODSTONE. Its green, with its round pond ringed by limes and chestnuts, must be one of the best in England. The Tudor inn still looks out at it across the road, a fine half-timbered place, much as it was when William Cobbett sat here eating bread and cheese.

Up the lane to the church, past another pond and a charming timbered cottage, we come to a hilltop group that might be old but is almost new, a 19th century company of almshouses by the church.

There are eight small houses for old people, built by a mother in memory of her daughter and designed by Sir Gilbert Scott. On a bank, with a small chapel at one end, they border the graveyard of the church Sir Gilbert Scott set up last century in place of a much more beautiful one which had stood 600 years. The nave still stands on its 12th century foundations, and the tower, behind its modern face, has stood since the 13th century. It has now been topped with a charming cap and spire of oak shingles, perhaps the most delightful bit of the group. The roof of the nave has still the 15th century timbers, and it has sheltered the font with its panels of Tudor roses all the time.

The great treasures of the church are the shining marble figures of two ancestors of John Evelyn the diarist. They lie on a magnificent altar tomb, their heads on tasselled cushions with cherubs at the corners and grotesque heraldic creatures at their feet. They are Sir John and Dame Thomasin Evelyn, and the tomb is a splendid piece of 17th century sculpture. Sir John supplied the crown with gunpowder from his mills at Godstone, an ancestor having been licensed to dig for salt petre after the Spanish Armada had revealed that our ammunition was dangerously low.

Worthy to keep this fine monument company is the white marble figure of Lady Macleay under the tower. She lived at the Jacobean house called Pendhill Court (still one of Surrey's charming homes) and there were still old folk who remembered her when we called. We see her as a charming figure with a graceful veil thrown about her, and a handful of flowers; the evening sun falls on her face, and she seems to have just fallen asleep. In a tomb in the churchyard four Macleay children lie, a pathetic group 13, 14, 15, and 16 years old.

The sculptured capitals of the arches are fine with ferns and foliage, and the oak chancel screen has a splendid canopy of grapes and vine leaves. There is much dignity in some of the faces looking down from the arches, and in a lancet window stands an attractive figure of Elizabeth of Hungary in a blue gown, carrying a basket of roses. A small picture below shows her giving to the poor. It is far the best of the 12 stained glass windows. One of the others, with Christ, the Madonna, and St John, is in memory of a mother by her only daughter. On one of the walls is a bronze medallion, set in alabaster between two winged angels, of Sir Walpole Greenwell who died in the year his son died on active service.

One of the great boulders known as sarsen stones, carried about the world by glaciers, marks the grave of a lover of little trodden pathways, known as Walker Miles; he was one of the founders of rambling clubs, and must have known every path for miles round Godstone, and thousands of paths about England.

Two Godstone men died for their faith in the days of the martyrs, Thomas Iveson and John Launder, both condemned by that astounding Bishop Bonner who pleased Mary Tudor and annoyed Elizabeth, and died in Marshalsea Prison after sending many men to the stake.

Marden Park, a few miles from Godstone, with beech trees in all their glory, fine wooded slopes, and a mile-long drive to a modern house something like a French chateau, was the home of William Wilberforce in the days when he was thinking out his crusade to save the slaves. In the garden is a pillar to the memory of our great philanthropist, the 17th century Thomas Firmin; he used to stay here with his friend Sir Robert Clayton, who became owner of Marden. A walk in the grounds is called Firmin's Walk. He was known as the Charitable Samaritan. Through the reigns of the Stuarts and during the Protectorate he remained a tolerant man, always in sympathy with the oppressed. His appetite for helping the poor grew with each success or failure. He put up a building to store corn and coals to be sold at cost price to the poor in hard times. He started a workhouse for employing men in linen manufacture, paying them more than they earned; his workhouse was maintained at a loss to the day of his death.

He was a prison philanthropist, deeply interested in the condition of prisoners for debt. Many he freed out of his own pocket. No deserving case escaped him. He set up French Protestant refugees in their own trades, and was the Prince of Beggars when money was to be raised for any good cause. Christ's Hospital remembers him as one of its best governors, and we may like to remember as an original member of a forgotten society which might well be revived in these days, the Society for the Reformation of Manners.

The People of the Old Church

GREAT BOOKHAM. It is a growing place with age and beauty still for those who seek. Its church is one of the prettiest in Surrey, keeping company with the flourishing stump of a great elm planted three centuries ago. The village hall was once an ancient barn, and the three walnut trees in the churchyard have been growing since 1734. The ancient timber tower of the church rises oddly from a stone base, the first part of a Norman tower which was never finished.

Approaching the church door, we pass a cross in memory of a man who was killed in Africa by a buffalo, and a seat put here for " those who have borne the burden and heat of the day." Outside a chancel window are two quaint heads, carved 600 years ago and nicknamed the Parson and the Clerk. The clerk has a wry mouth and is thought to be singing Amen.

The nave, with its round and pointed arches, shows very clearly the development of building, but older than both arches are two simple windows discovered in 1913. They were made about the time the Conqueror's Domesday Book was written, when Great Bookham was described as having a church and three serfs. One of these windows used to look down on the altar in the 11th century building, and still has patches of wall painting by Norman artists, a clear pattern of red and yellow.

The 14th century chancel tells something of its own story. In the sanctuary is a dedication stone describing how the chancel was rebuilt in 1341 by John of Rutherwyke, a famous Abbot of Chertsey who repaired churches, made roads, and encouraged farming. Close by is a stone once believed to be the top of his coffin, carved with a cross and disfigured by iron studs driven in to prevent boys from sliding on it when it was outside the church. Also in the sanctuary is a stone inscribed to Sir Francis Howard of 1651, a grandson of the great Lord Howard of Effingham; and at the other end of the church

Great Bookham The Church and its Timber Tower

Little Bookham The White Norman Church

The Two Mills on Outwood Common

Ockley   Reigate Mill Church   Wray Common

FIVE SURREY WINDMILLS

is one to a great-grand-daughter of the Admiral, a pathetic infant of one year, with this verse about her:

> *If peerless beauty could have swayed,*
> *This rose-cheeked child had longer stayed.*
> *But death refused her friends' desire*
> *And sent her to the heavenly quire.*

The Slyfield chapel was added to the church 500 years ago and is full of interest. A Tudor screen cuts it off from the chancel; and the patched-up remains of a 15th century rood screen, carved with falcons and dragons, cuts it off from the aisle. The piscina in the chapel is beautifully cut, and the east window is filled with glass in memory of Lord Raglan, who lost an arm at Waterloo and commanded the British forces in the Crimea. It was this Lord Raglan who, as they were carrying his lost limb away, called out, " Don't take that till I have taken off my ring"; he could more easily bear the loss of his arm than the ring his wife had given him.

There is a brass portrait of Elizabeth Slyfield of 1597, with a rhyme to tell us how well she was descended; and a brass inscription to her and her husband tells us that "in her lips no ill was ever found," and that her husband was beloved of all the poor. Looking down the nave is a fine family group in brass, Henry Slyfield of 1598 with his wife, six sons, and four daughters. There is a portrait of an earlier Elizabeth Slyfield who died 500 years ago, and another of Robert Shiers of 1668, who looks as if he were reading aloud. He lived at the great house named Slyfield, three miles away by the River Mole, newly-built in his day with red brick pilasters, fine plaster ceilings, and a gate at the foot of the stairs to keep the dogs from going up. The house is shown to visitors on request. In addition to his brass portrait there is an elaborate monument to him, with three fine busts of himself, his wife, and their son. A marble figure in the same aisle is of Thomas Moore of 1735, an English officer shown in Roman armour. Next to him is another marble monument with a medallion bust of William Moore who died about 200 years ago, the last of his family; two delightful cherubs perch on the cornice below him. A more curious monument is the weeping willow of stone, which for the last century has been climbing the chancel wall. On the south wall is a bust of Cornet Francis Geary, set above the relief of a scene from the American War of

Independence, when he was killed by an ambush hiding in a wood.

At the Norman font of Sussex marble, neighboured by a century-old barrel organ, was baptised in 1795 the little son of Fanny Burney and General D'Arblay. Here at Fairfield Fanny Burney set up housekeeping after her marriage, and here she wrote Camilla when her son was born. Pleasant it is to think of Fanny busy with her book and her housekeeping, while her husband, a refugee from France, found peace at last in a Surrey garden.

Bookham is closely associated with another famous novelist, for to the stately Georgian house known as the Old Rectory came Jane Austen to pay occasional visits to her godfather, Samuel Cooke. Polesden Lacey is connected with a dramatist, for in an earlier house on its site lived Richard Brinsley Sheridan after his second marriage. To the present building, with its terrace 300 yards long, came our King George and Queen Elizabeth on their honeymoon.

It is good to know that Bookham's commons, with their 438 acres of oak and holly, are in the keeping of the National Trust.

The Street of a Thousand Years

GUILDFORD. It has one of the finest streets in the south of England (Dickens declared it the most beautiful in the kingdom) and at the top of it we seem to be higher than the tower below. In and about this street of a thousand years (it is mentioned in Alfred's will), are eight monuments of the past that nobody should miss, and before we have finished with the town the eight will be eighty.

Yet, rich as it has been through the centuries, we found Guildford, when we called, preparing to build a new cathedral, and on Stag Hill, with its view over miles of glorious countryside, a great wooden cross 35 feet high, stood as a challenge to those who declare that faith is dead. The cross was made of teak from the timbers of the old battleship Ganges, and it marked the spot on which the great new cathedral will rise.

Round this fine street cluster all Guildford's ancient places. They are up and down like Time itself, with hardly a level space; even the floor of the middle church is on three levels. At the top of the street is the fine 16th century Grammar School, the 16th century Hospital, and the 18th century church. Halfway down hangs out the 16th century clock of one of the quaintest Guildhalls left in England. Beyond it is the Saxon tower of St Mary's, and at the bottom is the 19th century tower of St Nicolas. Up above, on a hill on each side of the river Wey, stand Guildford's ruined walls, the great walls of the castle and the small walls of St Catherine's Chapel. From either of them we look out on one of the finest views round any town, with the Hog's Back stretching out to Farnham, Lewis Carroll sleeping at one end and William Cobbett at the other; with Pewley Hill and the old semaphore tower (now on Semaphore House) by which Portsmouth signalled to London before the telegraph came; and the great height crowned by St Martha's Chapel on the Pilgrim's Way.

It is the stately charity house of Archbishop Abbot, founded a year or two after Shakespeare's death for ten old men and ten old women, which draws every eye in Guildford, for it crowns the top of the street with its fine red brick turrets and its charming chimneys. The turrets are capped with copper and crowned with weathervanes. The chimney stacks are of quaint shapes and have been called the best in Surrey.

The great black doors are painted in scarlet and gold with the mitre of Archbishop Abbot and his sign of three gold pears, and the gateway leads us into one of the most charming squares in the country. Round it live twenty people, with a guest room, a chapel, and a common hall. We reach the guest room by the old stairs up which everybody has walked who has ever seen this lovely place; little has the place changed since 1619. The same charming doors engraved like shells still swing on their hinges, the same bell still rings in the quadrangle for late-comers at night, the same brick summer-house is in the kitchen garden, the same clock still tells the time—we opened a cupboard door and saw its works still running. There are the same tables and stools and benches, the same almsbox, the same old Bible with vinegar printed for vineyard, the same portraits on the walls. Among the 17th and 18th century pictures is a charming one of a lady and two children, some by John Russell, the Guildford bookseller's son who became an RA, and one of Admiral Pollen with his wife and daughter which is thought to be by

Hogarth. Over the altar in the chapel is a 16th century Italian painting of the Entombment.

Guildford has some lovely rooms (few towns have more), and one of the best is the guest room here. The old table made in 1633 stands in the centre, and the splendid mantelpiece is a marvellous reminder of the feasts it must have seen. It is in black oak, like all this woodwork, and it tells the story of a banquet in a way reminding us of the humour of the ancient monks who carved queer faces on the walls of our cathedrals. Four upright figures stand for the server, the cupbearer, the carver, and the usher, and along the bottom runs a row of faces with mouths wide open and teeth anxious to bite; they are the guests. In the centre are masks of a jester, a singer, and a reciter, those who entertained the feasters; and along the top run the heads of boar and water fowl, with which the feast was spread.

We come down into the chapel and find this delightful too, a small place of rich and glowing treasure, with 50 painted figures in its windows. They tell the story of Jacob. We see Isaac sending Esau hunting, with Rebecca looking on, the boy with his sheaf of arrows. We see Rebecca tempting Jacob to steal his brother's birthright from old Isaac in his canopied bed, Rebecca watching from behind as Isaac gives his blessing, and Esau coming back and threatening Jacob, dogs barking about them. We see Jacob at the foot of his ladder with angels mounting and descending, the meeting with Jacob and Laban at the well, Rachel and her flock in the distance, and the patriarch with his wives and children about him. The pictures are all splendid, in the style of Albert Durer, and the artist has introduced into them attractive small windows through which the distant landscape is seen; in the great east window the three tiny painted windows have a remarkable perspective.

In the Master's House over the gateway is a very charming room, and in it the chair in which Daniel Colwall, one of the founders of the Royal Society, died a tragic death; he is buried in St Mary's Church near the Saxon tower.

Facing the Archbishop's gateway (in which the wretched Duke of Monmouth spent a night after Sedgemoor), we may cross the street, climb 20 steps, and stand at the tomb of Archbishop Abbot in Holy Trinity. His body was seen about 50 years ago, and the beard we see in his portraits was still intact. He is sculptured with his feet against the eastern wall on the right of the altar, under a canopy raised on black columns which rest on stacks of books carved in stone, with gilded clasps and bookmarks all complete. Between these stacks of books is a grille behind which the sculptor has chiselled a heap of bones and skulls as in a charnel house—a ghastly sight fashionable in those days, seen again in a monument under the tower.

The canopy above the tomb is, we cannot but feel, a little out of keeping with the old Archbishop, for it is elaborately worked out with figures from the Faerie Queen of Edmund Spenser, small figures crowning it showing the Archbishop as a Red Cross Knight, the Faerie Queen with the victor's crown, another holding a golden chalice, and companions from the story. Amid all this lies the simple Archbishop in his robes, and the inscription, after reciting his progress from a small cottage in Guildford to the throne at Canterbury, tells us that when he could go no higher on Earth he ascended into Heaven. This tomb, which Pepys came many times to see, was set up by the Archbishop's brother Maurice, the Lord Mayor of London. Archbishop Laud came to Guildford for the funeral, and the famous street was hung in black.

Trinity Church has been made new while the Archbishop has lain here with the skulls and bones about him and the knights and ladies over him; as we see it it is 18th century, and not a lovely place. Yet it has much beauty within—the finest modern windows in the town; splendid banners, including one embroidered with a charming Madonna and another of St George with trappings of real jewels on his horse; a huge Jacobean pulpit with a canopy, attractive iron screens, an apse with no window but with its vaulted roof and panelled walls covered with paintings. It has also one of the last chantries ever founded, for its vestry is part of the old church, and was built for Sir Richard Weston of Sutton Place in 1540, a few years before the Great Suppression.

A memorial chapel is filled with memories of battlefields in Europe, Asia, and South Africa, and the church is rich in tributes to West Surrey heroes of the famous Queen's Regiment. A book in a small shrine has the names of 8000 officers and men, and a great window has splendid figures of St Alban, St George, and St Martin on a white horse. Fine companion windows in the nave have figures of

St Michael, St Oswald, and St Catherine in a black robe being received by Christ; and above a painted marble reredos in memory of officers of the Queen's hang tattered flags that have waved on many a tragic field.

Near the tomb of the Archbishop is a charming brass with portraits of his father and mother and their six sons. The old couple are kneeling at a desk and the sons kneel at a desk below them. It is comforting, as we look at her, to think that the old lady narrowly escaped death under Mary Tudor, and it is pathetic to read that Maurice and Alice Abbot lived together here for 58 years and then, leaving six sons alive, died within ten days of each other in 1607.

Looking across the nave, sitting in a Roman robe and resting his arm on a heap of books, is a man who was known to every member of Parliament in the reign of George the Second, for he presided over the House of Commons through every year of the reign. He is Arthur Onslow, third member of his family to be Speaker, and in one of the open books on which he rests his elbow we read of the thanks of the House of Commons for his constant and unwearied attention in the chair for 33 years in five Parliaments. His monument is here, but he was buried at Thames Ditton and now lies at Merrow Church, near to the ancient yews of Newlands Corner. His portrait is in the National Gallery and in Guildford Guildhall; he is the chief figure in Hogarth's painting of the House of Commons, and there is a curious portrait of him in his seat at St Margaret's, the Commons church at Westminster.

There are fragments of the old church still left in the tower, where lie the figures of a Lady Weston wearing a ruff, with skulls and bones below her, and Sir Robert Parkhurst, a Lord Mayor of London in Stuart days, with his headless wife kneeling at his feet. On the wall of the tower is a small brass portrait of John Wheeler, a 15th century civilian with a pouch on his girdle. Let into the floor is a small brass telling us that below lies Sir Charles Knowles, a captain's servant who became an admiral in the 18th century.

Trinity Church crowns the top of the fine street; the tower at the bottom by the River Wey crowns the 19th century church of St Nicolas, an unlovely place but with much interest, and with a 15th century chapel to which for centuries they brought the Mores of Loseley, the Elizabethan house by the Hog's Back, a little way from

SURREY

Compton. It is impressive with its gables and has panelling said to have come from Henry the Eighth's extravagant palace of Nonsuch.

The ancient chapel is locked, but through the glazed arches of a modern arcade we see the sculptured figures on four tombs. Sir William More lies in armour with his wife in Elizabethan costume, with his two daughters kneeling on a tomb at one side, and on a tomb at the other side two small figures at prayer—Sir George More and his wife Ann. Sir George received Queen Elizabeth as a guest at Loseley and had the task of waking up James the First in the middle of the night to tell him that Protector Somerset refused to appear for trial. On the fourth tomb in the Loseley chapel lies the marble figure of Arnold Brocas, a 14th century rector. The roof of the chapel is borne on rather crude corbel heads, looking as if they were chiselled yesterday in chalk.

The best modern possessions of St Nicolas are its extraordinary font, its fine brass, and its pulpit with 30 or 40 figures sculptured in marble panels. The brass, centred in the floor of the chancel, is a fine portrait of William Skipsey Sanders, who saw the 20th century in as rector here; he is shown lifesize holding a chalice, and is under a canopy with side panels containing small portraits of the Madonna and St Nicolas with his three apples. The font is a massive piece of red-veined marble, carved on each side with grouped Bible scenes. It has a wooden cover with figures under canopies, and over font and cover too is a huge canopy, the whole structure being enclosed in iron rails.

On the west wall is a tiny brass portrait of Caleb Lovejoy, in whose memory a sermon has been preached every year since Queen Elizabeth died; he was a Grammar School boy, and an inscription tells us all about him; he sold waggons to Cromwell's army. There are many paintings on the brick walls of the aisles and the nave, the best of a poor collection being St Helena and St George. The best window is in memory of the most famous rector here Dr J. S. B. Monsell, whose hymns have been sung all over the world. He was killed by a fall when the church was being rebuilt, and a brass inscription on a fragment of an old column in the churchyard marks the spot where he fell. His window has eight Bible scenes and four big figures. One of the rectors before him preached here for 55 years.

To many it will seem that the most pathetic memory of St Nicolas is the tablet over the grave of a boy killed in the Crimean War, Henry Arthur Wight, of whom we read that

He was prayed for and soothed in his last moments by a ministering angel, Florence Nightingale, to the eternal gratitude of his sorrowing mother.

The oldest church in Guildford, and the town's oldest building, lies between the other two, nestling in a dip a stone's throw off the street; it is St Mary's, one of the quaintest churches we have seen, with a remarkable sculpture gallery, some charming windows, fine Norman arches, and a Saxon tower.

This tower was standing when they built Guildford Castle. It has seen its rise and fall. It has seen the whole history of Guildford from the beginning till now; there are those who think it was here when Guildford was mentioned in Alfred's will.

Centuries ago, and down to our own time, St Mary's had a remarkable group of frescoes said to have been painted about 1260, but they have crumbled away and nothing but a fragment of colour is left. They were in the vaulted roof of the chapel of St John, which has still the most charming peep we have in St Mary's. The chapels on each side of the chancel have apses, and St John's apse, reached by a flight of steps, is given a touch of rare beauty by a lovely triple window with delicate stonework which has been here 700 years. We stand on the threshold of this chapel and look through two Norman arches piercing the Saxon tower; above each arch is a small crude window through which the sun came in Saxon days. The arches of the nave, with charming capitals, were built when Norman work was merging into English, and from the same time come the grotesque sculptures bearing up the roof of the aisle. They are the work of artists who lived at least 700 years ago, and are remarkable for their queer expressions. One is a sort of half-human toad, another is said to have been meant for Judas in the mouth of Satan. The artists of St Mary's were first-rate men; we have only to look at the little piscina with its vaulted roof and at the daintily carved ribs of the chancel vaulting to see that.

Keeping company with all this good craftsmanship are three fine Jacobean chairs, a fragment of a 15th century screen which was once a reredos, brass portraits of a civilian and a lady of the 16th

Guildford   **The Castle Gateway**

Guildford   The High Street

Guildford   The Grammar School

Guildford — St Catherine's Chapel

Guildford — The Ruined Castle

Guildford   The New Cathedral as Drawn by the Architect

Guildford   Holy Trinity Church in High Street

century, and a fine candelabra given by our Mohammedan fighting men in the war to the mother of their squadron commander. One of the odd things of this place is a low square window in the western wall which once had a shutter and an iron grating, but the oddest impression of all is the impression of the three levels here. There are steps everywhere, and we feel that generation after generation has been adapting this fine church and moulding it to its heart's desire. Part of the difficulty as to the levels of the church is due to the fact that a great piece of the east end was cut off at the urgent request of the Prince Regent, who said the road was too narrow at that point for his coach to pass on the way to Brighton. The prince offered to bear the whole cost of the alteration, but when the work was done refused to pay a penny.

One of its parsons was preaching here when Napoleon was a little lad at school; he was preaching here through all his trials and triumphs, through Trafalgar and through Waterloo; and was preaching here when Napoleon died on St Helena. He was James Weller, vicar of Trinity and St Mary's for 50 years.

A great ruin and a little one speak from hill to hill across the Wey; the great one is, of course, the Castle, the little one is the Chapel of St Catherine, on the old Pilgrim's Way. It is believed there was a chapel on St Catherine's Hill 700 years ago, but the walls we see are early 14th century. Nobly have they stood the storms of time, for they are solid still with their pinnacled buttresses, three doorways, and eight lovely windows open to the sky. It is a fine little place, with a small tower which has three tiny windows; we are delighted that the town has now taken charge of St Catherine, and will keep it beautiful.

The castle walls, some of them 12 feet thick, are older than Magna Carta, and they have seen great times, the coming and going of many kings. The castle was once held by the Dauphin of France, in the days when he was chasing King John about England.

The gateway has been refashioned, but we can see the work of the men who set up this place on a Saxon mound with a ditch about it. There is herringbone work in the walls, Roman tiles, and pilaster strips on the Norman buttresses.

So thick are the walls that some have chambers within them, one an oratory with Norman arcading and carvings still recognisable of the

Crucifixion, a bishop lying under a crown, a Madonna, and St Christopher carrying the Child.

We can climb to the top and look down on the red roofs of Guildford, on the three church towers that have no steeples and on the two chapels that have steeples, on St Catherine's across the valley, on the little timber cupola of the Guildhall, on the six acres of castle grounds made into gardens, and on Surrey far away. In the gardens below stands a memorial arch with the names that live for evermore, and close by, at Rack's Close, are some ancient caves, into which we can walk for 100 feet.

One of the best-known clocks in England hangs before the old Guildhall; in this street are at least three clocks that have been working since the 17th century, but the town hall clock is the oldest of them all. Its case was made when it was hung in 1683, but its original works were made about 1560. The case is original but only a little of the ancient works remain. The clock was given to Guildford by a foreigner who wished to settle in the town but was not allowed to have his workshop there; he set it up outside the boundary, made this clock, and gave it to the town; and they put it on the new Guildhall and gave John Aylward his freedom.

His clock gives a touch of character to this street in which it has told the time for 250 years in the place where it still hangs. The bell in the quaint turret over it is new, having replaced the old one when it cracked; the old one is in the museum. It is one of Surrey's historic bells, having been brought from St Martha's Chapel on the high ridge above Chilworth visible from St Catherine's Hill. The 17th century Guildhall has two main rooms, the court room and the council chamber, both charming and full of interest. There is a mantelpiece carved in chalk and another in stone with four strange figures representing four phases of human character. What is called the Sanguine temperament is shown by a lover vowing fidelity; for the Choleric temperament stands a warrior surrounded by weapons, for the Phlegmatic a heavy man is in a boat fishing, and for the Melancholy is a solitary figure musing. Over this mantelpiece is a frieze of pine wood eight feet long, carved with heraldry.

The Guildhall is rich in civic treasures, for it has the finest silver mace existing of the 15th century, the oldest and the biggest of the few 15th century maces still left in England; its head has three lions and three ostrich feathers, and is decorated with roses and fleur-de-lys. That is the small mace known so well to 14 members of the Smallpiece family who have been mayors of Guildford from the reign of Henry the Seventh to our own day; the great mace with the silver stem is 34 inches long. Guildford is one of 32 towns in England with a state sword, which by a rare privilege it is allowed to have carried before the mayor; and it has a mayor's staff, a slender rod of campeachey wood, given by Queen Elizabeth. The silver head is engraved with a castle and the date 1563, and round it are the words, Fear God, Do Justice, Love thy brother. It is Queen Elizabeth's message to the Mayor of Guildford. Here also are four bronze measures given to the town by Queen Elizabeth.

Guildford has not only the oldest mace but the finest ewer and basin in existence; it was made in 1567 and given to the town by Bishop Parkhurst. The mayor's beautiful badge is of gold, and is dated 1663.

On the wall hangs a fine group of portraits. One by John Russell, RA, shows Admiral Onslow receiving the Dutch flag after the victory of Camperdown. One shows Arthur Onslow in his Speaker's robes. Two of the biggest Peter Lely portraits in existence show Charles the Second and James the Second, one by Paul Van Somer is of James the First and one by John Riley is of William and Mary.

The quaint front of the Guildhall is in keeping with the old charm of this famous street, and it is

> *A poor world this if, full of care,*
> *We have no time to stand and stare*

at the grotesque wooden brackets carved as long thin figures which reach out across the pavement.

But we cannot here exhaust the interests of Guildford, for it has a hundred things to see, innumerable peeps high and low, and a museum of ancient treasure, odd things used in cottage homes of Surrey long ago, tiles from ruined abbeys, old seals, relics of old fires and lighting, and a good chalk mantelpiece. It has the old grammar school with its fine stone front, gables crowned with red balls, a little wicket gate with a fine old knocker, all as they have been since 1552. Inside are the great beams on which boys have cut their names, the great seats for the masters, and about ninety chained books that have been here all the time. Here the three

Abbot brothers (the bishop, the archbishop and the lord mayor of London) were educated, and here Sir George Grey, the famous Colonial Governor, was at school; they must have handled half these books. Older still are some of the inns and houses in the High Street. The Angel has a wooden gallery, a 17th century clock, and a vaulted crypt 600 years old. It is one of two crypts facing each other under this street, the other being under the Savings Bank; and they are remarkable because there are only about six examples of early 14th century architecture in Surrey and these are declared by an expert to be the most important. The house Number 25 has been overhanging the pavement for centuries, and has still its old plaster ceilings and a marvellous staircase. Off Quarry Street, leading to the castle walls, is Old Porridgepot Alley, which has now given itself the more elegant name of Rosemary Alley; it is a remarkable sight with its 29 steps and just room to see the sky between the roofs. In Quarry Street is a medieval doorway, with wonderful ironwork, which may have belonged to the castle. In a shaded corner of North Street is a little garden in memory of G. F. Watts, called Quaker's Acre.

With all its enchantment, we do not wonder that William Cobbett thought Guildford the most agreeable and happy-looking town he saw in his rides. We have found happy towns all over these islands, but we have seen few more captivating in so small a space, and none in which we would rather spend a quiet and delightful day.

One house on the rising hill above the castle gateway will interest a multitude of people, for it saw the passing of Lewis Carroll. It is called The Chestnuts, and an enamelled plaque of much interest tells us that Lewis Carroll died here on January 14, 1898.

We owe this plaque to the enthusiasm of the children of Guildford, and it is a characteristic piece of work, bright with colour. On the big letter C of Lewis Carroll's name stands Alice, and above her on the top is Humpty Dumpty, looking as if a little shake from Alice would send him toppling down. Here also is the White Rabbit blowing his herald's trumpet, the Cheshire Cat grinning comfortably from his perch on the letter L, and the nodding Red King snoring loudly in the tail of the figure 9. The funeral service for Lewis Carroll was at St Mary's; he lies in the cemetery below the Hog's Back, visible from his old home.

SURREY

The Creator of Alice in Wonderland

LEWIS CARROLL was Charles Lutwidge Dodgson, who was born at Daresbury, near Warrington, Lancashire, in 1832, one of the 11 children of Charles Dodgson, who became archdeacon of Richmond, Yorkshire, and a canon of Ripon.

Charles was a precocious genius who, on being told that logarithms were too difficult for a child to understand, answered, "Yes, but please explain." From an early age he wrote plays and stories for the home, was a capital conjurer, and a schoolboy letter-writer who, with a tender, whimsical epistle to a sister, would enclose a note to a baby brother:

My own Skeff, Roar not lest thou be abolished. Yours etc.

At Rugby he was unhappy but diligent; at Oxford his genius for mathematics carried him to the foremost place; but for history and philosophy he had no taste or talent. He revealed the profoundest ignorance of Herodotus, and the examiner at last said, "Well, Mr. Dodgson, is there any fact mentioned by Herodotus that you do remember?" At that Dodgson brightened up, and named with much satisfaction a Libyan tribe of which the historian recorded nothing but that they painted themselves red and ate apes. That came home to him indeed, for he had had friends among the frogs and snails of his father's parsonage, and armed worms with tiny tubes with which to conduct defensive war.

He reached Oxford in 1850, and except for holidays never left it until he died, 48 years later. In order to qualify for a lectureship in mathematics he had to take orders, but he never entered the Church. Three reasons deterred him: he stammered, he could not endure parochial duties, and he thought his love of opera and the theatre incompatible with clerical functions.

He did preach from time to time, sometimes to undergraduates, but more commonly to the Christ Church servants, and to children, with whom he was always most at home. Among his friends were Tennyson, Ruskin, Millais, and Rossetti; but little girls were always dearest to his affections, hence the immortal Alice.

There were two Dodgsons, in temperament as in name. He adopted his psuedonym as a writer for London humorous papers, retaining Dodgson for his many mathematical works and papers on religious and social subjects. Although his fame was worldwide as Lewis Carroll, he imagined that few beyond his little girl friends knew it, and was deeply offended if Lewis Carroll or his works under that title were referred to him in a general company.

The immortal story of Alice sprang from a tale told on a summer afternoon to the little daughter of his friend Dean Liddon. He wrote it out, and presented it to her in 1865 as A Christmas Gift to a Dear Child in Memory of a Summer Day. The manuscript was sold at Sotheby's in February 1928 for £15,400, taken to America, and sold again with two copies of the first printed edition, for £30,000. The Looking-Glass followed five years later.

Dodgson was as good a comic artist as Thackeray and W. S. Gilbert, but fortunately he left the illustration of his masterpieces to Sir John Tenniel. Other illustrators he drove almost to lunacy, for he developed into as whimsical a crank as any of the deathless company in his pages, not only in his dealings with other men, but in his work.

Original writing was very slow; he told one of his girl correspondents: "I don't think I've done 60 pages in 18 weeks. I write a bit in one part of the book, then a bit in another part, and so on, all consecutively, and send it off to the printers to be set up in slip and arranged hereafter."

We have had no stranger character in literature, none greater of his kind. Children alone understood him and were at ease with him. He died at Guildford in December 1898 while on a visit to his sisters at The Chestnuts.

Surrey's Great Cathedral

GUILDFORD is giving to Surrey the proud distinction of being a cathedral county, and there is rising here on Stag Hill, a site given by Lord Onslow (reminding us of the bold sites of Lincoln and Durham), a cathedral to which travellers will come in a hundred or a thousand years as we now come to Winchester, not far away.

It is to be a noble place, built with rose-coloured bricks made from the clay of the hill on which it stands, the facings and the piers of stone. The main vaulting will be of concrete, and will be sprayed with asbestos plaster which it is hoped will prevent

SURREY

echoes. The cathedral is being built in the shape of a cross, and from end to end will be 365 feet. It will be 70 feet high and 40 feet wide, and the top of the tower will be about 180 feet from the ground, the flag flying 20 feet higher.

Mr Edward Maufe, the architect of the cathedral, has declared his intention of relying on proportion of mass, volume, and line rather than on elaboration and the repetition of ornament. No more typical English country exists, he says, than in the diocese of Guildford, and he is striving in his cathedral to express the heart of all this beauty. He believes his building will express the English spirit; it should be serene, and grow out of its site, "a calm, untroubled shape." The simplest of naves will lead up through a lofty choir to the richest of altars, and the cathedral itself will be tall and aspiring, quiet in colour except where special emphasis is wanted, as in the lady chapel, which will have a richly coloured roof and painted walls.

It is intended that the first part of the cathedral to be completed will embrace the choir and sanctuary, the ambulatory, the chapel of chivalry, the children's corner, and certain offices; that the nave and the west end shall follow, and that the lady chapel with the sacristy on the left and the chapter house on the right, shall complete the work.

This vast cathedral (which is to cost £250,000) is being set on a sort of concrete raft. It will stand on 780 concrete piles joined by concrete beams. Each pile weighs five tons and is 50 feet long; that is to say, the cathedral foundations will be 4000 tons weight and seven miles length of concrete pillars.

The foundation stone (brought from Jarrow, to mark the link which has formed with Jarrow by the relief fund Surrey raised for it) was laid by the Archbishop of Canterbury on July 22, 1936, and rests on stones brought from the fabric of Canterbury and Winchester cathedrals. The great stone therefore links the new cathedral with the Mother Church of England and the Mother Diocese of Winchester, as well as with the home of the Venerable Bede, who died at Jarrow. Inscribed at the top of the stone, on which are the diocesan arms of Guildford, Canterbury, and Winchester, are the letters A M D G, standing for the Latin version of To the Greater Glory of God. The name of the cathedral is to be the Cathedral Church of the Holy Spirit.

THE KING'S ENGLAND

Jacobean Splendour

HAM. A bare nine miles from Hyde Park Corner, its Common, at the foot of Richmond Park, might be in the depths of the country. Hawk and heron fly above it, and it is the haunt of badger and fox. Old Georgian houses peep at it from among the trees. To one of them Sir Walter Scott in his Heart of Midlothian brought Jeannie Deans to visit the Duke of Argyll; at another lived the Duchess of Queensberry, the Kitty of the poet Gay.

From a lodge on the Common runs a magnificent avenue of limes and elms leading to Ham House, one of the finest Jacobean mansions in England. We view its dignified garden front through a pair of stately gates made in Restoration days. On the bottom bar is a row of arrow-pointed uprights to keep out dogs, and at the top is a pair of scrolls capped by a spray of drooping tulips. Here the garden is nearly hidden by the wilderness, with some of the oldest Scotch firs in Surrey, and we must pass another fine avenue to get a proper view of the great lawn below the terrace.

In front of the house is another pair of iron gates, plain, grim, and prison-like, with a row of spikes on top. There are scarcely any gates round London as old as these, and beside them are some of the small number of 17th century railings now existing in the open. On the lichened garden walls painted lead busts of English poets and Roman emperors look out through trees to Twickenham Ferry. A stone statue of the river god faces them, backed by the handsome house front, red and white, adorned with many more busts of famous men above window, arch, and doorway.

The house has long been noted for its fine works of art, though Horace Walpole described it as pomp and tatters. It is not so now, and privileged visitors may wholeheartedly admire its fine furniture and pictures. The entrance is still under the ancient elms by the door described in Walpole's letters. The dignified hall is paved with black and white marble, and is surrounded by a graceful gallery. Among the fine pictures by Hoppner, Kneller, and Reynolds is the Duke and Duchess of Lauderdale by Sir Peter Lely, and another portrait of the duke by Van Dyck.

The grand staircase has walnut balustrades curiously carved with military trophies and weapons, the posts capped with urns of carved

St Mary's Church   Abbot's Hospital

The Peaceful Quadrangle of Abbot's Hospital

OLD GUILDFORD

A Doorway in Abbot's Hospital    A Doorway in Quarry Street

In St Mary's Church    A Quaint Byway

CORNERS OF OLD GUILDFORD

SURREY

flowers. The doors to the rooms are also richly carved. The ceiling of the drawing-room is in elaborate plasterwork. The coved ceiling of the picture room is painted by Verrio, and there is a little panelled chapel in which is kept a prayer book in gold and silver filagree, a present to the Earl of Dysart from Charles Stuart. Another room is hung with tapestry made at Mortlake 400 years ago, and forming one end of the house is a gallery nearly 80 feet long, with many portraits by Peter Lely and Van Dyck.

Most historic of all is the room where the notorious Cabal Cabinet, named from the initials of its members (Clifford, Arlington, Buckingham, Ashley Cooper, and Lauderdale) met in Charles the Second's reign. Inlaid in the floor is the cypher of the Duchess of Lauderdale, an unusual piece of decoration.

The library is famous for its early printed books, the 14 Caxtons including a first edition of the Canterbury Tales. The dining-room has a picture of the first pineapple grown in England, and a treasure of the house is a lock of the hair of Elizabeth's Essex.

Treasures all may share are the memories of the great house built in 1610 by Sir Francis Vavasour, fellow judge of Francis Bacon. It passed to Lord Huntingtower, whose uncle had obtained for him the post of whipping-boy to Charles Stuart, a post which entitled him to the beatings which could not be inflicted on the sacred body of the king. Charles the Second took refuge here after the Battle of Worcester, and James the Second was ordered to retire here by William of Orange. Ten years before was born here the Good Duke of Argyll, who figures in the Heart of Midlothian and commanded a regiment of infantry before he was 17. Pope, who knew the house well, wrote of

> *Argyll, the State's whole thunder born to wield,*
> *And shake alike the Senate and the Field.*

Horace Walpole, who disliked the house for its drear decay, though he praised the pictures and the china, said it made him think himself a hundred miles off and a hundred years back. John Evelyn came here and praised the house and garden "by the sweetest river in the world." Leigh Hunt called it a nest of repose, and Thomas Hood wrote his long poem on The Elm Tree (81 verses) after sitting under one of these elms:

THE KING'S ENGLAND

Twas in a shady avenue,
  Where lofty elms abound,
And from a tree
There came to me
A sad and solemn sound.

The church on the common was built last century, and its chief interest is that it has the grave of Sir Richard Owen and a small brass which is of interest because it is engraved with part of the map of North Australia, in memory of an explorer who met his fate in the Northern Territory in 1874. He was Edward Borradaile, one of the early explorers of Australia, lost with his companion Pearmain. Mount Pearmain in Australia is named in memory of their exploration, and a small red cross on the brass map here marks the place where they disappeared. The chancel screen has linenfold panels, the white font is in memory of a parish clerk for 46 years, and the pulpit with its beautiful canopy is in memory of a vicar for 47 years.

Building Up an Extinct Giant

SIR RICHARD OWEN, who sleeps at Ham, was born at Lancaster, in 1804, son of a West Indies merchant. He hoped to become a naval surgeon, but the need of bread drove him to science, and science nearly starved him.

He worked for a pittance in a minor position at the Royal College of Surgeons, where he catalogued the incomparable collection of anatomical specimens which had lain neglected since the death of John Hunter, their donor. He married the curator's daughter, and succeeded her father at the college, where he became professor of comparative anatomy, and began a series of valuable monographs on animal life and structure, ranging from sponges to man. He probed the deepest mysteries of life-processes; he made the dead dry bones of extinct creation declare their wonders. One of his greatest triumphs was, on receiving from New Zealand a leg-bone supposed to be that of an ox, to reveal it as the bone of a great bird. He lived to piece together the entire skeleton of such a bird, being the first man to reconstruct the extinct giant moa.

Owen's scientific triumphs won him worldwide fame, with honours from innumerable learned bodies, but he remained miserably poor, and was saved from poverty-stricken old age only by a magnificent letter of Macaulay's, which gained for him the post of superintendent of the Natural History Museum. He revolutionised the museum, as he had revolutionised the Zoo, making each the finest institution of its kind then existing. Unable to accept the theory of Evolution, he primed Bishop Wilberforce for his attacks on Darwin, but with that exception his genius as an investigator and expounder was unerring, and his position in the science of zoology was unique.

A Yew of Magna Carta Days

HAMBLEDON. It is a village of narrow lanes and high hedges, of old red roofs and wide views into Sussex, with a little hillside church beside a house with a delightful garden.

The church was made new last century, and the only old parts now to be seen are the 14th century chancel arch and arches in the nave. There is a richly carved seat and some oak panelling in the sanctuary, and a sad little tablet to a nurse who "spent herself" at Haslemere tending the wounded men of the war.

The east window is in memory of the wife of one of the best journalists of our countryside, Mrs Eric Parker; it shows Our Lord with his mother and other children, St Peter and Sir Galahad, Francis with the birds, and St Dorothea with fruit and flowers.

In the churchyard are two great yews of which any place would be proud. One is a fine straight tree 18 feet round, the other is a mighty veteran of 30 feet. Twelve people could get inside it, and it may well have been growing when Magna Carta was sealed in a Surrey meadow.

The little windows of Hambledon church peep across at the tall windows of Charterhouse Chapel four miles away, with the Hog's Back beyond. Nearer at hand is a fine hill known as Hydon Ball, 92 acres of which were given to the nation in memory of that good friend of the people, Miss Octavia Hill, one of the founders of the National Trust, who lies at a great viewpoint across the Kent border. Hydon Ball rises almost 600 feet and has a spacious view all round.

Seeing the North and South Downs

HASCOMBE. Its chief beauty is in its setting among the thickly wooded hills, the highest of them Hascombe Hill, which rises 644 feet and is a fine viewpoint for the North and South Downs and the Hog's Back. On the top have been found the earthworks, arrowheads, and pottery of our Iron Age ancestors 2000 years ago, as well as the iron ore and slag, showing that they were smelting or refining iron in this very place.

On the ridge called Telegraph Hill there was a signal station in Napoleon's time communicating by a black and white shutter with Bexley Heath in Kent on one side and Blackdown in Sussex on the other.

Two quaint arches of trimmed yew lead into the well-kept churchyard. The little 19th century church is over-decorated, but has something old and good in its medieval screen, made from Jerusalem olive trees and carved with flowers and tracery. Most of its modern paint one would wish away, saving only the 12 attractively painted panels of men and women from the Bible. The square font was given by a rector in 1690.

One of the Hascombe inns has a charming sign of a white horse painted in 1926 by Gertrude Jekyll, who sleeps in Busbridge churchyard. She was 83, and this little picture was one of the last of her innumerable contributions to the beauty of England, which was to her as one glorious garden.

Memories of Tennyson

HASLEMERE. It is 500 feet up in the lovely country where Surrey meets Sussex, between Hindhead and Blackdown, with much of the old-fashioned world in its broad High Street, with two churches to see, with a quite exceptional museum, and with a reputation among music-lovers the world over. Coming to it along the Chiddingfold road we pass a charming group of cottages forming the old Toll House; built for almshouses in 1676 from the profits of the market tithes, they have porches supported on great wooden balusters.

In the High Street stands a fine chestnut planted when Napoleon was beginning his career, and all about this little town there are old houses and memories of famous people. Here lived Josiah Wood Whymper, the water-colour artist and wood-engraver whose son Edward became famous as a mountaineer; here lived the poet and novelist George Macdonald; here, in a cottage on Shottermill Common, George Eliot wrote most of her Middlemarch; and here, under a nameless mound by the gate of the new churchyard, sleeps

SURREY

John Tyndall, whose life was given to science and whose death was filled with deep pathos.

But the abiding memory here is of one who loved this place and made his home not far away in Sussex, one whose memorial window is the first thing to draw the traveller in this church. Tennyson, coming to Haslemere from Aldworth, must have known this rugged 17th century tower, and in this Burne-Jones window something of his immortal spirit is expressed. It shows Sir Galahad kneeling in the little chapel where the vision of the Holy Grail came to him, and in the glass there are these words:

*I Galahad saw the Grail, the Holy Grail descend upon the shrine,
And in the strength of this I rode, shattering all evil customs everywhere.*

Tennyson was fond of this Surrey countryside and his house is up a long climb towards Blackdown, really in Ludgershall, where we come upon the poet and from where began his last ride to Westminster Abbey.

The church has a handsome modern pulpit and tower screen, a little old chest and a big new one, a memorial to a naval captain honoured by George the Third for his brilliant services, and three attractive angel figures in memory of James Stewart Hodgson, head of Baring Brothers and a benefactor of this place; his mother danced with Robespierre. In two of the west windows there is glass painted probably by Swiss artists in the 16th century, in which we see a variety of quaint and vivid scenes—Matthew with an angel looking over his shoulder, Mark with a lion, Luke with an ox, John writing his book while an eagle holds the ink pot, the Nativity, and the conversion of St Paul. One little picture shows the birds and beasts and people going into Noah's ark, and another shows Adam and Eve with the serpent winding round a tree and with several animals including an Alice-in-Wonderland cat.

The modern church of St Christopher, by a pleasant green, has its own canopied saint to welcome us at the door, and an attractive window of the Nativity; but its chief possession is a finely painted reredos, a triptych showing Our Lord worshipped by men and women and children down the ages. Nearest to him are an unknown man and woman, both of them with a little child; and grouped in the side panels are many figures ancient and modern—St Martin with his cloak, St Francis with his little sisters the birds, Sir Thomas More in his Chancellor's robes, little Hugh of Lincoln whose story is told by Chaucer's Prioress, Florence Nightingale, John Keble, Sir James Paget, General Gordon, and the heroic Father Damien who gave his life for the lepers. It is all very charmingly done, painted by Mrs Dibdin-Spooner, as the medieval artists used to paint, in the medium known as tempera. In the little panels below are saints representing the Beatitudes, St Agnes in the centre because she was pure in heart.

In an old house in the High Street is the museum, a model of what such places should be, for any child can find his way about it. The story of rocks and fossils is made easy to understand, and so is the story of the rise of man; but the museum is chiefly remarkable for its almost unique collection of Peasant Art from northern countries, things useful and beautiful, made in humble homes without thought of reward. The pilgrim will want to spend hours in this fascinating place, and will perhaps remember more than anything else, as we did, the extraordinary collection of mangle-boards, of which it is said that custom bound every lad to carve one for his future bride. Many of them are striking and beautiful, and one from Denmark goes back to the years before the Spanish Armada.

The Discoverer of Our Lost Music

HASLEMERE has its own peasant industries, but it is known far and wide to music lovers through the labours of its grand old musician Arnold Dolmetsch.

Seeing the ancient musical instruments years ago in the British Museum, Arnold Dolmetsch was fired with enthusiasm to re-create them and play old music as our ancestors actually heard it. Like Bach's family 200 years ago, his family are all musicians too, and we found them in their little factory making viols and recorders and harpsichords. Those who come to the Haslemere Festival hear the music of Bach and Handel and the Elizabethans as it was heard in those days, the same kind of instruments and methods of performance; and Mr Dolmetsch was always fond of saying that his art is not a revival but a survival, for his ancestors were instrument makers back to the time of Beethoven.

The reviving of our fine old English music has been a difficult operation. Musicians knew there had been such instruments as viols, lutes, recorders, virginals, harpsichords, and clavichords, but how many had ever heard them played? There are very few of them still in existence, and to play music composed for these instruments on a modern piano is like playing a piece for full orchestra.

It is here that the craftsmanship of Mr Dolmetsch came to the rescue. He made exact copies of these instruments, so that now the music of our great musical Englishmen can be performed on the instruments for which it was written.

Would you like to hear a concert of viols such as was played to Drake and his sea captains as they dined on the Golden Hind? Would you like to listen to a tune on Queen Elizabeth's favourite virginals? Would you like to hear some of the best of our English instrumental music? All this Mr Dolmetsch made possible.

Michael Faraday's Successor

JOHN TYNDALL, who sleeps here, claimed descent from the family of William Tyndale. He was born in Ireland, the son of a small landowner, and worked his way up from the local grammar school to an engineering post on a Manchester railway, where he was paid a pound a week. He became a teacher of mathematics in Hampshire, and began to study chemistry, and on his scanty savings went to Marburg University and gained his degree as Doctor of Philosophy. Returning to England, he vainly sought appointments at colonial universities, but, being given an opportunity by his great hero Faraday, he won fame in a single lecture at the Royal Institution. Here he eventually succeeded Michael Faraday (whose place he also took on other bodies), and years of intense activity followed.

He solved the mystery of the movements of glaciers and conducted searches into the acoustic properties of air, the travelling of sound, the illumination of lighthouses, the radiant properties of heat, and many other subjects now part of common knowledge. He made the valuable discovery that decay cannot originate in air which is free from germs. He taught preservers of food the best method of preserving it. He not only had a brilliant intellect, but was a master of clear language, and his expounding of Darwin's theory of Evolution made a great impression on the British Association. He had no financial ambition, and the thousands of pounds he once made on a lecturing tour in America he gave for founding scholarships for students at Harvard and elsewhere.

He did not marry until he was 56, when he found the ideal partner of his joys and labours in a daughter of Lord Claud Hamilton. They built a home at Haslemere for their old age, and here they were living when his health broke down. As an old man of 70 he suffered much from insomnia, and in December 1893 his loving wife, by a terrible mischance, gave him a fatal dose of an opiate for his sleeplessness. The professor realised it too late, and a few of his last words are among the saddest ever spoken: "Darling, you have killed your John."

The Spire Above the Downs

HEADLEY. It is a place of stirring beauty, whether carpeted with the golden gorse of spring, or glorious with the mellow tints of autumn bracken. The long line of the North Downs stretches far away to Ranmore Common, the horizon softened with rounded clumps of trees. Towards Box Hill rises White Hill, now held in trust for the nation.

Fine beeches grow on the steep banks of the lane to the church, where on a clear day we may see the towers of Westminster and the dome of St Paul's. In the churchyard sleeps the first Lord Cunliffe, Governor of the Bank of England in the anxious years of the war. Close-clipped yews are growing where stood the 14th century church pulled down last century. Some of the old stones have been built into a vault where lies the father of Emily Faithful, who was born at the rectory here in 1835. She became Printer-in-Ordinary to Queen Victoria for her work in starting a press for women.

The shingled spire of the modern church is a landmark for miles, and in it rings a great bell made in Sussex 500 years ago. The damask altar cloth was woven in the 17th century by Mary Stydolf. In one of the windows is a lady of our own time with a beautifully tranquil face, holding a baby in her arms, while a little golden-haired girl clings to her side.

In the chancel stand two bronze soldiers with arms reversed, guarding the names of 11 men who never came home again.

Friend of the Village

HERSHAM. This growing place by the banks of the River Mole still keeps much that is green, though more people come to live beneath its sway each year. One of the earliest to know it was William Lilly the famous astrologer who, with a pension from Oliver Cromwell, settled in the village to pass his closing years. He was one of the forerunners of the quacks who tell our fortunes from the stars, but with more excuse than they.

The gracious church with its shingled spire is 19th century, its effective west window glowing with Bible figures. The churchyard is bright with colour, and by an avenue of clipped yews lies one whom Hersham will long remember, Frederick Loring Vaux, who died on Christmas Eve in 1933. For over 40 years he was churchwarden, and he gave the village the eight bells in the tower, as well as the church house, the boy's club, and the house for girls. This elderly bachelor rode about on an old tricycle till he was 90, seeing year by year with growing dismay the houses encroaching on the fields. His dying gift was an open space, a bequest literally keeping his memory green.

Panorama Over England

HINDHEAD. Far seen and far seeing, it is one of the finest and best known heights in Surrey, and one of the most unspoiled, over 1600 acres of its hillsides and commons belonging to the nation.

At the highest point we stand 900 feet above the sea, gazing over a magnificent panorama reaching into the haze in every direction, except where Blackdown looms up over the Sussex border. Most impressive, perhaps, is the view to the north and east, looking across a mighty sweep of Weald country to the long line of the North Downs, with Leith Hill rising up 16 miles away. All below us on this side is a marvellously rich sea of trees and bracken. On the other side we look down into the fine sweep of the Devil's Punchbowl, and southward across to the many lines of Sussex hills.

The flat summit of Hindhead is marked by a tall granite cross with four Latin mottoes, put here in 1851 by Lord Chief Justice Earle. Close by is a toposcope given by his brother, showing the places we see from here, and a little apart is another stone one would gladly forget. Far too long it has perpetuated something that seems to hold this lovely place in its grip, the memory of a sailor murdered here in the 18th century, and of the three murderers who hung in chains on this spot. The story is ugly, with no grain of romance, and we should like to see the stone taken down so that a sordid memory may sink into oblivion.

Almost over the hilltop runs the old Portsmouth Road of the coaching days, many feet higher than the present main road, and along it tramped Nicholas Nickleby and Smike in the days when people did not seem to appreciate the grandeur of a wild and lonely place. Dickens does not mention the beauty all around them, but only how Smike listened with greedy interest while Nicholas read on the stone about the murder; and it is no less surprising to find that William Cobbett, riding through Surrey, only a century ago, thought Hindhead "the most villainous spot God ever made." Surely he would have been amazed to see car after car slow down where he himself had only hurried on.

Along the Tilford road is the handsome modern church of St Alban. It has an attractive reredos delicately painted with the Crucifixion, a fine window of the Good Shepherd, and a huge square font carved with arches. On the peace memorial cross outside is the name of Colonel Philip Bent, who won the VC for saving a section of the line in the Great War during an intense hostile attack. Our troops were being forced back so heavy was the shell fire; but Colonel Bent led a brilliant counter attack, stopped the advance, and captured an important position. "Come on, Tigers!" he shouted to his men during another battle. They were his last words, for he was shot dead while leading the charge.

The Architect Builds and Gives a Church

HOLMBURY ST MARY. It lies in the beautiful hilly country near Leith Hill. On Holmbury Hill, 857 feet high, something can still be seen of the ramparts of a Stone Age camp. Here about 500 of our ancestors would live, pasturing their flocks, growing corn, hunting wild boar in the Wealden forest below, and making the pottery that we dig up after 20 centuries. The view from this hilltop rivals that from Leith Hill, embracing both the North Downs and the South Downs and a mighty expanse of the Weald.

Holmbury church is built of stone from the hill, and was designed and given to the village last century by George Edmund Street, remembered as the famous architect of the Law Courts in London. He was buried in Westminster Abbey two years after this church was consecrated, and there is a cross to his memory in the churchyard, where his second wife was laid to rest.

Three old art treasures adorn the church, two in the chancel. One is an altar cross made about 800 years ago at Limoges; another is a beautiful triptych of the Madonna and Child with saints and angels by a 14th century Italian artist; and the third is a sculpture in enamelled terracotta of the Madonna and Child by Luca della Robbia.

A Little Piece of the Roman Road

HOLMWOOD. Along the Dorking road it has two 19th century churches, and buried in the woods it has a thrilling sight for those who love a peep into the past.

St John's at North Holmwood stands boldly by the wayside, and has two stained windows rich in detail. They show four saints, Augustine, Hieronymus, Ambrose, and Gregory, with smaller scenes of the first Easter Day. At South Holmwood the church is strikingly set among trees and has caught a little austerity from the Early English builders. It has an attractive corner within, the font standing between panelled walls with a painting of the Descent from the Cross. There is a tablet to a young mother who had helped to build the church, Olympia Henderson, whose baby Olympia lived only two days after her. The carving is quaint, and shows an angel kneeling by the monument which marks her grave in Switzerland. Another tablet has an engraving of a bridge in memory of George Rennie whose father gave London its old Waterloo Bridge. The son helped to carry out his father's schemes, and had great mechanical skill of his own. He was in charge of the Grosvenor Bridge at Chester, and under him the firm made the first biscuit-making machinery and the first ship of the Navy to be propelled by a screw.

But it is at a point between these two churches that the visitor must turn aside to discover the great thrill here, a little piece of the Roman road which ran 58 miles from Chichester to London. It is the famous Stane Street, and its course hereabouts is roughly parallel to the present highroad. The part to be seen is in Redlands Wood, and so that none may miss this rare sight we give exact instructions for finding it.

A signpost near the Norfolk Arms points along a narrow byroad. Walk along this for about 100 yards and then bear left across a field, passing close to the left of two square grey houses. Walk on, under the electricity wires and over a stile, and then bear farther to the left along a rising path.

It is only a few minutes walk altogether, bringing us to a scene of peace and beauty in which we are surprised to come upon a notice with the words *Stane Street, Roman Road*. Here the Surrey Archaeological Society has brought to light and restored a hundred feet of the ancient Roman surface of Stane Street, with the original metalling of flint and sandstone. It is one of Surrey's finest historical monuments, going back to the very first years of Roman rule when this route was fashioned by Roman soldiers to serve as a highway of peace and commerce. Long stretches of Stane Street elsewhere are used by the busy motor road and have lost their character, but here, in an almost eerie stillness, the dawn of our history comes back to us in the beauties of nature herself.

The modern highway at Holmwood has its unusual sight too, a wayside tribute to one who was a familiar figure on this, his favourite road. He was that romantic and gallant gentleman Alfred Gwynne Vanderbilt, who perished in one of the most dastardly outrages of the Great War, the sinking of the Lusitania.

A son of the famous house of Vanderbilt, whose fortunes were founded with the rise of New York, he was a millionaire with many interests in banking and railways. He loved coaching, and pursued it in England with a lifelong enthusiasm. Along the Brighton road his coach was a daily sight, and he used to say that when he handled its ribbons for the first time in making the journey it was the proudest day of his life. He made innumerable friends in this country, and those who shared this pleasant form of sport with him erected this granite memorial to his memory. A moving story is told of the last hours of this kindly and generous sportsman on the sinking ship after it had been torpedoed off the Head of Kinsale in 1915. He organised search parties for children and got them into the boats, and just before the end, unable to swim a yard himself, he took off his lifebelt and gave it to an old woman. The story of his sacrifice, even in those days when a multitude of men were showing great courage in the face of danger, should never be forgotten. It is a striking example of the truth that no man can tell till his last hour has come what is the most important day in it.

The Australian Conqueror of the Atlantic

HOOK. It has nothing much to see, but it has something to remember, the memory of a man who did a thing that will never be forgotten.

He lies facing his home in the shadow of the 19th century church, which has a fine weeping willow near its walls, and two interesting pieces of timber inside. One is a table of oak and cedar neatly carved with vine leaves and inset with panels of olive, cut from a tree on the Mount of Olives, and inscribed:

> *Upon the tree that flourished where Thy footsteps trod,*
> *Thy sacrifice we here show forth, O Son of God.*

The second piece of timber is a priest's chair with a back panel carved after Holman Hunt's Light of the World, in memory of the rector through whose energy and devotion the church was built.

The man who went out from Hook to do an immortal thing was Harry Hawker. Young, with the life-blood of Australia surging in his veins, his heart aglow with hope, a confidence that never failed, a brain as clear as crystal because he neither drank nor smoked, he set out, first of all the Atlantic flying men, to cross the ocean. It is one of the first thrilling chapters in the history of flight.

Though he made his home at Hook he was not a native of our Motherland. He was a boy in Australia when the first airmen were taking their machines into the air. Thrilled by tales of the pioneers in Europe and America, he determined to go among the flying men, and he came to England while still a boy. He had a natural aptitude for mechanical things, and secured a position as mechanic with Mr Sopwith, who had an international reputation in flying. He taught the young Australian to fly, and in 1911 Hawker secured his pilot's certificate. Before long he was in the public eye as a record breaker and pilot of no ordinary skill. In 1913 he created British height and duration records, and in 1916 made a world record for height.

During the war Hawker was chief test pilot with the firm which supplied to the British forces more aeroplanes than any other. Hundreds of machines came straight from the workshops into his skilled hands, and he would take them into the air for the first time.

Such was his skill that he could usually detect faults at once. It was an occupation requiring a quick brain and steady hands, both of which Hawker had, for he was a lifelong teetotaller.

Hawker was no stranger to success, but the greatest exploit of his career was a glorious failure. With Commander Mackenzie Grieve as navigator, he set out from Newfoundland in May 1919 to make the first aeroplane crossing of the Atlantic. For several days nothing was heard of the bold adventurers, and they were given up for lost. Then a Danish tramp steamer passing by the Isle of Lewis signalled that it had Hawker and Grieve on board. They had flown about a thousand miles when a defect in a pipe brought them down at sea. Luckily they were seen after an hour and a half, and taken on board the little Danish tramp, but the tiny vessel had no wireless and the world knew nothing of the rescue for a week.

Hawker's safety thrilled the world after the anxiety about his fate, but he was unspoiled by his fame. He had other miraculous escapes and became known as Lucky Hawker, but it was sheer skill and a cool head that carried him through. In July 1931 he was testing a plane when he crashed. He had been taken seriously ill while flying, and the doctors said he should not have gone up, for he was a sick man when he went out; but that was like Hawker. He knew the machine was wanted and the idea of his own safety would not enter his mind.

So ended a brilliant career at 31. His name still lives in flying, for the Hawker Aircraft Company has grown out of the old Sopwith concern which taught him all he knew; it was named in Hawker's honour by his old friend and chief.

Old Yews and Tudor Inn

HORLEY. The Brighton road, the railway, and Gatwick racecourse have destroyed its peace and brought it much modern building; but there is still a little quiet by the church, where two grand yews have been keeping watch for hundreds of years, and the windows of a Tudor inn look into the churchyard.

The interest of the big church is in its north side. The timber tower and spire (both shingled), the broad aisle, and the unusually tall porch are all very good examples of early 14th century building. The doorway is finely moulded, but has had too much attention from scribblers in the last 300 years. There is a little original glass in the windows, including some odd faces.

Lying in the aisle is a 14th century knight in armour, with a lion at his feet and a two-headed eagle on his shield. Two figures are in brass in the chancel; a big 15th century lady on one wall is looking across at a 16th century man, about half her size, on the other. A sad little tablet of 1817 tells of the death of "Miss Louisa Adams, aged ten months and eleven days."

There is an attractive modern screen with six traceried panels and a frieze of vine carving, given by the friends and admirers of Henry Webber, who lived here for 40 years. Though he was 65 when the Great War began he joined up as an officer, and died in battle on the Somme in 1916.

Near Horley is the very old castle of Thunderfield, which is thought to be the Dunresfield mentioned in the will of King Alfred.

HORNE. A little village in the Weald, with a church much rebuilt last century, it has a 13th century doorway, a 15th century font carved with quatrefoils and angels, and the stairway that once led to the roodloft. The roof is held up by timbers 500 years old, and the oak of the carved organ case is said to have come from Reading Abbey. On the chancel wall John Goodwine kneels in black Tudor costume, facing his wife Margaret.

A Group of Memorials

HORSELL. Almost a part of Woking, its individuality is preserved in the church, the tower and some other parts being 14th century. Its interesting memorials seem to tell us more than usual of the occupations of the people whose name they bear.

One shows Sir John William Rose in a wig, standing by an urn with his wife. He was 14 years Recorder of London and died in 1803. Another shows James Fenn in his robes kneeling towards two other figures; he was a citizen and skinner, and rose to be Sheriff of London in 1787. A tablet tells of John Green, citizen and mercer, who died in 1651; and a most interesting brass shows us Thomas Edmonds of 1619, a "carpenter to the Chamber of London," who married the daughter of a London fishmonger. Here they are with their children, five boys and two girls, two of the boys carrying skulls to indicate their early death.

On the wall are several brasses of the Suttons, all of whom seem to have died in 1603; and under each, as if to show that there were litter louts even then, is the courteous request: Gentle Reader, deface not this stone.

We see John Sutton, who was a widower for 24 years out of 74; his son Thomas, who died at 38, a month or two later; and Fayth Sutton, who was only 24, attended by two men who make with her a charming little group of three from Shakespeare's time.

The Wonder Garden of the Empire

KEW. All the world comes to Kew. In lilac time or bluebell time or any other time it is a matchless place.

It is the Empire's garden and the Empire's botanical museum. Nowhere else can we see so many flowers or learn so much about them. There are about 25,000 species and varieties always growing, and in the vast collections of specimens the great Herbarium, gathered together with great stores of information during 150 years, there are about four million examples of plants and trees and flowers. It is a marvellous place into which we step through the great gates that face Kew Green.

And yet there is another Kew. As we stand at Kew Bridge, one of the finest of all the bridges built by the 20th century to span the Thames, the river flowing beneath it marks the parting of the ways between the old order and the new. On the Middlesex shore the view stretches past Brentford, the ancient county capital, to the foreshore called Old England, where Britons built their wattled huts on piles before the Romans came. On the Surrey shore, the river path to Richmond, beloved of poets, runs past Kew Green and Kew Gardens, where, when Dutch William had gone and Queen Anne was dead, the Georgian Era began.

It is marked for us as soon as we step on to Kew Green, for there are stately Georgian houses on both sides. Those nearest the towpath have fallen from their highest state, but those looking on the Gardens preserve a regal state and dignity. One is Cambridge Cottage, where the last of the royal tenants, the Duke of Cambridge, lived for many years and where Queen Mary spent much of her girlhood; it now houses a museum belonging to the Gardens, and has collections illustrating British forestry, and the uses to which British grown timber is put.

Haslemere   Bracken on the Hills

Hindhead   The Devil's Punch Bowl

Witley   Iron Almsbox 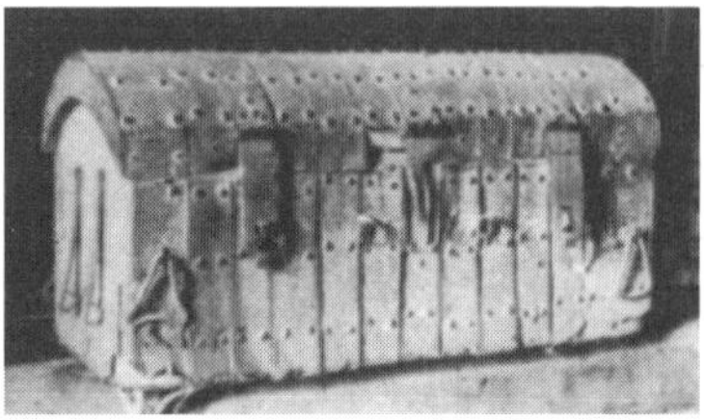   **Burstow**   Medieval Chest

Walton-on-the-Hill   Lead Font 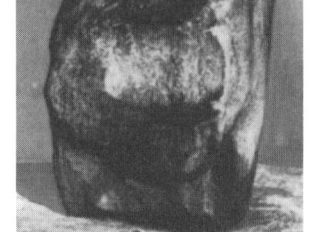   **Kingston**   Coronation Stone

Merton   Norman Door    **Pirbright**   Stanley's Tomb

SIX LITTLE SIGHTS OF SURREY

SURREY

Before we enter the rich domain of Kew Gardens we may pause at the old church on the Green, built in 1714. It is of red brick, pleasantly rather than magnificently designed, with a green copper dome at the east end and a copper-topped turret at the west. It has an interior that is light and boldly coloured. Five steps lead to a domed chancel with golden stars spangled over the blue, and in the apse of the sanctuary a golden sun gleams in the blue vault. Red marble pillars with gilded capitals support the dome of the choir, and the windows of the chancel glow with stained glass.

Two rows of round pillars support the coved ceiling of the nave. The west gallery is the old royal pew where George the Third and his queen sat. Their prayer-books are still kept in the vestry; their retiring-room has been made into a children's chapel. The organ was given by George the Fourth, who used to play on it, though it once had a greater organist than he, for it is said to have belonged to Handel himself.

With few exceptions the memorial tablets on the walls recall those whose names are linked with the Gardens. There is a tablet by Westmacott on the north wall to Francis Bauer, botanical painter to George the Third; his bust, said to be an excellent likeness, stands above carvings of his brushes and palette, with plants beside an inscription telling us of his 50 years of life here. Near it are busts of Sir William Hooker, first director of Kew Gardens, and his son Sir Joseph, giant of the Darwinian Era. There is another tablet to William Aiton, first gardener at the Royal Gardens, who is buried in the church. He compiled a famous catalogue of plants, and was so respected that at his funeral Sir Joseph Banks and Zoffany the painter, were pall-bearers. Zoffany, who lived on the other side of the river, at the charming little Strand-on-the-Green, offered an altarpiece to the church, which, however, rejected it, so that he gave it to Brentford. But when he died he was buried in this churchyard, all differences forgot, and here he lies not far from Gainsborough, with a tablet to his memory on the wall. Sir William Hooker and Jeremiah Meyer have also their memorial stones.

Jeremiah Meyer, who was a miniature painter, rests in the churchyard with Zoffany and Gainsborough and Gainsborough's friend Joshua Kirby, father of Sarah Trimmer, whose children's books won the admiration of Dr Johnson. Another man of small renown is buried not far away, John Dodd, the greatest of all the English makers of bows for violins and cellos in the 18th century. It is sad to say that he died a pauper at 87, in Richmond workhouse.

It is interesting to find lying here two immortals of the great days of English art, Gainsborough and Zoffany. Zoffany lived and died here, but they brought Gainsborough from the house we may still see in Pall Mall, where, as he lay dying, he remembered his estrangement from Sir Joshua Reynolds and sent for Reynolds to come to him. Sir Joshua came, and they parted after a pathetic scene, with the words on the dying man's lips: "We are all going to heaven, and Van Dyck is of the company."

Johann Zoffany was the son of a Bohemian Jew of Frankfort, but he was always regarded as an English painter. His father had risen from being a cabinet maker to the post of court architect. Young Zoffany, inspired with the same desire to rise, refused to mix colours in a studio and ran away to Vienna, going down the Danube on a timber raft with very little in his pocket. He made a living by copying pictures for 12 years. Then he went back home to find his father dead and no career waiting for the prodigal, so he packed his bag again and set out for England with a German wife and a fortune of £100. In London he bought a suit, a goldheaded cane, and a gold watch; but these did not help him much, and he came down to a Drury Lane garret.

At last fortune turned for him. An Italian told Rimbault, the great clockmaker, about him, and for this patron he painted some of the backgrounds on the faces of clocks that Rimbault made for Holland. Three of the clocks still exist; they struck the hour for Zoffany's success. From Rimbault he went on to do backgrounds for an artist in whose studio David Garrick found him. He painted portraits of Garrick and his wife and followed these with pictures of the actor in famous parts. These and many portraits of other actors mark one of Zoffany's chief contributions to painting and the story of life in the 18th century. The burly Bohemian painter with his strong foreign accent and boisterous humour now became popular and fashionable; his time was spent in painting the portrait groups of rich and titled families known today as Conversation Pieces.

We come into Kew Gardens through the beautiful iron gates which Decimus Burton, in the middle of the last century, hung on the tall stone pillars carved with festoons of flowers. If it is a summer's day we feel that it is a heavenly place, with all the glory of 288 acres of lawns and flowerbeds, woodlands and dells, tropical houses and little Greek temples and marvellous trees, spread out before us. We should give ourselves a day to wander round, for there is much to see and learn, and 15 miles of paths to walk along.

There are six gates by which we may come and go: the main gate on Kew Green, the Brentford and Isleworth ferry gates on the riverside, and Cumberland, Victoria, and Lion gates on the Kew side. There are four little museums in which those who study flowers may spend hours and days or weeks, and there are, scattered about the Gardens, small classical temples (the Temple of Aeolus, the Temple of Bellona, and King William's Temple), a remarkable gallery of hundreds of water colours of plants and flowers, a pagoda of ten storeys rising 163 feet high, and the Queen's Cottage among the bluebells. The classical temples belong to the 18th century when it was fashionable to adorn gardens with these things, and when their builder, Sir William Chambers, architect of Somerset House, saw nothing absurd in building a Ruined Arch which still stands there, one of the few shams in this great place.

There are two statues and two sundials which we should note. One of the statues is Hamo Thornycroft's Sower, presented by the Royal Academy; the other, on the Iris Lawn, is Mr A. G. Atkinson's Out in the Fields. One of the sundials was designed and given by Sir Charles Boys, FRS, and stands on a pilaster of old Kew Bridge, set in Cambridge Cottage Garden, full of old fashioned flowers; the other is a memorial of two important discoveries made in the Gardens long ago, and it stands on the spot where they were made. Here was Kew House, with a garden John Evelyn loved, where was an Observatory in which the Astronomer-Royal (James Bradley) in 1725 discovered the principles of the aberration of light and the mutation of the earth's axis. The house has gone and the sundial marks the place where this scientific history was made.

Kew as we know it has grown out of the old gardens of Kew House and Richmond Lodge, a house which once stood in the Old Deer Park. As long ago as Henry the Eighth there lived here William Turner, known as the Father of English Botany, and there is still something to be seen on the riverbank of an elm known to Queen

Elizabeth, who lived close by as a child. Elizabeth's favourite, Robert Dudley, was here when he received the news that stains a page of English history, the death of his wife Amy Robsart at Cumnor.

But it was in more modern times that the Gardens began to take their shape; it was the mother of George the Third who converted Kew into a botanical garden, and when she died, and Kew came under the control of George the Third, the Gardens entered on a new and supremely important phase. Sir Joseph Banks was appointed director, and it was under him that Kew became the repository of collections of every kind of plant known to men. It was George the Third who built what is called Kew Palace, which we see on our right as we enter from Kew Green.

The palace rests its attractions on its history; it is not in any way a palace, but is almost all that now remains of the buildings in which George the Third and his Queen Charlotte spent so much of their time with their children. Here Queen Charlotte died, and the place remained forlorn and neglected during most of the Victorian Era, but was restored at its close. It is a red brick Jacobean building, and its most pathetic memories are of the days when the mind of George the Third would break down. Thackeray has left us the picture in language that is not to be forgotten, the picture of the old king in a purple gown, his snowy white beard flowing over his breast, the star of a famous Order still shining on it:

He was not only sightless; he became utterly deaf. All light, all reason, all sound of human voices, all the pleasures of this world of God, were taken from him. Some light lucid moments he had, in one of which the queen, desiring to see him, entered the room and found him singing a hymn and accompanying himself at the harpsichord. When he had finished he knelt down and prayed aloud for her, and then for his family, and then for the nation, concluding with a prayer for himself that it might please God to avert his heavy calamity from him; but, if not, to give him resignation to submit. He then burst into tears, and his reason again fled.

We may all visit this three-storeyed gabled house of which the original walls still stand, though the windows are 18th century. Some of the linenfold panelling is Elizabethan. We may see King George's library, his dining room and breakfast room, the Georgian staircase probably built by the royal architect Kent, the bedroom in which Queen Charlotte died and her boudoir, and the actual bedroom (plainly decorated and rather commonplace) occupied by the king during his insanity. There are hundreds of exhibits, frames of small medallions, charts, drawings, and pictures. There are six framed Indian figures made of embroidered silks, a woolworked picture of a bunch of grapes, pieces of old English needlework, painting on stone, letters and drawings, portrait prints, a collection of Queen Charlotte's poems, with pictures by George Stubbs, David Wilkie, and Bogdani.

Perhaps more interesting as a collection is what is known as the North Gallery, in which one room has a collection of Sir Arthur Church's water-colours of plants, and another room has the remarkable series of drawings which give their name to the Gallery.

Here is one of the most remarkable collections of botanical pictures to be found in the world, 848 of them painted by Marianne North, who travelled to all parts of the world to complete the collection. She was born at Hastings in 1830, daughter of the MP for the town, and she very early developed her natural gifts for music and painting. It was her painting that was to make her famous, and after her father's death in 1869 she gave her life to this collection. She visited every continent. She went to North America and the West Indies, to Japan and Borneo and Java, to Singapore, Ceylon, and India, to Australia, Tasmania, and New Zealand, and to South Africa. Once in South Africa she was warned that there was a leopard about, but she went on searching and painting, saying: "One can but die once; anyhow, it does not much matter to me."

Having completed her collection she presented it to Kew in 1882, and gave with it the gallery in which it is housed. The paintings are closely packed on the walls from dado to cornice, all grouped under countries so that we may easily identify any plant or flower. Together they make up the most vivid impression of the colour and beauty of tropical vegetation that anyone could behold, and in the midst of them is a white marble bust of Miss North, to whose courage and industry the nation is so greatly indebted. The pictures are all painted in oil on cardboard, and they have now been backed with a continuous sheet of plywood, completely filling the frame, so as to prevent the air reaching them. Miss North was not only a fine colourist but a decorative artist and a sound technician, for no degeneration has been noticed in any of her pictures after more than half a century.

THE KING'S ENGLAND

Not far away from the North Gallery stands the great flagstaff of Kew. It is the biggest flagstaff in England and the proudest, for it was one of the noblest trees that ever grew in a forest. It is the gift of British Columbia to the mother country. The foresters of British Columbia scoured the country for the noblest tree they could find, and the distinction fell upon a magnificent Douglas fir, 214 feet high and 6 feet thick at the end, tapering down to 18 inches inside the bark at the top. Not the slightest warp mars the straightness of this giant. It is not every ship that can carry a tree like this, and there was much ado when it was proposed to the shipping companies that they should bring the mast to London. One company offered to bring it if they might bend the mast to the shape of the deck, so that it could lie cosily against the bulwarks without rolling, but the woodsmen indignantly rejected the proposal, and at last the mast was put on board the Merionethshire, of the Royal Mail Steam Packet Company, which picked up the unwieldly burden at Vancouver and brought it safe to London docks.

Not an ounce of its virgin strength, not an inch of its straightness was lost when the great tree fell with a mighty splash into Father Thames; it was towed up the river and at last arrived at the end of the Sion Vista, and there it lay, waiting to be set up on its new base as it had stood in its forests so far away, 18 tons of timber standing higher than the monument, and half as high again as Nelson's Column in Trafalgar Square. The sum of £1500 was set aside as the cost of setting it up, and as a beginning a tower of scaffolding 100 feet high was built, strong enough to hold the machinery for hauling the monster slowly upright. Twice while the tree was rising there was a thrilling risk that the lofty staging might crash and the great mast might snap. Once, just before the base of the tree slid into its socket, one of the blocks that helped to control it began to slip and there was a fierce struggle for safety between the engineers and the unfaithful block; and again as the last heave was about to be made, one of the great stays slackened and it seemed as though the end must be disaster. But all was put right, and then, majestically and steadily, the huge mast came to rest, plumb and true, and began its survey of the Empire's Garden.

The four museums of Kew are for botanical students, and are, of course, part of the great educational work of the Gardens. Two of them deal with various kinds of plants, and two with British forestry and Empire and foreign timbers. Here we may see almost any kind of timber we wish to see, and there are some odd exhibits, such as the hollowed trunk of an elm used as a water pipe in medieval London, and a Zulu piano made from resonant woods with gourds to increase the sound, an anticipation of the Loud-Speaker Age. One of these museums was originally the Orangery, built to grow oranges in tubs, and in one of the others is a remarkable copy of a Japanese gateway and a model of the mausoleum of a Shogun of Japan. It is one of the national works of the Far Eastern Empire, and this copy of it was set up by three Japanese craftsmen.

There is a lake which is filled from the Thames at high tide, a lovely lily pond made from an old gravel pit, a bamboo garden, an arboretum with four or five thousand species and varieties; an aquatic garden with hardy water-lilies, marsh marigolds, and swamp irises; one of the best bits of natural woodland near London, with 80 kinds of birds in it (near the Queen's Cottage); a herb garden with 7000 species of herbs, a rock garden made of limestone from the Mendips and boulders from the Yorkshire moors and sandstone from Sussex; an Alpine house; an azalea house; a rhododendron dell laid out by George the Third, and 19th century glasshouses, four of them filled with 1800 orchids.

Kew, we see, is more than a beautiful garden: it is a living university where all who would learn may do so. It is the Empire's vegetable garden, where everything growing wild in the Empire, between the Arctic and Antarctic Circles, comes to be tried and tested. Its great glasshouses grow palms and tree ferns native to India or the East Indies, and the plants of the desert or the frozen lands. Kew is the world's clearing-house of plants, especially the economic plants for food or industry. Here men study the way to grow these plants, what strains are strongest, where they will grow best, how they can resist disease. Kew is the Hospital as well as the Nursery.

A story more fascinating and immensely more important than that of its royal patrons is the story of the work Kew has done in the world. It has introduced breadfruit and quinine to the Empire. It has had a romantic share in the development of the rubber industry. It has cheapened the production of tea and developed the cultivation of cocoa and cloves, limes and bananas, camphor and sisal-hemp, all captivating chapters of science, and behind all this are immense collections numbering about four millions in the great Herbarium.

Perhaps we may look at the story of what Kew has done for rubber. It begins with the story of Sir Joseph Hooker, who followed his father here as Director of the Gardens. He was one of the great botanist-adventurers of the world. At 22 he sailed with an expedition in the Erebus and Terror to the Antarctic. In Tasmania they met Sir John Franklin, who was destined to sail with these two ships to his death. He noted the high ability of the young botanist. With their ships locked in the ice 50 yards apart, the explorers made a great ballroom on the surface for Christmas festivities in 1842, and Hooker fashioned a mighty statue of Venus from the ice. After great discoveries and escaping from many perils he returned home to write a classical account of land and sea in the great south, and 50 years later, the last survivor of those who had known Franklin, he helped to start the new era of Antarctic exploration, which ultimately sent Captain Scott to the South Pole. Seeking not gold or diamonds but plants, Hooker spent three years exploring the Himalayas, afterwards botanising in Morocco and America, before settling down for 27 years in Kew Gardens in succession to his father. He wrote many famous works and was an unfailing source of information to Charles Darwin. He lived on until 1911 and died at 94, one of the first men to receive the Order of Merit.

It was Sir Joseph Hooker who started the wonderful tale of rubber, by sending out an assistant to South America to bring back seeds of Para rubber. The man who found it was Henry Wickham, with whom was Mr Cross, the man who introduced the quinine plant into India. Few people know the value of the work of these two men.

The great difficulty was to transplant the seeds of the wild Para rubber tree from South America to Europe, for the seed loses its vitality in seven weeks, and this experiment was being tried as far back as 1873, before the coming of the Speed Age. Wickham, ascending the Tapajos River, collected 70,000 of these seeds, but he was far from the coast and knew too well the difficulties of getting them to Kew in time to germinate there. He worked his way down the river as fast as he could, haunted by the fear that he would not find a ship when he got to the coast, and that every seed would be dead before he got afloat. But luck was with him. He found a British

Kew   Daffodil Time in the Gardens

Avenue Leading to the Pagoda

A Springtime Idyll
IN THE WONDERFUL GARDENS OF KEW

The Iris Garden

Bluebell Time
KEW IN ALL ITS GLORY

The Beautiful Iron Gates by Decimus Burton

Victoria Regia Lilies

THE SPLENDOUR OF KEW GARDENS

tramp steamer waiting for a cargo, and he offered it his three boxes of seeds with a promise that the British Government would pay.

It was a stroke of good fortune that the shipmaster believed him; but even then Wickham's troubles were not over, for he did not find it easy to pass the Customs. Happily, he arrived safely in England, reached London, and took a hansom cab to Kew. Sir Joseph Hooker was delighted. He cleared all the greenhouses and put on all his staff to plant the seeds. They were just in time, and in a fortnight 1700 tiny rubber plants were showing their heads above the soil, the first ever grown in the Old World. As they grew up they were packed in miniature hothouses and shipped out to Ceylon and Malaya, where they were at first received with the doubts so often manifested by practical men for new ideas; but today they have grown into vast plantations, and have given the world one of its most valuable possessions. In those days the annual output of rubber was one or two thousand tons, today it is about a million tons, and the amount produced as the direct result of these three boxes of seeds is 450,000 tons in Malaya and 250,000 tons in the Dutch East Indies. The novelist's Mystery of a Hansom Cab is nothing compared with the romance of Sir Henry Wickham's hansom.

Such is the work that goes on continually at Kew, where they will tell us anything we want to know about any plant we send them. There is no collection on earth to equal the living collection here, or the collection of specimens preserved. There are some of the oldest living exotic trees from foreign lands, among them a magnificent Ginkgo, one of the most ancient trees known to botanists; it is familiarly called the maidenhair tree, and has been at Kew since the middle of the 18th century. Within sight of it are the tropical and temperate fern houses, which together present to us all the ferns of the world, and another house in which flourish plants of the deserts and hot regions of the world. This house has a companion (named the Sherman Hoyt House, after its donor) where the cactus and plants native to the Mohave Desert of California are scenically arranged. Somewhere in the Gardens is still growing a descendant of Shakespeare's mulberry tree, the tree hacked down in his garden at Stratford by the ill-tempered Parson Gastrell, who hated the people who peeped over his wall to see the tree Shakespeare planted, and so pulled it down and sold it as firewood. Most of us may prefer the wonderful Out-of-Doors at Kew, but there are those to whom Kew Indoors is little short of miraculous. Children love the Victoria Regia House, especially when the leaves of the giant water-lily of the Amazon, one of the vegetable wonders of the world, are floating in their tank. They are sometimes seven feet wide and a child may sit on them. We may see the remarkable pitcher plant, the plants that eat insects, and a host of other remarkable kinds. We may see an unequalled assemblage of Australian and New Zealand plants and trees in the connected buildings called the Winter Garden, which has a splendour of vegetation from the Antipodes unrivalled in any plant house in the world. We may see in the towering Palm House built by Decimus Burton giant bamboos, screw pines, and all the food plants of the Tropics. It is like an ordered tropical forest, and it is a remarkable contrast to come out of this great house and find radiating from its steps three broad grass avenues with splendid vistas. The one on the right is closed by the finest Cedar of Lebanon in the Garden; the middle one (called the Sion Vista) carries the eye beyond the Gardens and the Thames to the woods at Sion House at Isleworth; the one on the left carries the eye to the picturesque Pagoda, a rather incongruous structure painted red and blue, but a familiar landmark that Kew would be sorry to lose. Perhaps we may remember that William Cobbett was a gardener here in his youth, and that he never forgot, as he was sweeping up the leaves on the grass near the Pagoda, that the King passed by and laughed at his queer dress.

We do not laugh at Kew today. Rather we stand spellbound in this garden unmatched in the world. Solomon in all his glory was not arrayed like this. It is the chief garden of the chief country of gardens, and we could wish our kinemas could pour their crowds out on a summer's day and send them here to see a glory compared with which theirs is often but fading trash.

The Ancient Town of Kings

KINGSTON-ON-THAMES. The very thought of it must stir all Englishmen, for if we run back through the thousand years of our great Island Story it is at Kingston by the Thames that we find one of the oldest visible monuments of English power. Here in the wind and the rain, with Old Father Thames running by, is the old

Farnham
Sibil Jay and her children

Guildford
Maurice Abbot and his family

Oakwood
De La Hale

Ockham
John and Margaret Weston

Oxted
John Hoskins

Shere
Robert Scarclyf

Mickleham
William and Joan Wyddowson

Stoke D'Abernon
Anne Norbury

OLD SURREY FOLK ENGRAVED ON BRASSES

throne of England, one of two great stones that must forever be counted among the most precious possessions of our race.

The Stone of Scone on which our kings are crowned today is sheltered in Westminster Abbey near the Confessor's tomb, but the Kingston Stone is in the street, within the sound of ever-tramping feet, as if this oldest symbol of English power should say that the People and the Throne are one.

The kingly story of Kingston goes back to Egbert, who held a Great Council here in 838; the story of this old stone (the stone that named the town, King Stone) goes back to 901, when King Alfred's son was the first of a line of Saxon kings to be crowned on it. Edward the Elder, Athelstan, Edmund, Edred, Edwy, Edward the Martyr, and Ethelred, are all believed to have sat on this stone for their crowning, and set in the base of the stone are coins of seven of these kings. Great kings they were, carrying on the work of Alfred and driving the Danes back to their ships. There was Athelstan, crowned in 925, who won back Northumbria by his victory at Brunanburh; Edmund the Magnificent, crowned in 940, who conquered Cumberland and gave it to Malcolm, King of Scotland; Edgar the Peaceful, crowned in 958, who at length won a respite from warfare and with his famous Archbishop Dunstan revived religion and learning; Edward the Martyr, who was slain by the Danes under an oak at Hoxne; Ethelred the Unready, who tried in vain to buy new invaders off; and, perhaps last of all crowned here, Edmund Ironside, crowned in 1016, of sterner stuff, and only just failing to drive Canute from our shores.

Rising proudly in sight of this 10th century stone is the 20th century Guildhall, one of the noblest civic buildings set up by any English town. Its two wings sweep round in a triumphant circle to meet at an impressive square tower. Indoors and out it is a place of beauty, with a suggestion of compactness and efficiency and with something about it that touches the imagination. It is built of russet brick faced with Portland stone, and the red tiles of its roof converge on the tower which rises 122 feet above the pavement. The great doorway in white stone is in the centre of the tower, and above it four prancing horses, one pair on each side, hold up a lofty balcony, fronted at the corners by magnificent stone columns. Above the balcony are the Kingston arms, three silver fishes on a blue back-

SURREY

ground. The iron gates are painted blue and have silver carvings. Crowning the tower is a golden weathervane, a fine spectacle in keeping with the traditions of the town by the Thames, for it takes the shape of a river barge, with a bargee and his dog on board.

The great windows give a feeling of lightness to the interior, a feeling which is helped by the internal decorations which are mainly in the official colours of Kingston, silver and blue. The iron balustrades of the stairs are blue and have an aluminium bronze rail, and on them are the emblems of seven kings crowned on the stone outside. The council chamber is of light oak and has a jarrah floor from Australia, and there is an ingenious arrangement by which three of the committee rooms can be made into one, the partition walls disappearing into the floor. In the mayor's parlour hangs a portrait of Queen Anne for which Sir Godfrey Kneller was paid £2000. The architect of this fine place is Mr Maurice Webb, son of one of the great architects of the last generation.

From this civic centre of Kingston with its historic stone we may pass to gaze on stones that are much older still than this ancient throne of kings. It is not to be denied that the most historic spot in this old town is the site of the Saxon Church of St Mary by which the Norman church of All Saints now stands. The older building has now only its foundations for us to see, the stones of that Saxon church in which Alfred's son and six of his successors were crowned on the Great Stone.

Kingston welcomed the Coronation year of George the Sixth in a noble way, by marking out the site of the Saxon church so that all who pass by may see it. A tablet of bronze has been placed at each corner of the ancient shrine, let into the actual stones used by the Saxon builders, each forming a base 30 inches wide, the actual thickness of the original walls. From the position of the tablets we see that the church was 60 feet long and 25 wide, and there is still a fragment of the east wall in its original position, but when Edmund Ironside's brother built the Abbey at Westminster the church of St Mary lost its great pride of place. The old church was here, however, when the Normans came, and in the year 1130 the Normans laid the foundations of All Saints Church just outside its north wall, and joined the old church to its new neighbour as a lady chapel. So they stood together, the Norman church with the Saxon chapel, until

1729, when a pitiful thing happened. Sexton Hammerton was digging a grave, and his daughter Hester was helping him, when the Saxon chapel fell suddenly, killing the sexton and another gravedigger. Happily the daughter was protected by a pillar falling across the grave and saving her from harm; the pillar which saved her is now inside the church, and on it has been set a small stone engraved with a pattern, and appearing to be part of a Saxon cross.

There are few churches with a more interesting story, or with more interesting stones than these surrounding All Saints, but the church has received new interest from succeeding centuries. The central tower is 14th century, topped by 18th century bricks, but it enshrines, intact within it, the chalk tower of the Normans (probably one of the oldest chalk structures in this country); the interior of the church has traces of all our great building centuries. The 15th century chapel has stone corbels of angels, and there are 15th century roofs on the chancel, chapels, and transepts. One of the pews was made from a 15th century screen and there is still, swinging on its medieval hinges, the old oak door from the chancel to the vestry, opened by the lock made by an ironsmith 500 years ago. We come into the church by a door near which are two works of art separated by five centuries, a 14th century painting of St Blaise and a Chantrey sculpture of the wife of Lord Liverpool. The old painting of the patron saint of woollen drapers is on a column, and shows the saint wearing a green robe and carrying a staff and a comb. On a remarkable tomb in the south chapel lies Sir Anthony Benn, Recorder in the reign of George the First; he lies in his red robe and white ruff.

Near him is the record of a bitter tragedy, for here were buried, in the time of the Commonwealth, the ten children of the vicar, Edward Staunton. There is a stone to a Court physician who was one of the first Fellows of the Royal Society; he was George Bate who, after attending Charles Stuart, became physician to Oliver Cromwell, and after the Restoration was Royalist again. He made notable contributions to medicine by his studies of rickets. It is recorded also in the chancel that here lies Mrs Mary Morton, who died 300 years ago, after living long enough to see nearly 400 descendants. There are two sets of brasses in the church, one showing Robert Skerne, Keeper of the Old Deer Park; he is with his wife, who was the youngest daughter of Alice Perrers, the favourite of Edward the

SURREY

Third. It is a magnificent brass, on which the robes of the Keeper have wide sleeves and a fur-trimmed collar, his wife wearing a horned headdress, veil, and mantle. There are tiny brass figures of John Hertcombe and his wife on a pillar in the tower, but John has lost his head, though his wife keeps her 15th century butterfly headdress.

The modern pulpit of this old church is a piece of fine craftsmanship in oak. In a transept hangs an old lantern which once lit the belfry, and standing in an aisle is an old font, its duty done, and a clock of 1827, no longer telling the time; we may say that only by its works do we know it.

Divided from the chancel by an oak screen is the peace memorial chapel with two panels interesting for having above them copies of the Victoria Cross, in memory of two heroes who won it in the Great War. They were Corporal Dwyer and Private McNamara.

Edward Dwyer joined the army as a boy of 16 and is said to have been the youngest soldier who ever won the VC; he received it from the hands of King George in 1915, and was killed at Guillemont a year after. In the Retreat from Mons his battalion of the 1st East Surreys were terribly hard pressed, and Dwyer, who early in the day had gone out into the open to bandage the wounded under heavy shell fire, found himself alone in his trench. He could hear the Germans talking 20 yards away, and knew that if they took his trench his comrades behind it would be at their mercy. He climbed on to the parapet and began throwing hand grenades, and a shower of bombs came back to him. But he managed to keep the enemy at bay till reinforcements arrived, and the trench was saved.

John McNamara was a Kingston boy. He was working a telephone in enemy trenches which his battalion had occupied, when he realised that a counter-attack was gaining ground. He seized a gun and fired it till it jammed, and, being then alone, he destroyed his telephone, joined the post near him, and maintained gunfire till reinforcements came, so helping other posts to hold on.

The throbbing hub of this busy shopping town is the marketplace across the road from the Guildhall, and in it stands the century-old town hall, guarded by a gilded statue of Queen Anne cast in lead in 1706. She is the first of the royal company gathered in the marketplace of this town of kings, for on the front of a shop close by are statues of Queen Elizabeth and five kings, Edward the Elder,

Athelstan, Henry the Third, Edward the Third, and John. A neighbouring shop has a fine Elizabethan staircase, its panels carved with vines, grapes, and the infant Bacchus; it was brought from an old coaching inn which is now no more, though near its site still stands the 600-year-old post house, a gabled building now turned into shops. Farther down the road is the old Tudor Malt House, still with its louvre-covered chimney, though it is now a shop. The biggest building in Kingston, with dignified white walls crowned by a clock tower, is the County Hall, where the Surrey Assizes are opened with much pomp and pageantry.

Kingston's peace memorial is in a quiet little Garden of Rest amid the busy streets, with a figure of a child looking up at a man holding a flaming torch of freedom. There is a stone cross in the cemetery to the soldiers who died in hospital during the war. Among those sleeping here are Thomas Hansard, editor of the Parliamentary Debates, which bear his name, and Arthur Cowper Ranyard, a diligent worker in the cause of science who was for many years secretary of the Royal Astronomical Society. There is a stone angel on a tall pillar over his grave.

Among Kingston's group of old buildings is Cleaves Almshouse, a mellow brick building with the sundial over the central gable dated 1668. Not far from it is St Peter's Church, designed by Sir Gilbert Scott, and there is an inscription on a block of flats across the way recording that George Evelyn, the diarist's brother, lived here. A 14th century clustered column standing outside the museum is from a royal palace which has been entirely swept away, being less fortunate than Lovekyn's Chapel, standing by the London road. This interesting little building, with turrets at the corners and a carved head of Edward the Third on one of the brackets of the east window, is the only separate chantry chapel in England to survive the Reformation. It was built in the middle of the 14th century by John Lovekyn, four times Lord Mayor of London, and Queen Elizabeth turned it into a grammar school, where Gibbon the historian was one of the scholars.

The museum, a building lit by gay heraldic windows, has one window of 17th century glass with eight coats-of-arms in it; another showing the fanciful arms of the Saxon kings crowned on Kingston Stone, and another copied from a famous window at Cleobury Mortimer, Shropshire, which survived the Reformation. This

The Modern Guildhall

The Old Marketplace
KINGSTON, ANCIENT TOWN OF KINGS

Leatherhead   The Old Church above the Valley

Leatherhead   The 18th Century Bridge across the Mole

window serves to illustrate the May Games, so popular in Kingston long ago, and is gay with figures of the Fool, the Moor, the Spaniard, the Minstrel, the Peasant, the Franklin with his curly hair, the King of May on a hobbyhorse, the Lover with a flower in his hair, the Discard wearing a child's bib, the Friar in sombre brown dress, and the Queen of May in a golden crown. The museum has some remarkable fish caught in the Thames, and a collection of prehistoric stone tools and weapons found in the river, with Roman remains discovered in the town. There is a good collection of birds from the Thames Valley, another of the domestic antiquities of Surrey, and many pleasant pictures of bygone Kingston. But by far the most interesting museum exhibit in Kingston is the original kinema apparatus used by Eadweard Muybridge, the Kingston man to whom the kinema owes so much. The exhibit is like a huge magic lantern, with pictures set on revolving discs, and Muybridge used it to illustrate his lectures on animal locomotion.

Through all its long years Kingston has been a famous town. As long ago as 838 it was a royal town, clustering below the point where the little Hogsmill River joins the Thames. Today the Norman Clattern Bridge still helps to carry the Portsmouth Road across the Hogsmill, but Kingston has long had a noble bridge across the Thames; it had for centuries the first Thames bridge above London. The one here now was opened by Queen Adelaide and is handsome with its graceful arches and balustrades. Timber barges cluster thickly round it, and above and below it stretches long lengths of delightful public gardens where anglers fish the stream.

Eadweard Muybridge and His Moving Horses

EADWEARD MUYBRIDGE, as he chose to be known, was the son of a Kingston corn chandler, John Muggeridge. He was a photographer of genius, who long before the Kinema Age presented to the world a new idea of animals in motion. He was the first man to find a means of showing moving pictures.

His discoveries and inventions were both made in America, where, when still a young man, his ability as a photographer made him director of the photographic surveys of the United States. While holding this position he was able to settle a dispute between two American millionaires on the position of the four feet of a horse as it gallops. To do this he took a series of photographs of a horse as it moved past a row of cameras. There were no films then, and he had to use wet plates, but he obtained his instantaneous photographs from his cameras, placed in a line, by employing electric circuits and a clock for making and breaking the current.

This was the foundation of the method, still used, for instantaneous photographs, but Muybridge's experiments led to two other important developments. They revolutionised the artistic conception of animals in motion and led to a much more natural reproduction of all animals in painting and sculpture. This was what made Muybridge famous and led to invitations to show his photographs throughout Europe and the British Isles. He showed them at the Royal Institution before an audience including the Prince of Wales of that day.

The second outcome of his photographs arose from the invention he devised to impart an appearance of motion. The first part of it was an optical toy which he called the zoopraxiscope, a Wheel of Life which in its simplest form was like a tambourine with a succession of instantaneous photographs pasted along its inner edge. When the wheel was rapidly revolved anyone looking at the moving photographs through a hole permitting only one to be seen at a time received the impression that the figures were moving. To this apparatus he attached a form of magic lantern which projected these moving images on to a screen. The illusion of movement was thus obtained, as it is now in another form with Mickey Mouse.

Muybridge returned to his native Kingston and died there in 1904, bequeathing to the town's museum all his scientific instruments, including the zoopraxiscope, which he particularly requested should never be moved from here.

John Wesley and Judge Jeffreys

LEATHERHEAD. Most of us know its busy crossways and the High Street sloping down to the River Mole, here crossed by a long 18th century bridge.

Many of us know the old cedar in front of the dignified council offices on Bull Hill, under which John Wesley preached his last sermon a few days before he died. He was 88, and after preaching in Kingston House he came out to address the people waiting there.

SURREY

Kingston House has gone, but it is pictured on a memorial tablet outside the new building.

Less pleasant is the memory of an 18th century house behind a wall in Church Street, for it marks the site where lived Sir Thomas Bludworth, whose sister was the second wife of the brutal Judge Jeffreys. The story is told that the miserable judge, fleeing to avoid capture after the Revolution of 1688, came here disguised as a soldier to see his dying daughter. He hid in a vault under one of the cellars, but was betrayed by his butler. The daughter's death comes into the records of the church.

The massive tower of Leatherhead Church has been looking over the valley of the Mole for 500 years, and now looks down on a delightful public garden with attractive yew tunnels, near the church. Parts of the church are older than the tower. The nave arcades and chancel arch are 12th century, and the narrow chancel was built with the transepts in the 14th. Rather unusual are the dormer windows in the red-tiled roof, modern copies of the 15th century ones.

The chancel has a few signs still left of one of the medieval anchorite's cells we sometimes find in our churches. Blocked up in a wall is a square opening with a doorway, and just below the ground are the foundations of a room eight feet square. In this tiny cell the hermit spent his days, looking at the altar and receiving his food through the square opening, and passing through the door into the chancel only to tend the light or to take Communion.

One of the oldest treasures of the church is a long 13th century chest, and there is another chest covered with leather, a beautiful sanctuary chair carved with cherubs and foliage, and a Book of Homilies chained to a pillar. In the vestry is an old keyboard on which Handel is said to have played; it belonged to an organ built by the famous John Snetzler, who came over from Germany and built for Handel the organ used at the historic first performance of the Messiah in Dublin.

The big font is 500 years old and has eight panelled sides decorated with roses in quatrefoils. It may have been used to baptise the children whose portraits we see in brass in one of the aisles, six tiny figures with one of their parents, who died about the time Caxton was printing the first English books. A memorial to Robert Gardiner has his helmet hanging high above a long inscription composed by the Court Poet; Gardiner was Chief-Sergeant-of-the-Cellar to Queen Elizabeth, and the lines of Thomas Churchyard tell us that:

Four children for to furnish forth the table round he had,
With sober wife most matronlike, to make a man full glad.

There is tragedy and pathos on these walls too. One memorial tells how in 1806 a lady attending the Princess of Wales was killed at the entrance to Leatherhead by the overturning of her carriage. Another in the porch is a tribute to a paralysed lady, Diana Turner, who asked to be buried where her sedan chair used to stand during the service. She would come here to listen to the sermons of Robert Johnson, who was vicar 63 years before they laid him in the churchyard in 1752. Not long before him Richard Levytt had been vicar for 56 years, coming soon after the Great Armada and staying until the middle of the Civil War. Not only at its altar but in its homes the town has had fine records of long service: there is a memorial to Ann Goodes, who was more than 50 years a faithful servant of one family, and a stone in the churchyard to the faithful servant Ann Neaves, whose record was the amazing one of 70 years.

All Saints, built by Sir Arthur Blomfield, is another church here, its best possession being a beautiful window of the Annunciation. The chapel of Leatherhead School has some stained windows, and the big block facing the road boasts a fine oriel. One of the new laboratories here is in memory of an Old Boy, Paymaster Gedge, the first British officer killed in the war; he lost his life when HMS Amphion was mined on August 6, 1914. Another British officer, Colonel Drinkwater Bethune, lived at Thorncroft, an 18th century house at the bottom of Gimcrack Hill. He is said to have designed the lodge at the entrance, but lives in memory as the author of a book on the famous siege of Gibraltar. His daughter wrote a popular poem on the river which runs through the grounds.

The town has the biggest school for the blind in the world (the Royal School founded in 1799) and it has in the grounds of Cherkley Court some of the finest yews in Surrey, one over 20 feet round.

The Free Men of Shellwood

LEIGH. The old houses near the green are charming, and the church is worth a visit if only to see the brasses. It is a 15th

Limpsfield   The Norman Church

The Tower on the Summit

A Magnificent Panorama
LEITH HILL, CROWN OF SURREY

century building made new, and has a font and a little old glass (in the vestry) from the time when it was built.

The chief brass has figures of John Arderne and his wife in costumes of the 15th century. With them are three rather stiff-necked daughters and an incomplete group of three sons. Across the chancel are the remains of a similar brass to John's grandson Richard, who died 50 years later. Only the shaped recesses of the chief figures are left, together with the inscription and an odd little brass picture of the Trinity. God enthroned is holding a crucifix on which a dove is sitting. We see again one of the daughters of old John Arderne in a portrait on the chancel floor.

The Ardernes lived at Leigh Place, a little way along the road. The house is not as they knew it, but the wide moat of their day is still full of water, and its borders have become a rockery. After their day Leigh Place passed to one of Shelley's ancestors, and then to Sir Thomas Copley, a distant cousin of Queen Elizabeth, who supported her claim to the throne.

In an old farm near Leigh Ben Jonson is said to have had a retreat from the bustle of London; and on the common at Shellwood a Royalist stand failed in the last year of the Commonwealth. Shellwood Manor is a gabled 17th century house, and has a memory 400 years older than itself. There was a time when its lands belonged to the Priory of Merton, and the old feudal records tell a remarkable story of a long dispute between the men of Shellwood and their landlords. The Prior demanded that every tenant should come with his household to help the Priory at harvest time, and offered each man who came two meals. He also claimed that no tenant could get married, or sell an ox or horse, or cut down oaks, without his permission. The men of Shellwood replied that they would give their service, not as a legal duty, but as the courteous act of free men; and, although they allowed many of the claims which were customary in those days, the dispute went on for several generations.

The Roof of Surrey

LEITH HILL. It is the crown of Surrey, a hilltop of delight for thousands of walkers, and a matchless place to stand and see the world below. It is right that it should be ours for all time, and it is now in the safe keeping of the National Trust.

THE KING'S ENGLAND

At the top of the tower on Leith Hill we are 1029 feet above the sea, standing in the highest place not only of Surrey but of a great area in England. Nothing as high comes between us and the coast to south or east, and the nearest rival height to the west is 100 miles away in the Mendip Hills.

All round us is a vista hard to beat. To the south is the huge patchwork plain of the Weald, and beyond it the South Downs, with Chanctonbury Ring and a glimpse of the sea through Shoreham Gap 24 miles away. To the west are Godalming and Hindhead and Tennyson's Blackdown; to the east we look across at the Kentish hills; and to the north, beyond the line of the North Downs, is the dim ridge of the Chilterns 50 miles away.

Nearer at hand is Broadmoor Valley, still lovely with those of its trees not felled in the mad days of the war; and not far away is a peep of Dorking spire. The Crystal Palace and St Paul's are seen on a clear day. It is a place where a man must stand and hold his breath with wonder as he looks out over all south-eastern England from Kent to Hampshire and from Buckinghamshire to the Channel.

It was Richard Hull of Leith Hill Place who built the tower in 1766 (as a tablet tells us in Latin) for the delight not only of himself but of his neighbours and everybody else. Beneath it he was laid to rest a few years later. A quaint tradition says he had himself buried upside down, believing that the world would have turned on its axis before the Day of Judgment, and *wishing to stand before his Maker right way up!*

In his day the tower had two furnished rooms, and glasses were provided for people to look at the view. Yet there were louts who did not know when they were well off, people who would carry away the very brickwork of the tower, so that it was reduced to a dilapidated shell. To save it from ruin its doorway was blocked, and it was filled up inside with cement, remaining for more than half a century as nothing but a landmark. But in 1864 Mr Evelyn of Wotton decided to give the public a second chance, and, finding the cement by now too hard to be broken, he made another way to the top by building on a new stairway.

In our own time a generous friend of Surrey has given the tower and five acres of this incomparable hilltop to the nation, and anyone may now climb its 75 steps to stand on the roof of Surrey. Those who do so will be aghast to find the names of half the litter louts of Surrey on the wall. The fine memorial on the parapets at the top has been designed to resist the efforts of these name-scratchers. It is a series of bronze tablets giving the names and distances of the chief landmarks in the view, put here in 1929 by the rambling clubs in memory of Edmund Seyfang Taylor, a London printer who gave all the time he could spare to discovering and making known the fieldpaths and byways of the countryside. Walker Miles he was nicknamed, and since 1908 he has lain in the churchyard at Godstone.

It is recorded that one clear day in 1844 a group of Ordnance Surveyors looked out from here with their "small glass" and saw no less than 41 of London's church towers. More remarkable still, they were able to pick out on Dunstable Downs 50 miles away a staff four inches thick! Let into the turf a few yards from the tower is a small tablet dated 1792, believed to be a relic of the earliest official survey of this enchanting part of Surrey. On the high ground towards Abinger is a lonely offshoot of Greenwich Observatory, a place where men study not the stars but the Earth itself. Here it is that the changes in the Earth's magnetism are recorded hourly on delicate instruments housed in huts built of non-magnetic material. No iron or steel must come near them; even the locks and keys and nails of this remote temple of science are made of copper and brass.

The Quiet Village of Famous Folk

LIMPSFIELD. We are not surprised that it has gathered many famous folk about it, for it is one of Nature's lovely places. Its winding ways, its tiny green, its Little Heath and its Great Chart, make it a pure delight.

Its street is full of lovely timbered houses mixed with homes of red and grey, with the ancient Court House which is thought to have come from the 13th century. A fine Georgian rectory faces the church and across the way is a manor house which has a place in history because it was here a widow sent out into the world a book which made a great sensation in its time. By Limpsfield Chart is a house fashioned from the old Salt Box of medieval days, where salt was stored before its distribution, and on the lovely common hereabouts Major Baden-Powell and Colonel Cody used to fly man-lifting kites in the days when men were learning to fly. For centuries famous people have loved to walk among the gorse and heather here.

As for the village street, we felt when we called that with all its charm it has nothing lovelier than its churchyard, full of sunshine and fine trees, and with a rich green carpet from which rise the Norman walls and the low Norman tower known to multitude of Surrey folk.

Here we found a friend from Aberdeen sleeping under a stone from his granite city, with a Scotch fir shading his grave—John Arthur Thomson, gallant knight and learned scholar, professor of natural history, and writer of many books.

He would write about the dawn of life far back in the mists of Time, or about the beauty of the little wren, or the colour in the heart of the rose, or the shimmering gleam on the sunlit sea; or he would write about the wondrous way in which we are made, the astonishing workings of the human mind, or the faith that keeps us going through hard times. Life and its mystery, the incredible wonder of the past, the loveliness of the present, the immense and boundless hope of the future were his ceaseless themes, and every word that was printed of his was written with his own hand, *mostly on sheets marked out in fifty squares for convenience of counting.*

Here sleeps also Florence Barclay, whose Rosary novel has been read all over the world. We remember these lines on her stone:

> *My Lord, come home with me,*
> *And, when the morning rush of life is o'er,*
> *When all the things of Earth have ceased to be,*
> *Then, for the sake of Thy great love for me,*
> *Let me come home with Thee.*

And here in this garden of memories sleep two old ladies who will not be soon forgotten in this Surrey countryside.

One is Harriet Kennard, who gave her life for strangers. It is a story of the coming of the railway in the 19th century, when cholera broke out among the French navvies working here. No one would go near them, but Harriet Kennard could not bear it; she was 83 but she nursed those French navvies till she caught the plague and died.

The other old lady sleeps by the north door, with two friends whose home she shared. She is Elizabeth Frances Harley, and we read her story on a sculptured stone carved by one who loved her well. It is one of the most charming stones we have seen in a churchyard, with a scallop shell to show that she was a pilgrim of Eternity, living in this world for all but a hundred years, and with two child angels guarding a rose, which is here because they took a rose to her every day. She was an old lady greatly loved, and we found a gardener cutting the grass who could not speak of her without a tear.

In a little rock garden close by Sir Arthur Thomson's grave sleeps a young scientists, killed in an accident, who lies here with his mother, "a brave, wise, and loving woman." On the stone are these words:

> *For death takes toll*
> *Of beauty, courage, youth,*
> *Of all but truth.*

Inside the church sleep a Groom-of-the-Chamber to Charles Stuart's wife, the widow of Lord Chesterfield who created a sensation by publishing her husband's famous letters, and the 13th Baron Elphinstone, who spent much of his life as a Governor in India and when he died in Limpsfield was given an extraordinary funeral with a procession of Chinese servants in their picturesque costume.

He is a handsome figure in white marble wearing a chain and badge, a remarkable likeness by Matthew Noble, the Yorkshire sculptor who carved the Dream of Eugene Aram for Tom Hood's grave, and has statues in many of our cities. He made the statue of Lord Derby which faces the Houses of Parliament, that of Sir John Franklin in Waterloo Place, that of Sir James Outram on the Thames Embankment, and the Wellington monument in Manchester.

The low tower of the church stands rather oddly in the south wall at the east end; it was set up by the Normans. The nave and aisle are 12th century and the chancel 13th. The altar, with a reredos which has 15th century fragments worked into it, stands between an open arch through which we walk and a tiny lancet window near the ground—one of the most curious we have seen. Near it on the chancel wall are four peculiar recesses. Let into the wall in the north chapel is a fragment of stone carved with a spray of foliage by a 14th century mason.

There are small fragments of 16th century heraldic glass, but the oldest touch of the painter at Limpsfield appears to be the painted rosettes on the splays of two chancel windows. They look rather like stars and are thought to have been here 700 years. The glass in these windows, with Peter and Paul, was given by 365 parishioners in memory of a rector for 30 years. We noticed tablets to three men who were vicars for 34 years each, two of them brothers.

Inside and out, Limpsfield draws the pilgrim to it. We found a thorn growing from a sprig of the holy thorn at Glastonbury. We found a peace memorial with beautiful lettering erected to those who live for evermore "by those who loved them." We found a comic little face on a gravestone between two scallop shells, and a stone with three 18th century cherubs.

Into all this interest and beauty and history we come through a lychgate which has stood inviting pilgrims here since 1350, before the days of Joan of Arc and Agincourt. It seemed to us like one of the places where Time comes home to sleep, and under an old yew in the churchyard lies the blind old musician Delius, who wished to come home to England to sleep after his life in France, and after burial in France was brought to Limpsfield and laid to rest here at midnight. His wife, crossing the Channel with his body, caught a chill and was laid in his grave two days after him. For a long time music-lovers will wend their way to this little churchyard.

The Tragic Story of Frederick Delius

IT was one of the last wishes of Frederick Delius that his poor body might be laid in the peace of an English country churchyard, and it was to Limpsfield they brought him. Blind at the last, and stricken with paralysis, yet working heroically to the end, he had come to feel that only such a place as this could be his last home on Earth. He stands alone in the story of music, a solitary figure, like no other and copying none, masterly within his limits, personal in his utterance, a seeker after pure emotion and its expression in sound.

He was born at Bradford in Yorkshire, but was the son of German parents settled there, and at only 20 his rebellious spirit took him away to Florida to spend several years among the orange groves. Coming back to Europe, he studied in Germany, and then for most of the 40 years of his working life made his home in France. His story has very little to do with his native England, yet in his music he sought to express her magic, her quiet and rolling countryside, her simple people, and her natural and peaceful charm. It is not that Delius was an imitator of the sounds of nature, but that (as someone has said) he seems to show us the influence of nature on our souls. The very names of his works are poetry, for who can think without enchantment of A Village Romeo and Juliet, Sea-Drift, A Song of the High Hills, a Summer Night on the River, and Songs of Farewell?

It is in his works for the orchestra and for voices that we hear his genius at its best, and even in his last tragic years he was labouring on at them, dictating note by note when an hour or two's work in a day was all that his broken body could stand. He has a sure place in the affections of music-lovers everywhere.

Eugenia Stanhope, who lies at Limpsfield with her son and lived in the manor house, has a strange place in literature.

The Remarkable History of the Chesterfield Letters

EUGENIA STANHOPE lives in memory by virtue of a treachery for which posterity is thankful. To his infinite surprise and disgust, she became the daughter-in-law of the famous Lord Chesterfield, who wrote the well-known letters to his son (Philip Stanhope) never dreaming that Eugenia existed.

The letters, witty, cynical, often wise, reflecting the morals of an immoral age but enjoining the faithful discharge of duty to God and man, extended over more than thirty years. Philip Stanhope, whose mother was French, and not married to his father, was to be modelled by these letters into the perfect gentleman, at ease with princes and peasants, learned but modest, a diplomat, an orator, the accomplished, shining man of the world, to whom the most exalted office was to be opened by wit, finesse, scholarship and honest deserving.

Chesterfield wrote in the expectation that no eye but his son's would see the letters, but all his hopes in his son were falsified. Philip was shy, awkward, and loutish, and but for one or two terms in Parliament he lived mainly abroad, where he filled minor diplomatic posts. He died at Avignon of dropsy, in 1768, aged 36. The same letter that told the news of the death informed Chesterfield that Philip had been for some years secretly married to the obscure and unamiable Eugenia, and that their two little boys, Charles and Philip, were living. At a stroke the old statesman found himself sonless, a father-in-law, and a grandfather.

With stoical courtesy he took Eugenia and the boys to his heart. He clothed, educated and endowed them. He housed Eugenia handsomely. He cannot have known that she had the letters; at any rate he cannot have divined the purpose with which she preserved them. He died in 1773, aged 78, and within less than a year Eugenia had sold the letters to a publisher for £1500. It was an ungracious betrayal of a man who had behaved with great generosity to her. Members of the dead writer's family invoked the aid of the Law Courts in an attempt to suppress the volumes, but the widow's legal right was unassailable, and for over a century and a half the letters have been read in every European language with amusement, admiration, and deprecation, but not without profit.

Eugenia's ingratitude and treachery were flagrant, yet she, and she alone, secured the immortality of the writer of the letters. But for them he would be forgotten.

Surrey's Westminster Abbey

LINGFIELD. It touches the meadows of Kent; we can stand near the fine yew in the churchyard and look across the border.

A pretty old house on the west of the churchyard has a stone roof which is said to be much as it was when the builders left it in 1431; it was then part of the college built by Sir Reginald Cobham for a master and a few brethren. The lovely timbered building on the north, with a stone roof covered with moss when we called, has developed from the guest house, reconstructed from 15th century materials. The old homes of the Cobhams, Starborough Castle, is in ruins, but still has its wet moat. The fine stone-gabled house called New Place, facing us as we leave the station, was built about the time when Shakespeare died at his New Place. What is called St Peter's Cross, under an aged hollow oak, is the village look-out, a pretty little building with a turret and a stone roof, probably 18th century, now used as a rough and ready museum. In it we found a flail, a mantrap, a boneshaker, and (framed on the walls) a number of local anecdotes taken down from ancient inhabitants.

It is the most delightful corner in Lingfield that brings us to the church, a little street with quaint and beautiful overhanging shops on one side and the fine long front of a 16th century inn on the other.

The great church has been called the Westminster Abbey of Surrey, for its rich array of monuments of the great lords of Starborough Castle. It is much as it was when Sir Reginald Cobham finished its

Lingfield						The Way to Church

Miserere 　　　　　　　　　　　　　　　　Miserere

Bench End　　　　The Tudor Font　　　Bench End

Reginald Cobham and His Wife 　　　The First Lord Cobham

Three of the Carvings on the Panelled Seats of the Choir

IN LINGFIELD CHURCH, SURREY'S WESTMINSTER ABBEY

rebuilding. There was a church here in the time of Alfred and the work of the Saxon builders may still be found in the south wall and in the tower. But the main tower is 14th century and the church has been as we see for just 500 years. The projecting stone tower on the north has the old rood stairs. The deep cuts in the doorway to the south transept are believed to have been made by knights who blunted their swords on these stones before entering the church.

The eye is drawn, as we stand looking up this nave with its graceful piers of clustered round columns and its fine oak roof, to the noble altar tomb in the middle of the chancel. In it lies the man who raised this noble place and died 15 years after its completion. He lies in alabaster with his wife, his face remarkable for its expression of character. He is in armour, his bearded head resting on a helmet with a crest of a bearded Saracen's head; his feet are on a lion, and his gauntlets and dagger are chiselled at his side. A stately figure he must have been at Agincourt. His wife has a gentle face and her head is on a cushion held by two golden-haired angels.

The tomb of another Reginald Cobham, the first lord, is in the north chapel and shows him as a painted figure with his head on his helmet and his feet on his enemy. His enemy was the Turk of the day, and at Lord Cobham's feet reclines a Turk in a loose white tunic and a white turban, his face, hands, and legs curiously painted olive green. The knight's helmet is of iron with a Moor's head in stone and two small figures like attendant sprites with glowing hair seated by the helmet.

Exceedingly rich in brasses is this great church. The best of all is of a third Reginald Cobham, belonging to a generation between the other two. He is in armour, his head engraved as resting on a Saracen's, and his feet on a dog. He carries a dagger and a long sword with a rich scabbard, and the inscription tells us that he was as brave as a leopard and in all lands bore off fame and honour. The portrait of a knight he may have known is near his own, that of John Hadresham of 1417, shown in armour with his long sword, his face looking out of his helmet in a way reminding us of Sir John Tenniel's version of Lewis Carroll's White Knight.

Four of the brasses are of priests of the college in their 15th century robes, one with a fine embroidered collar; they are John Knoyll, John Wyche, James Veldon, and John Swetecok. Three others are women.

One is Katherine Stoket, whose hands are pressed together in front of her; she was chief chambermaid to the first Lady Cobham, who left her £30 with which to make a good marriage. The second is of a young lady with long hair bound round her forehead in the fashion of the 15th century; she has a dog in the folds of her dress with bells on its collar. The other lady was the first wife of the third Reginald Cobham, and her brass shows her with a veil falling to her shoulders, her cloak drawn across the shoulders by a cord fastened with two floral brooches. In the folds of her dress are two dogs with bells on their collars, both looking up at their mistress, whose slender fingers are clasped in prayer. She is under a beautiful canopy supported by pinnacled buttresses, and the canopy has battlements from which a flag is flying, a very rare thing in brasses.

The chapels and the chancel are enclosed by three oak screens by medieval craftsmen, and their magnificent handiwork is still in the stalls of the choir, with the familiar tip-up seats richly carved with the usual curious and heraldic conceptions of medieval craftsmen. On some of the panelled seats of the choir are carved a striking bird, a man in a big helmet, and a severe-looking woman in a high collar; it is thought they may have come from a private house and may represent Philip and Mary.

The Tudor font has flowers in quatrefoils, and we noticed two quaint little faces peeping out among the petals. The Jacobean lectern has on it an early 17th century Bible attached by an old chain. The brass candelabra in the nave is 18th century. The helmet on a bracket in the chancel was carried at the funeral of one of the Cobhams. In a chancel window is glass like a patchwork quilt. Under the window is written, "Gather up the fragments that remain, that nothing be lost," and the reference apparently is to the fact that in this window are fragments of the original glazing of the east window of 1431 which were found in a box in the crypt.

One rare and lovely thing we found at Lingfield that we do not forget. In the part of the village called Plaistow Street is the peace memorial by a pond, and it is crowned with a light which never goes out, but burns in memory of those who live for evermore.

The Tale of an Only Son

LITTLE BOOKHAM. A secluded place half a mile from its bigger brother, it has a little white church built soon after the

Norman Conquest. Round the church is a high hedge, and shading its toy spire (with a wind vane dated 1744) are a stately cedar and a gnarled yew 24 feet round, the yew said by authorities at Kew to be 900 years old.

A curious thing has happened to one of the nave walls. Arches were pierced in it by the Normans when they threw out an aisle, but the aisle has vanished, and the arches have been filled up again to make a solid wall, leaving only their rounded outlines and the capitals of their pillars to tell of an arcade once inside the church and now part of its walls. There is a cracked Norman font held together by metal bands, and a lancet window with a delicate 15th century medallion of Our Lord. By another window is an ancient scratch dial. Carved panels of the 17th century are worked into the pulpit and the vestry door.

Among the many tablets one tells an unusual story. It is to George Augustus Pollen, a rector's only son, who became an MP, raised the regiment of Loyal Surrey Rangers at his own expense, and when still a young man was shipwrecked in the Baltic in 1808. Many months after his body was miraculously washed ashore, and, being brought home again, it was recognised by his widow and laid to rest at North Berwick.

In the churchyard sleeps General Coote Manningham, who died a General at 43. We read that his health was weakened by long service in the West Indies, and that he fell an early victim to the fatigues of the Peninsular War. He too raised a regiment of the British Army, the "95th Regiment of Foot," which became known as the Rifle Brigade. It fought in almost every campaign in the 19th century, and played its part at Ladysmith. In the Great War ten of its men won the VC. In 1933 its officers reconstructed this tomb.

LONGCROSS. We come to its 19th century church by a road gloriously shaded with great trees, one tall acacia overhanging the memorial lychgate to Cyril Mullens, killed in an air fight in 1916.

Many of the memories in this simple church are of soldiers and sailors and the things of war. There is a tablet to a Crimean officer who might have been nursed by Florence Nightingale, a proud White Ensign flown by HMS Lord Nelson in the Dardanelles, and a Turkish cannon ball (made of stone and about a foot across) which she brought home with her.

Yet there is Peace here too; it is the one blessed word carved on the lychgate, and it is in the group of Nativity figures looking out from the altar into the road.

Close to the church is the entrance to Barrow Hills, the fine house and park of Lord Camrose. In its delightful grounds is one of the wonders of this lovely countryside, a famous Japanese garden.

£100 from Cromwell

LONG DITTON. A little lane shaded with elms brings us from the busy Portsmouth Road to the church, by the lovely black and white rectory which has been here for centuries; it has a good cluster of chimneys. The church is modern but has brass portraits of people who were probably here when the rectory was built—Robert Casteltoun who died 400 years ago and is here with his wife and six daughters; and Richard Hatton, who died in the same year as Shakespeare and is in brass with his wife, who wears a hood and farthingale.

There is a tablet to a mayor of Calcutta during the Mutiny, who lost a leg in battle, and three tablets to men who died for us in France; and in a case is kept a book written by a rector here from the days of Charles Stuart, through the Commonwealth, and into the Restoration. He was Richard Byfield, son of a vicar of Stratford-on-Avon, and may have seen Shakespeare. The uncle of John Evelyn complained to Oliver Cromwell that Byfield preached against him, and Cromwell reconciled the two, and, after advising Sir John Evelyn to "search his way," sent him £100 for repairing the church.

A marble tablet at the east end of the church is a memorial to a rector here for over half a century, Mr Pennicott, who preached here for 53 years, embracing the period of Napoleon's wars.

Treasures to Stir the Imagination

LOWER KINGSWOOD. In this lovely country round Reigate, the little Church of the Wisdom of God should draw every traveller who rides this way. Humble enough from outside, and with a weird wooden tower standing apart, it has an astonishing interior to delight the eye and a remarkable collection of treasures to stir the imagination; and it is of our own time, built in 1892.

We have seldom seen modern marble look so beautiful as here, where it lines the apse, paves the chancel, and makes a central aisle.

Very lovely are the shades of grey and green and mauve, and proudly were the mats raised and the beauty pointed out by one who, in the evening of her days, was caring for this place when we called. She took us to the font, perhaps the simplest and certainly one of the best modern fonts we have seen, just an exquisite column of cream marble hollowed out to a bowl.

The woodwork is strikingly original, much of it finely inlaid. The nave ceiling is richly coloured with flowers and leaves; from it hang two great iron rings, each supporting 18 candles. Part of the fabric itself is in memory of those who fell in the war, their names being carved on one of the pillars.

The ceiling of the apse is a fine mosaic in gold, green, and blue, and bears the names of Edwin Freshfield and his wife, the good friends of this church for many years. From their garden came the ancient treasures, mostly on the walls, which make this place a museum as well as a House of God, and take our minds back to the earliest Christian times.

Two of them are mounted on the floor, great stone capitals carved in the fourth century of our era. They come from the church built by the Christian emperors Constantine and Theodosius over the traditional site of St John's tomb, in that part of Ephesus where the Temple of Diana had stood. The carving of them includes spirals, acanthus leaves, and patterns like grotesque faces. On the walls are other ancient capitals and carvings, ranging from the sixth century to the 11th. Some are from Constantinople, and one has a Christian cross defaced by the marks of Turkish bullets.

One of several ancient carvings is a very quaint picture of Adam and Eve who are hiding their nakedness, while the oddest serpent in the world climbs an equally odd tree.

The Children's Trees

MALDEN. It has a link with the famous Walter de Merton, Lord Chancellor of England and one of our earliest college founders. Some of its lands belonged to him, as they have belonged to his college at Oxford ever since, and here in 1264 he founded what was called a college, though it was actually a little house of priests who looked after the estates, collecting the money to keep 20 scholars at Oxford. From these lands of Merton College Henry the

Eighth took away 120 acres to add to the great park of his Nonsuch Palace; they make up Worcester Park here, with a great house built in the 18th century.

The old church of Malden also helped to pay for Walter de Merton's scholars, but it has nothing left from his day. It overlooks the pleasant valley of the little Hogsmill River, and has a 19th century nave and chancel built beside the old ones, which are now an aisle and a chapel. The chapel is probably 16th century; the aisle and the tower were built in 1610 by John Goode, a lord of the manor whose memorial stone is on the wall. Also from his time are four carved panels from a pulpit, and a medallion of heraldic glass in one of the windows.

Near Malden runs the Kingston bypass road, part of it with a Children's Avenue of double-white cherry trees. Each tree has the name of a child, and they grow up together. Close to the road is the new and very attractive church of St James, with walls and arches of brick, and stone windows in the style of 500 years ago.

Surrey Delight

MERROW. Everyone who has rambled in Surrey knows it as the village for Newlands Corner, where thousands turn aside between the church and the old inn to walk over gentle downs to a superb viewpoint 567 feet up. Standing at the top we are at one of the superb heights of England, looking forward and backward over a vista of eight or nine counties, from Windsor Castle to Essex, from the heights of London suburbs to far villages of Sussex and Hampshire. It is a feast of delicate colour and outline, worth a day's run to see.

The Pilgrim's Way ran over the downs here, marked by gnarled and twisted yews; it must have been of this lovely spot that Kipling was thinking when he wrote:

> *There runs a road by Merrow Down,*
> *A grassy track today it is,*
> *An hour out of Guildford town*
> *Above the river Wey it is.*

Certainly it was of these yews that William Watson was thinking when he wrote his fine poem on Emperor Yew, for he wrote it under these very trees of Merrow Down:

SURREY

Old emperor Yew, fantastic sire,
Girt with thy guard of dotard kings,
What ages hast thou seen retire
Into the dusk of alien things?
What mighty news hath stormed thy shade,
Of armies perished, realms unmade?

Ah, thou hast heard the iron tread
And clang of many an armoured age,
And well recall'st the famous dead,
Captains or counsellors brave or sage,
Kings that on kings their myriads hurled,
Ladies whose smile embroiled the world.

A broad green pathway of a very different sort is the one marking the old Merrow racecourse, remembered as the training ground of the greatest racehorse that ever lived. Born on the day of an eclipse in 1764, he was called Eclipse, and he eclipsed all other horses for he never lost a race. It is said that he never had a single blemish, that he had a perfect temper, and that his blood flows today in the veins of every English thoroughbred. We may see his skeleton today at the Royal Veterinary College in Camden Town.

Approached along paths darkened by more yews, the church porch has a handsome bargeboard 500 years old, and the doorway inside it has a Norman arch. One of the chapels is 13th century and has some old blurred painting on an arch; the other is dedicated to Ronald Pease, a boy of 19 who fell in the Great War. In it hangs the simple cross from his grave in France, and on the beautiful dark panelling his name keeps company with 39 others from Merrow who never came back.

In an unknown grave by Clandon gates lies an old man who saw the execution of Charles Stuart; and living not far away when we called was the first Earl Midleton, who told a remarkable story of a link with the old man who had this dramatic experience. He said that when he was young he met Lord Lovelace, who as a boy had been to see Lord Onslow, and Lord Onslow had made the boy write down these words:

Today I saw Lord Onslow, who had dined with Boisragon, who was present at the execution of King Charles.

As if this were not romantic enough, Lord Midleton, in telling this story, added that he had lunched with Lord John Russell and helped him on with his coat, and as he did so Lord John said to him, "Remember that you have met a man who lunched with Wellington at Torres Vedras and dined with Napoleon on Elba."

Sleeping in the churchyard are the Onslows from Clandon Park, a family with perhaps a unique record for its association with Parliament as Speakers in the Commons and Chairman of Committees in the Lords, having produced five of these. Here lies Sir Richard, the first Lord Onslow, a staunch whig who married the daughter of the Lord Mayor of London and was Speaker in Queen Anne's third Parliament. Here is Arthur Onslow, who was Speaker through every hour of the reign of George the Second, seeing the fall of our first Prime Minister, Sir Robert Walpole, and the rise of the elder Pitt. When failing health drove him to retire the Commons thanked him for his constant and unwearied attendance in the chair in five successive Parliaments, and, as we read on his monument in Trinity Church at Guildford, he told them in his reply that being within those walls had ever been the chief pleasure of his life. Horace Walpole tells us that no Speaker was ever more firm or dignified, and that he died after long agony borne with great patience. His portrait is in the National Gallery and in Guildford Guildhall and there is a curious sketch of him engraved in his pew in St Margaret's, the Commons Church at Westminster. His only son George also spent many years at Westminster, became an earl, and was described as a noisy, indiscreet man. His grandson Thomas Onslow, the 2nd earl, was something of an eccentric, with such a passion for driving four-in-hand that someone wrote of him:

> *What can Tommy Onslow do?*
> *He can drive a chaise and two.*
> *Can little Tommy do no more?*
> *Yes, he can drive a chaise and four.*

The fine iron gates of Clandon Park are 18th century, and the grounds were laid out by Capability Brown, the fashionable gardener, who laid out Blenheim and helped to lay out Kew. The great house itself was designed by the Venetian architect Leoni, who settled in England and built many country seats; two of the fireplaces are the work of the Flemish sculptor Rysbrack. The home farm in the grounds is known as Temple Court and may once have been a grange of the Knights Templars.

In Merrow churchyard lies Sir Edmond Elles, a remarkable man who had lived here many years when he died in 1934.

Across the Hindenburg Line at Seventy

AT the beginning of his military career he served in India, being transferred to Egypt in 1882 when the rebellion broke out in the Egyptian Army. He returned to a long period of staff work in India, and was there under Lord Curzon in 1901. He was concerned with the administrative side of the army, and when Lord Kitchener arrived as Commander-in-Chief, with the idea that administrative and executive powers should be in the same hands, there was friction between them. Lord Kitchener was unable to establish any of the charges he made against Sir Edmond, but soon after Lord Curzon resigned and Sir Edmond followed suit.

At home he took a big part in encouraging the Boy Scouts. He was County Commissioner for Surrey for 25 years. He was 67 when the war began, but he went round the country addressing meetings and appealing for recruits. In 1918 he went out to the front to see things for himself. His son was an officer of the Tank Corps, and Sir Edmond took the opportunity to do a daring thing: he went across the Hindenburg Line in a tank when he was 70, surely the oldest soldier to make such a journey. It was only when he was 84 that he gave up driving his own car.

When he died Sir Edmond had spent 40 years in the army and over 66 years in public service. His administrative and executive genius was apparent in all he undertook, and perhaps even more noticeable was his sustained enthusiasm and interest in public matters; he put to shame many a younger man in his whole-hearted discharge of the duties of a good citizen.

The Door Seven Centuries Old

MERSTHAM. The London to Brighton traffic swirls round the corner, missing a quiet little backwater which is the great charm of the village. It leads between houses old and new to the grey gateway of Merstham House, guarded by rampant lions and watched by the pretty overhanging storey of a 15th century house which was once a forge.

North and south the great road goes today, but there was a time when the Canterbury Pilgrims were trudging by from west to east, passing a few yards from the church and pausing to refresh themselves at the little wayside pool. Already in those days the Merstham quarries were famous for their sandstone, which was used in 1259 for the king's palace at Westminster and a century later for Windsor Castle. It was used, too, for old St Paul's and London Bridge, and we see it in the walls of the church.

At the time of Domesday Book the rents of Merstham were helping to clothe the monks of Canterbury. Centuries later the wealth brought to the shrine of Becket built the chancel of this church, and there is evidence that the architect who designed it had a hand in several other churches not far away.

The church is mostly 13th century, but the timber spire and the stone porch are 14th, and the two chapels 15th. One of its treasures is the 13th century west doorway, in which the original door still swings on its beautiful iron hinges.

At the top of the tower arch is a carved heraldic stone from Old London Bridge, and in the tracery of a chapel window are some little figures in 15th century glass. They are Peter, the Virgin, and St Katherine, the fourth figure being modern. The big marble font is Norman and the little screen by the chancel door is made from screenwork 500 years old. One of the five bells is 14th century, and their five old clappers are in the aisle, mounted on ancient belfry oak.

There is a battered stone figure of Nicholas Jamys, found under the pavement where it was hidden in Cromwell's day. He was mayor and alderman of London 500 years ago, and one of his daughters married a Merstham man, John Elingbridge. She is seen in brass (with a second wife exactly like her) on his tomb in one of the chapels. The other brasses are John Ballard of 1463 and his wife; John Newdegate of 1498 looking very warlike in armour; Thomas, the grandson of John Elingbridge, and his wife; and two little brothers who died just before Armada year. One is in swaddling clothes; his brass is a copy of the original which was stolen.

Unusual and striking is the brass portrait of Reginald Woodhouse, a rector's son who fell in Mesopotamia in 1916; he stands to attention in his officer's uniform.

There is a tablet to George Jolliffe, who was killed on the Bellerophon at the Battle of the Nile, with a carving of the battle taking place and a reference to his father who was the victim of " a casualty awful as unforeseen."

The list of those who have served Merstham as rectors is full of interest. Over 500 years ago there came the adventurous Welshman Adam of Usk, lawyer, petty thief, papal chaplain, and parish priest. A century later the rector for a month was Thomas Linacre, one of those who brought the New Learning to our shores. He founded the College of Physicians in London and was buried in St Paul's. In 1584 came Richard Wood, who comes into the first of the famous Marprelate Tracts as Richard Never-be-good; and after him was Thomas Ravis, who helped to translate the New Testament under King James. In the 18th century one name stands out, that of Jeremiah Milles, whose letters of travel through Europe are in the British Museum.

The lychgate is said to be made from the oak timbers of an old mill pulled down when the railway came this way. Another railway memory lingers in the empty cutting with a little bridge, beside the Brighton road. It is a relic of the first public railway in England, made for goods traffic in the earliest years of last century, drawn by horses, and used chiefly to carry the stone and lime from Merstham to the Thames at Wandsworth. One of the humble labourers who worked on it rose to be the builder of three London bridges. He was Sir Edward Banks, who sleeps in the next village of Chipstead.

History's March Through Merton

MERTON. Houses by the thousand and factories by the score now stand where Nelson came for country air, but it has great memories of the days before Greater London engulfed it. Far back in the mists of history its story goes, for in the days when Merton can have been no more than a small settlement among the fields the Wessex King Cynewulf was murdered on Roman Stane Street, and here, a century later, King Ethelred was mortally wounded in the last of the eight battles he fought against the Danes. After that the English throne passed to his brother and second-in-command, our great Alfred.

Time passed by and here at Merton Parliament met in 1236, the meeting taking place in the priory that had sprung up and has now disappeared. It was to the altar of this priory that the gallant

Hubert de Burgh fled to avoid the king's displeasure, pursued by 20,000 angry citizens, who were happily recalled in time to avert a clash. The monks of Merton had among their scholars at the priory young Thomas Becket, and it is believed that in the next century after him another scholar was Walter de Merton, who was to become famous as the founder of the college system at our universities.

Time marches on and brings us to Lord Nelson. It was at his home here (Merton Place, surrounded by a moat which his daughter fondly called the Nile) that he and Lady Hamilton lived through the last chapters of their life together, and these two dazzling figures flit like shadows through the twilight of Merton.

Alas, for the March of Time! Nothing is left of Nelson's house, and the stones of Merton Priory are scattered far and wide. Its destruction was the work of Thomas Cromwell and his royal master, and from its ruins were built the famous Nonsuch Palace at Ewell, perhaps the most spectaclar of all the palaces of the Tudor Age, though in its turn this too has vanished.

It is the church that has the only visible link with Merton's historic past. Here are the only remains of the ancient priory, and of the Merton Nelson knew. In the churchyard is a splendid Norman arch from the priory guest-house, found in 1914 when Abbey House (close to Merton Abbey Station and within the precincts of the old priory) passed into the hands of the housebreaker. Workmen were stripping the outer layers from the front of the house when suddenly this fragment of the Conqueror's England was revealed, a Norman doorway. Steps were immediately taken for its preservation, and now after many years it has been transferred to the best possible place for it, between the old church and the vicarage.

The church has a Norman doorway adorned with zigzags and scalloped capitals, and, most thrilling of all, it has still swinging on its hinges the original Norman door, its timbers bound together by the scrolled ironwork fashioned and fixed by a Norman blacksmith. It may be that the great Hubert de Burgh opened this very door. For 500 years the door and its doorway have been sheltered in an exquisite timbered porch with a traceried bargeboard and a grotesque little head finely carved, looking at all who come up the churchyard path.

SURREY

Much-worn heads of a medieval king and queen adorn the 14th century west doorway, and the shingled spire above completes a charming picture. Inside is another picture of a fine old age. The three walls at the west end, each with its little window, are all Norman, and here hangs a painting of Christ Falling Under the Cross, believed to be by a pupil of Van Dyck. The roof beams across the nave, lighted by new dormer windows, were made from Windsor Forest oaks given by Henry the Sixth. Above the nave arcades hang six hatchments, including those of Nelson and Sir William Hamilton, both brought into the safe keeping of this church by Lady Hamilton.

The chancel is 13th century with a beautiful chestnut roof of the 14th, and one of its windows has a head of Christ delicately drawn 500 years ago. Here is a beautiful marble group of Gregory Lovell, Cofferer to Queen Elizabeth's household, showing him with his two wives and nine children, all kneeling in Tudor costume with ruffs.

A monument in the north aisle, with a woman kneeling before an anchor, recalls one of the great figures of the 18th century. It is to the memory of the Smith family buried in a vault by the chancel, and was set up by the widow of the immortal Captain Cook. Her mother was a Smith. The beautiful kneeling figure represents Mrs Isaac Craig Smith, and was sculptured in Rome by her brother, the famous Richard Wyatt, who was one of Canova's pupils and spent nearly all his life in Rome. One name on this monument is that of a cousin of Captain Cook's wife, Admiral Isaac Smith, of whom a romantic tale is told. He sailed with Cook on two of his three voyages of discovery, and it is said that on Sunday, April 29, 1770, when Cook had anchored his ship in Botany Bay, he took Smith with him in a small boat and called to him, "Jump out, Isaac," so that young Smith was the first Englishman to set foot on Australia's Pacific coast.

Merton church is, of course, very proud of its association with Nelson, and in the vestry, guarded by a 600-year-old door (the second ancient door doing duty here), is the plain unbacked bench on which he used to sit, preferring this, it is said, to the box pews then in fashion. In a frame near it is a fragment of the red cloth which covered the seat in his day. The plain bench is cherished as a treasure, for this was the last church in which Nelson worshipped, and this was doubtless the last seat he sat on in a church. With him on the Victory was the son of the vicar here, a midshipman of 14 who must often have seen Nelson in this church and must have talked of immortal scenes at Trafalgar to his dying day.

There is a curious link with the admiral in the parish register, which has an entry recording the christening of the son of William Suckling, "which christening was postponed on account of Lord Viscount Nelson (one of his godfathers) being out of England on His Majesty's service." Nelson's association with Merton is also recalled by the name of the Nelson Arms, standing where the carriage-drive to his house began; and his name is more worthily perpetuated by the fine Nelson Hospital, built in 1911.

Sleeping in Merton churchyard is Charles the Second's Embroiderer, William Rutlish, who left money for the schooling of poor children. Nearly a century later they laid here Francis Nixon, who first discovered how to print calico, and set up his works on the space then enclosed by the priory walls. Two hundred years ago over a thousand people were engaged in fabric printing here, and the old tradition is still maintained here by the House of Liberty.

The vicarage with its fine trees and paddock, and the lovely lanes about the church, are like a rural oasis in a desert of busy streets. Many of these trees were planted by John Innes, whose memory is kept green in Merton by a playing-field bearing his name, and by the John Innes Institution for the practical study of scientific horticulture. Another welcome touch of Nature is Wandle Park, with a fountain recording its gift to the people of Wimbledon and Merton in memory of John Feeney, "who loved Nature and his fellowmen." On one side of the fountain, facing the never-creasing flow of traffic, are inscribed these lines written in Kensington Gardens by Matthew Arnold:

> *Calm soul of all things! make it mine*
> *To feel, amid the city's jar,*
> *That there abides a peace of thine*
> *Man did not make, and cannot mar.*

They strike a happy note in this quiet corner of a town where often we may think with Wordsworth that the world is too much with us.

Nelson's Country Home

MERTON PLACE was Nelson's only country home. He lived there with Sir William and Lady Hamilton as his guests. There the drama played itself out and reached its climax in the birth of Horatia, who was actually born with Sir William in the house, yet, so it is said, knowing nothing of it. The child was got away within three days.

It is an exciting chapter of this rather piteous story. Here the social round of life went on with parties from morning till night. Nelson and Lady Hamilton still with all their vital powers, and old Sir William nearing his end. Lord Minto, a great friend of Nelson, who had no patience with Lady Hamilton, has described the scene:

The whole establishment and way of life are such as to make me angry as well as melancholy, but I cannot alter it, and I do not think myself at liberty to quarrel with him for his weakness, though nothing shall ever induce me to give the smallest countenance to Lady Hamilton. She looks ultimately to the chance of marriage, as Sir William will not be long in the way, and she probably indulges a hope that she may survive Lady Nelson. In the meantime she and Sir William and the whole set of them are living with him at his expense. She is in high looks, but more immense than ever. The love she makes to Nelson is not only ridiculous but disgusting; not only the rooms, but the whole house, staircase and all, are covered with pictures of her and him. The celebrated Jew singer Braham performed with Lady Hamilton; she is horrid, but he entertained me.

The day came in the spring of 1803 when Sir William was taken seriously ill in Piccadilly, and for six days Nelson and Lady Hamilton watched at his bedside in turn until at last he died in their arms. He left his favourite picture of his wife to Nelson, "the most virtuous, loyal, and truly brave character I ever met with." Nelson continued to live at Merton Place, and she with him. When Horatia was about four she went to live at Merton too, and a little sister was born, to live only a few days.

In the summer of Trafalgar year Nelson was back himself, and within a few days had assembled under his roof as many old friends and kinsfolk as he could get together. At five o'clock on September 2 a captain from the Admiralty brought despatches, and it was resolved that Nelson should take command of the Mediterranean as soon as the Victory could be ready for him. On his last day here Lord Minto called and found that Lady Hamilton had been the day before "in tears all day, could not eat, and hardly drink, and near swooning, and all at table." The next night Nelson was creeping upstairs to kiss Horatia as she lay asleep, and at half-past ten he drove "from dear, dear Merton, where I left all I hold dear in this world." He saw it no more.

The Founder of Our College System

MERTON has established itself as one of the most famous names in Oxford, and in no way can the name now perish; its fame hangs on its association with Walter de Merton. He is Walter de Merton because it is felt that he may have been born here or that he may have been educated at the priory. We know nothing of his father save that his name was William, and both his parents lie at St Michael's, Basingstoke, where he founded a hospital in their memory.

Fortunate it is for Merton that, by whatever chance, this famous name was linked with it, for he was one of the founders and forerunners of learning, and it is his proud claim that he established the college system in the life of our universities. He himself was one of eight children, having seven sisters but no brother, and he had also eight nephews to educate. Here he may have had the inspiration of his great work. He founded a school for his nephews at Malden, and after ten years (in 1274) he transferred the school to a new college he had founded at Oxford. Merton College was the first college to provide education and home life in one building. Its students were not to train for the priesthood or the monastery, but were to be made masters of all the knowledge available to their age. A man of immense liberality and great learning, with a practical knowledge of the world, his generous endowment of his college was an inspiration for all college founders who followed him, and upon Merton all other colleges at Oxford and Cambridge have been modelled.

He served his country in other noble ways, for he went on a mission to the Pope, and twice he was Lord Chancellor. Then he became Bishop of Rochester, the last high office he held, for in the third year of his bishopric he was fording the Medway when he was thrown by his stumbling horse, and received injuries from which he died.

The Yews of Druids Grove

MICKLEHAM. It lies in the lovely Mole Valley between Box Hill and Leatherhead, Surrey's newest bypass road below, and Roman Stane Street climbing the hill above. Here the Mole

SURREY

lives up to its name by playing curious tricks. We look over Burford Bridge a mile away and see it flowing by; we walk beside it at Mickleham in dry summers and see nothing but an empty river-bed with a few pools. The explanation is that the waters disappear into the chalk and flow along in subterranean clefts, appearing normal again when we take another look at Leatherhead.

A Norman tower has been watching Mickleham through the centuries, and it draws us to the church. Just inside the lychgate we are greeted by the last message of old John Walker who died in 1813, boldly written on one of the wooden memorials:

> *Farewell all my friends so kind,*
> *I hope in Heaven my soul you'll find.*

The Norman chancel has four windows enriched with moulded arches and pillars, and its Norman arch is beautifully decorated with carved patterns. Under a carved arch in the Tudor chapel are 16th century brass portraits of William Wyddowson and his wife, and the chapel is lined with 17th century panelling from St Paul's School in London. The square arcaded font of Sussex marble is 13th century. The pulpit is rich with Bible scenes and figures of apostles. Some parts of it are old Flemish work, and the other panels were carved and put together by two Mickleham boys who were sent to learn carving in Belgium by a 19th century rector. He was Alfred Burmester, who was here for half a century. Next but one before him on the list of rectors is Thomas Roger Filewood. He lost his sight, and was able to repeat the services only with his daughter's help; he lost his property through family troubles; and with the strain of it all he lost his reason and his life.

Hanging in the chancel are the helmet and banner of Sir Francis Stidolph, who died in 1655. In that year he was visited at Mickleham by John Evelyn, who wrote in his diary of his host's "goodly walks and hills shaded with yew and box." Over the vestry door is Continental glass 400 years old, showing part of a Pentecost scene.

Walking in the churchyard we noticed the grave of a Mickleham man who went to Rome and was Chamberlain to three Popes. We were looking for the simple grave of a man who was laid to rest here only a few months before we called. He was Frank Cole, who for more than 40 years was the gardener and friend of George Meredith at his house below Box Hill. In his lifetime he met many of the great Victorians who came to visit his master, and was a familiar figure in the village, leading the donkey which drew Meredith in his bath-chair.

Let into the small stone at the foot of another grave in the churchyard is a small metal aeroplane. It marks the resting-place of one of the earliest pioneers of flight in England, Douglas Graham Gilmour. He was built in the heroic mould but was too reckless to live, and he crashed in Richmond Park at 26. It was in the days before the war, soon after Wilbur Wright had flown in France. Gilmour had learned to fly in Paris in the autumn of 1909, and bought a little two-seater Bleriot monoplane which he called Big Bat. He joined a Bristol aviation company and flew dangerously in spite of spill after spill. He flew over Hampton Court at a height of 200 feet, flew to Henley Regatta with his landing-wheels actually touching the water, and flew up the Thames at Westminster. The Royal Aero Club protested and put him on trial, suspending his flying certificate; but the warning deterred him little, and on February 17, 1912, he took the risk again and crashed, one of the first victims of the Flying Age which has robbed the world since then of so much brave youth.

Beside the village street stands an imposing house of 1636, where lived the well-known William Rogers of St Botolph's in Bishopsgate. The front door came from a 17th century house in Paradise Row, Chelsea. Juniper Hill, hidden on a height and believed to have been designed by Adam, is a fine house with a stately staircase and magnificent marble mantelpieces.

Farther along towards Box Hill is Juniper Hall with fine old cedars in the garden. Here during the French Revolution came the fugitive General D'Arblay, with Talleyrand and Madame de Staël, and here Fanny Burney took her French lessons from the General, afterwards marrying him in Mickleham Church. Across the road at Fredley lived Richard Sharp, who was hatmaker, poet, and MP, and counted the greatest among his friends. They nicknamed him Conversation Sharp, Macaulay adding that, whatever he said, he never talked scandal. Another famous resident was John Stuart Mill, who protested against the railway running through Norbury Park. He failed in this, but later became a founder and active member of the Commons Preservation Society, which has protected 2000 square miles from enclosure or encroachment.

Now much of Norbury Park has been preserved by the County Council. It is one of the loveliest estates in Surrey, and is wonderfully wooded. Its most famous trees are the ancient yews of the Druids Grove. Two of the biggest are over 22 feet round, and the path passes under one remarkable specimen whose branches touch the ground for a circumference of 230 feet. Just above this is the dead trunk of a beech 24 feet round, with moss-covered roots stretching more than 50 feet from the trunk. Some of the yews have assumed fantastic shapes, and bear such names as King of the Park, the Horse and its Rider, and the Fallen Giant, coiled on the ground as if writhing in pain. It is said that the rare Dotted Chestnut Moth is to be seen here at midnight in October, gorged with the juice of the yew berries. A remarkable oak farther up the hill bears branches creeping along the ground.

George Meredith loved to send his visitors to see the yews, and at West Humble is the little weatherboarded chapel where his sister-in-law talked to the railway navvies on Sunday evenings. This building was once a barn, and was being beautified with new panelling when we called. There are ruins of a much older chapel up the lane; the chapel was probably built about 1200 for the tenants of Merton Priory. The ivy has been removed from the walls and the site laid out as a garden.

Up the road at Bagden Farm an earthenware pot was found in the middle of the 18th century. It contained about a peck of little brass coins, the latest of the year 268. At that period Britain was in a disturbed state under the usurper Tetricus, and we may conclude that the hoard was buried for safety.

Queen Elizabeth Calls on Sir Julius Caesar

MITCHAM. It is famous for the cricket on the Green, for the ancient Fair which is held there every August, and for the lavender which is now but a fragrant memory. It deserves to be famous also for having preserved its open spaces during its transition from village to town while London has crept haphazard to its gates. Of its five square miles a sixth has been saved in this way, and for all who live in Mitcham there is a walk by the river, or a seat in the shade, or a game on the heath. In addition to the furze-clad common fringed with trees, there are many scattered areas of pleasure-grounds, and across one corner, Cranmer Green, runs the avenue of prunus and tulip trees planted in King George's Coronation year.

Mitcham's cross of memory is in another green corner, and what is called Lower Green has one of the most famous cricket pitches in England, nursery of Surrey cricketers and once the practice-ground of Australian Elevens. The fast bowler Tom Richardson and the famous wicket-keeper Herbert Strudwick are among the giants of the game who learnt cricket on this green. Mitcham has also 18 beautiful acres by the Wandle preserved for the people forever, the land called Watermeads, with its delightful walk under the willows. The birds love it all, and over 70 kinds (including the kingfisher) have been observed. A strip of bank called the Happy Valley is dedicated to the memory of Octavia Hill, one of the founders of the National Trust, and we are sure it would have delighted John Ruskin, who fought his hardest to save the River Wandle from pollution.

Not far from the river have been found graves and skeletons of our ancestors 1500 years ago, with bronze brooches worn by their women and iron blades used for weaving. Found in a gravel pit was the skeleton of a young man wounded in the skull, the weapon that made the wound lying near him.

Mitcham has several modern churches, and one old one, St Peter and St Paul, still with the medieval base of its tower, though it was all rebuilt after Waterloo. Outside are many quaint heads, including a demon with horns and huge ears grinning at a modest-looking bishop; inside is a graceful iron screen, and clustered columns supporting a vaulted roof; but the interest is mostly in the monuments. In a dark corner by the west window we see medallion busts of Sir Ambrose Crowley and his wife, the man Steele satirised as Sir Humphrey Greenhat. By the pulpit are two portraits in relief, one in bronze of George Parker Bidder, who "never turned his back but marched breast forward," and one in marble of a Fleet Street man, Henry Hoare, who lived 40 years at Mitcham Grove and lies at Morden. Close by on the chancel wall is a relief sculpture of Canon Wilson, vicar for 59 years before they laid him by his church in 1918. A tablet by Westmacott has a lovely little figure of a woman holding a cup; and another by the altar shows John Hyde in his wig, with a beehive to remind us of his industry as a London merchant of Trafalgar days. Sleeping in the churchyard is the actress Anne

Mitcham   Cricket on the Common

Ockley   Cricket on the Green

Merton
Nelson's Church

Mickleham
Norman Church Tower

Mortlake The Old Parish Church

SURREY

Hallam, famous in the 18th century for her playing of Lady Macbeth.

Among the modern churches is St Barnabas, built in 1914, a fine building with tall lancet windows and a lofty bell turret. Among the old houses is the 18th century Eagle House seen through attractive iron gates; it has a lantern turret on its balustraded roof.

Mitcham's richest memories are of some of the great figures of our Golden Age. Here lived John Donne, laid to rest in St Paul's in 1631, the last preacher of the Elizabethan Era and the man Dr Johnson called the founder of the metaphysical school of poetry. Here, too, Sir Walter Raleigh inherited a house which he sold to raise money for his expeditions; and here came Elizabeth herself, visiting the judge Sir Julius Caesar, whose own story of her visit makes it clear that only a very rich man could hope to entertain the great queen. He tells how she supped and lodged and dined next day, going away with exceeding good contentment—as well she might after he had given her a richly embroidered gown of silver cloth, a mantle with a fringe of pure gold, and a white taffeta hat bejewelled with rubies and diamonds. She had promised to come before, and with the cost of this disappointment it all came to £700 sterling, not counting "mine own provisions and what was sent by my friends."

London in Surrey

MORDEN. Trees still line the roads leading to it, and others still cast a beneficent shadow on its ancient church, but for the most part Morden has given itself up to the builder. Almost everywhere he has taken possession, and his work goes steadily on.

Here at Morden are the fine Haig Homes for our war heroes, each block of buildings with a medallion of Earl Haig. Here are the houses of the St Helier estate with new roads running beside some old Surrey lanes instead of swallowing them up. Here are new houses by the hundred and new shops by the score. Here is a transformation scene of our own day, for Surrey fields have become homes for Londoners. In the wide High Street are red buses from London, and here, too, adding a dignity all its own, is a new Underground station of simple straight lines.

Half a mile away, in a quiet corner where trees still dominate the scene, is a lychgate leading to a red brick church, originally built about 1136. It was built anew in 1636 by Richard Garth who sleeps in the chancel, and its oldest part is a pointed 15th century doorway in the porch. It was one of the Garths of the next century who gave the panelled pulpit, its sounding-board inlaid with a star, and its staircase with twisted balusters; and it was the physician-poet, Sir Samuel Garth, who moved his friend Pope to say that if ever there was a good Christian without knowing it, it was Dr Garth.

The church has a sanctuary chair and an almsbox, both probably carved by 17th century craftsmen, the almsbox with rich foliage and a tiny cherub's head. The altar rails are Georgian. The east window is aglow with striking 17th century glass, said to have come from Merton Abbey, showing Moses in red and blue, Aaron in the vestments of a high priest, the Tablets of the Law, and two kneeling figures thought to be the donors of the window.

Twice here we come upon the influence of Chantrey, for the font was made by his pupil James Legrew, and one of the memorials has a fine face carved by Henry Weekes, who had been his assistant. On the wall is a big monument with two urns and the bust of Peter Leheup; and in the vestry hangs a genial picture of old Dr Peers, who came as rector in 1778 and stayed for 57 years.

Where the Boat Race Ends

MORTLAKE. It lies between Richmond Park and the Thames, and once a year its name is on everybody's lips, for here the Boat Race ends. But for 364 days every year the appeal of Mortlake is in the proud collection of celebrated names enshrined in and about its church. They are a remarkable company, for among them we find a Prime Minister, a great reformer, astrologers, writers, and lord mayors.

The church was rebuilt by order of Henry the Eighth and has the year 1543 on the tower. The attractive little belfry is modern. The tower doorway facing the fine lofty nave is well moulded and has tracery and flowers in the spandrels. The altarpiece in the south aisle is a picture of the Entombment painted 300 years ago by a Belgian artist and given by a Mortlake picture dealer. The unusual-looking altar below it is a 15th century walnut chest, dedicated as an altar after it had been in the church about three centuries. Said to have come from the Spanish Armada, it has decorations round the keyhole, and a carved lion at each end. Another fine chest in this aisle is several generations younger. The beautiful 15th century font is almost the oldest thing here and was given by Archbishop Bourchier to the chapel of the manor house. On its bowl are quatrefoils with shields and flowers.

Two 18th century lord mayors of London we think of in this place, one remembered by a tablet, the other sleeping under an unnamed stone. The first is John Barber, who knew Swift and Pope and put up Samuel Butler's tomb in the Abbey. The second is the merchant and politician Sir John Barnard, so modest that when they put up his statue in the Royal Exchange he never went in again.

There is a tablet to Sir Philip Francis, who is thought to have written the celebrated Letters of Junius, and is known to have helped to prepare the case against Warren Hastings. On another tablet we find the name of Henry Addington, Speaker during the trial of Hastings and Prime Minister just before Trafalgar. He became the first Viscount Sidmouth. In a frame at the back of the vicar's stall is a good example of 17th century Mortlake tapestry, showing the head and shoulders of Peter with his keys. In an alley leading to the river (nearly opposite the church) is a Jacobean house now converted into mean dwellings. Here, in an inscription fading away, we read that the famous Mortlake tapestry-making was established under the patronage of James the First, and that here were copied the celebrated Raphael cartoons bought by Charles Stuart on the advice of Reubens.

The church has a 19th century chancel, but far older are two men laid to rest within it. One is Augustine Phillips, who played on the stage with Shakespeare, and who, when he died here in 1605, left "a thirty-shilling piece of gold to my fellow William Shakespeare." The other is the Elizabethan astrologer Dr Dee, whom we see on an engraving in the vestry. Less than two generations after his death was born not far away the second great astrologer of Mortlake, John Partridge, who made himself famous for his almanacs, and spent his last years trying to convince the world that he was still alive. He lies in this churchyard in company with Sir Edwin Chadwick, the friend of Jeremy Bentham, and one of the greatest reformers of the Victorian Era.

In the Roman Catholic cemetery lies Sir Richard Burton, who died in the same year after a life given to travelling and writing; he is buried under a huge tent-shaped stone bearing stars and moons.

It is said that it was at East Sheen, by Mortlake, that poor Amy Robsart was married to Lord Robert Dudley, in the presence of the boy King Edward the Sixth.

The Remarkable Traveller

SIR RICHARD BURTON, born in Hertfordshire in 1821, was educated at Oxford, and in France and Italy. He was only 21 when he found himself in India, the beginning of a remarkable lifetime of travel. He learned native ways and languages as to the manner born, and in 1853 he set out to map unknown Arabia.

Disguised as a native, he was one of the first Englishmen to enter Mecca. Assuming the guise of an Arab merchant, he made his way to the mysterious Harar, Somaliland, and after service in the Crimea set out in 1858 with John Speke on his memorable expedition to Central Africa.

In spite of malaria and paralysis, they were the first white men to see Lake Tanganyika. Soon afterwards, while Burton lay ill, Speke discovered Victoria Nyanza. The mystery of 30 centuries, the source of the Nile, was also solved.

Burton's later travels included Dahomey and the Gold Coast; he twice crossed the Andes, travelled 1500 miles by canoe down the San Francisco River in Brazil, and made extensive explorations up the La Plata River and the Amazon. He was subsequently British consul in three continents, each post serving as a base for new explorations.

For the last 30 years of his life he was accompanied on his travels by his heroic wife, who, when he died at Trieste, brought his body to Mortlake for burial, and prepared the grave at his side which she herself was to occupy in due course.

A man of great strength and courage, Burton felt that he could go anywhere and do anything; and he had few failures. Master of 35 languages, he wrote brilliant volumes on his travels and discoveries, in addition to a full translation of the Arabian Nights, of which his wife issued an edition for household reading. His translation from the Arabic of the Scented Garden she destroyed after his death.

The Forerunners of Our Quacks

JOHN DEE and John Partridge, divided by a century in life, are united in the common earth of Mortlake. Dee was born in 1527 and Partridge in 1644.

Dee, educated at Cambridge, travelled widely on the continent, but turned his great learning to poor uses. He declared that he could transmute base metal into gold, and was able to forecast the future. Even Queen Elizabeth believed in him. On his professing to raise spirits to prophesy, a mob broke into his house and scattered his library, and, his reputation blasted, he died, a melancholy quack.

Partridge was a shoemaker who taught himself Greek and Latin, and began the life of an astrological fortune-teller. He was making a fortune for himself when Swift, writing as Isaac Bickerstaff, produced a mock almanac predicting that Partridge would die on a certain day the next year. In due course this was followed with a pamphlet declaring that Partridge had died as predicted, a detailed description being given of the deathbed scene, and the astrologer's confession of his imposture. Partridge had not died, but he could not prove it to all those who read Swift's pamphlets. He spent the rest of his life in trying to prove that he was alive, but he had become the laughing stock of Europe and is forgotten, with all the quack astrologers of his time, though not, unhappily, with the quack astrologers of our time.

He Saved Our Generation

SIR EDWIN CHADWICK, who lies at Mortlake, was one of those immense forces behind the life of a nation which act like purifying winds. He found England a breeding ground of fever, and left it a sweeter place. He saved millions of lives. Wherever life is spared and illness is prevented as the result of sanitation and good water, the cry should rise from the hearts of men, Thank God for Edwin Chadwick.

He came of old Lancashire stock, born in a suburb of Manchester, and arrived in London one day by a slow jogging coach to earn a pittance in a lawyer's office. He wrote articles for papers and became a barrister, and one day, on writing an article on public health, it came to him that there was too much that was wrong in this country. He threw up the Bar and hurled himself into a crusade for cleaning up the country. He had the courage of a bulldog. He knew that England was reeking with preventable disease, and he went up and down the land declaring it.

He drew up a report that frightened the Government, but his facts were fully borne out. One in ten of the people of Manchester, and one in seven in Liverpool, were living in hovels underground. Water teemed with the germs of death. Houses were built back to back with no ventilation. In great towns not half the children born lived even to be five years old, and the length of life in a town was only half that of the country.

Edwin Chadwick started the science of living decently. He started sanitation. He was the inspiration of those laws of public health that have saved a countless multitude of lives.

His fame was far and wide. Napoleon the Third sent for him and asked his advice about Paris. "Sir," said Chadwick, "they say that Augustus found Rome a city of brick and left it a city of marble. If you, finding Paris stinking, will leave it sweet, you will more than rival Caesar." When he died, at the great age of 90, this was the verdict passed upon him by a high authority:

The sanitary works that have been undertaken during the last half century in every civilised nation are so many monuments to Chadwick.

That is true; this fiery reformer who toiled so long without fee or reward, sacrificed health and ease to give health and strength to posterity. He told the truth to the nation and made it clean, and, by laying the foundations of a healthy state, he saved our generation.

Relics of the Forests

NEWDIGATE. The Weald is all about it, and if most of the ancient forest has gone we can still see some of the splendid trees that grew here 500 years ago. They are the massive timber pillars and interlocking arches of the church tower, one of the finest pieces of oak building in Surrey.

The church has a 13th century chancel and an aisle added a century later, with a peephole from one to the other. The modern screen is richly carved, and the organ case is beautified with carved panels. Under the mighty beams of the tower is an ancient chest, made from a single piece of oak, and the carved front of a Jacobean gallery.

There is a brass inscription to the wife of George Steere, who was rector for 52 years, and managed to hold his position through the Civil War. He founded the village school. In a window of the modern aisle are fragments of 15th century glass, showing the tops of three ornamental canopies and a red shield with three lion's paws.

SURREY

The shield is the arms of the Newdigates who lived here for several centuries. One of them gave £25 towards the English fleet that beat the Armada; and the founder of the Newdigate Prize at Oxford belonged to a younger branch of the family in Warwickshire.

Old Cobbett

NORMANDY. It is one of two places near the Hog's Back with surprising names: the other is a growing hamlet called Christmaspie, a mile or two away.

Normandy has a few old cottages and many new ones, and it has the great house and finely wooded grounds of Henley Park, an estate which Queen Elizabeth gave to her favourite Essex. Parts of the house are said to be unaltered since the time the Earl lived in it.

Essex is not the only public figure to be remembered here, for about a century ago this place saw something of that turbulent writer and politician William Cobbett. Here he had a farm where he made experiments in agriculture, and here in the summer of 1835 he died, an old man of 73, working and debating to the last. They took his body to Farnham where he was born, and among those who followed it in the procession from Normandy was the great Irishman Daniel O'Connell, an impressive figure in black.

The Burne-Jones Window

NUTFIELD. From its cross-roads above Redhill a lovely lane goes between walls of rock to glimpses of the Weald, and another runs down to the old church on the hillside.

Its 15th century tower was patched up by later builders, and its 13th century chancel was lengthened after a century of use. The general impression is of a wide church, one aisle being 15th century and the other modern.

We step into the chancel through the arch of a beautifully carved screen 500 years old, and find it lighted by a delicate Burne-Jones window, showing a choir of angels in reds and greens with the deep blue sky above. Under an arch is the 14th century tomb of Sir Thomas de Roleham, and on the wall in brass are William Graffton and his wife of the 15th century. He is described as "sometime clerk of this church" in the days when a priest might not marry, and it is thought he was in minor orders before he had a wife.

There is a seat with two Tudor poppyheads, a pulpit with carved Tudor panels, a little jumbled glass 500 years old in two windows, and a 17th century collecting-box which says, Pray Remember the Poor. The font is 15th century with eight carved panels, and its date, 1665, is probably the year when it came back here after the Commonwealth.

Among the memorials is a tablet to an old army surgeon of many campaigns who died in Trafalgar year, and to his son, who fell in storming the forts at Salamanca.

The Arrow From Nowhere

OAKWOOD. A little place a mile from Sussex, it hides its possessions even from the few cars that pass along this lane. They are in the church across the fields, reached by a delightful walk with Leith Hill. Here, in this place of woodland peace, in what was once the Wealden forest, people were coming to worship 700 years ago, and there is still left a little stained glass and a faded wall-painting they must have seen. Some other fragments of glass and another faded painting are two centuries younger; and beneath the pieces of old glass are lovely modern windows of the Madonna and an angel.

Like hidden treasure under the chancel floor is an interesting brass, the portrait of Sir Edward de la Hale of 1431, in full armour. The story goes that when hunting one day in the forest with his son he wounded a wild boar. At that moment the boy slipped from his horse, and was in great danger from the rush of the dying beast until an unexpected arrow (apparently from nowhere) disposed of it. Out of gratitude to God for this deliverance Sir Edward made a vow that he would restore and endow this church, and but for him, if the tale be true, it might be a ruin today.

The stone roof comes from his century, and other changes in the building are known to have been made in his time. Yet any restoration he did cannot have lasted too well, for in 1701 John Evelyn wrote in his diary that he subscribed towards the rebuilding of Oakwood Chapel, "now after 200 years almost fallen down."

A tablet on the wall tells how the estates belonging to the church had been taken away at the Reformation, how Queen Elizabeth gave £3 6s 8d a year for the chaplain, and how the poor man and his successors had to manage with this until in the 18th century new endowments helped to make their living less beggarly. Among those who gave the much-needed money were a later John Evelyn, and Dr Godolphin, the Dean of St Paul's.

Grocer's Son and Invincible Doctor

OCKHAM. Its 15th century tower stands in Ockham Park close to the great house. The church is in a fine setting of trees, and most impressive as we walk to it is the beautiful east window of seven lancets, sometimes called the Seven Sisters. Probably 13th century, it is a striking sight from outside, and attractive from within, with painted glass of Our Lord, saints, and happy children.

But there is other and older glass to delight us. Two beautiful 14th century windows are partly filled with Dutch glass of the 17th and 18th centuries; and very quaint some of it is. A medallion of 1659 shows a Dutch mariner in a big hat standing by a globe, with a ship on the sea behind him. Another, painted 28 years earlier, shows Susanna with the Elders, Susanna doing her hair by a bath sunk in the ground. Still older glass in other windows shows angels forming part of a heavenly choir, some knots and leaves, and two little round pictures of grizzly, squinting monsters with their tongues out. Close to one of these is a small pane giving us a glimpse into village history 150 years ago. On it these words have been scratched:

W. Peters new leaded this in 1775 and never was paid for the same.

The nave is spanned by three medieval beams of oak, that are above the chancel arch still with the three holes which held the Rood and its attendant figures before the Reformation. The lower panels of the 500-year-old rood screen are worked into the two front pews, and are pierced with holes that children might see the service. The 16th century ceiling is made of panelled wood, and was probably set up by a local carpenter. It still bears traces of its original painted pattern, but its great beauty is in its bosses. There is the twisted knot which was the badge of Lord Berners; the fleur-de-lys; a hemp bray on a trestle table; a grinning face with outstretched tongue; the Weston arms with heads of wolves; and the magpie badge of Lord Rivers. Most curious of all is the tail of a fish disappearing into a basketwork trap fitted with ropes for fastening it to the weir. An old painting of daisies is on the wall above the chancel arch. The tower arch is Norman, the roodloft stairway is exposed to view, and the chancel stalls have some old bench-ends. A gem of sculpture is a maiden's head beneath a niche in the wall, carved 600 years ago by someone who must have loved a little girl, surely a portrait from life.

There are two good brasses in the sanctuary, one showing a 14th century rector Walter Frilende, and another of a 15th century couple, John and Margaret Weston, he in armour and she tall and graceful, with an elaborate headdress. A modern brass tablet is in memory of Stephen Lushington, a keen reformer and a clever advocate, who worked among other things for the abolition of the slave trade and of capital punishment, and died peacefully at Ockham Park at 91.

Looking over the locked gate into the King chapel, we have a peep into the life and politics of 18th century England. In the centre is Rysbrack's elaborate sculpture of Peter King, the Exeter grocer's son who became Lord Chancellor. As a boy he spent his pocket-money on books, and some of his early writings attracted the notice of his kinsman, the philosopher John Locke. He became a lawyer, went to Parliament as a Whig MP, and was knighted by Queen Anne. Rising to be a judge, he had to try some of those who had been implicated in the Jacobite Rebellion of 1715. As a peer he called himself Lord King of Ockham, and in 1725 took his seat on the Woolsack. His reputation did not increase during the years he was Chancellor but he established certain principles in law, and was responsible for the act ordering English to be used instead of Latin in writs and other documents. He was a Fellow of the Royal Society, and a pall-bearer at the funeral of Sir Isaac Newton.

With the death of the first Lord King in 1734 Ockham Park passed to each of his four sons in turn. Two generations later it was inherited by his great-grandson, another Peter King, of whom there is a fine bust in the King chapel. This Peter succeeded to his title as a boy of 17 and sat in the House of Lords when he came of age.

One of his two sons, Peter John Locke King, was an enterprising politician who introduced many bills to Parliament, threw out old laws as well as making new ones, and in one session alone obtained the repeal of 120 useless statutes. Another of Lord King's sons married Byron's daughter and became first Earl of Lovelace; there is a memorial here to their son, the second earl, Ralph Milbanke. He was a remarkable man. At 22 he spent a year in Iceland. For his bold climbing a peak of the Dolomites is named after him. He was an excellent scholar, a much travelled man, and a fine linguist, but his chief zeal was devoted to a vigorous vindication of his grandmother, the poet's wife, Lady Byron, from the attacks made on her after Mrs Beecher Stowe's revelations concerning Byron. He believed that Mrs Stowe's story was true, and defended Lady Byron against all her critics.

More than 600 years ago there was born, perhaps in this Surrey Ockham, a man who became one of the greatest philosophers of his day. He was William of Ockham, the Invincible Doctor, who received his training at Oxford and became a Franciscan friar. As a result of his heresies the Pope had him imprisoned at Avignon; but William with other friars of his order, escaped by night and went in a boat down the Rhone with a cardinal in full chase. The Pope excommunicated him and gave elaborate orders for his capture, but without avail, and he finally arrived at the Franciscan house in Munich where he was to be laid to rest many years after.

The books he wrote, and the arguments he put forward, were used as valuable weapons by those who opposed the papal authority in later times, and they are said to have helped Luther to think out his doctrines. William of Ockham was a great figure in the life of the 14th century, and is remembered as much for his work in philosophy and logic as for his arguments about politics and religion.

Roses Beyond Memory

OCKLEY. The road that runs by its village green is the great Stane Street of the Romans, a piece of their way from Chichester to London. From Sussex it comes up as straight as an arrow, making for the gap in the downs near Dorking, where it crosses a corner of the churchyard. It is the oldest thing in Ockley, and has probably been used without a break since Roman times.

Many a sight it must have seen, but nothing more thrilling than an event occurring here about two centuries before the Normans came to our shores. Historians believe this village to be the place mentioned in the Saxon Chronicle as Aclea, the place where King Ethelwulf of Wessex fought a great battle with the Danes. Here the armies gathered, the Danes marching victorious from London and Ethelwulf hurrying with his forces from Winchester, and here the invaders were defeated. Looking out on this battlefield of long ago is a crumbling windmill 200 years old.

The chief attraction of the church is the view of it from outside. It is set in a churchyard delightful with oaks, yews, and tall white-leaved poplars.

Some of the walls and windows are 14th century, and the charming timber porch is 15th, with balustrades added later. The tower is dated 1700; the old roof is made of stone and has graceful kingposts within. The handsome mosaic and marble decoration of the chancel is in memory of John Lee Steere, a boy of 19 who was killed in the first months of the Great War.

Growing in the churchyard are roses that keep alive in Ockley the memory of a quaint and pretty custom. Writing in Stuart times, John Aubrey tells us how in those days there had been red roses among the graves beyond man's memory, and how if one of two lovers died the other would always plant roses to bloom where the loved one was laid.

The Old Windmill

OUTWOOD. Side by side on the common its two old windmills stand 400 feet above the sea. They are the only things to see in Outwood, but they are enough.

A charming picture they make in this breezy place, the older and better of the two still in working order when we called. It is nearly the oldest mill in England, and was built in the year before the Great Fire of London. From the top of it, the story goes, the people of Outwood watched the red glow over the city 22 miles away. Its sails were given to it in our own time by the Society for the Protection of Ancient Buildings.

The other is a tall eight-sided black mill, and was built as a rival by the brother of the owner of the old mill. When trade was bad it had to close down, and it now stands idle with two of its sails missing. It seemed to us that the old mill of Outwood was saying:

> *In sixteen hundred and sixty-six,*
> *When London was burning like rotten sticks,*
> *To tell the news to the neighbouring farms,*
> *I, Outwood Windmill, swung wide my arms.*

SURREY

The wind blew high on this Surrey down
And fanned the fire in the crumbling town.
Folk cried It will burn till the great wind calms.
(And wildly and wildly I turned my arms.)

How the timber crashed! There were terrible falls.
London Bridge went and the great St Paul's;
The folk gathered round me were filled with alarms,
But I stuck to my post, and I swung my arms.

I'm not quite the mill that I once used to be
When I swung my arms for the world to see,
For those were the days of my youth, you must know,
Now nearly three hundred years ago.

The Home of the Nightingale

OXTED. All motorists know its steep old street with the 17th century and 18th century cottages reached by steps, and at the top the old timbered inn, a fine bit of Tudor England.

All BBC listeners know its nightingales. They are the best-known birds in the world, and have been heard on every continent. In millions of homes in our Motherland and overseas Oxted nightingales have been heard singing to a lovely cello, but long before the BBC began these nightingales were known, for they were famous enough in those days to be put on the gramophone.

Oxted has grown into two, the old and the new, and it is odd that the oldest place it has is among the new. One of the new places is Mr Frederic Lawrence's striking Union Church for united Non-comformists, an impressive structure with a low tower, great arches, and many fine windows. On the front of the building is a stone to the Architect, Builder, Foreman, and "to the workmen who built this place." Known as the Church of the Peace of God, it is a dignified building in the shape of a cross, with an interior charming with plain cream walls, wide arches open to the tower (which has 20 windows) and neat oak seats. The apse, approached by five steps, has three narrow lancet windows in blue, green, purple, and gold, giving a glow of colour contrasting with the plain walls. In front of the building is a little pond with goldfish and water lilies, and a fountain.

The oldest place in Oxted, of course, is the ancient church with the great low tower the Normans built very little higher than the chancel. The 15th century porch, shaded by a magnificent yew in front of the old manor house, has two trefoiled windows and shelters a 14th century doorway with the original door still on its hinges. It has tiny heads carved on it of two men and two women fading out of recognition after exposure to 600 summers and winters.

The chancel arch is 14th century, the nave arcades 15th, and there is a 13th century priest's doorway, one of those of which it is said that they were made small to teach the priest humility. It is odd that such a door should have so proud a lady over it, represented by an angel and with an inscription which tells us that her astounding qualities were hardly paralleled, so that

Perfect happiness she could not miss
Led by such graces to eternal bliss.

More modest is the floor stone on which we stand to read of this proud lady, for it tells us, with skull and cross-bones, of one of whom we would gladly hear a little more, Mrs Charles Hoskins, whom they laid here to rest in 1651 with these words:

Let this
 Pattern of Piety
  Map of Misery
  Mirror of Patience
 Here rest

On the chancel wall beside the proud lady is one of the most delightful family pictures we have seen in stone. It is the family of John Aldersly, a London merchant who died in the same year as Shakespeare. Two small cherubs look down on John and his wife kneeling at a desk, and below them are two charming processions of their sons and daughters looking towards each other. There are 10 sons and 7 daughters, six sons with beards and five daughters with quaint caps, and none of the figures are more than eight inches high, some little more than half as high.

The chancel is rich in small brass portraits. One of a rector who has been here 500 years has lost its head, another of the same century shows the wife of John Haselden and a fragment of John. Two quaint brasses are of three little brothers who lived three centuries ago, one a few months old and two aged five. John Hoskins (of the family of the humble lady) has ribbons tied in bows at his knees and a short cloak with a stand-up collar, and his brother, who has lost his wise little head, is commended to us because a quarter-of-an-hour before he died he said, suddenly and surprisingly, Lead us not into temptation, Deliver us from evil.

The windows of Oxted have much good glass, old and new. In the east window are 14th century paintings of the symbols of the Evangelists, a gold angel with red wings for Matthew, a brown lion with green wings for Mark, a red bull with yellow wings for Luke, and for John a yellow eagle soaring over all. The colours glow richly after 600 years.

The nave has four modern windows made by William Morris's firm from designs by Burne-Jones, all charming. One, in memory of all Oxted folk who have suffered uncomplainingly, has a beautiful Madonna in a garden of lilies, lovely in silver and gold as she listens to the good news from Gabriel. A companion window has two angles of the heavenly choir. Facing these two are windows with St Cecilia and St Catherine in a garden, and Christ and St John with little children, this being a thank-offering from many who have been baptised in the 15th century font. The east window of a small chapel has St George and St Martin in memory of two brothers killed in two Octobers of the war.

A remarkable possession of the church, which we found under its 18th century gallery, is a wonderful old iron box with an amazing lock covering the whole of the lid; it has 13 bolts all shooting together when the key is turned, a miracle of ingenuity.

The way to the bells in the tower is by a surprisingly elegant oak staircase of the days of Queen Anne, and there is an oak table of the same age. On the north chancel wall is a small iron ring which it is thought held the Lenten veil in the days before the Reformation.

The churchyard, with old gravestones carved with cherubs and comical faces, is dominated by a charming 20th century cross slenderly and beautifully made, with St Catherine and the Crucifixion at the top and 24 traceried panels at the base.

A little way out of the village is Barrow Green Court, a Jacobean house made new, in which lived Grote the historian, who sleeps in the Abbey. The house has a glorious park, fine greens surrounded by yew hedges, and a farm with ancient oak beams in its barns.

A Life of Adventure

PEPER HAROW. It is the home of the Midletons, not far from Godalming, an 18th century house standing with its church, its cottages, and its mellowed 17th century granary in a splendid park crossed by the Wey.

In the churchyard sleep lords of Peper Harow and their servants, among them Thomas Welland, who served his masters faithfully for 68 years. Near him lies Lawrence Eliot, who was rector here for 60 years of the 19th century; and there is another rector who was here for 55 years of the 18th century, Robert Holdsworth. In the churchyard also lies Sir Henry Dalrymple White, who led his regiment in the Heavy Cavalry charge at Balaclava. There is an immense double yew perhaps 600 years old, and here in the park, as if to crown it all, has been found a black flint worked by a man who lived perhaps 12,000 years ago.

The church has a plain Norman doorway and a Norman chancel arch enriched in modern times. On a corner stone of the nave is scratched an old sundial. There is a brass portrait of Joan Brocas of 1487, kneeling at prayer in her widow's veil and mantle. Her first husband John Adderley was Lord Mayor of London a generation after Dick Whittington; her second was William Brocas, Lord of Peper Harow. Another attractive brass shows Elizabeth Woodes of 1621, the daughter of a rector, in a peaked bodice and high collar. There is a brass inscription put here in 1635 to Henry and Jane Smith, who owned Peper Harow and were married 48 years; and outlined on marble is a portrait of Christopher Tonstall, "a faithful pastor of this place" in Stuart times. There is a monument to the fourth Lord Midleton who died about a century ago: it shows him reclining with a book.

On the chancel wall is a memorial to Admiral Thomas Brodrick, a distinguished 18th century sailor who lived here at the old gardener's cottage. As a lieutenant he commanded the storming party when Admiral Vernon took Porto Bello, one of the few successes in the miserable war over the ear of Robert Jenkins (who stirred the nation to madness in 1738 by producing at the bar of the House of Commons an ear which the Spaniards had cut off, he said, with taunts at the English king). Later, in the Seven Years War, he was sent to the Mediterranean with reinforcements for Admiral Byng, and, when Byng was brought home under arrest for his failure at Minorca, he sat as one of the courtmartial that sentenced the admiral to death. One of the most thrilling events in Brodrick's career took place a

Godalming   **Charterhouse Memorial Chapel**

Oxted   The Church of the Peace of God

Pyrford   Newark Priory

Pyrford   Newark Mill

year after, when he was second in command in the Mediterranean. His flagship, the Prince George of 90 guns, caught fire off Ushant, and only 250 of her 800 men were saved. Brodrick himself had to swim about for an hour until he was picked up stark naked by the boat from a merchant ship which had come to the rescue. In 1759 he served under Admiral Boscawen in the naval victory at Lagos Bay, and went on to blockade the remnants of the French fleet in Cadiz, doing it so thoroughly that even the Spaniards who were their friends could not help jeering at them. It is said they put up a notice with these ironical words:

> *For Sale—Eight French Men-of-War. For particulars apply to Vice-Admiral Brodrick.*

But in the end a gale drove the English into Gibraltar, and the blockaded ships managed to escape. For the last years of his life Brodrick lived in retirement, until he died in 1796 and was laid to rest in this most peaceful corner of Surrey.

A Marriage That Gave Us a Queen

PETERSHAM. It lies below the gloriously wooded slope of Richmond Hill, with meadows sweeping down to a fine stretch of the Thames. Here are quaint boarded cottages, fine 18th century houses, and a little wooden lock-up by an inn; and here, from the top of a bus in springtime, we look over high walls, expecting to see costumes of 200 years ago among the lilac.

A gracious air has Petersham, with its two churches, and the cottage (Elm Lodge) where Charles Dickens came when he was creating Nicholas Nickleby (mostly written here), playing all sorts of games, going to the races, and starting a fire-balloon club to amuse the children of the village. In the magnificent grounds of Petersham Lodge are huge cedars, and a chestnut avenue leading to the wooden summerhouse where John Gay is said to have written his Fables for the young Duke of Cumberland.

The old church of the village stands where a Norman church once stood, but it was rebuilt in the early Georgian period. Set behind a garden wall, it is small and quaint, one of the best places near London to see how our Georgian forefathers worshipped. It seems to consist mostly of two long transepts, and its box-pews fill even the tiny chancel up to the altar rails. It has a very lofty pulpit, a raised reading-desk with a box for the clerk below, a pair of old sanctuary chairs with carved backs, a blocked lancet window 700 years old in one of the outside walls, and an 18th century font with a tiny marble bowl on a thick stone baluster. Kept here as a relic is a bag left in the churchyard by a body-snatcher who was disturbed at his gruesome work.

The oldest monument is in the chancel, where, under a richly carved recess, are the figures of a 17th century lawyer, George Cole, and his wife and grandson. We see him in an unusual embroidered cap and a long black gown, and his wife in a black hood; the grandson is in a niche in front of the tomb. Near the tomb of a family she faithfully served for 60 years sleeps Sarah Abery, who died in 1795.

On the walls we find tributes to two 18th century men buried in the churchyard: Charles Stuart (though not Prince Rupert's Charles) and Captain George Vancouver, who sailed on a voyage of discovery round the world. By Vancouver's grave grows an arbutus tree, named after his botanist and sent here from the Canadian island that bears his name. Here also lie Mary and Agnes Berry, who suggested to Horace Walpole that he should write his Reminiscences; Mortimer Collins, an old-fashioned Tory politician, poet, and novelist, of the middle half of last century; and Theodora Jane Cowper, who comes into Cowper's poems as Delia.

She was Cowper's lost love, one of the three daughters of Ashley Cowper and a cousin of the poet. They fell in love in the days when she was a merry and accomplished and beautiful girl, and the poet used to visit at the house; but the father forbade their marrying on account of their relationship and the poet's poverty. After two years the young couple drifted apart, and never met again. Cowper put her into his poems:

> *Fear not that time, where'er we rove,*
> *Or absence, shall abate my love.*

She kept up her interest in him and helped him in his struggling by sending anonymous gifts and furnishing him secretly with a small annuity. Once he said to her sister, the famous Lady Hesketh of his Letters: "I still look back to the memory of your sister, and regret her, but how strange it is that if we were to meet now we should not know each other." Theodora remained faithful and never married, though she lived long after him.

It is the proud distinction of this little old church that the Earl and Countess of Strathmore were married here, the marriage that has given a queen to the throne in our time. Queen Elizabeth, daughter of the Strathmores, traces her ancestry to Robert Bruce, whose 21st lineal descendant she is. The Strathmores originally held the Glamis barony, the ninth Lord Glamis becoming an earl. The first Lord Glamis was a grandson of a daughter of Robert the Second of Scotland, and this Robert was the son of Marjorie Stewart, Robert Bruce's daughter. It was because Marjorie married a Stewart that the name of the royal line of Scotland and England was known as the Stuarts.

The big 20th century church of All Saints is built of brick in the Italian style, with a figure of Christ on its lofty campanile. Its chancel is raised very high above the nave, and has an imposing reredos with a carved Resurrection scene supported on marble arches. The rood shows Mary and John kneeling by the cross, and was carved by Oscar Zwink. The font, fashioned by the King of Italy's sculptor (Signor Nicoli), has three beautiful kneeling angels bearing on their wings a bowl of red marble veined with white; it stands in a baptistry of mysterious gloom, poised above a well intended for total immersion.

Among other possessions of the church are a pleasantly coloured rose window, and a Boy Scout peace memorial which shows in mosaic a knight kneeling in armour. Outside is a sundial with a little touch of London's history, for its pedestal comes from the parapet set up on old London Bridge when the famous houses on the bridge were pulled down.

One of Captain Cook's Boys

GEORGE VANCOUVER, who sleeps at Petersham, was one of a fine school of navigators of the 18th century. He sailed at 13 on Cook's second great voyage, being promoted midshipman. At 22 he began his militant career, fought under Rodney and Gardner, and was then appointed to the command through which he lives on the map.

Sailing in 1791, he followed the course of Cook, rounded the Cape, surveyed the south-west coast of Australia, where he found and named harbours and headlands, then crossed to New Zealand. Entering Dusky Bay, which Cook had marked on his map *Nobody knows what*, he carefully mapped it and entered on his chart *Somebody knows what*.

After a survey of Tahiti and the Hawaii Islands, whose submission he accepted without authority, he reached the west coast of North America, and explored far north, minutely investigating all inlets, discovering the Gulf of Georgia, and sailing round the island which bears his name.

Renewing his work to the north, he for the first time correctly mapped the coast beyond San Francisco, reaching England in 1795 after a voyage of four years, rich with results. Bred to rigid discipline at sea, he was himself a strict disciplinarian, and there was an outcry over his having flogged a midshipman (Lord Camelford), put him in irons, and discharged him from the ship. His voyage completed, he settled down at Petersham to write its story, and had just finished it when Death ended his voyage through this world.

The Unknown Charles Stuart

THE Charles Stuart who lies at Petersham was the son of that Marquess of Bute who served George the Third as Prime Minister, and concluded the Seven Years War with France and Spain.

His great opportunity came just after Napoleon had driven the English out of Toulon. A local patriot had suggested to Admiral Hood that Corsica should be set free from French domination, and Hood, with a fleet and a military force under Dundas, arrived at the island. Admiral and General could not agree, so Charles Stuart was made General in command of all the army in the Mediterranean, a post in which he was very successful. Another enterprise was now planned to secure a naval base in the Mediterranean, for Corsica had been evacuated. The idea was to take Minorca, and Lord St. Vincent told Pitt and his Ministers that there was only one man who could be entrusted with the undertaking, for his soldiers would go to the devil himself for him!

General Charles Stuart was accordingly sent to Gibraltar to collect four battalions from the garrison, which, with a mixed force from Portugal, made his numbers 4000. Escorted by men-of-war, the expedition set out to effect a surprise attack, but the secret had leaked out and the Spanish garrison were waiting for him. He succeeded in landing his forces under cover of the warships guns, but found himself on a rugged island with impossible roads. No transport had been provided and only six light cannon. There were two fortresses and two ports to be captured, a difficult task; but Stuart had an audacity and a resource equalled only by Nelson's. Two roads led to one of the fortresses, and he spread his troops over both to make them look like a great army. The trick frightened the Spaniards out of their advance trenches into the shelter of the town walls. The next night he threw up two siege batteries big enough for powerful guns (though he only had six small cannon to place in them), and spread his redcoats on a still wider front. What they saw in front of them the next morning so alarmed the Spaniards that they surrendered the island. Minorca was won without the loss of a man by one of the greatest bluffs in history, and very soon the island was made impregnable.

Early the next year an urgent letter reached him from Nelson at Palermo, hinting that 1000 men might save Sicily from impending disaster. Realising that Sicily must be saved from falling into French hands at all costs, Charles Stuart sailed with two regiments, and so improved the defences of Messina as to secure it from attack. His next and last effort was an attempt to persuade the Government to land an expedition to deliver Italy from Napoleon's yoke, but enough soldiers could not be found, and the scheme was dropped. In 1801 Charles Stuart died, mourned as a brilliant soldier whose leadership was unsurpassed in his day.

For Valour

PIRBRIGHT. Looking out over the green is a child reading a book. She seems to be coming home from school, and is part of a drinking fountain set up in memory of Queen Victoria's Diamond Jubilee.

The church has a battlemented tower from which a narrow spire rises up; but it is not this that strikes us most as we walk here from the green, it is a huge block of unhewn granite standing in the churchyard above the grave of Henry Morton Stanley. He lies with his wife, with whom he spent several quiet years here before his death. The great stone marking his grave is from Dartmoor, meant to be a symbol of Stanley's rugged nature, and on it is his African name Bula Matari.

The interest of the church is chiefly in its walls. A brass tablet tells of a hero of the Empire who lived at Pirbright, loved and honoured, for 21 years, dying a year after Stanley was laid to rest. He was Ross Mangles of the Bengal Civil Service, and he won the VC in the Mutiny for carrying a wounded soldier six miles over swampy ground to safety, though he himself was wounded. The VC was awarded two years later, when the rule was altered to include civilians. Here, as part of his tablet, is a medal, *his actual VC*.

Another tablet tells of a man who won quiet distinction at home. He was George Dawson who died in 1755, "minister and presbyter" of this church for 50 of his 76 years. Hanging on the wall is a photograph of a British Museum treasure, a document of great interest to this village because it was witnessed over 700 years ago by Jordan, the first known parson of Pirbright. It is a charter in which a man makes over to someone else his lands at Hadlow in Kent.

Not far away at Brookwood is the biggest cemetery in England, several hundred acres made beautiful with trees, rhododendrons, and flower beds. Parts of it are allotted to various London parishes, and to such communities as the Chelsea Pensioners, the Corps of Commissionaires, and the Parsees. Here, too, are Actors Acre, Oddfellows Acre, and graves of soldiers from the Antipodes who died in the Great War.

It is thrilling to see here the little bit of bronze which is the most coveted British reward for valour, the only one we have come upon in a church.

The Victoria Cross

THE Victoria Cross is a patent of nobility for men and women who serve their country with courage in the presence of an enemy. Its cost is little more than that of the laurel crown bestowed on the heroes of ancient Greece, but, like those bays, it takes precedence of all other distinctions. A man may be a Doctor of Divinity or a Knight of the Garter, but the VC follows his name before all other degrees or marks of rank.

It consists of a small bronze Maltese Cross, with the Crown surmounted by a lion, is inscribed *For Valour*, and is worn in the place of honour on the left; it is the most cherished decoration in the world. Instituted in 1856 for "conspicuous bravery or devotion to the country in the presence of the enemy," it came into being in the

Crimean War. In the next 58 years there were 525 awards; during the Great War it was won by 581 heroes.

Until 1911 the honour was confined to white troops, but then Indian soldiers were included. In 1920 the decoration was extended to women: matrons, sisters, and nurses, and the staff of the Nursing Services, and to civilians of both sexes regularly or temporarily under the orders or supervision of the Naval, Military, or Air Forces of the Empire.

The cross is accompanied by an annuity of £10 a year, where the recipient is below commissioned rank, with an additional £5 for every bar added for fresh acts of bravery which would have entitled the owner to the VC if he had not already received it. Should a VC be unable to obtain employment when leaving the service the annuity may be increased to £50.

The distinction is democratic in range; it may be won by general or private; its possessors are a unique order, each of whom has hazarded life and safety for the weal of the nation. Many ancient orders of chivalry, with their spurious romance and glittering pretence, are one with the wreckage of Feudalism; the VC is a true Order of Chivalry, in which only valour and sacrifice are counted meritorious.

It is inspired by the spirit of Henry the Fifth in his great speech to the Earl of Westmorland on the eve of Agincourt, when he declared that every man who fought with him that day should be his brother; however lowly his rank, "This day shall gentle his condition." The VC gentles the condition of every man who wins it.

The Man Who Found Livingstone

SIR H. M. STANLEY, one of the greatest African explorers, here lying under a great stone, was born in 1841 at Denbigh, his name being John Rowlands. His father dead, his poverty-stricken mother sent him to the workhouse, from which ill-usage drove him to sea. Reaching New Orleans, he was befriended by a man named Stanley who adopted him and gave him his name.

Stanley served during the American Civil War, sent descriptions of sea-fights to the papers, began exploration in Asia Minor, and accompanied the British expedition against Abyssinia as war correspondent for the New York Herald, whose proprietor, Gordon

Bennett, one day sent him an order to "find Livingstone," who was lost in Africa, and for whose safety there was grave national concern.

Starting inland in March 1871, Stanley was attacked by fever and deserted by his porters, but at the end of eight months, at Ujiji, he met the lost missionary with the question, "Dr Livingstone, I presume?" Together they explored the north of Lake Tanganyika, and then, leaving stores with Livingstone, Stanley returned home. In 1874 he was sent out by the Daily Telegraph and Gordon Bennett to complete Livingstone's work. After circumnavigating Lake Victoria Nyanza and determining the outline of Lake Tanganyika, he traced the course of the Congo to the sea, a great feat which dispelled an age-old mystery.

His last great expedition was to rescue Emin Pasha from Equatorial Africa, and resulted in his discovering Lake Albert Nyanza and Mount Ruwenzori. Afterwards he served the notorious King Leopold in organising the Belgian Congo, a success attended by unhappy results for the natives. Re-admitted to British citizenship, knighted, and elected to Parliament, he bought an estate at Pirbright, and here, four years later, found his last rest.

Quiet Ways

PURLEY. It leaves speed to its neighbour Croydon, the Charing Cross of the Air, and while Londoners dash through it on the way to Brighton it seeks more peaceful attractions in the three walks which make it unique among suburbs, Silver Lane, Rose Walk, and the Promenade de Verdun.

Silver Lane is a long avenue of silver-trunked birches crowding two or three deep on each side of a gated road where motors may only crawl.

In summer it needs no notice to arrest the few cars allowed down Purley's Rose Walk, for the sight of this unbroken line of rose beds, bowers, and trellises is enough. It is one of the loveliest sights for miles. We know no road quite like it.

For nearly half a mile the rose of England is supreme; then comes the poplar of France, and for nearly another half-mile Lombardy poplars shade a grassy walk. It is the Promenade of Verdun, a tribute to French soldiers killed in the war, and the poplars stand with their roots in a scattering of French soil brought from Armentières.

France is here with her earth and her poplars, and in the 19th century church by the Brighton road are four wooden crosses from French soil which will be for ever England. In the glass of the west window a soldier is receiving the Crown of Life.

St Mark's on Peaks Hill was finished four years before the war, with a clerestory to chancel and nave and a rich west window of Christ in glory. The war came and then peace, and a memorial of stone and mosaic was put here with figures of Christ, St Michael, and St George and the names of 49 men for whom peace came too late.

It was here that William Tooke lived, the man who persuaded his firebrand friend John Horne, the clergyman who became a notorious political agitator, to add the name of Tooke to his, after Horne had successfully fought an Enclosure Act which would have affected his friend's Purley property. John Horne Tooke wrote The Diversions of Purley, and it was obvious that he hoped to be heir to at least half his Purley friend's fortune; but in this he was disappointed. The story of this agitator with the name of a Purley man. He loved nothing better than a battle of wits in which he could use his legal knowledge, he sympathised with every cause of liberty, with the French Revolution, and with the American Colonies, and he was chiefly instrumental in obtaining the printing of parliamentary reports.

Three Rectors in Nine Reigns

PUTTENHAM. Almost on the slope of Hog's Back, it is a place of peace and charm, with a trim churchyard and a church so inviting that its altar cross can be seen from the road.

The grey tower patched with red is 15th century, and lost its spire in a fire two centuries ago. Two little fragments of old stone carving are outside one of the chancel windows, the heads of an angel and a bishop. There are four Norman arches, a Norman window, and a chest made in 1705 with good panelling. The chancel is very attractive with its modern oak carving and panelling.

There is an expressive brass portrait of Edward Cranford in his robes, a rector who died in 1431; and a brass inscription telling of two later rectors each called Henry Beedell, father and son. The father came here when Shakespeare was writing his plays, and remained 38 years; the son succeeded him for 56 years, and they were followed by Thomas Swift who served for 59 years, three men whose service covered more than a century and a half, linking up nine reigns, from Elizabeth to George the Second.

There is a tablet to Hugh Pope, a young man from an Oxford college, who died in 1912 while climbing alone in the Pyrenees, where, we read, "he rested for nine days in God's most holy sight." Five friends went out from England to search for him, and by their hands he was lowered into his grave.

A mile along the road to Seale is Shoelands, a Tudor house with a porch added by Sir Nicholas Lusher in 1616.

The Norman Builder and the Norman Painter

PYRFORD. It is all charming, whether we stay in the meadows by the River Wey, or go up to the church on the little hill, or seek the striking mill with white boards and red roofs which would tempt any artist; or come to the field with the ruins of one of the old religious houses of Surrey, gaunt and forlorn after seven centuries. They are all that is left of the church of Newark Priory, a few arches and windows in roofless walls.

If the old priory church has fallen into decay the still older village church is far from it. A charming little place, it has a Norman nave and chancel and a delightful Tudor porch of brick and timber. There are solid 15th century pews, a Norman doorway with zigzag moulding, two Norman consecration crosses painted on the walls in red, and a chalice said to have been given by Queen Elizabeth. The 14th century east window has in its tracery a little of the original glass, showing Our Father of Pity, a picture of the Creator with one hand raised in blessing and the other holding a crucifix. The beautiful pulpit is Jacobean, and has a carved sounding-board.

One of the rare treasures of English art is a Norman painting, and there can still be traced on these walls some of the paintings made by Normans 800 years ago. One looks like Moses standing by the rock when the water rushed out; another shows Jezebel and Jehu and a procession of six figures, the last leading Jehu's horse; a third is a vigorous painting of a man swinging a scourge weighted with stones.

There is some faded 15th century colouring in the roof above the place where the rood stood before the Reformation.

This little church must have been a place of solace to a remarkable young man who found a friend at Pyrford over three centuries ago.

He was John Donne, the poet who became Dean of St Paul's, and had been the secretary of Sir Thomas Egerton, Keeper of the Great Seal. Unfortunately he had also made a secret marriage with his master's niece Anne More, who was only 16, and when the secret came out Anne's angry father was able to see that Donne was sent to prison and dismissed from his post. So it was that the young couple were in disgrace and had nowhere to go, until they found a welcome here in the house of Anne's cousin Francis Wolley.

The Remarkable Energy of Thomas Cubitt

RANMORE. It stands serene on a Surrey hill 600 feet high, and its people can see Windsor Castle, St Paul's, and Westminster Abbey. When these towers are hid in the mist they still can see the slopes of Box Hill and the Wealden fields.

But it has no need to search for beauty far afield, for its own common is glorious all the year round. The 19th century church, with firs and spreading oaks shading its churchyard, has a spire which is a landmark for miles. It has a noble chapel with a portrait of the first Lord Ashcombe who built the church, and beautiful frescoes in memory of his three grandsons, Henry, Alick, and William Cubitt, three brothers in their twenties who went out from the great house here to die in foreign fields. On the chapel door is a simple wooden cross from the grave of the eldest brother.

The frescoes in this gracious shrine were the work of Reginald Frampton, and are among the loveliest examples of his inspired genius. Over the altar is the Adoration of the Magi in soft pastel shades, with the Madonna in a pale blue cloak and pink dress, sitting under a canopy with Joseph looking down at the Child by her feet, while the Wise Men reverently offer their gifts. On the side frescoes are St George of England, St Joan of France, a charming figure of St Gudule of Belgium, St Denis beside a kneeling Galahad, and others of the saintly company. So long as these pictures last will Ranmore remember the men who went down the hill never to return.

In the churchyard lies the founder of the church, Lord Ashcombe, whose father was Thomas Cubitt, builder of the family fortunes. Beginning life in 1788 he worked as a carpenter, setting up in business when he came of age. He became the first man to do building in all its branches. In the year of Waterloo he built the London

Institution in Finsbury Circus, but he was mostly engaged on houses. He used to buy ground for building in order to provide continuous work for his men, and large parts of London were built by him, including Belgrave Square. He built one front of Buckingham Palace.

He was keenly interested in keeping London clean above and below, making great efforts to stop the smoke nuisance, and writing a pamphlet on drainage reform. Though his business was covering land with buildings, he was one of the prime movers for preserving Battersea Park.

When hearing of the loss of £30,000 which fire had caused to his Thames bank premises he said: "Tell the men they shall be at work within a week, and I will subscribe £600 towards buying them new tools." This was in 1854, and he died in the following year, leaving a million pounds and the longest will on record, and closing a life of remarkable energy which has left its mark on London to this day.

Old Daniel Gumbrell

REDHILL. It is Reigate's young and lively neighbour, gathering about the busy Brighton road and the Brighton railway which Reigate refused to have.

Redhill has a common with fine views of Leith Hill and the Kentish Weald, and it has among its modern churches four with something to see. In the Roman Catholic church is a handsome reredos richly carved and elaborately canopied. In St John's is an impressive screen of delicately-wrought ironwork, and a font which must be nearly unique, for its bowl is a great shell held in the arms of a kneeling angel; it is a tribute to one who was vicar 36 years. In St Matthew's we come upon the best glass in the town, one window showing King David and Miriam, another a charming scene of Gabriel bringing the good news to the Madonna, and another a knight kneeling with his sword before the Master. A fourth window shows the scene by the Sea of Tiberias where Our Lord says to Peter, Feed My Sheep, and is a tribute to the 42 years work of Henry Brass, the first vicar. It was in his memory that the 20th century church of Holy Trinity was built; its chief possession is a beautiful peace memorial window in which we see Peter and John at the tomb, the Risen Lord, His appearance to Mary Magdalene, and a little picture of doubting Thomas.

If it has little history, Redhill, a place which millions pass through, has a garden which a mighty multitude has seen, for it has been made from an old homestead into one of the most remarkable daffodil gardens in the world. It is Wiggie, the home when we called of Mr Arthur Trower, whose devotion to it for a long lifetime has made it a much-loved place for thousands every time Spring comes round. There is no more wondrous spectacle for miles around than Wiggie in its daffodil days, and it is open to everyone, for Arthur Trower's garden was perhaps the first of all our English gardens to be open to all who pass by.

Here we found a willow flourishing vigorously, one of the two trees of old Daniel Gumbrell. For over two generations he was part of the life of Redhill. In this old-world garden he lived with Nature nearly every day of nearly eighty years.

Daniel began his working life at nine, and every day's work he ever did was done in this garden. Mending a fence in the days of his youth, he drove into the ground a piece of willow, four inches across and five feet long. It strengthened the fence between two meadows, but it did more, for it took root and grew, and it rose in its might until its trunk was 15 feet round and its branches spread out for 80 feet, and in its shade old Daniel would sit.

His second monument is also a tree, the tree of his other lives—a hundred and thirty men and women and children who have descended from Daniel Gumbrell, who have seen him alive and touched his hand.

A thrilling thing it must have been, one day not long ago, when Arthur Trower walked into his garden to find a crowd of people there, old men and babies in arms, and to realise that Daniel was bringing his children to see his garden. The old man walked in front of his people, his immortality, over the scene of his long toil.

The Prayer Book of an Armada Conqueror

REIGATE. Here lies Lord Howard of Effingham, one of our Armada men, the friend of Drake and Raleigh, of that immortal group which gave to England the sceptre of the sea. They buried him here at dead of night on the eve of Christmas in 1624, and he sleeps under a stone in the chancel, with a brass inscription. He has no monument, but his name is enough, and one small thing there is that brings him near to us, for Reigate has his prayer-book. It is here in the church, in the library of 2000 books founded by the vicar over 200 years ago. The books are in the upper room of the Tudor vestry, a little place packed with much wonder, for it has precious manuscripts, the old locks of the doors, fragments of old glass, a shilling of Henry the Third found in the base of one of the pillars, and a complete stone coffin which is an astonishing thing to see, for it was made for a child only 15 inches long.

But it is the manuscripts that fascinate us. One was written by Stephen Byrchington, a 14th century monk; it probably runs to a hundred thousand words and is beautifully done. Another is bound as a little book three inches thick, and the writing is like printing, almost too small for the naked eye, yet clear as noonday after about 500 years. The prayer-book of Lord Howard, the gem of gems at Reigate, came into the world after Caxton's day and is printed; but was ever printing so lovely and so neat? It was printed long before the Spanish Armada and the pages are still so beautiful that we dip our pen in memory of the men who did it—John Cawood and Richard Jugge, who no doubt handled this very volume in 1566.

In the 14th century chapel behind Lord Howard's inscription is one of the most beautiful ladies we have seen in Surrey: Katherine Elyott. She died in 1623, and here she kneels in a niche of the wall, a daintily chiselled figure wearing an elegant ruff. Across the chancel in the other chapel, among such a jumble of sculpture as we have rarely seen, lie her father and brother, one above the other; and beside them under a canopy lie Sir Thomas Bludder and his wife, who died within a week of each other in 1618. He is in armour and she wrapped in a cloak as if for stormy weather. On the windowsill above them are four much battered figures, and at the window looking down on Katherine Elyott is a charming stone figure of a child in 16th century costume, very uncomfortably poised on one of her elbows. She is a daughter of Sir Thomas Bludder, moved away from her proper place at his tomb.

The church has much fine carving—leafy capitals on the Norman columns, and a little gallery of sculptured heads in the chancel. They are extraordinary, some fiercely showing teeth, some rudely showing tongues. A remarkable font has 25 queer faces in two lines round the bowl, all very small. The 15th century chancel screen has

SURREY

fragments of carving along the top, and the choir stalls have 24 carved misereres with heads on the arm-rests. The charming pulpit, with a canopy now made into a table, is probably 17th century; the handsome candelabra is 18th. By the west door is a medieval coffin lid with a raised cross.

The 15th century chancel has a very rare and beautiful possession in its original stone reredos, brought to light only about a century ago. It stands about eight feet high, with a cornice of Tudor flowers, and has a row of rich canopied niches filled with modern figures of Our Lord and the Twelve, and on each side two bigger niches with saints. The 15th century sedilia and piscina are handsome for all their ugly paint. On the wall hang three old helmets, a gauntlet, and flags, above the roll of names that live for evermore; we noticed among them a woman, Sister L. M. Stevens. There is a tablet to a father and a son who preached from this pulpit for 65 years, their successor being vicar for 54 years, from 1847 into the 20th century. There were only three vicars here from the time of the French Revolution to the end of the South African War.

The modern church of St Mark has three attractive things: a pulpit deeply carved with scenes from the life of Paul; a group of coloured mosaics showing Christ teaching, healing, and blessing the children; and a reredos with elaborate sculptured panels of the Resurrection.

Reigate rose to importance as a town through the influence of William de Warenne, who fought for the Conqueror at Hastings, but the ancient glories of both castle and priory (which he and his ancestors built) have passed away. The great mound and ditch of the Norman castle have been made into a flower garden open to all, with a little stone gatehouse pretending to be very old, although it is only 18th century; under the mound is what is called the Baron's Cave. But we must summon up in imagination an important fortress on the way from London to the coast, one which came more than once into history. For generations it lay partly ruined, and its end is thought to have come with the Civil War.

The name of Reigate Priory, founded 700 years ago, is kept alive by a great house in beautiful grounds, standing where the ancient priory stood. We see it as the 18th century refashioned it, with a cupola and a steep-tiled roof; but some of the walls are those the monks knew. It was Lord Howard's father who converted the monastic buildings into a mansion, in due time the home of the great admiral himself. He did not die here, but we are told that he constantly lived here. In our own time, after the Great War, it became the home of another great sailor, a man after Lord Howard's own heart, Admiral Beatty of Jutland.

Reigate, by virtue of its setting below the chalk-capped Downs, is one of the most attractive towns within 20 miles of London, and it has grown rapidly in the last few decades. To keep pace with this development an imposing town hall has been built (in the mayor's parlour are some attractive water-colours of Reigate by W. Tatton Winter), but the quaint old town hall with its open arches still stands in the marketplace to pay tribute to the more leisurely days of Queen Anne, although its ground floor is now a kind of waiting room for those who wish to travel, and its top storey a library for those who wish to read.

Fanny Burney, who came this way in 1779, remembered Reigate as a "very old half-ruined borough in a most neglected condition," but today it is a pleasant town with infinite charm in its parks and in the neighbouring countryside. To the north it has Wray Common with an old brick windmill, Reigate Hill (given to the town by Sir Jeremiah Colman), with marvellous views over four counties, and on a clear day as far as Chanctonbury Ring; also Queen's Park and Colley Hill (750 feet high), with the view William Cobbett admired so much. There is the delightful Reigate Park of 90 acres with the tree-clad slopes of another splendid viewpoint called Park Hill, and farther west are the 130 acres of Reigate Heath. Here among the bracken we came upon one of the biggest surprises we have met in going about the country, still another windmill, fitted up as a church. Most intriguing is this Mill Church, no more than seven or eight paces across, with two windows barely lighting up a simple altar and a few chairs. The gigantic central post of the mill, a wooden beam a yard thick, comes down within six feet of the floor, and there are four lesser beams going out like spokes to rest on brick piers against the walls. To the passerby it looks like many another old windmill fallen out of use, with a brick base, black boards, and four sails, and we may wonder how many of those who walk or play on this beautiful heath have taken a peep inside it.

On the road to Betchworth we pass a third old windmill by a big

Reigate — Colley Hill

Reigate — On the Heath

Reigate — The Medieval Church

Gatton — The Town Hall in the Park

house among the trees, and also June Farm, a lovely old house of brick and timber with a great sloping roof. Not far off is Little Santon Farm, still with one of the hiding-holes made for priests in the days of persecution. It is a space just big enough for a man to stand in, cleverly made between two chimneys, a bedroom wall, and the back of a landing cupboard.

The Howards of Effingham

TWO Howards of Effingham who sleep at Reigate, father and son, have a great place in history. The first baron, son of the victor of Flodden Field, was at first high in favour with Henry the Eighth, attending his marriage to Anne Boleyn and seeking a French wife for him in succession to Jane Seymour. But his own kinswoman, Katherine Howard, was the next of Henry's queens, and the baron was sentenced to perpetual imprisonment for not having disclosed her misconduct. Pardoned and released, he carried out royal missions, was enriched by Edward the Sixth, saved Mary and London from the Wyatt insurrection, and championed Elizabeth when she was in danger of following her mother to the block. He served her as Lord Chamberlain and Lord Privy Seal.

His son Charles, second baron and Earl of Nottingham, helped to suppress the Northern rebellion against Elizabeth in 1569, and urged the execution of Mary Stuart as a danger to the throne. Like his father, he became Lord High Admiral; and, like him again, was much beloved by the sailors.

It fell to the son to win immortal fame as commander of the fleet which defeated the Armada. Himself a daring sailor and a dauntless fighter, he had the mighty aid of Francis Drake as his vice-admiral, with Hawkins as rear-admiral, and he knew better than to ignore their judgment. He played a valiant part in the great battle, handicapped by vagaries of weather and shortage of ammunition, and at the end had the crowning glory of seeing the rule of the seas pass from Spain to England. His last outstanding service was to put down the insurrection of the Earl of Essex, but he continued Lord High Admiral under James, and until he died he was the sailor's hero.

Here Ended the Reign of Queen Elizabeth

RICHMOND. It stands nobly on its hill with the silver Thames winding about its feet. Its ancient name was taken from the

Thames—Sheen for the shining river. The great park is its birthright, the fragment of the palace and its courtly old houses are its proud heritage.

Though it is almost London, it seems to take delight in eluding the bands of brick that would enclose it, and from its great heights it looks joyously towards a landscape with Windsor Castle on its far horizon, but with six counties visible on fine days. It is this hill above the river that is the one thing everybody knows of Richmond. It climbs up from the river to the Great Park, and brings us to that glorious Terrace view which Sir Joshua Reynolds looked on so often, which Turner loved to paint, and which inspired Sir Walter Scott. If we count Richmond as part of London this is the noblest view that London can command. Trees clothe the side of the hill, dipping down to the Petersham meadows and the glorious reach of the Thames with its wooded island. On a summer's day the river below is crowded with Londoners in steamer, skiff, or punt, and spread out before us are the Berkshire hills, the famous chestnut avenue in Bushey Park, and that most marvellous ridge in the south of England, the Hog's Back, running between the two old Surrey towns of Farnham and Guildford.

But we must come down to Richmond Green to feel what Richmond has been down the centuries. Here is the gateway of the royal palace, and the wing called Wardrobe Court, which is all that is left of one of the most famous buildings in our royal story. It goes back to our first King Edward, who received his nobles here. The unhappy Richard the Second was here in his happier days. Henry of Agincourt rebuilt it, and Edward the Fourth gave it to his queen Elizabeth Woodville. Henry the Seventh came here soon after his triumph and changed its name from Sheen to Richmond, and here he died. Cardinal Wolsey used it, and here our royal Bluebeard put away one of the wives he did not want, giving Richmond to Anne of Cleves. Here before her lived Catherine when her lord was away at the wars, and here one day (it was in the days when he still loved her) Henry came to surprise her after the Battle of Flodden. Here came Catherine's nephew Charles the Fifth of Germany, to be entertained with 2000 men and 1100 horses, on his betrothal to Princess Mary, aged six. Here the terrible Mary Tudor brought the terrible Philip of Spain, after she had married him in Winchester Cathedral.

SURREY

But it was the Golden Age of Queen Elizabeth that brought the Golden Age to Richmond. She was born by the Thames and she died by the Thames; Greenwich and Richmond were her riverside palaces, but it was Richmond that she loved. It became her favourite home. Here Sir Philip Sidney came to see her, in the days when he fell in love with Sir Francis Walsingham's daughter, greatly to the indignation of the queen. Here Sir Walter Raleigh brought Edmund Spenser to read to Elizabeth his Faerie Queene, she being so enthusiastic about it that she declared it to be of wondrous worth and promised him a hundred pounds, until her Treasurer expressed his horror at such a price for such a song, upon which Elizabeth said: "Then give him what is reasonable," so that Burleigh gave him nothing. Then it was that Spenser wrote this to the queen:

> *I was promised on a time,*
> *To have a reason for my rhyme.*
> *Since that time until this season,*
> *I have had nor rhyme nor reason.*

on reading which Elizabeth insisted on Spenser having his money.

In her old age she would take her daily walks on Richmond Green, and here it was that she refused to die or even to go to bed. She had cushions placed for her on the floor, and there she lay for four days or more and would not eat or move. It is thought it may have been in the room above the gateway, behind the oriel window that is there today, but certainly it was hereabouts. As she lay there she had her wedding ring (she was wedded to the Crown) cut from her finger, but the ring Essex had given her she refused to have removed. When she was told that she must go to bed she shook her finger at the greatest man in England and said: "Little man, little man, if your father had lived he darest not have said so much." When at last she went to bed she would sit up with her eye fixed on one thing for hours; and she took a great delight in prayers. She would hug the archbishop's hand when he spoke of heaven and its joys, and at last, in the middle of the night, she who had stormed so much, the greatest queen in history, the inspiration and delight of the most wonderful group of Englishmen who ever lived, passed out of the world as quiet as a lamb. A ring was thrown out of this very window to be carried by a rider on horseback through England, to tell James the Sixth of Scotland that Gloriana was no more.

THE KING'S ENGLAND

The great days of Richmond were over. Prince Henry added to its glory and Charles continued his good work. Henrietta Maria lived here, and Charles the Second made one of his ladies Duchess of Richmond because he loved this place. But the shadows were falling over it. In the Commonwealth Richmond was made over to the City of London, and the people hated the passing of the old palace which Henry the Fifth had rebuilt, where Henry the Eighth had made merry, and where Gloriana had held her court with her lovers about her. The place was sold for ten thousand pounds.

Of all that glowing story the gateway is the solitary witness, the gateway and Wardrobe Court, which was occupied by the Wardrobe Keeper, who must have kept here some of the two thousand dresses Queen Elizabeth wore. Wardrobe Court as it remains is 100 feet long, and the garden side of the house was refronted in the reign of Queen Anne, probably by Christopher Wren, but the Tudor front looks down on what is now called Old Palace Yard. The garden's beautiful old walls remain, and a sundial stands where Elizabeth planted a yew tree. The herb garden is filled with rosemary, lavender, angelica, mint, thyme, and rue, and there is a little Dutch garden. It is a tradition that a pomegranate should always grow in the garden here, and Lady Cave, when living here with her husband in the days before he became Lord Chancellor, planted one. It is supposed to be in memory of Catherine of Aragon, whose pomegranate was blended into the Tudor Rose, in the days when the king cared enough for her to do such things.

Next door to Wardrobe Court is the Trumpeter's House, built in the days of Queen Anne, and named from two stone figures of boys blowing trumpets, which are now in the garden. It is an enchanting place, lovely indoors and out, with an imposing portico overlooking the garden and the lawn running down to the river. It belongs to the Crown. It was built by Queen Anne's favourite Mrs Masham, and Marconi lived here in the days when he was building up the Wireless Age. The embattled summerhouse crowning the riverside wall is said to be part of Henry the Seventh's palace. Close by stands Asgill House, with a great window overlooking the Thames. It was built for a rich merchant who became Lord Mayor in 1757. Its foundations are in part of the old palace, and in its cellars the ancient walls are still seen.

SURREY

On the Green is Maid of Honour Row, a group of four beautiful houses built for the ladies of the Court in the time of George the First. There was not room for them at Richmond Lodge, for which they may have perhaps been thankful, for a more dignified terrace of houses than these it would be hard to find. Their scrolled iron gates and canopied doorways are delightful, and they set the note for other houses like them scattered about Richmond, in Ormond Row, and on the hill, and on the way to Petersham. About the Green are many other attractive houses. Garrick House stands on the site of the old Richmond theatre, which in a hundred years of acting numbered among its actors Helena Fawcett, Edmund Kean, and a young amateur named Charles Dickens. Queensberry Villa, built at the same time as the Trumpeter's House, has gone; it was there that the old Duke of Queensberry stood in his ballroom looking out on the river, and said: "What is there to make so much fuss of in the Thames? There it goes—flow, flow, flow, always the same. I am weary of it."

Richmond's pride is its Great Park, 2300 acres enclosed by a wall eight miles long, with 1500 red and fallow deer, herds of cattle, innumerable rabbits, and a wealth of old trees. Wordsworth loved it. Its nightingales are famous. We may often seen herons at its two ponds, both well stocked with fish, and may always see the graceful deer as we ride through this spacious park. Sidmouth Plantation is a wondrous sight when the rhododendrons are in bloom, and Isabella Plantation is famous for its bluebells. One of the best views from the park is from Bloomfield Hill, from where we see the lofty towers of the lost Crystal Palace, the brick tower of Westminster Cathedral, and the round stone tower of Windsor Castle. From the western ridge with its fine hawthorns we may see Ranmore church on the North Downs, and a mound near Pembroke Lodge is the view-point which Henry the Eighth is said to have chosen for seeing the rocket from the Tower which announced the death of Anne Boleyn. In the park stands the historic house known as White Lodge. It has a classical front and was built originally by George the Second. It has had, as guests of the Ranger of the Park, William Pitt, Sir Walter Scott, and Richard Brinsley Sheridan, and it was here that Nelson traced with his finger on a little table the plan of attack he was to adopt at Trafalgar. The Lodge has been a royal home for generations, and in it one of our kings (Edward the Eighth) was born, and it was the first home of George the Sixth and Queen Elizabeth in the days when they were Duke and Duchess of York.

Richmond has another open space which has no deer today but is called the Old Deer Park, now playing fields for archers, footballers, bowlers, and golfers, and the scene of a famous horse show every year. It was used by our kings for hunting, and it lies between Kew Gardens, old Richmond Palace, and the Thames. Here are the handsome buildings of the Mid-Surrey Golf Club, and near them are some carved stones found hereabouts on the site of a monastery to which the body of James the Fourth of Scotland was brought from Flodden Field. It was at a mansion on this spot that Swift, visiting Sir William Temple, met Stella, daughter of Sir William's steward. Reached by a road beyond the club house is Kew Observatory, which belongs to Richmond. It has a little dome in the middle of its balustraded roof, and was built for George the Third by Sir William Chambers to enable the astronomers to observe the transit of Venus. It is now used by the Air Ministry for the study of the weather, atmospheric electricity, and earthquakes.

Overlooking the Old Deer Park is Richmond Royal Hospital, which has been described as an architectural sandwich because its modern wings flank a gracious old house on the site of the cottage in which lived James Thomson, the poet who wrote The Seasons. Here he lived and here he died, leaving behind, among all his poems of Nature, one on Richmond Hill. Many old houses hereabouts have had famous people living in them; in Gothic House lived Madame de Staël, drawing to her salon a dazzling company of intellectuals. Her garden joins the delightful riverside Mear's Walk, stretching downstream to Richmond Bridge, the fine stone structure painted by Turner when he lived at Twickenham. It was opened in 1777 and has now been widened for this Traffic Age. A little downstream is a magnificent new bridge with broad wide-span arches, an important link in the Chertsey arterial road. Below this bridge again is a footbridge built in conjunction with the famous half-lock, the only one of its kind on the river. It is the lowest down the Thames and ensures that Richmond's riverside, with its lovely trees and gardens, shall be ever free from mud. This lock, which cost £60,000 and was opened in 1894, has three big sluices, each 66 feet wide and weighing 32 tons. At flood-tide these sluices are drawn up, out of use, and at other times are lowered partly into the river, so that while some of the water is held back above a certain amount can pass below, rendering a weir unnecessary. When these sluices are in use big boats use a lock on the narrow Surrey bank.

Richmond's church is tucked away in an angle of two main streets. Its massive tower, with a clock set up between the days of Trafalgar and Waterloo, comes from the end of the 15th century, but the spacious nave is 18th century and the chancel and its chapels are modern. The fine 18th century pulpit rests on six curiously twisted legs, and has panelled sides and cornices carved with foliage. In the chancel are three handsome Queen Anne chairs with carved backs, and over the tower arch are royal arms finely carved in Georgian days.

There is an interesting group of monuments. On the north wall of the nave Robert Cotton kneels on a brass with his wife and their eight children; he was an officer of Mary Tudor's Wardrobe, who, by the queen's special choice [we read] was taken from the Wardrobe to serve as a groom in her privy chamber all her lifetime, and at her death became an Officer of the Wardrobe to Queen Elizabeth. High on the wall are small kneeling figures of Lady Margaret Chudleigh, 300 years old, and from the same time come the kneeling figures which face them, of Sir George Wright and his wife Dorothy, with their three sons and four daughters. On the south wall is an 18th century bust of William Rowan which Chantrey thought excellent, and a monument by the younger Bacon to George Bean, a major killed at Waterloo, as a relief of a cannon and some swords reminds us. High above this is a bust of Robert Lewis, a 17th century lawyer of whom we read the curious epitaph that he died "not from length of days, but from being such a studious lover of peace that when a contention sprang up between life and death he immediately yielded up his spirit to end the dispute." There are two monuments by Flaxman, one set up by the pupils of Robert Delafosse, his monument having a mourning schoolboy at each side; the other a weeping figure with a lovely lily, in memory of Barbara Lowther, whose portrait is in marble.

On the west wall is a brass plate to the poet James Thomson, who lies here, and there is a portrait medallion of the actor Edmund Kean. Here Kean lies, having died at Richmond at the end of his remarkable career. Beginning as a strolling boy player, he appeared at Drury Lane as Shylock after ten years in the provinces, and sprang suddenly into fame. His career was broken, however, by his irregular life, and in the end he became a physical and mental wreck. Close by the Kean medallion is a bronze relief of a lady novelist who was a best-seller of Victorian days, Miss Braddon. She is shown with frizzled hair and lace collar, and is wearing a locket, and we read that she was "a writer of rare and refined scholarship, who gave profitable and pleasurable literature in her library of threescore-and-ten works of fiction." She began unpromisingly while writing for a Brighton newspaper, but succeeded with Lady Audley's Secret, and was wise enough to marry a publisher. By Miss Braddon's memorial are three busts from Cromwell's days of John Bentley with his wife and daughter.

One of our great tragic actresses kneels in a niche over the inside doorway of the south porch. She is Mary Anne Yates, and with her is the comedian Richard Yates, her husband. She was much praised by Oliver Goldsmith, and it was said that her acting moved David Garrick to tears. Richard made a great reputation as a comic character in Shakespeare's plays, but was stupid enough to fall into a fit of rage and die because he could not have eels for dinner.

On the outer wall of the church is a monument to Lord Fitzwilliam, the Irish peer who founded the Fitzwilliam Museum at Cambridge, and in the churchyard is the grave of the father of Sir John Moore, and that of Nicholas Brady, the Richmond rector who joined with Nahum Tate in the 17th century to produce a metrical version of the Psalms. Through this work Tate and Brady have probably become the widest circulated poets known to English literature. Neither had one spark of the divine fire, but both could rhyme a verse, and they started from favourable positions. Tate was poet laureate and Brady a royal chaplain. At Richmond Brady kept a school for boys which Steele slyly advertised in the Spectator, but whether in kindness or derision is doubtful. Besides his work on the Psalms Brady published sermons and translations, and had a tragedy acted at Drury Lane, but none of these count now. He had an Irish way with him, and was fluent and lucky.

Richmond's cemetery has a famous company of honoured dead. Here sleeps Miss Braddon, whose memorial is in the church. On the

SURREY

tombstone of Charles Garvice is a quill pen to remind us of the countless stories he wrote for a countless public; he died in Maid of Honour Row soon after the war. There is a cross to Sir Charles Hawtrey, the actor-manager with so many great successes to his name. Here is the grave of Leslie Stuart, composer of so many popular songs of Victorian days (Soldiers of the Queen among them). His songs went round the world and back again in his own day, but have been broadcast since his day to multitudes that no man can number. At one grave in this place all who love London may pay tribute, for here lies one who served the great city well as a writer and literature well as a poet, Arthur St John Adcock. He knew Fleet Street for half a century, and everybody in Fleet Street knew him. Never was a kindlier or more lovable man, giving away more than he had. It was he who discovered W. H. Davies when he was living in a lodging house and nobody would read his poems, and Adcock himself was a poet not unworthy to keep our tramp poet company; he wrote:

There is nothing so beautiful now as it used to be;
Something has gone from the grass and the flower and the tree,
Something, O thou who art gone! that faded with thee,
And there's nothing so beautiful now as it used to be.

There is an imposing obelisk carved with a springbok to South African soldiers who died in England during the Great War, and in the cemetery lie two men who won the VC. One is Sergeant Harry Hampton, who won it in the South African War for his courage in forgetting his wounds and enabling his outnumbered men to withdraw from a difficult post; the other is General Olpherts, who has a gun carved on his gravestone. He was a famous figure in the Indian Mutiny, where he captured guns under heavy fire. He missed death a hundred times and lived to be 80, when they brought him here on a rumbling gun-carriage, firing a volley over his grave amid the flash of lightning and the crash of thunder.

The land sloping away from Richmond Hill is partly a field, partly a wood, and partly a public garden with glorious rockeries and herbaceous borders. The Terrace along the top is a dignified row of old houses, with handsome blocks of modern flats among them. At Wick House lived Sir Joshua Reynolds, who painted the Terrace View, and one of the old buildings here is Doughty House, with one of the finest private art collections in the country, built up by Sir Francis Cook and his son Sir Frederick. Students and visitors may sometimes see these noble examples of Italian, French, German, Spanish, and English Schools of painting. Near the best-placed building on the Terrace (the Star and Garter) is a fountain with a bronze relief of the Duchess of Teck, Queen Mary's mother, and close by stands Ancaster House, which the Auctioneers Institute gave to Queen Mary for the use of the Star and Garter Home. It is occupied by the nursing sisters. One of its windows lit the room of Sir Lionel Darell, who was often visited here by his friend George the Third. When Sir Lionel died his daughter kept his room shut for nearly 60 years, and when she died the room was found as he had left it, his old cocked hat on the table, and The Times for one morning in 1804 ready for him to read. But of all the buildings on this famous Terrace none has so brave a tale to tell as the Star and Garter Home.

It is, of course, the home of disabled soldiers and sailors, one of the finest memorials of the Great War. It was designed, free of all charge, by Sir Edwin Cooper, and was built from a fund raised by the women of the Empire. Imposing with its tall columns and its stone parapet, it has dormer windows and red tiled roofs, giving it the appearance of a real home for those broken in our wars. Another real home, the house of Lord Cardigan, who led the Charge at Balaclava, has been transformed into a delightful row of flats, with gardens and lawns in front, where live the disabled men who make the poppies. Their poppy factory, run by the British Legion, is close by. Nowhere is there a happier family than these poppy men, everyone disabled by the war. Of the 360 nearly a third are totally disabled, half have lost a leg, and there are almost as many missing limbs as there are men. They were brought together and organised for the making of the poppies by one of the bravest men of all time, Major George Howson. Himself disabled in the war, where he won the Military Cross, he was eager to help when it was over, and he founded the Disabled Society, out of which grew the idea that the men might be set to work making things. He set them to work making flowers, and the first beginnings of poppy-making were in a room he hired off the Old Kent Road. Now this factory at Richmond, the House of Remembrance that never forgets the men who won the war, produces over forty million poppies in a year. The Major is no longer among his men, for at Armistice-time in 1936 he lay dying on a bed of pain, but would not be denied his longing to see once again the Field of Remembrance at the Abbey. The inspiration for it had come to him in a dream, and they laid him in the ambulance and drove him there, and, as he lay watching the pilgrimage to this little garden of crosses and poppies, the King came to the ambulance and talked to him. It was his last sight of the Garden of Remembrance. He went back to Richmond, and his last words at the factory spoken to one of the original five members of the staff were: "Remember, if I peg out I go in the factory van." As the ambulance moved away he led the singing of Are we Downhearted? and that is how his men remember him.

Though the Lass of Richmond Hill was a Yorkshire lass there is a delightful medallion of her on an inn round the corner, showing her carrying a pair of pails. Across the way from it is a Gothic building of the 19th century, with a high tower dominating a frontage of nearly 250 feet. It is the Methodist College, with one of the best of all John Wesley's statues, one of his old pulpits, and many of his books. The tower has a beautiful view from the top, and the chapel has a beautiful window by Frank Salisbury. Near the Methodist college is another tower, with a spire, belonging to the 19th century church of St Matthias, designed by Sir Gilbert Scott. The tower is nearly 200 feet high.

Of Richmond's other modern churches by far the most interesting is the Barn Church of St Philip and All Saints, tucked away in North Sheen, not far from Kew Gardens Station. It is one of the most extraordinary churches we have come upon in our travels. Seen from outside, it looks not unlike a barn; inside it *is* a barn, for its splendid timber roof and the avenue of columns supporting it, and forming the arcades, came from a 16th century barn of Stonehall Farm at Oxted in Surrey. A striking spectacle are all these rough-hewn timbers, and we look round half-expecting to see men in smocks, with scythes and sickles thrown aside.

The owners of the barn generously offered it in 1926, when new churches were called for in the diocese, and two years later it was pulled down, and each timber numbered. Brought to its new site, it was set up again with as little change as possible, and in February

929 this splendid church, which had cost only £5000 to build, was dedicated by the Bishop of Southwark, and stands now as a tribute to the generosity of the Hoare and Lambert families.

Nearly all the fittings for the church have been given or inspired by other old buildings. The porch is made of old timbers, and the slates in it were once the barn's threshing floor. The walls are made of bricks baked at Basingstoke, of a type contemporary with the barn; the windows are modelled on those of the great house of Compton Wynyates in Warwickshire; the tower frame was copied from Tandridge church in Surrey, and the little spire was inspired by that of Martyr Worthy, near Winchester. The oak pulpit is a copy of a 16th century one in Hereford Cathedral, and the design of the square grey font is based on a 13th century font in Hertfordshire. The Jacobean altar rails came from Writtle church in Essex, the old poppyheads of the choir stalls from St Dunstan's in Fleet Street, and the bell was given by Holy Trinity at Wandsworth. Nearly all the new oak came from Godstone, and the cedar wood used in the lady chapel and for the sanctuary chairs came from one great tree blown down in the churchyard at Godstone in Surrey. It is remarkable, seeing that so many places have contributed to this fine barn church, that it should appear so complete and harmonious.

Royal Richmond has provided almshouses for its aged poor with royal munificence. There are six groups, each with an old-world charm like a mantle of serenity. Three groups are in a road off Richmond Hill called the Vineyard.

The first are Michel's Almshouses, looking on to a lawn, founded in 1695 by Humphrey Michel; they were rebuilt in 1810, six others being added in 1858. Across the road are two more old neighbours, Duppa's Almshouses, founded in 1661 by Brian Duppa, Bishop of Winchester, grey brick buildings with tall chimneys, enclosed by iron railings, and having over the gate the words "I will pay the vows which I made to God in my trouble." Next to these are the little stone-faced cottages called Queen Elizabeth's Almshouses, founded by Sir George Wright in 1600 and rebuilt in 1767; high up in the wall is a worn stone panel with the Queen's arms. The three other groups are off the Sheen Road. In Worple Way are Houblon's Almshouses, founded in the 18th century by Rebecca and Susanna Houblon, low red-tiled cottages ranged round three sides of a lawn, and hiding a little shyly behind a high wall. The two others, not far off, are 19th century neighbours, the Church Almshouses with sharp gables and rounded windows, and Hickey's, handsomest of all, with windows and comfortable-looking porches looking on to a fine lawn; they have their own church, and are guarded by a kind of battlemented gatehouse.

Here Lies the Poet of the Seasons

JAMES THOMSON spent a quarter of his life at Richmond, and, dying at 48, was laid to rest here in a scene far dearer to him than his native land. Trained at Edinburgh University for the ministry, he was irresistibly drawn to poetry. As Johnson said of him, "He could not have viewed two candles burning but with a poetical eye."

He reached London at 25, had his introductions stolen by a pickpocket, and was driven by want to write a poem on Winter, the first of his Seasons, which appeared successively between 1726 and 1730. He wrote a poem on the death of Sir Isaac Newton, and in the same year, when England was ringing with the capture of Porto Bello, and Anson was starting on his world voyage, he introduced into a masque his immortal Rule, Britannia.

His work brought him useful friendships and the patronage of the Prince of Wales, who awarded him £100 a year. Much of his work, including his five forgotten dramas, seeks to exhibit the Prince as the champion of freedom in opposition to the Court.

His last long poem, The Castle of Indolence, the fine drowsy music of whose early stanzas influenced Tennyson's Lotus-Eaters, has a picture of the poet himself, "A bard here dwelt, more fat than bard beseems." Lazy he truly was; he would not trouble to take his hands from his pockets to pluck a peach in his garden, but would nibble its riper side as it hung on the bough. Yet he nobly influenced our literature. Breaking away from the artificial conventions of his age, he went back to Nature: sunshine and storm, mountain and valley, trees and flowers, birds, beasts, and insects, sound and scent, movement and colour—he wrote of all with the ardour of a lover and the accuracy of the artist. He ruled the world of poetic thought until Wordsworth rose to eclipse him. His grave is here at Richmond, but his monument is in Westminster Abbey.

On the Portsmouth Road

RIPLEY. The roaring, rushing Ripley road is known to every motorist, and the old houses lining the village street witness a never-ending procession of traffic. Half a century ago the place was a Mecca of London cyclists, and half a century before that dozens of coaches rattled through every day. The White Horse Inn of Tudor times is now a chemist's shop, while the 17th century George Inn, with its beautiful windows, is now called Cedar House, a coaching sign by Cecil Aldin reminding us of the old days. The neighbouring Anchor Inn was new when Queen Elizabeth passed this way, and old-time cyclists still remember Annie and Harriet Dibble, who served them here. In the church next door is a window to them, put up by "their cycling friends."

A gloomy yew tunnel leads to the west door of the church, and cobbles form a patterned path to the porch. The chancel is one of the best pieces of Norman work in Surrey, enriched inside by a beautiful band of carved leaves and flowers running round the wall. Clusters of shafts with scalloped capitals look as if they were intended to carry a vaulted roof. The frame of the east window is 700 years old. Lovely linenfold panelling screens the Children's Corner, with its picture of white-winged cherubs by Glyn Philpot.

The great green, fringed by tall trees, was a cradle of cricket. Ripley had a club to be proud of even in the 18th century, and many exciting matches were played here in the days when county cricket was unknown, and a wicket had only two stumps.

Through this Arch Passed Catherine of Aragon

SANDERSTEAD. It comes into Saxon records more than a thousand years ago, and from its lovely countryside even the 20th century has spared 200 acres for a bird sanctuary and a Nature Reserve.

The two great houses are now hotels sharing 230 acres, yet each has kept much of the spirit of the old world. Selsdon Park has turrets like a castle and a great array of stone mullioned windows. Beneath its case of brick the oldest parts are 15th century; and older still, standing by itself not far from the house, is a bit of ancient London framed against the holly trees in these beautiful grounds, an entrance arch from the monastery of Blackfriars. Through it, in their black hoods and cloaks, the monks were passing to and fro 700 years ago, and through it they must have gone their ways for generations. Through it also, we may believe, passed Catherine of Aragon on her way to the trial which lives for ever in Shakespeare's noble scene.

Sanderstead Court (now Selsdon Court) is a Tudor building made into a fine Queen Anne House. Its hall is attractive with tapestries and Corinthian pillars, and many of its rooms are panelled. Queen Elizabeth stayed here when it was the home of her Master of the Horse, and she is said to have planted the splendid old cedar.

The church goes back to the 13th and 14th centuries and is rich in memorials, a group of them being to the Atwoods of Sanderstead Court. On one wall are Tudor brass portraits of John Atwood and his wife in fur-trimmed gowns, and on the opposite wall is a brass of ten little boys thought to be their sons. The third son Nicholas has an inscription saying that he died in 1586, having served Queen Elizabeth from the second year of her reign.

The chancel is paved with Atwood graves, some cut with very clear coats of arms. Kneeling on the wall is the most beautiful little figure in armour of John Ownsted, another servant of Elizabeth, "Master of Her Most Dread Majestie's Horse for 40 years." His hands are broken off, the hands that served the queen for 40 years, but the colour on this alabaster gem is still here. His wife Joanna has a brass inscription in the nave floor. There is a beautiful 17th century figure of Mary Audley, shrouded in a flowing cloth tied at head and feet; and a big monument to George Mellish who died at 23, with a sculpture of him in his wig and a verse attributed to Dryden. Two tablets in a corner of the church tell their little stories of tragedy in our own time; one is to a girl of 16 who was killed in a railway collision, and the other to a man who was drowned when his ship was torpedoed in 1917.

Those who come to Sanderstead will notice the remarkable number of modern memorials with the name of Smith, and they will not be surprised to read on one of the tablets that Henrietta Smith, who was born in the year of Trafalgar and died in 1891, left no less than 111 direct descendants.

There are two fine yews in the churchyard, and in a corner by the gate sleeps Sir Francis Head, a distinguished officer who was Governor of Canada and wrote A Ride Across the Pampas.

The Old Clarinet

SEALE. Its church has a timber porch through which people have been passing for 600 years, and one of the six bells in the tower was made three centuries ago. The porch looks its age and is perhaps the most impressive thing in Seale, but there is interest and tragedy in the memorials in the church.

On the chancel wall are several brass inscriptions and coats-of-arms from the graves of the Woodroffes, including Sir Nicholas of 1598 and his wife Grissel. A modern brass tells of George Woodroffe, the last male of this ancient family, for more than 200 years lords of the manor of Poyle, just across the Hog's Back. He sleeps with his two wives beneath the altar, and there is a tablet to his first wife Anne, who died in 1762 from "a second sudden stroke of the palsey."

A marble tablet tells of a sad accident at sea and has a carving of it in relief. It is to Edward Noel Long, who, with others of his regiment, was on his way to join the British forces in Spain a few weeks after they had laid Sir John Moore to rest at Corunna. Another tablet is in memory of Dudley Ralph Turnbull who won the DSO in the Great War. He fought at Mons, and was killed when commanding his regiment. In a case on the wall is an old clarinet played in the church by a lady in the days when the music came from an orchestra in a western gallery. The font is Norman.

Along the lane towards Puttenham is East End Farm, a group of buildings round a fine old timbered house with striking chimneys.

The Clever Men at a Tudor House

SEND. The hamlets of Send are dotted here and there and the River Wey twists and turns between them. Send church is charmingly set among farms and fields close to the river, and in one of the river's broad sweeps stands one of the most impressive houses in England, the Elizabethan Sutton Place. We have a peep of it from the lane crossing the river near Burpham, but it lies in the heart of its great park, and its red roofs and its Tudor chimneys are almost lost among the trees.

The church has a 13th century chancel and much of its original

Richmond   The Wonderful View from the Hill

White Lodge

Two Glimpses of the Old Palace

The Barn Church at North Sheen

IN ROYAL RICHMOND

roof; the unusually wide nave and the tower are 15th century. There are a few fragments of painted glass, an ironbound chest, benches with moulded tops, and a traceried chancel screen five centuries old. The gallery is Tudor, and it is thought that the porch may have been built by Thomas Marteyn, a vicar of 500 years ago, who has a brass inscription. There are brass portraits of Laurence Slyffeld with his wife and their three sons dressed as in the days of Henry the Eighth. There are many tablets on the walls to the Onslows, whom we frequently come upon in this part of Surrey. One tells us of George Onslow, who died in 1844 after being vicar 51 years, and of the tragic deaths of his two sons, a midshipman lost in a hurricane and a Woolwich cadet crushed by an iron roller. There is a tablet to Sir John Strachey, a distinguished administrator in India.

By the lychgate is a veteran elm struggling hard for a new life. It is 20 feet round and has still many youthful branches rising from the ancient stump; but it is hollow inside and has been filled with cement and bound with an iron belt.

Sutton Place goes back to the days of Henry the Eighth, being built by one of the king's devoted servants, Sir Richard Weston. He helped his master to build up the power of the Tudors, and took part in all the royal pageantries of his time. He was at the Field of the Cloth of Gold, he sat on the jury that condemned Buckingham, and was given Sutton Manor on the day the duke was executed at the Tower. It is thought that when building this great house he was influenced by some of the noble chateaux he must have seen on his travels in France. Built of brick and terracotta, Sutton Place is remarkable as one of the earliest examples of a great house without fortifications. It dates from 1530, and the quadrangle is 80 feet square. A hall 50 feet long runs along one side, and the great gallery is 140 feet long. Queen Elizabeth stayed here in 1591, and so great was the fire in the hall that soon after her departure the hall itself was burnt to ashes. So it remained till 1721, when it was repaired.

During Sir Richard Weston's time both the king and Thomas Cromwell came to Sutton Place, and Sir Richard's heir, Francis, became a popular young man at court until he was accused of loving Anne Boleyn and lost his head, as all such lovers did. He never lived to inherit his father's estate, but the child he left grew up to fight at the Siege of Calais, and it was he who entertained Elizabeth at

Sutton Place. It is said that there is still in this house the ruff of Sir Thomas More stained with his blood and a crystal pomegranate which belonged to Catherine.

Two generations later came the Richard Weston who spent his time in this great house working out schemes for improving canals and for making navigable the River Wey. He was a great agricultural reformer, and it was he who introduced clover into this country, establishing a new system of rotation founded on the cultivation of clover, flax, and turnips. It is recorded that he introduced into Surrey also the grass called Nonsuch, and raised rich crops of hay from irrigated meadows.

So that this famous old house has contributed something to agriculture, something to navigation, and something also, we believe, even to wireless, for in the early years of our own century, when Lord Northcliffe bought this house and used to say that the quiet he found here was the best thing money had given him, one of the clever men of our time conducted scientific experiments here with Lord Northcliffe's help. He was Major Baden-Powell, the Chief Scout's brother, and one of the things he did at Sutton Place was to fix up a wireless telephone long before such things were familiar in the world.

Not far away from Sutton Place a Roman Catholic church stands near the spot where Edward the Confessor had a hunting lodge. The lodge is the oldest building of which we have any note on this site, and traces of it have been found in a field. Here is still kept a chasuble with a view of Sutton Place embroidered by the ladies of Henry the Eighth's Court.

In this Roman Catholic church (St Edward's) lies Maude Valerie White, composer of hundreds of songs. She was born at Dieppe and educated at Paris and Heidelberg, but she herself would probably have said that it was at the Royal Academy of Music in London she received her life's inspiration. She had a gift of melody, and it has been said that the better the words she chose the better the song she produced. She set to music the lyrics of Herrick, Browning's Cavalier songs, and poems of Victor Hugo. The British Government recognised her services to music by granting her a pension of a hundred pounds, which she received until she died in 1937. Her grandfather was a naval lieutenant with Nelson, and was on the Victory at Trafalgar when Nelson died.

SURREY

Ferguson's Gang

SHALFORD. White cottages, the peace memorial, a yew, and the old stocks make up a delightful corner by the church. Across the Tillingbourne stream stands a charming 18th century mill, now in its years of rest the property of the National Trust, and farther along the road is the common on which the great fair of Shalford was held for centuries.

King John gave a charter to the rector, and for a long time the fair took place in the churchyard. It grew in size and fame and was moved to the common, where it covered 140 acres and was visited by merchants from all over the kingdom. John Bunyan, it is said, lived for a while in a cottage on the common; and if this is true his account of Vanity Fair in the Pilgrim's Progress may well have been influenced by what he saw at Shalford. The real Pilgrim's Way runs close by, and Shalford must itself have been something of a Vanity Fair to those tramping along to Canterbury. The common is now a fine place for games. A remarkable cricket match took place on it one day in 1877, when a team of 11 Mitchells, all related, played against a team of 11 Heaths, all of one family.

The church is modern, with a little Tudor brass of the three boys of Roger and Margaret Elyot, preserved from a former church. There is a tablet to a vicar's son who, with his wife and four young children, was among the 77,000 victims of the Messina earthquake of 1908; and, let into the chancel floor, is a memorial to Colonel Haversham Godwin-Austen, who explored and surveyed the North-West Himalayas, and won the Founder's Medal of the Royal Geographical Society. It was his father, the geologist, who also lived and died here, who in the middle of last century predicted that coal would be found in Kent.

The pulpit, carved with linenfold and ships and shields, is a most attractive memorial to a young English sailor, Maurice Hervey Bagot, who was drowned when HMS Monmouth went down with all her crew in the battle off Coronel in the Great War. Inscribed on the pulpit are the words:

And many fell that day, and there was much valour.

Of another such day in England's history we think as we look at the tablet to Colonel Frederick George Shewell, who died here in

1856. He fought at Alma and Inkerman, and led his regiment in the charge of the Light Brigade at Balaclava, by his courage and coolness saving the remnant of the broken brigade from total destruction.

It was interesting to find as Vicar of Shalford the man who inspired the sublime idea of the Unknown Warrior. He was David Railton, who came to Shalford as vicar in 1931. He had served as a chaplain in France, and after the war the idea of the Unknown Warrior occurred to him, and he took it to the Dean of Westminster, who placed it before the Cabinet. The Union Jack which hangs above the grave in the Abbey is the very flag which Mr Railton used in France as a pall for the bodies of the soldiers he buried.

In the roll of vicars of Shalford is William Oughtred, a famous mathematician of the generation before Newton. He was here five years, before going on to be rector of Albury, a few miles away.

By the church is Shalford House. It goes back to Tudor times and belonged to the Austen family for 300 years. The dining-hall has a carved stone fireplace of 1609, and its walls are hung with old pictures and family portraits. Other rooms have fine panelling and magnificent old fireplaces, and the drawing-room is a good example of the Adam period.

It was at Shalford that there first appeared that mysterious company of gangsters going about the countryside making observations of England's treasures, the company known as Ferguson's Gang. It is impossible to discover who they are, but in addition to their leaders there are nine others: Bill Stickers, Black Mary, The Bishop, Sister Agatha, Arris, Erb, P.P. Unde Gregory, Kate O'Brien, and White Biddy. Their activities first came to light over two years ago when they presented the 18th century watermill at Shalford to the National Trust.

Nothing was heard of them for some months. Then one cold and wet January evening a taxi stopped outside the National Trust offices in Buckingham Palace Gardens, and Biddy got out, heavily masked, carrying a big bag filled with silver coins. This she laid on the secretary's desk, saying it was the first £100 of the endowment fund the gang had agreed to raise for Shalford Mill.

More than nine months passed. Then, early one November morning, a masked man sent his card in to the secretary of the National

Trust: Erb the Smasher, it said. Erb laid two banknotes for £100 each on the desk, the balance of the endowment fund promised.

Again the gang disappeared from view, this time for nearly a year, and then the nerves of the National Trust's office staff were tested anew by the arrival of another masked member, Kate O'Brien. Hers was one of the briefest business visits in history. It took her exactly 30 seconds to leave a banknote for £500 for the purchase and repair of Newtown Old Town Hall in the Isle of Wight. They have also raised £1750 for buying land to protect our Atlantic coastline in Cornwall from the builder.

The methods of the Ferguson Gang are an improvement on the Chicago type of gangster, and their anonymous way of keeping an eye on England's treasures can do nothing but good.

A Thousand Coins of Caesar

SHAMLEY GREEN. Its cottages and houses, many of them centuries old, are charmingly laid out round two wide greens. Up the hill is Farley Heath, where the Romans had a camp, approached by a branch road from their main thoroughfare, Stane Street. Remains of buildings and over a thousand coins of the Caesars have been found here.

A little away from the village is the modern church, with six tubular bells given by friends of Henry Scott Boys, an Indian Civil Servant. In one of the windows is attractive glass showing Our Lord with knights in armour, in memory of two officers who fought in Palestine in the Great War; and outside the window is the wooden cross that marked the grave of one of them in the cemetery at Cairo.

All these men went out into the world and gave their best for England, but they are not alone in being remembered on these walls. In the chancel is a brass inscription to Walter Hemming, above the seat in which he sat while other folk came and went for 40 years.

Shere Beauty

SHERE. One of the prettiest of all our villages, it has drawn many an artist to paint the quaintness of its narrow streets and tinted cottages, the odd little footbridge over the road and the charming line of willows weeping by the Tillingbourne. We remember it as a village of old houses and gentle slopes, seen at its best if we enter by the road from Newlands Corner.

In a little house here Sir James Barrie wrote one of his earliest plays, and in the construction of the White Horse Inn are many old ship's timbers, brought in the barges that used to ply between Deptford and Guildford.

The old grey church adds much to the delight of the scene and has scarcely changed in 600 years. It comes into Domesday Book, and some of its masonry may be Saxon. Certainly the tower is Norman, rising up from massive 14th century arches, one of them pierced within its Norman predecessor. The shingled spire is a remarkable piece of medieval carpentry.

There are two fine doorways. One is a Norman arch that has lasted better than the 13th century shafts on which it rests. It is richly carved with chevrons and foliage, and several mass clocks are scratched below it. The other is 13th century and beautifully moulded, framing a big studded door of 1626.

Several of the windows have beautiful 14th century tracery, and there are many fragments of glass nearly 700 years old. The best of the remains show the symbols of the Evangelists, Matthew's angel, Mark's lion, Luke's bull, and John's eagle, all well preserved; and below are two heraldic medallions of a later century. The modern east window, seen from a distance, is an effective mosaic of colour.

There is a carved Norman font with four pillars, an ancient red painting of a vine on the stone round the east window, and a long 13th century chest, no doubt made to collect alms for poor crusaders.

Of the five brasses the oldest is Robert Scarclyf, a rector of 1412, with every graceful fold of his vestments still distinct. Three others are from the time of Henry the Eighth, and show Oliver Sandes, John Redfford (a quaint little figure with his wife and six children), and a demure maiden lady with long hair. The fifth brass is a fine big portrait of John Touchet, who became Lord Audley and died in 1491. His son, the seventh Lord Audley, was beheaded for leading the Cornish Insurrection in 1497, and must have come marching through Shere with his men on the way to their crushing defeat at Blackheath.

John Touchet was buried in this church, and held the manor of Shere as the tenant of Sir Reginald Bray, the statesman and architect who is believed to have designed Henry the Seventh's chapel at Westminster. Ever since his day the Brays have had their estate here, and many memorials to them are on these walls. One tablet is to William Bray of 1832, who lived to be 97 and joined with Owen Manning to write a famous history of Surrey. Others are to Sir Edward Bray and his brother Reginald, both of them judges in the present century. And it was Miss Bray of the manor house here who started the Anti-Litter League to keep our lanes and commons free from rubbish.

There is another remarkable collection of family names on the list of rectors. Six in succession, from 1658 until 1843, were Duncombes, and four of the six were called Thomas, one Thomas being rector for 40 years and another for 56.

The Home of the Shirley Poppy

SHIRLEY. It has given the world the fairy-like Shirley poppies, first grown here after ten years of study to perfect them, and still growing in the vicar's garden behind a wonderful holly hedge.

It was the vicar here, Mr William Wilks, who gave the new flower to the world. He was Secretary of the Horticultural Society, and, taking the ordinary wild poppy, experimented with it in his vicarage garden and established the new variety, the exquisite poppy now found in gardens everywhere. The discoverer of this flower lies in the churchyard near where the flower was born.

We found here another touch of vivid colour, for the winter sunlight was streaming into the modern church and lighting up its reredos pictures of saints under elaborate arches of gilded stone. The church has a handsome font of polished marble, but its chief interest to many will be the inscription to William Purdie Treloar who was laid to rest here in 1923. He was one of London's most popular lord mayors, and one of the best friends crippled children ever had. He got an Act of Parliament passed to enable him to turn a war hospital into a cripple hospital at Alton in Hampshire, and its work has been one of the romantic chapters of modern surgery, as well as a great story of philanthropy.

Under a fine tree in this churchyard sleep the parents of John Ruskin, with his own incription to their memory :

Here rests from Day's well sustained burden John James Ruskin. He was an entirely honest merchant, and his memory is to all who keep it dear and helpful. His son, whom he loved to the uttermost and taught to speak truth, says this of him:

Here beside my father's body I have laid my mother's; nor was dearer dust ever returned to earth, nor purer life recorded in heaven.

It was in memory of his aged mother that Ruskin cleaned out a pool at Carshalton and called it Margaret's Well. His father had inherited a business with many debts, all of which he paid before he began to lay by anything for himself.

No one can altogether understand John Ruskin who does not know something of the two old folk who lie at Shirley.

Two Springs from Which Flowed a Great Force

IF ever parents moulded the life and character of their child they were Margaret and John James Ruskin.

She was the daughter of a skipper in the herring industry, and he was her cousin, son of an Edinburgh calico merchant. They married in 1818 and in 1819 their only child was born at 54 Hunter Street, Bloomsbury, the father having become partner in the London wine firm of Domecq, Telford, and Ruskin, of whom it was said that Domecq provided the sherry, Telford the capital, and Ruskin the brains. He was a shrewd business man with a real love and knowledge of literature and pictures to fill his leisure hours, or even to combine with work, for summer after summer he and his wife, with young John perched on the dickey seat of a private chaise, would tour the country in a leisurely fashion, visiting old customers and gaining new ones for the firm, while noting the beauties of the country as they went along. They would stop at a museum or a private house for the sight of a famous picture, and look in on literary or artist friends, several of whom were the giants of those days. Before John was twelve he had seen in this way most of England, Scotland, and Wales, and his father's pockets were bulging with odd sketches or poems on this or that place done by the boy.

But that was in the summer and the child was growing up. Winters and earlier days give a very different picture of the home ruled by a stern, unbending mother, whose admirable qualities were overlaid by a narrow evangelical faith. She loved her son, but controlled her love as she controlled her life. As a child he never heard a harsh word to disturb the orderly peace of the household, but neither did he hear one word of warm affection. He was happy in a way, but there was a wall between him and the world. It was as if he were brought up in a monastic cell. All her life Margaret Ruskin tried to protect him from what seemed to her the ever-threatening menace of the world. She could see evil in toys and in playfellows. Companions her child had none, and his only toys were a box of bricks and a bunch of keys. It was a memorable occasion when his mother counted out to him three raisins as a treat. Sunday was a day of gloom with every story book put away. He was 39 before he made his first sketch on a Sunday.

Every day his mother read to him a passage from the Bible, beginning with the first verse of Genesis, on to the last of Revelation, and back to Genesis again. Soon he was able to read alternate verses, while she watched every syllable to see that it was neither mispronounced nor misplaced. All his life he was grateful to her for a knowledge of the Bible possessed by few, from which came his critical attention in all reading and the perfection in taste which was the basis of his work. Against that she gave him a childhood with nothing to love but himself, and kept him as long as she could dependent in the narrow world she had made for him. She was his only teacher till he was ten, even learning a smattering of Hebrew that she might pass it on to him. When he went as a student to Oxford she went too, taking rooms for herself and staying there the three years that he was in residence. Never once did he miss tea with her every evening, and at weekends the father joined them. If he wanted to go rowing it had to be done in secret lest the mother should fear for his safety.

They still travelled together, but now farther afield, to the Rhine, Switzerland, Italy, and other European countries. Sometimes he would stay abroad, and letters would pass almost daily between them, Ruskin's being nearly always to the father, to whom he owed his introduction to art; he had never let him look at a bad picture, and was his son's literary agent till he died. The father had concurred in the rigid upbringing, but had managed to combine it with a literary and artistic training. He arranged for the boy to have his own table at which he could write and sketch at home, and he was for ever filling his pockets with his son's latest productions that he might show them to friends in the City.

He it was who one day ran up the stairs waving a paper in his hands, his eyes shining, his cheeks wet with tears. "What is the excitement?" asked Mrs Ruskin. "It's—it's—only a print," said he. It was the proof of his son's first printed prose, and he had burst into tears of joy when he saw it. Many years later he insisted on printing in book form all John Ruskin's juvenile verse, distributing copies among his friends and thereby annoying his son extremely, for by then the young man had realised that in this his mother's judgment was the better; she was right in believing him to be but a poet in prose. Later, when the art critic became a fierce teacher of political and social economy, the father grew puzzled and worried, but still went on seeing the essays through the printers, and still the son bore patiently with parental interference, sparks flying now and then, but no question of severance arising.

The father was a wealthy man, always buying pictures and always ready to hand to his son large sums to help this or that artist or this or that struggling cause.

The father died in 1864, and the mother, now a difficult, imperious old lady of 83, bore her loss stoically, though not from lack of feeling, for when she herself came to die she asked to be laid by the side of the husband whom she trusted to see again, "not to be near him; not to be so high in heaven, but content if I might only see him."

Only during the few years of his unsatisfactory marriage had Ruskin any home but that of his parents, and for some time after his father's death he stayed with his mother on Denmark Hill, bearing with a patience that was almost saintlike her constant criticism and her rasping tongue. She was as worried over his change in religious thought as the father was over his socialist tendencies. Here were two things strange to them in the son who had seemed so utterly theirs. The old lady still ordered John about like a child, but to the end he loved her and was grateful to her. He knew that she loved him beyond all else on earth. He saw her in arms at once at any criticism of her son from the outside world. When she died her simple will was: "I leave all I have to my son."

This son once wrote that the happiest bit of manual work he ever did was when he washed the stone steps of an old inn at Sixt because his mother had complained of them. It must have been his mother's spirit working in him, too, when he hired a little band of crossing sweepers and himself worked with them to clean the streets that London would not keep clean for herself.

SURREY

A Bullet at Majuba Hill

STOKE. Now swallowed up by Guildford, its 15th century church on the Woking road catches the eye with its cheque-patterned tower, made up of alternate squares of stone and flints. A few yards down the road is a leaning brick and timber house of 1663, oddly packed in among modern villas.

In the church are several brass inscriptions to the Stoughtons, important local people of the 17th century. Bridget, the wife of one of them, died in 1631, and a quaint verse tells why she went home to Hampshire for her last sleep, ending:

> *She at her father's, by her sister's, side,*
> *Lies buried where she thrice was made a bride.*

The east window is a memorial to Sir George Colley, a distinguished soldier and a fine administrator whose career was cut short by a bullet at Majuba Hill in 1881. He had set out to relieve the British garrisons under siege in the newly-proclaimed Boer Republic, and, marching through the night with 500 men, climbed for eight hours to scale the hill. In the morning the Boers made an unexpected attack and rushed the height, Sir George being killed by a shot in the forehead and half his little force lost. With him England lost a man destined to be one of the leaders of her army, a man loved by his comrades and described by one of them as "the ablest soldier I have ever served with." It was his brother officers who gave this window of Our Lord and the Evangelists in his memory.

In this place in 1830 was born Commodore Goodenough, who met at Santa Cruz the same tragic fate which had struck down Captain Cook on another Pacific Island.

Fate Stops a Great Career

FROM the day that James Graham Goodenough, the son of the Dean of Wells, entered the Navy at 14, his career was one of continued progress and brilliance.

He saw the world. In 1848 he was off the coast of Africa. Three years later he was sailing down the east coast of South America. Another three years and his ship took 1500 Frenchmen to the Baltic Campaign, and returned with 1200 Russian prisoners. Another three and he was at the capture of Canton. Next he is off on a special mission to enquire into the advance of American naval armaments during the Civil War.

Admirals almost tumbled over themselves to put him in command of their flagships; the Admiralty appointed him to a committee considering the designs of ships of war. Serious, extremely intelligent, with varied gifts and fluency in seven languages, there was no knowing where he would end, but the end came tragically at 45 with a grave in Australia.

At that time he was Commodore of the Australian station, having voyaged from England in a wooden ship fitted with steam and sails. After the occupation of Fiji and the capture of King Thakombau, he started on a round of visits of the islands of his far-flung station. It was August 1875 when he landed on Santa Cruz with a few men. He thought the natives were his friends, and he was sitting chatting with them when an arrow struck him in the side. It was the story of Captain Cook over again. More treacherous shots followed, and six of his men were also wounded before they could get back to their boat.

Suspecting that the arrows might be poisoned, Goodenough steered to the cooler South, but eight days later, before the ship was within 500 miles of Sydney, two men had died and the Commodore knew his time was near. He lay on the quarterdeck while one by one his officers filed past him for a last handshake. His body was taken ashore at Sydney, and there they buried him.

His portrait bust is in the Painted Hall at Greenwich, an excellent likeness by his old messmate Prince Victor of Hohenlohe; and the Goodenough Gold Medal was founded in his memory.

England's Oldest Brass

STOKE D'ABERNON. The highway through this quiet little spot has but a few cottages by its side, and from it winds a chestnut avenue to the secluded church and manor house on the banks of the Mole. The 200-year-old manor house is a red brick building in a lovely garden, green meadows stretching all around, and over the churchyard wall the beautiful terrace bordering the river.

Standing by the manor house is the grey flint church, parts of which were already old when the Normans came to England, for the east part of the nave is ninth or tenth century work, and we can

Sir John d'Abernon, 1277   His son, Sir John, 1327

The brass of Sir John D'Abernon, Sheriff of Surrey, is the oldest in England, 1277; it is also notable as the only known brass of a knight with his lance.

THE MOST FAMOUS BRASSES IN SURREY—AT STOKE D'ABERNON

still see a Saxon doorway blocked up in the wall. Still older is part of the chancel, for it has a piece of Roman brickwork still in its original mortar; it is believed to have been brought from the ruined villa which is under the manor house lawn, or perhaps it belonged to a basilica which may have stood on the site of the church. It at least reminds us that human life has clung to this spot for nearly 2000 years.

The inside of the chancel is very lovely 13th century work. The roof is vaulted with stone, and on the eastern wall are the restored remains of a contemporary painting in red and yellow of the Adoration of the Lamb. We recognise a group of human figures, a crowned king playing a harp, and two angels, one beckoning and one playing a musical instrument.

In the chancel floor is the greatest treasure of the church, the brass of Sir John d'Abernon, who died in 1277. It is the oldest brass in the land, and the only one known of a knight armed with a lance. It is unusually large, being 6 feet 6 inches long, and the blue enamel still remains on the shield and the flowing pennon. Sir John was Sheriff of Surrey, and here we see him wearing a coat over his chain mail, his noble face looking out of a close-fitting helmet. A long sword hangs from the belt at his waist, and his feet rest on a lion which grasps the shaft of the lance in its paws and mouth.

Close to this famous brass is one of Sir John's proud-faced son, who died just half a century after his father. He is partly dressed in plate armour, for by this time chain mail was going out of fashion.

Beside the dim chancel is the light-flooded chapel, built and probably designed about 1490 by Sir John Norbury, whose funeral helm hangs on the wall. It is divided from the chancel by a beautiful panelled arch which once covered Sir John's original tomb. On the wall is a little figure of the founder kneeling at a desk in armour of the days of Charles Stuart. It was erected, as the inscription tells us, by his descendant Sir Francis Vincent. It was after taking a valiant part at Bosworth Field that Sir John built himself this chapel, and we may infer that he wished to be comfortable after his great perils, for here is one of the very few Tudor fireplaces in an English church.

The small and graceful font may have been given by Sir John Norbury, and we may be sure that Ellen Bray was christened in it. She died in 1516 before she was a month old; her quaint little brass figure, wrapped like a mummy in her christening cloth, is by the arch of Sir John Norbury's first tomb. Opposite are eight children, engraved on the skirt of their widowed mother, Lady Anne Norbury, one of the few instances of children grouped on the folds of their mother's gown. The four girls have their hair fastened in nets, and the eldest boy carries a purse attached to his girdle.

On the other side of the chapel is an ornamented arch beneath which lie coloured figures of Sir Thomas and Lady Vincent. Sir Thomas died in 1623, and we see his bearded figure reclining on an elbow, wearing the huge baggy breeches of his day. Below him lies his wife, in ruff and Paris hood, her head on two cushions; and high on the wall hangs the tattered coat of Sir Thomas.

It was Sir Thomas Vincent's son Francis who gave the church its magnificent pulpit on being created a baronet in 1620. He imported it ready-made from Flanders, but the fine sounding-board and backboard are additions in English oak. The seven sides are elaborately carved, and supported by weird human monsters with moustaches and beards. The lower panels are carved with heads of lions; those above show little flowers, and are flanked by tiny figures of men. The sounding-board is supported by scrolled iron stays, and in the middle of the board is an angel. This glorious pulpit is one of the loveliest in Surrey, and near it is a 17th century hourglass bracket of scrolled iron, the hourglass itself, a rarer sight, is in the vestry, brought back to the church from a school at Fetcham.

Lady Sarah Vincent, the wife of Sir Francis, did not live to see the fine pulpit her husband gave. Under a round arch in the Norbury chapel we see her prim figure in hood, ruff, and tightly-waisted dress, reclining uncomfortably on a tasselled cushion. Below on the front of the tomb are kneeling figures of her children, five model sons in cloaks, and two exemplary daughters with full skirts and carefully arranged hair.

Another family is shown on a square brass plate on the chapel wall. Here we see the interior of a stately building with massive columns and paved floor. Kneeling at a prayer-desk is Thomas Lyfelde in ruff, doublet, and gown, and facing him is his wife Francis, who died in 1592. She wears a hood and ruff, and kneeling behind her is her daughter Jane. Both have their gowns tied with ribbon, and left open to show richly embroidered petticoats.

The 18th century lectern is probably, like the pulpit, from the Low Countries. Its twisted stem of dark wood is carved with a climbing vine, and a gilded eagle supports the desk.

The church has two valuable chests; one of them 500 years old, among the earliest made for church use. It is thrilling to know that it was probably constructed to collect money for the Crusades, and if we are clever we may find the secret cavity for the coin. On the front are three roundels with starlike patterns, decorative devices brought back from the East. The other chest is 17th century, of panelled oak, and has a carving on the front. Also of oak are the modern panelled pews based on the old ones at Clymping church in Sussex.

There is some 15th century glass, a lion's head, an angel playing on a stringed instrument, and fragments of elaborate canopies. In the middle of the window is an early 16th century scene of St Anne teaching the little Madonna to read.

In the lancet windows in the south wall of the nave are six delightful roundels of yellow glass made in Holland in the 15th and 16th centuries. There is St Barbara with a book, a Crucifixion with the Madonna and St John, and a group showing Peter being rebuked for taking the sword against the High Priest's servant. Other panels show Christ in Glory, a prisoner kneeling before a saint who has released him from goal, and the Madonna with the body of Christ.

In the sanctuary is a tapering gravestone 700 years old, with an inscription to "Richard the Little, formerly parson of this church."

The churchyard with its smooth lawns and yews is delightful, and in it has been found a censer cover nearly 1000 years old. It looks like the top of a great pepperpot, and is attached to a pillar at the west end of the church.

Here sleeps Ellen Kate Green, whose record of faithful service can seldom have been excelled. As a girl of 14 she entered the family of a Birmingham vicar who became vicar of Dartford in Kent, and she brought up all his ten children. She passed into the home of two of the children and died in their service at 86. At her graveside stood six of the seven surviving children she tended from childhood, and one of them conducted the burial of this fine old lady at whose knee they had so often knelt during her 72 years with the family.

Shere   The Village Street

Albury   The Silent Pool

Frensham   The Great Pond

Virginia Water   The Beauty of the Lake

One of Stoke D'Abernon's rector's, preaching here for 32 years, was Thomas Neesham, who comes into a tragic story.

The Wife of Judge Jeffreys

INSTALLED here in 1629, he was the father of six daughters and two sons, and was glad to allow one of the daughters, Sarah, who was born in 1644, to go to London as servant to the daughter of a wealthy merchant.

At this time a hard-drinking, hard-swearing, unscrupulous young lawyer named George Jeffreys was carousing and joking himself into the favour of the city merchants. He got to know Sarah Neesham's rich young mistress, and carried on a correspondence with a view to a secret marriage which would give him possession of her father's fortune. Sarah Neesham was made the go-between, so that when the lady's father discovered the intrigue it was upon her that his wrath descended. He turned her penniless into the streets of London and left her homeless. Her own father was by this time in the grave, and the rectory at Stoke D'Abernon knew the Neeshams no more.

In her distress Sarah turned to the man who had brought her to disaster, and George Jeffreys did the one chivalrous and disinterested thing of his life; he married Sarah Neesham, she being 23 and he about the same age. She lived to see him become, by sheer audacity and unscrupulousness, Lord Chief Justice of England.

Happily she died before 1685 and so was spared the horrors perpetrated at his instigation during the horrible Assize, but her granddaughter, the Countess of Pomfret, was hooted in the West Country when it was known that she was descended from the brutal judge who had married a daughter of Stoke D'Abernon rectory two generations before.

The Town the Railway Made

SURBITON. Like so many of the suburbs of Greater London, it has attained the full dignity of a borough, and its boundaries have been extended from time to time, bringing its neighbours Tolworth, Hook, and Chessington under its governing wing. As a name Surbiton appears as early as the 12th century in the records of Merton Priory, and it comes into the annals of the Civil War, for in 1648 there was a skirmish between Roundheads and Cavaliers on

the now vanished Surbiton Common. But its real story begins with
the advent of the railway early in the 19th century. Ever since then it
has been growing, and its population is now fast approaching 50,000.
Thomas Hardy, who started his married life here in the days when
he had given up architecture and begun writing novels, would hardly
recognise it today.

Spacious houses of the Victorian Era still line many of its roads,
but Surbiton moves with the times, and its dignified civic buildings
and its kinemas, shops, and blocks of flats reflect the modern trend
of architecture. For those who would play games the town has
provided many fine recreation grounds and named them in honour
of kings and queens; for those who would swim there is the wonderful Lagoon, with a swimming bath 165 feet long and 90 feet wide;
for those who seek a tranquil corner away from busy streets there
are the charming Claremont Crescent Gardens, with lawns and a
waterfall and a little winding brook; and for those who would walk
and admire the river there is the magnificent Queen's Promenade
nearly a mile long, shaded by fine trees and shrubs and looking
across to Hampton Court.

The mother church of Surbiton is St Mark's, standing high on a
hill, a fine 19th century building with a graceful spire. It has a
window in memory of the town's VC, Major Robert Shelbeare who
died at sea in 1860, three years after he had won his cross at the
Siege of Delhi. Among the daughter churches of Surbiton is the
graceful St Matthew's, also with a spire. Its east window has Bible
pictures designed by Henry Holliday, and on the wall is a white
bust carved by a local sculptor, T. T. Arran; it shows a stern but
kindly man, Francis Stephen Clayton, "patron, warden, and benefactor of this church." There is also fine carving in the Congregational Church, again with a tall spire; it has a bronze relief by
Richard Goulden, and portrays a sorrowful figure of Victory crowned,
a memorial of the war. Near is St Andrew's Church, its tall tower
built by Sir Arthur Blomfield, who gave it a saddle-back roof.

The Fear of Elizabeth Gibson

SUTTON. It is one of Surrey's busy grown-up places, with a
pleasant little park, a pretty green, and a church of St Nicholas
refashioned last century. It has a lofty shingled spire and high-pitched

roofs. Hanging on the chancel is an iron helmet of long ago, and among the modern glass is an exceptionally attractive window showing figures of children and angels.

The churchyard is beautiful with shrubs, and more interesting than beautiful is its huge mausoleum of the Gibsons, to which a little story belongs. It is the 18th century tomb of five of the family, and in August every year, after a service in the church, the vicar and the churchwardens walk out to it, open the iron gate, look at the five coffins, say a prayer, and lock it up again for another year.

The ceremony dates back to the death of Elizabeth Gibson in the 18th century, when the practice of body-snatching made people fearful lest thieves should steal their bodies and sell them to hospitals for experiments. Miss Gibson determined that her family tomb should never be rifled, and in her will she left £500 to pay for regular visits to it. In some churchyards bodies were set up for watchers in those days. The fear of body-snatchers is long past, but the little ceremony at Sutton has been paid for, and so it will continue.

One of the best new churches we have seen in Surrey is the imposing Baptist Church quite close to Sutton's busy crossing. We should not be surprised if it were the finest church the Baptists have anywhere; it cost £33,000, and was paid for by selling the site of the old chapel, which had become very valuable in the High Street. The church is of brick, and looks a little severe from outside, though its windows carry on the spirit of the medieval builders. The interior is wide, impressive and beautiful, with windows handsomely framed in great brick arches. The east window shows little scenes from Pilgrim's Progress, and below is a medallion carved in relief with figures of Philip and the Ethiopian. With the church is a group of buildings containing some of the most charming Sunday school rooms we have seen anywhere.

Giants Indoors and Out

TANDRIDGE. It has a living yew guarding its church, a giant we can well believe has been growing for nearly a thousand years. It may have seen the workmen bringing the stones to build the tower, and ever since those days it has been throwing its branches across this beautiful corner of Surrey. They make a circle of 250 feet, and have such life that this great trunk, hollowed out and about

32 feet round, has given itself new strength since it was reported dying a hundred years ago.

And this great giant has a company of giants that it cannot see. It is possible that he may have seen them once, when they were giants and he a youngster of 300 years. The ruins of Roman houses must have been widespread over England when the four giants inside the tower were young. Here they stand, these four immense oak trees, one still in the ground where the workmen set it 700 years ago, three resting on great stones, holding up Tandridge tower.

The tower is one of the earliest of its kind in Surrey, and the rafters in the roof, which have been pierced for modern dormer windows, are of the same age.

This small church which has a parish ten miles long and one mile wide, is famous chiefly for its tower, but it has another claim to fame in its priest's doorway, now leading to the vestry. It is one of the oldest in Surrey, built by the Normans in their early days. The door is only 26 inches wide and has beside it a tiny lancet the Norman builders made at the same time. A 14th century doorway has been built into the modern porch.

Hanging on the ancient oak trunks in the tower is one of the most charming coats-of-arms we have seen. They are those of Charles Stuart and are carved right through the oak. It is said that they are by Grinling Gibbons.

The carving on the reredos is interesting. It has about 20 figures in three scenes which show the woman bringing the box of precious ointment, Thomas doubting at the Resurrection, and the Crucifixion, this scene being remarkable for showing a figure like a Scout holding Christ's girdle with one hand and the Cross with the other.

It was Sir Gilbert Scott whose restoration robbed this church of a Norman chancel arch. He lived at Tandridge and in this churchyard sleeps his wife. Round her tomb are medallions of Faith, Hope, and Charity, saints, and the Madonna. Sir Gilbert Scott himself carved the bluebells, primroses, and daffodils in which the medallions are set. Also in this churchyard lie three 19th century Earls of Cottenham who lived at Tandridge Court; one of the graves has a cross on stones sculptured with ivy by Westmacott the younger.

The big houses of Tandridge are new, but there are a few fragments of the ancient priory; they are outside the village by the old fishpond. The three poplar trees on the triangular green mark the site of the old lock-up.

Sussex, Surrey, and Kent

TATSFIELD. It has nothing to surpass the magnificent view from the churchyard nearly 800 feet up on the North Downs, a height used by the engineers of the BBC for their experimental work. In their station here the wave-lengths of European stations are checked, and short-wave transmissions are received from America and the British Empire. Hills and trees and fields of Surrey and Sussex and Kent roll out before us in a scene of unending delight. Three chief ranges we see, the Sevenoaks ridge, the high ground of Ashdown Forest, and the far line of the South Downs.

All this the little church has been watching for eight centuries, for it was set in this place by the Normans. The north wall they built is here still with two of their lancet windows, though one has been pointed. There are old beams in the roof, a 500-year-old font, a piscina and a double aumbry in the sanctuary, an Elizabethan cup, and a chancel window which draws the eye for the great beauty of its stonework, richly moulded 700 years ago with a pillar at each side, and looking as if it has strayed by accident from a cathedral into a village church.

There is no old glass, but the east window has a soft harmony of colour in a scene showing Gabriel bringing the good news to the Madonna. On the wall is a wooden memorial painted to look like stone in memory of John Corbett of Southwark, a carpenter in the time of Queen Anne, "a person truly ingenious."

There is a striking canopied brass engraved with the names that live for evermore, and by it are tablets to a soldier and a sailor who gave their lives at Gallipoli.

Here Was Written The Song of the Shirt

THAMES DITTON. It has grown up by the banks of the Thames and has an inn taking us back 600 years and a church tower which takes us back a century more. The inn is the Swan. Many interesting people have known it, and one of the most famous of all its visitors was Tom Hood. Here the poet of the poor would often stay, and it is recorded that he was staying at the Swan when he wrote the Song of the Shirt.

So from this old inn there went round the world and has come down the ages one of the most piteous of all human cries:

> *With fingers weary and worn,*
> *With eyelids heavy and red,*
> *A woman sat in unwomanly rags*
> *Plying her needle and thread.*
> *Stitch—stitch—stitch!*
> *In poverty, hunger, and dirt,*
> *And still with a voice of dolorous pitch*
> *She sang the Song of the Shirt!*

The church is famous for its brasses, a little gallery of five groups with about 70 figures from the 16th century. On one is Erasmus Forde, seen in armour with his six sons behind him, his wife kneeling before him with her 12 daughters; they would be neighbours of Robert Smythe and his wife, here with seven children, and of John Polsted and his wife, who kneel on tasselled cushions by a tablet with books on it, four charming little daughters in hoods and puffed sleeves kneeling behind the mother. The brass was put up by the youngest daughter Julian when she was 73. In another brass she herself is shown between two husbands, the first being Serjeant of the Confectionery to Henry the Eighth and the second Gentleman Usher to two kings. There are 11 children on her brass; another shows William Notte with his wife and their 19 children. We have rarely come upon a group of brasses so crowded with people.

There is a 16th century treasure chest with five slots for coins, a finely carved 15th century Easter Sepulchre, and the pillar of a Norman piscina. In the porch is a tablet to Thomas Merser, who was parish clerk of Thames Ditton for 50 years, and here was buried Arthur Onslow, who was Speaker through all the five Parliaments of George the Second. He is here no more, however, having been removed to Merrow Church. It was he who rebuked a member for keeping Parliament waiting for the king. Colonel Fitzroy excused himself for being late by saying he had been in attendance upon his Majesty. "Sir, (said Mr Onslow, indignantly) don't tell me of waiting; this is your place to attend in; this is your first duty."

Here, at Ember Farm, is a sort of flying school for birds, with aviaries in which caged birds that have lost the use of their wings can be given the opportunity to regain the mastery of flight, before being set free to look after themselves. The place was built by the RSPCA, largely in the interest of foreign birds which cannot be given freedom in this country, but which kindly folk wish to set free from their small cages.

In Charge of Admiral Byng

THORPE. It lies peacefully spread on the flat ground by the Thames, with red walls and old cottages, and a red brick tower built in the 16th century. The church was already old when they gave it this tower, and it still has its Norman chancel arch, with a 15th century peep-hole on either side, and 14th century sedilia.

Several pieces of old glass are scattered about the windows, the best being the 15th century painting (under the tower) of canopy work. In a nave window are five medallions of Flemish glass about 400 years old, showing the Madonna, John the Baptist, the Crucifixion, the miraculous draught of fishes, and a quaint scene of Jacob's sons raising their hats to their father as they set out for Egypt.

On the chancel wall are brass portraits of an Elizabethan family, William Denham and his wife and 15 children; and in the sanctuary is a tablet to Admiral Isaac Townsend, laid to rest here in 1765. He was a Fellow of the Royal Society, an MP, and governor of Greenwich Hospital, and it was his lot at Greenwich to take charge of his fellow admiral John Byng, then awaiting the trial which led to his being shot at Portsmouth for neglect of duty.

A Real Old Chestnut

THURSLEY. It lies among the commons on the way up to Hindhead, with delightful cottages along a winding lane leading to the church.

Walking this way we come upon two charming old houses, and a colossal chestnut which must be one of the highest and best in Surrey. It grows just inside the churchyard, and beneath its dipping branches we go toward the shingled spire with its blue sundial.

We are treading where men and women were coming to worship a thousand years ago and we still see some of the things their eyes rested on. The church has the appearance of being made new in the 19th century, but the 20th century has brought to light the fact that the core of it is Saxon, and some fascinating things have been uncovered after several hundred years.

They are mostly in the chancel: two little windows, an oven, and round the wall a ledge which once supported a room above for the priest. The oven is a plain square opening in the wall, and was used for baking the wafers and heating the charcoal for incense. Such a Saxon oven is a rare thing to find (East Horsley has another), but there is something not less rare in the deeply splayed Saxon windows above. They were shedding light on this chancel in the time of Edward the Confessor, and in those days the light came not through glass but through horn. Though the horn has vanished there still exists in each of these windows the wooden frame which held it in place, made from oaks that may well have been growing in Surrey when the Danes were invading our shores. We can see how the wood was shaped to take the horn, and the very nails with which it was fastened have been found. On the splay of one window the old red painted patterns are still clear.

Most of the chancel walls are Saxon; the nave stands chiefly on Saxon foundations and has a window (now opening into the aisle) dating from about 1060. The massive font is also thought to be Saxon.

The chancel arch, the sedilia, and the double piscina were added in the 13th century, and there is a piece of carved 14th century masonry found under the chancel floor. Another piscina is Norman, and there is an oak chest of 1622.

Three modern lancets at the west end throw a flood of light into the nave, showing up clearly a feature of the church said to be unique in Surrey. It is the astonishing structure of beams rising up from four moulded wooden piers in the middle of the nave; they have been supporting the steeple for about 500 years.

The churchyard has a good view across to the Hog's Back, and an attractive peace memorial cross. Close by is the grave of the sailor murdered on Hindhead by three villains in 1786; the gibbet on which they were hanged stood on a site marked by a stone at Hindhead. A little way off is a modern stone with three words that speak volumes:

John Freeman—Poet. He was one of the poets who died too young, not yet quite fifty.

He was little known in his lifetime though he won the Hawthornden Prize which made him known to a wider circle. Something of his appears now in most recent anthologies, and his work will be better and better known. He wrote intimately of what he loved, seeing visions in the everyday sides of nature and the countryside, and believing that love and gentleness are the things that matter most. These lines are from one of his poems during the war:

> *There is not anything more wonderful*
> *Than a great people moving towards the deep*
> *Of an unguessed and unfeared future; nor*
> *Is aught so dear of all held dear before*
> *As the new passion stirring in their veins*
> *When the destroying Dragon wakes from sleep.*
>
> *Whate'er was dear before is dearer now.*
> *There's not a bird singing upon his bough*
> *But sings the sweeter in our English ears:*
> *There's not a nobleness of heart, hand, brain*
> *But shines the purer.*

They laid him to rest at Thursley in 1929, and it is by his own desire that he lies in sight of Crooksbury Hill. We may believe that his grave with its single-word epitaph is just what he would have wished, and that he would rejoice to know that a green field by the church had been dedicated to his memory.

Philip Snowden

TILFORD. It has two attractive old bridges over branches of the River Wey, but it has nothing to beat the grand old giant watching over the spacious green, the King's Oak William Cobbett pointed out to his son in a ride through Surrey a hundred years ago. A fine bulwark of England it is, 26 feet round, hale and hearty, and nobody knows quite how many centuries old.

We should like to come to Tilford in 500 years' time to see how five little oaks on this green have been getting on. They were planted to represent events from the Diamond Jubilee and the Coronation of Edward the Seventh to the accession and Jubilee of George the Fifth and the crowning of George the Sixth.

Among the memorials in the modern church is a tablet to a young cavalry officer who was killed on patrol in the first days of the Great War. Here, too, are kept the flags of England and the Red Cross under which the VAD served continuously at Waverley Abbey Military Hospital from 1914 to 1919.

About a mile along the Farnham road from here is Woodlarks,

the first permanent camping site for crippled Girl Guides, given to the movement a few years ago. It is in beautiful country and overlooks miles of heath and woodland.

Here one of the most remarkable men of our generation, and one of the most remarkable statesmen of all time, Philip Snowden, spent the last few years of his life, and here he died. He and Ramsay MacDonald were the brains of the Labour Party. They built it up for thirty years, and they had the courage to break away from their old friends when they felt that their duty to the nation called them first. Philip Snowden was first of all a lover of peace, a friend of all mankind, and an English patriot. He dared to tell the truth. As Chancellor of the Exchequer he was not afraid to demand justice for his country from abroad, or loyalty from our people at home.

No man was truer to himself. He left the great fighting arena of Parliament with eternal honour to his name. He had made his name famous and respected in England and the world. He made it impossible that history should forget it. Physically crippled, he had a kingly intellect, and he would stand in the House of Commons, in those days when he stood high in the esteem of the nation, suffering great pain but making masterly speeches. Literally he suffered for his country and gave his strength for it. He came into Parliament as a party man, having built up a great class machine; he left it as a patriot, above all classes and with the esteem of the whole nation. It was as if England was saying to him, Thine island loves thee well, thou famous man.

Titsey's Long Past

TITSEY. It has known the primitive men who made flints on Titsey Hill, it has seen the Romans building a villa in Titsey Park; it has heard the tramp of feet on the Pilgrim's Way, and seen its old church taken down at the whim of a lord.

A steep road winds down the hill skirting the park, and beside it is the modern church with a group of old houses. One of them is dated 1673. Like many old churches this new one has a family chapel connected with those who have lived at the great house, and there are many memorials to the Greshams and the Leveson-Gowers who came after them. The oldest is a brass portrait of William Gresham kneeling at prayer with his wife and their seven children. He was a first cousin of the Thomas Gresham who founded the Royal Exchange, and, like him, died in 1579. His grandson John is remembered here by a big memorial which greets us as we enter. He was a stout Royalist, and, though he died early in the Civil War, his memorial was not put up till the Restoration.

From three generations later is a tablet to Sir Marmaduke of 1742. His heir was drowned at sea, and another of his sons became the John Gresham whose name must be remembered with mixed feelings in Titsey. He pulled down the house of his ancestors in the park, and pulled down the 14th century church because it stood too near the new house he was building. There is a solemn note in the church register of 1775, when the writer says grimly: "Begun to pull down the church. The church was a noble structure, with a strong tower and lofty steeple." Six days later they laid the foundation stone of another church across the way, and the church of today is its successor on the same site.

In the family chapel lies the dignified sleeping figure of Granville Leveson-Gower, sculptured by Sir Thomas Brock, who sculptured Britannia for Queen Victoria's pennies. Mr Leveson-Gower excavated the Roman villa in Titsey Park and wrote a full account of it. On the wall is a fine relief of his son, who died a young man.

There are two graceful candlesticks brought from a mosque in Salonika; a window of old glass showing shields and the grasshopper crest of the Greshams; and 14th century tiles from the old church, worn, we like to think, by the feet of pilgrims to Canterbury.

TONGHAM. Two things it has for the traveller to see, one behind the modern church and the other in it. The detached wooden bell tower is a son's unusual memorial to his mother, who lived at the great house in Poyle Park; and the stone font was carved on its eight sides by Colonel John Luard, when he was in his 83rd year. It is a remarkable feat for an old man, and shows among other carvings Our Lord on the Cross and with the children.

The Two Butchers

VIRGINIA WATER. One of the best-loved places in reach of London, it is on the edge of Windsor's Great Park and shares in its charm.

The beautiful lake among the trees is about two miles long, and its farther shores are in Berkshire. Looking anything but artificial, it was made in 1746 by that Duke of Cumberland who was known as the Butcher of Culloden. In designing it he had the aid of the skilful engineer and landscape gardener Thomas Sandby RA, who had been his secretary and was with him at Culloden and in Flanders. They planted delightful glades, made a cascade, and, after the fashion of the time, brought over a collection of ancient ruins from Tripoli. Very self-conscious they look in this English scene, some of the tall pillars erect, some broken, some carefully askew on the ground.

Half a mile away the church stands well in a spacious churchyard rich in fine evergreens. In it is a memorial to the Spanish Field-Marshal Ramon Cabrera, who, when this church was being built, was distinguishing himself as a Carlist leader in the civil war in Spain. In 1837 he captured Valencia, and two years later seemed to have won victory for the Carlists; but the tide turned and he was driven into France. He finally settled in England, and died at Virginia Water in 1877, leaving the memory of a brilliant soldier but a pitiless man whose cruelties earned him the title of The Tiger. Odd that this peaceful corner of Surrey should have been the home of two such men, the two butchers of Virginia Water.

Noah's Ark

WALLINGTON. Almost yesterday it was a hamlet of Beddington, but it has grown into a busy place with a town hall it shares with Beddington and a Cross of Remembrance it also shares, set up among the elms of the green. The town hall is a fine brick building set off by lawns; we may wish that all town halls were as good to see as this, and that all towns had libraries as fine as the one that Wallington shares with Beddington. It hides its delightful walls in a garden with a lily pond, and it has in it something that must be a sheer delight to every child, one of the finest specimens we have seen of one of the finest toys ever made for childhood. It is a Noah's Ark, probably the best example in the land, with over 400 animals walking two by two, all given, with the Ark itself, by four happy children who have found a new happiness in sharing this toy with other children.

Wallington has a dignified and spacious 19th century church with a spire 110 feet high, and when we called it had one of the tiniest kinemas we have come upon, made out of a stable but finely fitted up for 30 people by an enthusiastic group of amateurs who were writing, acting, and making their own films.

Hunter With Queen Elizabeth

WALTON-ON-THAMES. Here by London's river men were living and coming to church before the Conqueror landed on our shores; and long before that, it is said, their ancestors put stakes in the water to stop Caesar from crossing over. It was the old Walton Bridge, linking Surrey with Middlesex, that Turner painted by moonlight, but we doubt if he would care to paint the present bridge by any light at all.

The town is one of Surrey's fast-growing places, with pleasant new houses set among fine trees, but its greatest attraction is still the old church where its many monuments are gathered. One of the walls is Saxon at the core, another has Norman stonework below 17th century brickwork, and the tower with its huge buttresses is 15th century. The interior has its share of old things too, for there are Norman pillars with fluted capitals, a 600-year-old nave roof and chancel arch, and an 18th century gallery. The east window is enriched with two panels of 14th century glass, one showing a shield with three medallions representing the Trinity, and the other a shield with the instruments of Our Lord's Passion. Hanging in the nave are two Queen Anne candelabra, and kept in a glass case is a curious relic of punishment in the old days, a gossip's bridle with two iron rings to go over the head, and a bit to go into the mouth.

Most striking of all the monuments is the huge marble by Roubiliac to the last Viscount Shannon, who fought in the Battle of the Boyne and died in 1740, half a century after his great-uncle, the famous scientist Robert Boyle. Here he stands before his tent in his wig and cloak and top-boots, carrying his field-marshal's baton and leaning on a mortar. Looking up at him is a beautiful figure of his daughter, who set up the monument, and beside him is a remarkable display of carving of military equipment, a cannon with all its paraphernalia of powder, ramrods, and ammunition; also a powder horn, a drum, a trumpet, a pouch, and a standard. It is an extraordinary parade of martial pomp.

Near by on the wall is a brass much older, a portrait of John Selwyn, keeper of Queen Elizabeth's park at Oatlands not far away. He wears a tunic and has a horn at his side, and is standing with his 11 children and his wife, who wears something not unlike a bowler hat. Hinged up above is a little brass plate with pictures of the worthy John on both sides. They show him mounted on a stag and killing it with a dagger, a feat he is said to have accomplished in a hunt at Oatlands with the Queen, leaping from his horse on to the animal's back and skilfully managing that it should fall dead at her feet.

The chancel has several monuments. One is a fine work by Chantrey with a woman weeping for Sarah D'Oyley and her husband; she was a granddaughter of the celebrated 18th century doctor Sir Hans Sloane, and in her house at Twickenham, Chantrey did some of his first works. Near the altar are two figures by the 19th century sculptor Joseph Gott, Faith pointing to the sky and Grief leaning on a pedestal; they are to a sailor of the time of Napoleon's wars, Admiral Sir Thomas Williams, who was buried at Hersham, near Walton.

A stone in the floor has the names of the 17th century astrologer William Lilly and his friend Elias Ashmole, who put it here; and a quaint tablet over the vestry door is carved with oak trees in memory of Henry Skrine, who wrote books about his travels over England in the 18th century. The smaller trees represent his six children, two with bare branches being for little ones who died.

Sleeping in the churchyard is an Irish poet of last century, William Maginn, with a granite cross by the tower to mark his grave. He was the original of Captain Shandon in Thackeray's Pendennis, and his mocking epitaph by Scott's biographer Lockhart tells us that he is "With Homer and Shakespeare on the heights." The truth is that Maginn's poems were undoubtedly clever, and so was his disreputable journalism. He came to Walton in an advanced state of consumption, penniless after his discharge from a debtor's prison.

We found in the baptistry of this church a touching momento of the Great War keeping Walton in touch with the Empire beyond the seas. It is a banner embroidered with the flags of England and New Zealand, and with the names of 17 New Zealand soldiers who lie in the graveyard. It was worked by one of their comrades, and includes the names of a nurse and of a man who died when the war was over. The town has set up on a wall by the road a bronze tablet to the 27,000 wounded New Zealanders who were cared for in two military hospitals hereabouts, one at Oatlands Park in Weybridge, and one here at Mount Felix, a striking house with a tower by the bridge.

From Manor Place near the river we see a timbered gable of the Tudor manor house where John Bradshaw lived, and from which he may well have ridden forth to pronounce the death sentence on Charles Stuart. He became Lord President of the Council under Cromwell, and was one of those whose bodies were dug up and hanged on Tyburn at the Restoration of the Stuarts.

Of Walton's many new houses, built on the old estates, by far the most interesting is the King's House at Burhill.

The King's House

THE KING'S HOUSE is hidden away at Burhill near Whiteley Village, a magnificent gift from the Royal Warrant Holders to mark the Silver Jubilee of George the Fifth, that he might have in his gift a house in which some honoured servant might live. The dignified design was chosen by King George himself, and is remarkably appropriate to the surroundings of gently rolling slopes and woods. The house is crowned by a silver weathervane representing the royal yacht Britannia, and is fitted with every device science can suggest to add to its architectural beauties. Every room has an electric clock, and most rooms have a loudspeaker panelled in the soundproof walls. The kitchen walls and ceiling are lined with stainless steel, and the cooker combines electricity with gas. The best bathroom is panelled with amber-glass; a switch automatically opens the doors of the wardrobe. All the material in the house is British, home-made, home-grown, or sent by Dominions overseas.

The house was completed in the brief reign of Edward the Eighth, who opened it with a diamond-studded key which unlocks every door. In the study, panelled with Canadian silkwood, he signed the first name in the Visitors Book. He chose as the first tenant Admiral Sir Reginald Tupper, who commanded the fleet of armed merchantmen and trawlers which patrolled the sea between Scotland and Iceland in the Great War.

The Great Quack

AT Walton, where he was for nearly 20 years a churchwarden in the Stuart Age, sleeps one of the greatest quacks of his age, William Lilly. Born at Diseworth in Leicestershire, and educated at Ashby-de-la-Zouch, he reached London as a youth of 18, and served an illiterate shopkeeper, whose widow he married.

Not until he was 30 did he turn to astrology. The time was favourable to such pretensions; belief was general in witchcraft, in the power of demons to affect private and national fortunes; and in this field of folly Lilly reaped his harvest, as other quacks do in our own time. Permitted to practise his arts with a view to finding buried treasure in Westminster Abbey, he ascribed his failure equally to demons and the mocking laughter of onlookers.

His first wife dying, he married a second, whose extravagance drove him into retirement, but he saw in the Civil War a chance to restore his broken fortunes, and began the publication of his astrological almanac, which he continued for nearly 40 years. He was consulted as an oracle alike by Royalists and Roundheads, among his patrons being Lenthall the Speaker and among his credulous friends the founder of the Ashmolean Museum at Oxford, who erected the monument to his memory here. Receiving political information from a French priest, Lilly made it appear the fruit of divination, and enjoyed a pension from Parliament for two or three years. After predicting that England would never again be governed by a king, he bought a pardon at the Restoration, and died in 1681. His almanac lived after him.

Up Above the Downs

WALTON-ON-THE-HILL. A Roman camp once stood on the heath, which is radiant in spring with gorse and silver birch. Here, too, has been found a Roman villa, with a brass figure of the God of Healing and a coin of the Emperor Vespasian who conquered the Isle of Wight.

Tressady is a good old black and white house in the style of 400 years ago, and the manor house has work which is older still. It has arches which led to a 13th century chapel, and in the garden is a mound where an older house used to be. We think Henry the Eighth may have come here for the hunting,

Walton-on-Thames   **The Airman's View**

Whiteley Village   The Octagon from the Air

Waverley   The Ruined Walls of the Abbey

Waverley   Ancient Bridge Across the Wey

and certain it is that Anne of Cleves stayed here when he wanted her no more.

The church is chiefly of our own time, though in the graveyard is an 18th century yew. Some of the wonderful glass is a gift from Woburn Abbey, for the Duke of Bedford gave it away a hundred years ago. For a while it dazzled the windows of a parson's house at Tooting, and when its owner became rector of Walton he put it in a box. Years later it was taken out and put up in the church.

In the sunny side of the nave are remains of a nature scene by an English craftsman of Henry the Eighth's time; he drew a butterfly on a branch, a stork on a stump, and a snail on a rose.

The 16th century Flemish glass includes a fine medallion of St Augustine in his gold mitre and white cope, reading a book. Another shows St Catherine kneeling by her wheel, a prison beside her, three soldiers before her, and angels behind. A very fine 16th century scene shows Our Lord rising from the tomb, accompanied by an angel. From a century later is the scene of the Last Supper. We see, too, the Visitation of the Prisoners, the Prodigal Son, the Last Judgment and the woman sweeping for the lost piece of silver. Two merchants shake hands behind a pair of scales, a man lights a fire, another distributes fruit.

The treasure of the church is the 800-year-old lead font, said to have been brought from the manor chapel after the Reformation. Nine worn figures sit in Norman arches round the bowl, some with books and some with a hand raised in blessing. Round the top is rich ornament enclosed by lines of beads. This is one of the best of the 38 lead fonts in England, and Surrey has not another like it.

House, Church, and Barn

WANBOROUGH. It is little more than an attractive hillside group of a charming old house, a church, and an impressive 15th century barn, all nestling together under the Hog's Back.

The church goes back 700 years and is almost the smallest in Surrey. It is only 45 feet by 18 feet, and has a carved 15th century screen to mark off a chancel. It has a mass dial on its walls. Once it belonged to Waverley Abbey, and was in the care of six monks who lived and worked on the farm next door. Later, when the monks had gone and Civil War had ravaged England, this little place stood neglected for 200 years, and was even used as a carpenter's shop until a rector of Puttenham restored it for worship last century.

The old barn is twice as long as the church and nearly twice as wide. It has black weather boards outside, and its fine timbers are only seen within.

The great house (where Mr Gladstone often stayed) was built soon after Henry the Eighth seized the possessions of the monasteries. This piece of land he gave to his lord high admiral William Fitzwilliam, whom he made Earl of Southampton.

Cranmer Presents His Prayer Book

WARLINGHAM. Its houses cluster round the green, facing the stone figure of a soldier guarding a woman and her child, the peace memorial to the men of Warlingham.

A little road of new houses leads to an old church of great interest. The chancel and much of the rest have hardly changed in 700 years, and there are many old things to see. We go in through the original doorway put back in a modern wall; we look round at the original lancet windows and the holes where the scaffolding went when the church was building; and we see above us the great tie-beams of the original roof.

In the chancel is one of the old windows known as lowside windows, of such a height that a man standing on the floor could look straight out, and with a recess in which he could stand while looking. These windows never had glass, and this one has been given a new wooden shutter. It is thought that the priest would use it for hearing confessions or for ringing the sanctus bell to those outside, but the real purpose is still something of a puzzle.

A fine piece of medieval decoration is the 15th century fresco of St Christopher, a giant more than lifesize with the Child on his back. He has a red beard and a dark cloak, and his picture is well preserved.

There is some glass of the same century in one of the windows. It shows the clear yellow and white canopy work that once surrounded two figures, and is so good that modern figures of St Gabriel and the Madonna have been put in to complete the picture. What the old figures were is not known, but the fine canopies and borders are made up of the pinnacles, arches, and buttresses characteristic of the 15th century.

SURREY

Opposite is a window with modern glass in which these old canopies have been reproduced. It is to remind us of a tradition that makes this church a historic place. Here, it is believed, the English prayer book was first publicly read in the presence of its author Cranmer, who came from Croydon Palace to hear the experiment. The glass shows us the boy king Edward the Sixth on his throne, with Cranmer presenting his new prayer book, courtiers looking on.

Among the things to see are two fine chairs carved in the 17th century, three old piscinas, and a 15th century font carved with eight quatrefoils and a weird face.

A window showing Jesus and the children tells a tragic little story of the Great War. It is given in memory of Richard and Lilian Roberts, both much loved in Warlingham. They were father and daughter; she was helping him at his office in London one summer's day when a bomb fell and shattered their lives.

Its Fame is at the Ends of the Earth

WAVERLEY. It is without a church and has hardly a handful of cottages, yet its name is known to the ends of the Earth, for it was the inspiration of Scott's Waverley. And it has delightful scenes and memories, with all that is left of a famous monastery on the banks of the Wey.

The house now called Waverley Abbey looks out across a lake at the ruins of what was once the real abbey. The ruins are scanty, but of much interest to anyone who cares to wander in a lovely spot, trying to imagine how the oldest Cistercian monastery in England must have looked in the days of its greatness.

It goes back more than 800 years to William Giffard, Bishop of Winchester, who gave these lands to a little colony of an abbot and 12 monks from Normandy. Here they began to build, and, in spite of terrible damage and discomfort from the floods of the Wey, the community grew rapidly and began to send out parties of monks to found daughter houses throughout England.

The first simple buildings at Waverley were soon enlarged and rebuilt, eventually gathering about a splendid 13th century church 300 feet long and 150 feet across the transepts. At its dedication in 1278 a vast company of 7066 abbots, knights, lords, and ladies were entertained at a feast. The parts of it still standing are a good deal of one transept, a little of the other, and a corner of the nave. A magnificent old yew is growing not far from where the high altar must have stood, and an old coffin shaped like a man is embedded in the turf, in what was once the presbytery of the church.

The fine beech in the south transept spreads its branches over the high roofless walls of the chapter-house. Next to this is the tunnel-shaped room which was the parlour where the monks were allowed what little conversation was necessary. An ash tree is growing close by in what was the Norman treasury.

Nearer the river we see still the wall of the Norman dining-hall, three well-preserved lancets at the end of the long sleeping room, and the beautiful vaulted dining-hall of the lay brothers, its roof resting gracefully on slender pillars. On the floor above are one or two windows of their sleeping room.

It is sad to think of the destruction of these noble buildings which went on for generations. The abbot, we read, wrote to Thomas Cromwell "beseeching your good mastership for the love of Christ's Passion to help the preservation of this poor monastery." The reputation of the Waverley monks was unblemished, but their abbey went with the rest in the days of this destroying Cromwell. Everything of value was removed from the walls, the ancient tiles were torn up from the floors and sold, roofs were stripped for their lead, benches were used for firewood, and the masonry was carried away to be built into other houses. What is left gives little idea of the splendid group of buildings once existing here, and only the careful digging of experts has revealed to us how fine the abbey was in its prime. Yet if these poor ruins should themselves disappear the name of Waverley will last as long as there is anyone to read the novels of Walter Scott, for much of our knowledge of this place comes from the Annals kept by the monks, and it was through reading these that Scott formed the idea of giving his first novel the name of Waverley.

Memories of a different kind belong to another great house at Waverley. It was to Moor Park, at the end of the 17th century, that Jonathan Swift came as a young man to act as secretary to Sir William Temple. Here he wrote his satires The Battle of the Books and The Tale of a Tub, and here he met beautiful Esther Johnson, the famous Stella to whom he wrote his Journal. Her mother was the companion of Sir William Temple's sister, and Swift acted for a while as the girl's tutor.

During his time at Moor Park Swift was introduced to William of Orange; and it is said the king gave him a lesson in cutting asparagus and offered to give him a troop of horse. Later on Jonathan was sent on a fruitless effort to persuade the king to agree to a Bill for having a new Parliament every three years. Altogether he must have spent several happy years here, making his way as a writer and enjoying the company of the charming Stella. Years afterwards in Ireland he copied for himself, on a smaller scale, the Moor Park gardens he had loved in his youth.

Stella's charming cottage is still here by the roadside, and a little way up the drive to Moor Park is a strange cave she and Jonathan must often have seen. It is said to have been the home of Mother Ludlam, a notorious character in witchcraft days, and the story goes that the great cauldron in Frensham church came from this very spot.

The Strange Story of Swift and Stella

ONE of literature's strangest stories began at Waverley when, in 1689, Jonathan Swift arrived at Moor Park as secretary to Sir William Temple, and found a pupil in Esther Johnson, a beautiful child of eight, daughter of a widowed confidential servant of the family. Swift taught her to write and to love study, and she was the solace of his gloomiest hours.

Although appointed to a church in Ireland, Swift's connection with Temple continued until the death of his patron in 1699. Stella, as Swift called her, was now an accomplished beauty, and, inheriting property in Ireland from Temple, went there in 1701, accompanied by her friend Rebecca Dingley, and by Swift, who became Dean of St Patrick's.

He was 14 years older than Stella, but she loved him devotedly, and his Journal to Stella shows that he loved her. But he loved others too, as the tragedy of another of his adorers, Vanessa, reminds us. He declared that he never saw Stella except in the presence of a third person; but she was present at his dinner parties, occupied the deanery when he was absent, took lodgings with Rebecca near him when he returned, and accompanied him to England.

Tradition has it that he secretly married her in 1716, and Vanessa died from the shock of his treatment of her when she wrote to Stella asking if the story was true. In 1728 Stella was mortally stricken, and, lest her death at the deanery should cause a scandal, Swift ordered her to be removed, dying, to her lodgings.

Her funeral was at night, and he hid in his room so that he might not see the lights in the church. After his death, 17 years later, a packet containing one of Stella's tresses was found in his desk, inscribed, "Only a woman's hair." He is buried at her side in St Patrick's Cathedral, Dublin.

Rare Fragments

WEST CLANDON. It runs along the edge of Clandon Park, the seat of the Earls of Onslow, and several things in its church remind us of their family, who have been here since 1642. Some of the pews are richly carved in dark woods brought from abroad by one of the earls, and there is old glass showing three coloured badges and the family arms from the 15th to the 18th centuries, prominent in most of them being six Cornish choughs. On the wall is a tablet to eight Onslows who gave their lives in the Great War.

The chancel with its massive timbers in the roof is chiefly 13th century, and the beams in the porch may be the same age. Saved from an old screen are three fragments painted by a 15th century artist with figures of Peter, Paul, and Thomas Becket. They are among the very few examples of painted woodwork in Surrey, and were fortunate to survive a fire that destroyed the tower and bells in 1913.

The sundial on the wall, the pillar piscina, and the font of Sussex marble are all Norman workmanship, and there is a delicately worked Elizabethan chalice.

The Happy Warrior

WESTCOTT. With a church high above the road near Dorking, its chief beauties are the view across to Ranmore Common and the old houses in the lane leading from the green. "For One and All" says the seat (with a little thatched roof) standing with a dovecot on the green. The church was designed by Sir George Gilbert Scott, and fits in well with its surroundings. In the chancel is an attractive little carving of the Happy Warrior as G. F. Watts painted him, in memory of a young officer who fell on the Somme.

Where the Guildford road dips down over the stream we pass a splendid old elm and catch a glimpse of Rookery House, the birthplace, in 1766, of Thomas Robert Malthus, made famous by an essay originally published without his name. His theory that lack of food would keep down the population of the world has been contradicted by history, but his Essay on the Principle of Population, which appeared in its full form just before the Battle of Trafalgar, has been one of the most discussed essays in the English language. He has been much abused and misrepresented; he was, in himself, a warm-hearted man, whose work was of great value to Charles Darwin in building up his theory of Evolution.

Raleigh's Head

WEST HORSLEY. In a part of Surrey rapidly being devoured by the builders its church faces a lovely expanse still unspoiled when we called, and its great house, West Horsley Place, is an imposing line of Jacobean brickwork seen from the road. The pretty timbered cottage by the wayside was probably the priest's house centuries ago.

A church stood here before the Norman Conquest, and some of its masonry is still in these nave walls. The tower was built soon after the Normans came. One of the porches was made of timber 500 years ago and protects a doorway a century older; the other is modern and shields a Norman arch turned into an English one. The church is wide and well-lit, and gets much dignity from the dark woodwork of the pews and the three attractive 15th century screens. There is a Norman font, a 13th century chest bound with iron straps, the remains of a 13th century fresco, and a chandelier of 1652, made in Namur for a village church in Belgium.

In the 13th century chancel are several little treasures, among them two medallions of painted glass 700 years old. One shows St Catherine rescued by an angel from torture on the wheel, and the other Our Lord with Mary Magdalene at his feet. Probably part of the original glass of the chancel, they are now in two of the three lancets making up the east window. There is an alabaster carving in relief of the scene at Bethlehem, very quaint in its perspective.

The work of the 14th century, found under the floor in the 19th, it shows the Madonna and Child, a shepherd, an ox and an ass peeping over the wall, and the head of Joseph.

Sleeping in the chancel is the lifelike figure of a priest in his vestments, his hands joined in prayer and a little angel on each side of his head. He is Ralph Berners, who was rector here and died in 1348, and he lies under a rich canopy carved with leaves and monkeyheads, his family badge. From the same century comes the window above, with its flowing tracery and its glass portrait of Sir James Berners kneeling in armour. He was a follower of Richard the Second, and lost his head on Tower Hill when Parliament made a clean sweep of all the king's friends.

The portrait shows him in the prime of life, with yellow hair and beard, and we read underneath that he was the patron of this church. He lived at what is now West Horsley Place, and his daughter may have been the celebrated Dame Juliana Berners, who wrote a treatise on sport printed at the press of Wynkyn de Worde. A later kinsman who may have lived here was Lord Berners, who translated Froissart's Chronicles and was at the Field of the Cloth of Gold.

It is probable that the oldest parts of the great house were built by Sir Anthony Browne, Henry the Eighth's Master of the Horse; and if that be so, his wife, the Fair Geraldine of the Earl of Surrey's sonnets, may have lived in it. A century later the estate was inherited by Carew Raleigh, Sir Walter's younger son, who was born in the Tower and spent some of his early years there with his father. Through him the house passed to Sir Edward Nicholas, one of Charles the First's Secretaries of State, and there are monuments to his family in the Nicholas chapel.

But it is not by these that we are moved in the Nicholas chapel; it is for something much more stirring. It is believed that Raleigh's son buried here the head of his father, the noble head the King of England sacrificed to the enemies of his country. For more than a quarter of a century Lady Raleigh preserved the head and carried it about with her in a red leather bag, and it would be natural that it should pass into the hands of their son. In 1703 Sir John Nicholas's wife Penelope was killed in a storm at West Horsley Place, and her son William put it on record that when she was buried in the family vault in the chapel he saw the head of Sir Walter.

SURREY

We consider this fascinating question of Raleigh's remains at Beddington, where the body is supposed to lie, but there is little doubt that the head lies here. If not, then, as Raleigh said in his last words, "What matter how the head lie, so the heart be right?"

He Named the Conservative Party

WEST MOLESEY. One of the two Moleseys by the Thames, its chief attraction is the rugged grey tower which has stood as we see it for 400 years. Carved over one of its windows is the pelican badge of Richard Foxe, who founded Corpus Christi College at Oxford and was lord of the manor here.

The tower keeps watch over a 19th century church with one or two old things inside. The 15th century font is carved with flowers in eight quatrefoil panels; the pulpit, looking rather top-heavy with its big canopy, is Jacobean. There are three notable memorials of a soldier, a sailor, and a politician.

The soldier is Sir George Berkeley, and his tablet tells us that he fought in many campaigns and was severely wounded at Waterloo. His great desire, we read, was to make all around him happy. The sailor's tablet is to Admiral Cranfield Berkeley, who joined the navy at 13, and became page boy to little Caroline Matilda, the 15-year-old grand-daughter of George the Second, when they were taking her to Denmark to marry a dissolute Danish king. He went to Newfoundland with Captain Cook, and was an officer on the Victory 18 years before Trafalgar. Berkeley surveyed Newfoundland and the Gulf of St Lawrence with Cook, fought and lost an election costing £50,000, and won an action for libel which is still remembered.

The politican is John Wilson Croker, a privy councillor in three reigns, supporting Peel, attacking Keats, and introducing the word Conservative into the vocabulary of politics. Here he lived many years in daily intercourse with his neighbour, the fugitive king Louis Philippe. He sleeps in the churchyard, and there is a sculpture of his head and shoulders in the church.

The son of a Devon man, Croker entered Parliament at 28, and when Wellington left for the Peninsula acted for him as Chief Secretary for Ireland. So began a friendship lasting till the death of the duke, though the duke was often angered by the bumptious assertiveness of Croker, who would contradict him on the details of his own battles. For more than 20 years he was a faithful and efficient Secretary of the Admiralty, and was high in the counsels of the Tory party, to which, in 1830, he gave the name of Conservative. Hating reform, he retired from Parliament on a pension of £1500 a year, broke with Peel over the repeal of the Corn Laws, and devoted himself to the service of his party through the Quarterly Review, which he had helped to establish in 1809.

It was in this periodical that he launched his notorious attack on Keats, provoking Byron, on the death of the poet, to the rejoinder:

> *Who killed John Keats?*
> *I, said the Quarterly,*
> *So savage and tartarly,*
> *Twas one of my feats.*

Disraeli, whose dislike of Croker was as intense as Macaulay's, caricatured him in one of his novels. Macaulay lashed him in a famous review of Croker's Boswell. Croker bided his time, and retaliated with compound interest when Macaulay's History appeared; but Croker lost the battle, and it is Macaulay's essay on him that keeps his memory green, though he has a place in the literary history of Sir Walter Scott, whose Tales of a Grandfather were inspired by Croker's Stories from History.

Little Comedy and Jessamy Bride

WEYBRIDGE. It is indeed Wey Bridge, the town grown up where the Wey meets the Thames and the oldest locked waterway in England comes to an end. The Wey Navigation Canal was planned about 300 years ago by Sir Richard Weston of Sutton Place, and now Weybridge has one of England's latest waterways, the Desborough Channel, running 100 feet wide for a mile, and avoiding three miles of winding Thames.

The original bridges and locks of the Wey Navigation were built from the ruins of Oatlands Palace; the palace is gone but we can inquire today for the Palace Gardens as we might have done when Shakespeare was a boy. Instead of a palace we shall be shown an old red wall with a blocked gateway, running in and out among some of the newest houses in the town. Nothing is left of the palace built by Henry the Eighth save the memory that he made it for his fourth wife, the unwanted Anne of Cleves, and used it for his marriage to the fifth, his much-wanted Catherine Howard. Queen Elizabeth was often here, and so were the first two Stuarts.

The name of Oatlands is given to a hotel, and a spreading tree on its lawn bears a label telling us that this is one of the first Cedars from Lebanon imported into England, and adding that it was planted here by Prince Henry of Otelandes, youngest son of Charles the First.

The beautiful Oatlands grounds were laid out 200 years ago by the Duke of Newcastle, who made a lake a mile long and spent £40,000 on the extraordinary grotto, where the Allied Sovereigns lunched in 1814 during their visit to London. The Duke brought from Italy a father and his two sons, and for a generation these three laboured to make this place, covering its walls with shells and stones, rare minerals, shining crystals, and horse's teeth, making inlaid patterns and imitation stalactites, little rooms and winding passages, a gambling den, and even a place for a bath—a wonder in those days. There can be few better examples of misspent ingenuity and wasted effort than these walls with millions of fragments on them.

The great house was afterwards bought by George the Third's son Frederick, and then by Edward Ball Hughes, a young man so rich that Society called him the Golden Ball. The Duchess of York of those days was much loved in Weybridge, and there are many memories of her, chief among them the tall column on the green, which has a story of its own. There was a time when it stood in London at the place called Seven Dials, marking the point where seven streets meet. During a riot it was pulled down by those who imagined there was hidden treasure under it, and it was then bought by a Weybridge builder. For years it lay in his yard, until it was set up by the townsfolk as a memorial to their beloved duchess. The old stone with the dials long stood as a mounting-stone, and here it now stands in front of the museum.

We think of the duchess again in the church, where her memorial is a lovely figure by Chantrey, the most beautiful of all the memorials under the tower. Keeping it company are several brasses and a tablet with a chapter of naval history. One brass shows Thomas Inwood in his Elizabethan finery, with three wives in broad-brimmed hats, and five children; another, on which is a shield and an owl, shows his contemporary John Woulde with two richly-dressed wives and 16 children. A third shows three gruesome skeletons, a grim memorial of the three children of Sir John Trevor, who was park-keeper at Oatlands under Queen Elizabeth. There is also a brass inscription to Humphry Dethick, who lived at Dorney House by the river, and was the gentleman usher and daily waiter to Charles Stuart.

The memorial to Sir Thomas Hopsonn, who rose to be an admiral and spent 55 years in the navy, tells us that he fought for his country in 42 battles and received many wounds. At the battle of Vigo Bay his ship (the Torbay) was chosen to break through the Spanish boom nine feet thick. He succeeded, and Sir George Rooke sailed through to destroy the enemy and capture immense treasure. The Torbay had a narrow escape when a Spanish fireship grappled with her, and was only saved by the strange chance of a cargo of snuff putting out the flames of the fireship when she exploded. Hopsonn brought the prizes home and was knighted by Queen Anne, and he settled down at Weybridge to spend his last years in peace, calling his new home Vigo House. It stood where the fine new hospital stands now, and from it he was carried to his grave here.

History is sceptical about the most picturesque legend of his youth. A tailor's son at Bonchurch in the Isle of Wight, legend has it that he ran away to sea and was on board a battleship when she grappled a French man-of-war, and the two pounded each other terribly. In his innocence young Hopsonn is said to have asked how long the battle would last. As long as that white flag floated at the French mast-head, he was told. "If that is all I will see what I can do about it," he answered, and scrambling aboard the Frenchman he climbed to the masthead, tore down the flag, wrapped it round him, and returned to his ship. The French sailors, the story goes, fell into confusion and ceased to serve their guns, with the result that before they could rally their ship was in English hands.

The church was designed in the 19th century by John Loughborough Pearson, architect of Truro Cathedral, and the effect of the chancel with its big window is very pleasing as we look up the nave. The peace memorial chapel has an attractive reredos carved and painted with nine figures.

Sleeping in the churchyard are two sisters, Catherine and Mary Horneck, friends of Burke, Reynolds, and Goldsmith. When they were young and beautiful Oliver Goldsmith nicknamed them Little

SURREY

Comedy and Jessamy Bride, and long after his death Mary treasured a lock of his hair. She lived to be nearly 90, preserving her beauty and charm to the end, so that it was said of her that she went through all the stages of life adding a grace to each. She shared in the poet's wish, Let me grow lovely, growing old.

Fanny Kemble spent some of her girlhood at Eastlands, and Robert Louis Stevenson is said to have read the proofs of Treasure Island while staying at the inn on the common. At the Roman Catholic church, since made new, the French king Louis Philippe lay buried for some years before they took him back to France, and the church has a fine figure in white marble of Antonia of Saxe-Coburg, Duchesse de Nemours, calmly sleeping.

Weybridge museum has pictures of Oatlands Palace as it was in its great days, and there are here two stone carvings from the ruins of Chertsey Abbey; they are a little monkey and a grotesque face, and are believed to have been plundered from the abbey to be used as building material for Bluebeard's palace here. But the most interesting possessions of the museum are relics of two prehistoric settlements in Surrey, a dug-out canoe and a collection of coins and weapons.

The canoe, about 12 feet long with its high ends pierced to take a rope, but unhappily in pieces, was used by men of the Iron Age on the banks of the River Wey over 40 centuries ago. It is the most dramatic thing discovered in the prehistoric village found in 1923 at Wisley, and it is believed that the boat was used by the men who lived in pit dwellings dug four feet into the ground, with roofs supported on a central post.

The coins and weapons came from the prehistoric camp on St George's Hill, a beautifully wooded building estate which has lovely views. On the summit of the hill are remains of the biggest prehistoric earthwork in Surrey, covering about 14 acres. The bank round it was over 20 feet high above the bottom of the ditch, and appears to have been built in the Iron Age. In the time of the Commonwealth the hill was the scene of a curious social and agricultural experiment conducted by a number of people from Cobham led by a cashiered army officer called Everard, a self-styled prophet. They argued that as there was no king the crown lands belonged to the people, and proceeded to fire the heath, dig up the ground, and sow vegetables. Though a troop of horse was sent the Government seems to have taken little notice, and the Socialists were finally ousted by the local authority, and by neighbours incensed at their common rights being infringed. Some were imprisoned by the sheriff, others beaten by gentlemen, and Parson Platt pulled one of their houses down. Their cattle were maimed, their crops uprooted, and serious damage done by a surprise attack carried out by men of Walton disguised as women.

There is, hidden away in the chapel of the cemetery, a magnificent altar-table carved by 15th or 16th century craftsmen, but perhaps the greatest treasure of all belonging to Weybridge is a bronze bucket from Brooklands, which is not here to be seen. It is a relic of the trading days of Britain before the famous days of Greece and Rome, and is preserved for all time in the British Museum.

The Old Folks at Home

WHITELEY VILLAGE. Tucked away in the Surrey countryside not far from Weybridge, among the woods by the Cobham Road, it is one of the most wonderful villages in England.

Whiteley village was built for 350 aged people out of a million pounds left by William Whiteley in 1907, and is the biggest collection of almshouses in the country.

In the middle is a memorial carved by Sir George Frampton in memory of Mr Whiteley, "by whose munificent bequest this park was purchased and these cottage homes were built for the comfort of old age and as an encouragement to others to do likewise." Beneath a bronze-seated figure of Industry we see a plaque of this kind-faced, bearded man, and his life-story is briefly set out.

We read that he was born at Agbrigg, Yorkshire, on September 29, 1831, educated at Pontefract, and apprenticed at 16 to a drapery firm. He went to see the Great Exhibition of 1851, and the busy life of the metropolis attracted him. He spent ten years of thrift and constant study with a City firm, and then started a small business of his own. Before long he had won for himself the name of Universal Provider, and for his business a world-wide reputation. He was the pioneer of the great London retail stores of today.

Sealed in a bottle under the memorial is Mr Frank Atkinson's parchment plan of the village. The central part is in the form of an octagon, and from this monument in the middle radiate eight avenues and grassy glades. The cottages beside each vista are by different architects, and very charming they look, though all are built to only one or two simple standards. They are mostly of one storey, and are built with narrow bricks of a beautiful red colour.

In their delightful variety they must be among the most beautiful modern cottages in England, and they enable us to compare the work of such famous men as Sir Aston Webb, Sir Reginald Blomfield, Sir Ernest George, and Mr Walter Cave. Here their great genius has been devoted to supplying the simple wants of the poor. For those too infirm to live alone there is a quiet home of rest, and near by is the guesthouse where friends of the villagers can make a short stay.

The fine church among the fir trees was designed by Mr Walter Tapper, and has a beautiful oak chancel screen richly carved with foliage. The Nonconformist church is a lofty and light building of brick, its vaulted roof supported on fluted pillars. It was designed by Sir Aston Webb, and its gable is flanked by angels in stone.

The clubhouse and hall, with its little clock tower, was also designed by Sir Aston Webb, and here the villagers meet for lectures, concerts, plays, and talkie films. The village also has its own stores, library, post office, communal kitchen, workshop, and allotments. There are six bowling greens and a recreation ground where the old people can watch the play.

We look down on a small lake from the fine brick bridge of Mr Frank Atkinson, who also designed the lodges and the gates; and another delightful spot is the flowery terrace below the clubhouse. Indeed this wonder village is a miniature garden city, its ways fringed with borders of heather and flowering shrubs. There is a beautiful avenue of limes, and here and there stand pines and firs. Around are plantations of chestnut, oak, and larch, and along the western and southern sides of the village the rhododendron walks make a glory in the spring.

The lucky villagers are elderly men and women with but little money of their own, and here they may end their days with free medical attention and care, unworried by bills for electric light, gas, coal, and water. Interesting it is for us to share their paradise awhile, for we may wander round and peep into their small picturesque world at any time we choose.

Capital of the Tennis World

WIMBLEDON. It has leapt into fame and shares with Kew and Croydon the pride of place as the most famous of all the Surrey towns. The whole world knows it for its tennis. Once every year this busy, thriving place becomes a stage with a host of players (the world's finest tennis players from all corners of the globe). The play lasts for a fortnight, the curtain is rung down, and Wimbledon resumes its normal ways. That is the Wimbledon the world knows.

Most Londoners know it better for its glorious Common, which with Putney Heath covers 1000 acres and has the 2300 acres of Richmond Park for a neighbour. The Common has a site still called Caesar's Camp, though it was an earthwork before the Romans came; and it has the well called Caesar's Well in the belief that the Romans knew it. The windmill, built by a Roehampton carpenter two years after Waterloo, is a landmark and has a brick base now formed into dwellings. But the charm of the Common is not in these things, but in its beech avenues, ponds, patches of heather, and the tracks through the spreading bracken and the silver birch trees.

Near the Beverley Brook is an area of 40 acres known as the Richardson Evans Playing Fields, in honour of one who devoted much of his time to the preservation of the Common. Here among the sports grounds are five cricket pitches and eight football pitches, and here also is a Garden of Rest which, besides being a peace memorial, is also a bird sanctuary. On the Wimbledon side of the Common is another peace memorial, a cross with a lion's head and the cross of St George on its pedestal, and on the front a panel with a bronze figure of Peace.

One of the houses the traveller will want to see stands on the south of the Common. It is Lauriston House, with ceilings and staircase walls decorated by Angelica Kauffmann, and with memories of Wilberforce entertaining Pitt. Near the house is a stone seat with the inscription: "Site of Old Village Well. Once beneath this stone the softest water could be drawn, but now no more." From here lovers of sea stories will want to walk a little way to Gothic House in Woodhayes Road, for it was the boyhood home of Captain Marryat, and in other days of Lady Anne Barnard, remembered for her lovely ballad, Auld Robin Gray.

Richmond — A Herd in the Park

Wimbledon — Silver Birches on the Common

The Little Norman Church

The Famous Pond
WISLEY, BY THE PORTSMOUTH ROAD

SURREY

We come upon a memory of Pitt again in High Street, in the middle of the old village of Wimbledon, where a room in Eagle House is known as Pitt's room. The house was built in Shakespeare's last years by Robert Bell, Master of the Girdlers Company, and has a stone eagle over one of its many gables. Most of its brick front is plastered up, but the plaster is beautiful inside on four fine ceilings. Nelson came to Eagle House as a friend of Thomas Lancaster, the vicar of Merton whose son was a midshipman on the Victory at Trafalgar.

These places are as they were, but most of the rest of Wimbledon has changed. The trees still cast their shade on Wimbledon Hill and the heather still blooms on the Common, but the village of old has grown into a borough, and a population which was less than 1800 in the year 1800 has in our own time grown to 60,000.

In the Broadway, with bright lights to lure the shopper, is a handsome stone town hall, opened in 1931. In Lingfield Street is the John Evelyn Club and Museum founded by Richardson Evans to keep Wimbledon beautiful and to carry on something of the spirit of the diarist, who was often a visitor at the manor house. It has many documents, pictures, and relics of Old Wimbledon, and a library of about 900 volumes of Captain Marryat's works. Scattered about the town are over 40 buildings ministering to the spiritual life of the citizens, but only one of these churches and chapels is interesting to the casual visitor; it is St Mary's, a grey church in a secluded corner among the trees near Wimbledon Park. Its slender and graceful spire looks down on a building that is chiefly modern but has much beauty and many memories of the brave.

It has one bell of Henry the Eighth's time and another of Queen Elizabeth's; a fragment of 600-year-old masonry in the tiny low window in the chancel, discovered when the Warriors Chapel was built after the Great War; a brass of William Wilberforce as a kindly figure in knee-breeches; and a modern brass of Walter Reynolds, a 14th century baker's son who was rector here and rose to be Archbishop of Canterbury.

In the nave is a witness of the war, the tattered flag flown by the Inflexible at Jutland, and in a chancel window are two big medallions of old glass with heraldic shields. One shows the arms of Thomas Cecil, who died in 1623 after becoming first Earl of Exeter. He was the son of Queen Elizabeth's Treasurer Burghley, who built himself a house here when he was still Sir William Cecil. It is now the Old Rectory House by the church, the oldest house in Wimbledon, with the fig walk he planted still flourishing in the garden.

But it is the Warriors Chapel that thrills us in this church. Here is the great tomb of Lord Burghley's grandson, the Lord Wimbledon who commanded none too well the expedition sent by Charles Stuart to capture treasure at Cadiz; and on the wall is a suit of armour thought to be Lord Wimbledon's, and another suit belonging to a foot soldier.

In a window is a beautiful medallion of St George in white armour with his sword and lance, the finest figure in Surrey in 14th century glass. In a case is an embroidered stole given by a British officer, who found it among the ruins of a church on a French battlefield and carried it 300 miles in his haversack.

It is a moving thing to find ourselves reading in this Warriors Chapel the most famous lines written in the Great War, *They shall grow not old*, and to discover that they were written on this vellum by the hand of Laurence Binyon and presented to the chapel by him. On the walls are many bronze tablets in memory of those who grow not old, and we noticed among them two VC's: Arthur Harrison, who, wounded and in great pain, led the storming parties from the Vindictive on to the Mole at Zeebrugge through a storm of machine gun bullets; and George Cates, who, working furiously with his men to deepen a captured trench, struck a bomb with his spade, and put his foot on it, saving many lives but losing his own.

The church porch has a tribute to James Perry, who edited the Morning Chronicle in the early years of last century and was something of a hero in civil life, for he was more than once prosecuted for his Liberal views. We see him in relief by Westmacott, seated with a quill in his hand and we read of the courage and ability with which he put forward the principles of civil and religious liberty, attempting to convert the daily press into a great moral instrument. The monument was set up by the Fox Club, and has on it a portrait of Charles James Fox, who once had a house on Wimbledon Hill.

Sleeping in the churchyard are two men as different as men could well be, for one was a usurer and the other an artist. The usurer was John Hopkins, of whom Pope wrote:

SURREY

*When Hopkins dies a thousand lights attend
The wretch who, living, saved a candle's end.*

The artist was Gilbert Stuart Newton, who came from Nova Scotia as a young man and showed his first picture at the Academy in 1818. He painted many subject pictures, and numbered among his sitters Sir Walter Scott and Thomas Moore. His last years were saddened by mental trouble and physical illness, and he died at Chelsea in 1835, only just over 40.

Not far from the church the road goes steeply down to the All England Lawn Tennis Club which has made Wimbledon the capital of the Tennis World. The Club was founded in 1864 and for nearly 60 years had its headquarters in Worple Road. The first championship tournament was held in 1877 when Spencer Gore became first champion and the final was watched by 200 people, the men in top hats and the women in flowing gowns. The first championship for ladies was in 1884, when Miss Watson won. The Renshaw twins, William and Ernest, made their first appearance here in 1880, and held sway for many years. The gallant Doherty brothers, who are among the game's immortals, appeared in 1895 and reigned supreme for about ten years. The first foreign challenge came in 1883, when two American brothers named Clark appeared, but they did not win, and it was not until 1907 that a visitor from overseas, the Australian Norman Brookes, became champion.

Since then over 20 nations have competed at Wimbledon in a single year, and the championship has been won by the New Zealander, Tony Wilding; the three Australians, Norman Brookes, Gerald Patterson, and J. H. Crawford; the three French Musketeers, Borotra, Lacoste, and Cochet; and five Americans: W. Tilden, W. Johnston, S. B. Wood, Ellsworth Vines, and Donald Budge. After the inevitable break caused by the war, Wimbledon tennis started on a fresh lease of life, when spectators paid over £9000, and Suzanne Lenglen won the first of her championships, Mrs Lambert Chambers losing it after holding it for six seasons. Suzanne Lenglen's triumphal progress was at last to end, and the championship passed in turn to English and American girls. By this time thousands of people were watching the games, and in 1922 the present ground was opened, with its great concrete Centre Court holding 15,000 people, Number 1 Court holding another 5000, and many outside courts.

Every year sees a fresh triumph for the All England Club, for there is magic in the name of Wimbledon.

WINDLESHAM. Its fine red brick tower was built in the 17th century, and looks out over open country to the woods of the Berkshire border. The chief treasure in the church is a chained copy of Jewel's Apology, kept in a case made by a Windlesham man from two pieces of wood which played their part in the village life for centuries. Part of it comes from a yew blown down in 1896, a great veteran mentioned in an ancient chronicle as standing in the churchyard in the 11th century; and part from a charred beam belonging to an earlier tower struck by lightning in 1676.

Among the tablets is one to Winifred Simms, who, as village schoolmistress for 28 years, "inspired her pupils with love of righteousness and goodness." Another tells of the tragedy of a rector's youngest son, who was massacred with his wife and child in the Indian Mutiny.

25 Centuries Older Than Christianity

WISLEY. All motorists know its lovely pond, a flash of beauty for every car rushing along the Portsmouth road. It is flanked by firs a hundred years old. There is a Roman road between the lake and what is known as Currie's Clumb, running from Farley Heath to the Thames, but by the modern highway is something older still, the tree-covered barrow of Cock Crow Hill. It was opened in the early years of this century, when signs were found of a cremation that had taken place thousands of years ago. There are signs also of an excavation which is believed to have been made in the 18th century, during a search for iron ore; and certainly the parallel trenches which cut across the common were dug for iron. Now the heather has happily healed the wound, and we are left with its glorious glow and the wonder of the woods.

But Wisley is a very ancient place, and we find in a watery spot by the tiny Norman church a witness to the site of a British village 25 centuries before the birth of Christ. The fact is inscribed on a stone which tells us that the site of this ancient village was discovered in 1923, and that the village existed from 2500 BC to 150 BC. It was set on the sand by the River Wey, and some of the later huts were built in lines, with proper drains running between them. They were

Thames Ditton: Erasmus and Julyan Forde with their 18 children, 1533

Merstham
Peter Best, 1585

Walton-upon-Thames
John Selwyn, 1587

Merstham
Richard Best, 1587

Weybridge: Thomas Inwood with his three wives and children, 1586

BRASSES OF SURREY FOLK OF BYGONE DAYS

pit dwellings, dug about four feet into the ground, and in many of them were discovered remains of a central post, while outside was evidence of a circle of pegs, such as we use for tents. There was also a floor of beaten clay, probably used for dancing. The romantic discovery of this village of 4400 years ago was made by some boys bathing near by, whose bare feet detected something hard in the sand. It was found to be a dug-out canoe about 12 feet long, its high ends pierced to take a rope. It was presumably used by the Iron Age villagers, and is one of the most interesting prehistoric possessions of Surrey, now kept in the museum at Weybridge.

Older still is one of the possessions of the ancient church, for in the churchyard is a big block of sarsen stone lying over the grave of Farmer Hanford, who found it one day when he was ploughing. It must have been brought down to where he found it before England was England, or Britain was Britain, or Egypt was Egypt, for it was borne on a glacier in some distant Ice Age.

The little church the Normans built stands by a beautiful old farmhouse covered with vines. The timber porch is 17th century and shelters a Norman doorway, within which are the axe marks made by the Norman masons. The roof is modern but has beams in it 800 years old, and there are traces of medieval painting on the walls, including a red cross which was touched by the bishop on consecration day centuries ago. There is an Elizabethan hourglass-stand of scrolled iron, and an old chest standing on feet formed by an extension of its iron straps. In the churchyard are pathetic rows of white wooden crosses to children from the homes for cripples at Pyrford.

Wisley is known to a very wide public of garden lovers, for here is the great garden of the Royal Horticultural Society, where fruit, vegetables, and all sorts of plants are grown in garden conditions scientifically tested, and demonstrated to students. The laboratory building by the gate has the charm of an old country house, but is modern. It faces a formal terrace garden with a warmed lily pond. A path between rose beds leads us to one of the best rock gardens in the country, covering an acre and a half of steep hillside with a stream trickling slowly among the big boulders of sandstone into a pond below. The variety of this great garden is surprising. There is a sandy beach by the river for special kinds of plants, and vistas of grass lead us by borders of flowering shrubs and heather. There is a wood with winding ways and pleasant paths which are a riot of rare rhododendrons in due season, and across the arboretum are 40 acres of fruit trees grown for testing by the Ministry of Agriculture.

Here Lies Birket Foster

WITLEY. Its tower and spire call us from a busy road into a quiet village scene. Turning aside at the 16th century inn we come upon old cottages, the village school, and a church which takes us back to Saxon England.

It shows very clearly how the Normans would take a simple Saxon church and enlarge it into a finer cruciform one. They did it at Witley towards the end of the 12th century, adding a new chancel, throwing out transepts, and raising a sturdy tower on four slightly pointed arches. Still here from the Saxon church are some of the nave walls, and two small windows, one of them high up in the west gable and the other partly obliterated by a bigger nave window pierced in the 13th century. Both are fascinating, the first because it has kept its Saxon oak frame in which would be mounted a strip of horn or oiled linen to let in the light, and the second because it has on its splay the beginning of a remarkable series of paintings which are continued along the nave wall. These show scenes in the life of the Madonna, and are described by Professor Tristram as 12th century work in the Byzantine style. Some of the figures are hard to see, but we can make out the Nativity, the Flight into Egypt, and the Marriage at Cana.

The main doorway of the church was built in the time of the Conqueror and is protected by a porch with carved 14th century bargeboards brought from a Witley house. The later Norman building is well seen in the south transept, where there are two original lancet windows and an oak roof, probably as old as the walls.

Let into the chancel wall is an unusual old stone with four lines of lettering, two cut and two scratched ready to be cut. It is in Latin, and bears the name of the Duke of Clarence, brother of Edward the Fourth. He was treacherous and wished to be king himself, and is said to have been drowned in a butt of Malmsey wine. But he was also lord of the manor of Witley, and this stone with his name on it is thought to be part of an unfinished memorial to one of his bailiffs.

Clarence was not the only famous person to own Witley during the centuries. There was Earl Godwin, father of King Harold; and Peter of Savoy, who raised the village rents until his niece Queen Eleanor had the sympathy to lower them again; and there was Edward the First's Queen Margaret, who sent two oaks from Witley to make shingles for the roof of the king's hall at Westminster. Edward the Third gave the manor to his valet, and Richard the Second gave it to his nurse, who married the king's tailor.

A brass below the Duke of Clarence stone is perhaps the best memorial in Witley. It shows the figures of Thomas and Jane Jonys, with three boys and three girls, and we read on it that Thomas was a "sewer-of-the-chamber" to Henry the Eighth. His business was to find out by trial whether the king's food was good to eat, well cooked, and free from poison.

The manor chapel was added to the Norman church in the 13th century and is cut off by a 15th century screen. In it is a little heraldic glass of the 14th century, a little Tudor glass, a brass inscription to Henry Bell "Clerke Controwler of the Houshold" to the first Stuart king, a tablet to a 17th century lord of the manor, and the wooden Flanders cross of a boy who fell in 1917.

There is a 13th century font with eight pillars, an enamelled iron almsbox into which money has been dropped for 500 years, and a brass tablet praising Sara Holney, who married the vicar of Witley in 1621, when she was 16. The pulpit and lectern were carved last century by a village cripple, and the oak panelling in the nave was given by Canadian soldiers camping here in the Great War.

Not far from Witley is Rake Manor, a charming old house of brick and timber, with panelled rooms overlooking a lake. In its lovely garden is a pigeon-house with four gables.

We found here (at Wormley Hill, a mile from Witley) a beautiful memorial to a British general killed in the war, a little Chapel of the Good Shepherd at the end of a beautiful drive, open day and night for passing tramps. At the time we called it was usual for the tramps to walk up the drive to the big house, where they were given a hot meal at any hour. The chapel was a simple place with an altar, a few chairs, and a stove, and we were told that nothing had ever been taken from the offertory box in this friendly little room.

More than one artist has been attracted by this village and the countryside round it, and one at least will always be remembered here. He is Myles Birket Foster, who was laid to rest in 1899 under one of the fine chestnuts in the churchyard.

Born of an old Quaker family at North Shields, Birket Foster was educated at the Quaker Academy, Hitchin, and then apprenticed to engraving. For years he worked independently at his calling, drawing on wood charming designs to illustrate the poets. Not until he was about 35 did he take to painting, but so successful was he that within three years he was elected to the Royal Society of Painters in Water Colours.

Surrey was his favourite county; he painted its landscapes and rural scenes, its woodlands and byways, its rustics and its children in oils and water colours, his work distinguished by its delicacy and minute finish, its daintiness and happy sentiment. His critics said that his long career as an engraver had made him a slave to detail and over-elaboration, but the beauty and balance of his compositions was undeniable, and the public admired and enriched him.

He wandered at times beyond the county of his adoption and some of his best work resulted from a stay in Brittany, but it was here that he made his home and got together his collection of artistic treasures, and here he was laid to rest.

The Town Old and New

WOKING. A town as big as Surrey's capital, and mostly as new as Guildford is old, it is an astonishing example of mushroom growth springing from the building of a railway junction near an old village, and it is hard to believe that Woking station, when it was opened in 1838, stood alone with an inn on the heath.

In new Woking is Christ Church, standing in a garden beautiful with flowers in summer. It is a modern building, and has a dignified interior of brick with stone arches. Its reredos has five painted scenes from the life of Our Lord.

Built in the same year as Christ Church is the Mohammedan Mosque in Oriental Road, one of the only two mosques in the country and a surprising sight to see by an English railway, with its big dome and gold crescent and its little minarets. In it are a pulpit from India and a niche showing the direction of Mecca.

But it is to Old Woking that we must go for all that is old and historic in this place, even if its village street is losing character in these days. There is still here a big gabled brick house of the 17th century, and the old parish church round the corner seems safe from change and has much to show.

The chancel and lower half of the tower have stood 700 years. The fine east window and the top half of the tower are a century younger, and the aisle and its arches a century younger still.

The core of the nave is Norman, and in the Norman doorway under the tower is one of Woking's chief treasures, the actual door of the Norman church still swinging on its hinges after eight centuries, held together by its original ironwork. The timber of the door seems surprisingly thin, and only the ironwork can have saved it. There are long decorated iron bands, big sweeping circles, a cross, and a quaint little affair of legs that may be a spider. For a hundred years before the tower came to protect it, this door was facing the wind and rain, but it has happily survived, and is today one of the finest old doors in the south of England.

Some of the pews are 15th century and the others match them. The attractive pulpit is Jacobean, and its style has been very well copied in the chancel panelling and the table given in memory of a vicar who ministered for 33 years. The brick porch (now out of use) and the western gallery are also Jacobean.

There are many memorials, an interesting group being gathered together on the aisle wall. In the centre are brass portraits, 500 years old, of John and Isabell Shadhet standing at prayer, and Joan Purdon and her four daughters. The portrait of Joan's husband is missing. Beside the brasses is an 18th century tablet to Thomas Bund, vicar for 53 years, and another to the vicar John Merest and his son James, who spent 52 years as a clerk in Parliament. In a window above is a yellow Tudor rose in 15th century glass.

The Great War memorials include the White Ensign of Admiral Thomas Philip Walker DSO, who was churchwarden for 24 years until he died in 1932, and a beautiful brass with a relief of St George in memory of two naval officers killed in the first months of the war.

One more memorial there is to see, perhaps most fascinating of all; it is a brass inscription on the chancel wall to Sir Edward Zouch, who gave the western gallery to the church and is said to have been buried here by night because he was an unpopular figure in the village.

SURREY

He was one of the "chief and master fools" who assisted James the First in his court pastimes, and to him the king gave all that was left of the ancient royal palace of Woking. In exchange Sir Edward agreed to give the king £100 in gold and fish for dinner on St James's day, and to "wind a call" in Woking Forest on Coronation Day. The royal palace stood where Woking Park Farm now stands by the Wey, and we can still see among the farm buildings a gateway 500 years old, a derelict barn, and traces of the moat and palace foundations. But it was once a great pile of buildings with two chapels, and the home of several kings and queens. Henry the Seventh's mother lived and may have died here; Wolsey was here with Henry the Eighth when the letter came from Rome to say he had been made a Cardinal; Edward the Sixth was here in 1550; and Elizabeth came often.

It is likely that Sir Edward Zouch found the palace in a bad state when he received it from King James, so he pulled it down and built himself a new house half a mile away at Hoe Place. Some of the stable buildings of this house, with their ornamental brickwork, are still here, standing close to the later house built by his grandson James Zouch, with decorations by Verrio and Kneller.

Here we found the lovely garden at Pyle Hill where the iris blooms as if it were in paradise, for it was the home of Mrs W. R. Dykes, who might almost be called the mother of the Iris, so much did she love this flower. Her husband was a master at Charterhouse School and an outstanding naturalist. At a time when the iris was little appreciated he devoted himself to growing it, and produced some very beautiful hybrid varieties. He was made secretary of the Royal Horticultural Society, but his tenure of office was all too short, and he perished in an accident. Mrs Dykes devoted herself to the flowers her husband had so loved. A good deal of his work was unfinished, and she completed it. The hybrid varieties he had made reached maturity and perfection under her care at Pyle Hill.

A mile or two from Woking is the burial ground of Brookwood, which has been called a Great Camp of the Dead. It is the biggest cemetery in the country, laid out last century in 500 acres of sandy land, carpeted with heather and planted with flower beds, shrubs, and rhododendrons, a true Garden of Sleep. Some of the graves have been arranged in sections, for certain London parishes or communities such as bakers, foresters, actors, Chelsea pensioners, and so on, and a corner was set aside for Parsees, far from their Eastern Towers of Silence. Out of this great burial-place sprang the founding of the Cremation Society and the building of the first British crematorium; and here, in a charming Garden of Remembrance, the ashes of many famous men and women have been laid to rest.

The Great Camp of the Dead

THE most beautiful and in some ways the strangest burial-ground in England is Brookwood cemetery. A private railway station in London is the gate to 500 acres of Surrey, with the pine trees and the heather and the grassy knolls as they always were, save that here and there flowers and shrubs have been planted among them, and here and there a group of stones marks a last resting-place.

Nations and faiths and friends, each group in its own camp, lie together on this stage of their march to eternity. For the last half-century there has been a grave here for Italian, Parsee, Londoner, or Greek, each buried with the funeral rites of his faith. Many societies and London parishes have their allotted place. Behind one clump of trees is the Actors Acre; another screens the graves of the Foresters or the London Bakers. When the last bugle sounds for a Chelsea pensioner he joins the rest of the old campaigners here; and here is another batch of soldiers, young fellows who came from America to help in the war and to stay forever on our side of the Atlantic. The last of them joined his countrymen in a corner of the American Military Cemetery only a short time before we passed this way, brought from a stranger's grave in the island of Coll, off north-west Scotland, an unknown American soldier from a torpedoed ship, cast up four days after the Armistice, but only in 1934 brought to this final resting-place.

In this American corner of Brookwood stands an impressive Grecian chapel dedicated to the memory of the 540 United States soldiers and sailors who died in England during the war. They lie, as was said at the dedication in 1937, in the sacred soil of Britain, from which their ancestors sprang. The chapel is simply built in white stone, with a front supported on four pillars, and was the last of a series of eight war chapels dedicated by the American Battle Monuments Commission. It is the only one in England, the others being in France and Belgium.

Many are here who died as far from home, yet at the foot of these pine trees they were laid among their kind with all the rites of their faith, and for a moment the sand of Surrey became desert and the pine trees their palms. The Moslems, who have their own mosque at Woking, have also their separate burial-ground, but here is the Parsee resting-place, and not long after the American soldier was brought here there was a glow of flames from the funeral pyre of a Nepalese princess.

This strangest of all funerals ever seen in England took place, not in the Camp of the Dead, but in the grounds of the crematorium close by. It was here, to a house close by the crematorium, that Princess Shumshere Jung, the wife of the Nepalese Minister, was brought to die, that her body, on its journey from the deathbed to the funeral pyre, might have no contact with impurity—that is, with any person or any vehicle that was not Hindu. Four Hindus of highest caste carried her body to the grounds of the crematorium, and village children scrambled for the coins they threw as symbols that the princess had passed beyond the need of worldly things.

Round the pyre of fragrant woods the Brahmin priest walked seven times, chanting prayers, holding aloft his torch of sandalwood. Never has England seen the like of the fire he lit that day, and four hours later the ashes of the young princess (she was only 39) were gathered for their last journey to the waters of the sacred Ganges.

WOLDINGHAM. Its little church stands with an old yew and a fine ash in a churchyard that was beautiful with flowers when we called. No one knows its age, for it has been much restored, but it has the distinction of being the smallest ancient church in Surrey, and rivals Tatsfield for being the highest. Both are nearly 800 feet up.

From the high ground near Woldingham we see as far as the Chilterns, and from the edge of the chalk pits there is a magnificent view over Oxted and the Weald.

Little Elizabeth

WONERSH. Its winding street is full of old houses, many of them old enough to remember the days when Wonersh was a centre of Surrey's cloth industry. In them is a surprising wealth of 16th century work, with some much earlier. The Mill House, still preserving its great charm in a glorious setting, is probably from the

15th century, and has fine timber work, with a Tudor brick fireplace. The house, a mile from the village, is not seen from the road. What is seen by all who come is one of the most attractive bus shelters we remember anywhere. It is at the village centre, and above its coned and tiled roof is the signpost showing the road to Guildford.

Once hidden behind a high wall but now revealed to the road, the church stands among fine lawns. It is an unusual mixture of the centuries. The tower is Norman at the bottom and 18th century at the top, and stands among the oldest parts of the church. Joining it are a nave wall, probably Saxon, and a 14th century chapel with an odd little crypt with some tiles 600 years old. The chancel arch is 13th century. Most of the rest was built up again in 1793, after a fire, and the general impression of the interior is 18th century.

There is a nameless table tomb 500 years old, a fine old Flemish candelabra, a plain 15th century screen and a modern one with 11 carved figures, three old chests, and an Elizabethan chalice. The font has a ring of carving believed to be Saxon. On the chancel floor are 15th century brasses of the Elyots, Thomas and his wife, and Henry and his wife and 23 children. Within the altar rails a pathetic brass tablet tells of a baby born here while Drake was sailing round the world. She was little Elizabeth Bosseville, who lived to be "27 days old," reminding us of a little child of the same name in Kent whose epitaph tells us that she died so young that she was like a jewel taken out of a box, shown to the world, and put up again.

Much of the modern glass is good, especially the window showing Our Lord with our first martyr and our patron saint, St Alban and St George. The east window has 27 figures of Jesus and the saints, as well as many little angels; it is in memory of Edward Kennard and his wife, who lived at Great Tangley Manor, one of the finest Elizabethan houses in Surrey, said to go back to the days of King John. It stands among the trees not far from the village, and is a noble picture with its carved timbers and overhanging storeys. The moat is still wet, and the beautiful gardens have a fine yew hedge which takes the gardeners a month to cut.

A Great Feast

WOODMANSTERNE. The creeping hand of the builder is about it, but never, we hope, to threaten the superb cedars by the lychgate. Beneath them we pass to see a few old things still left in the rebuilt church.

They are chiefly in the vestry, a little 13th century window with Paul in 16th century Flemish glass, a Jacobean table and two chairs, and a Jacobean corner cupboard carved with Samson and the broken temple pillars. Two more Jacobean chairs are in the chancel with a 14th century piscina. The almsbox and font cover are 18th century, and both have carved faces.

There are several memorials to the old Surrey family of the Lamberts, including an inscription telling us they were being buried at Woodmansterne 600 years ago. With one of them Constable often came to stay, and painted his portrait. In another house Dickens spent much time when its tenant was his publisher, Edward Chapman.

Everyone who has heard of horse-racing knows the names of a great house in Woodmansterne and the man who was living in it two and a half centuries ago. It is The Oaks, and its owner was the 12th Earl of Derby who founded the two famous races at Epsom and called them after himself and his house. The densely wooded grounds border the road, and the great 18th century mansion, like a castle, can be seen through the trees; part of its grounds are public.

It was here in the summer of 1774 that Lord Derby gave a celebrated feast in honour of his son's marriage with Lady Betty Hamilton. This is what Horace Walpole wrote about it in a letter:

This month Lord Stanley marries Lady Betty Hamilton. He gives her a most splendid entertainment tomorrow at his villa in Surrey. It will cost £5000. Everybody is to go in masquerade, but not in mask. He has bought all the orange trees round London, and the haycocks I suppose are to be made of straw-coloured satin!

For this scene of costly splendour General John Burgoyne wrote a masque called The Maid of The Oaks, produced by David Garrick.

Hero of the War

WORCESTER PARK. Only its name is old, coming from a park formed by Henry the Eighth at the same time as Nonsuch, and now it is a populous suburb with a busy railway station, a busy high street on a hill (with kinema complete) and thousands of new houses reaching out to join hands with their new neighbours of Motspur Park and Stoneleigh.

At the top of a pleasant tree-fringed road is a church of brick and flint with tiny spire; it is Cuddington Parish church, consecrated in 1895 by the Bishop of Winchester. Inside it is just a village church and has a sculptured marble reredos of Christ and the Little Children. On a wall is a tablet with the never-to-be-forgotten names, among them that of Frank Wearne, who won the VC during the Great War for leading his men gallantly during a raid on enemy trenches, encouraging them although severely hurt, and refusing to leave them until he was carried away mortally wounded.

A Fine Array of Colour

WORPLESDON. Set back from the road is its tower, looking anything but 500 years old and standing in a churchyard with glimpses of wide landscapes through the trees. Except for the 14th century chancel, the church is mostly 15th century, and we enter it under the tower, passing through a doorway with Tudor roses in the spandrels. Near the high tower arch is cut an ancient inscription to say that "Richard Exford made xiv fote of yis touor," leaving us to wonder what village comedy or tragedy made him leave off where he did. The timber porch was put up a year or two after the Spanish Armada.

The ornamental font and the carved and inlaid pulpit are 18th century. They are said to have come from Eton College, and several tablets on these walls testify to the connection between rectors of Worplesdon and the school. One 18th century rector was Dr John Burton, a classical scholar who wrote not only tracts and text-books but also a description of the Epsom Races in Greek. A later rector was William Roberts, who came to Worplesdon at the beginning of last century and helped to restore to these windows some of their old glass.

What is left is a fine array of colour, painted by craftsmen in every century from the 13th to the 17th; and finer still it must have been before any of the windows went to ruin. In the tracery lights of the east window are 14th century roses on a background of black and white oak leaves. In the south aisle windows are shields with fleur-de-lys and lions, edgings made up of fragments, the arms of Henry the Eighth and Anne Boleyn, and the shield of Robert Bennet, who was Bishop of Hereford in Stuart times. In the north aisle is the best

Witley   The Ancient Church

Woking   Mohammedan Mosque

Stoke D'Abernon — Church by the Mole

Wotton — Where John Evelyn Sleeps

glass of all. One of its windows has two figures, nearly complete, against rich red backgrounds and under yellow canopies, St Etheldreda in green and St Cecilia in a yellow gown holding a book. Another has a 13th century bishop's head, a 16th century crown, and a little 15th century monk kneeling on a black and white floor. He is wearing a blue robe, a red cloak, and a brown hood, and his upturned, earnest face is beautifully drawn.

Worplesdon allows us to see the rich altar plate that is one of its finest possessions. It is beautifully wrought.

John Evelyn's Home

WOTTON. We come to the lovely home of John Evelyn, thinking only of him and his diary and the beauty he helped to make in England. Here he was born, here he spent the evening of his life, and here he lies with his family who went before him.

There is little in Wotton save his house and God's house, and many a car passes without seeing either. Those who look among the trees see a church peeping through across a little valley, in a setting hard to beat.

We come to it down a path and along an avenue of towering chestnuts, and it brings us to a halt with one of the most fascinating doorways we have seen. Fashioned 700 years ago, it is carved with eight little heads which have puzzled the experts, believed to be of people living at the time when King John was quarrelling with the Pope over the election of Stephen Langton as Archbishop of Canterbury. The idea fits them well, and, if it is true, the eight heads (beginning with the lowest on the left) are the papal legate Cardinal Pandulf, a modern copy of the original head; a peasant with a round-brimmed hat; Queen Isabella with her crown and wimple; a layman, probably lord of the manor; a priest, probably rector of Wotton; King John, with hair loose to his shoulders; Pope Innocent, with a tiara like a dunce's hat; and Stephen Langton. They are all the beautiful work of some old worker in stone, and they take our minds back to one of the darkest hours in English history.

This doorway is set in a wall of the tower, which is believed to be Saxon at the foot, though it opens into the nave with a Norman arch. Over the porch, within walls already 600 years old in his day, John Evelyn learned his lessons as a boy of four; and through a little 13th century window, with the Madonna in beautiful modern glass, the light falls on the place where he sat. Two of the bells up above are older than the Reformation; the third was new in Evelyn's day.

The chancel and the chapel beside it are 13th century, and it is in the locked chapel that the Evelyn monuments are kept. We look at them through the bars of a simple screen of 1632.

There are three generations: George Evelyn, his son Richard, and his grandson the great John. George Evelyn kneels with a wife each side and one of the longest processions of children we have seen. There are 20 of them, as well as four pathetic babes who scarcely lived. The two eldest girls are reading, and the two youngest boys are looking impish as they kneel at prayer. Richard Evelyn kneels facing his wife, with five children below and an angel drawing back the curtain on each side. He died in 1640, and she, John Evelyn's mother, was buried "at night, but with no mean ceremony." The middle one of the three sons is John, and at the top of the monument is a rare little carved Madonna, one of the very few that escaped destruction in Cromwell's time.

But these monuments are beautifully sculptured, in striking contrast to the simple raised tomb covering John Evelyn himself. We cannot see to read his inscription, but it includes these words:

Living in an age of extraordinary events and revolutions, he learnt, as himself asserted, this truth, which, pursuant to his intention is here declared: that all is vanity which is not honest, and that there is no solid wisdom but in real piety.

He asked to be laid among the laurels he had planted in his own garden, or, if not there, in this chapel; he begged them not to lay him in the red brick mortuary newly added to the church in his day.

A step away, under a tomb like his, lies Mary Evelyn, the wife he married when she was a girl of 12; and up on the wall is a bust of his sister Eliza, her dead babe in its cot.

Also in the Evelyn chapel is a 16th century font, with a very old painted cover on which a quaint bird stands. It is possibly the font used for John's baptism in 1620 by Parson Hyham, who comes into the diary as "a plain preacher but an innocent and honest man." A later rector Dr Bohun, whose tablet is in the chancel, has gone down to immortality as "a learned person, and excellent preacher." He may have preached the last sermon John Evelyn heard at Wotton.

Among the later memorials the most beautiful and interesting is the marble urn in the churchyard, carved with two fat-cheeked cherubs. It marks the grave of John Evelyn's nephew William Glanville, who left £30 a year for five poor boys of Wotton to be apprenticed to a trade. Every February the boys competing have to recite passages from the Bible and the Prayer Book, each boy resting a hand on the tomb.

Out of sight in the little valley of the Tillingbourne lies Wotton House. We have walked in its gardens in August, among lovely lawns, quaint grottoes, beautiful flowers, and the scent of roses; and have looked round at the wider park with its magnificent living witnesses to the love John Evelyn had for trees. Some of the garden he must have planned, and some of the house is still as he knew it, but all has belonged to his family ever since the time of old George Evelyn, who bought it.

Among the many treasures of Wotton House are the Prayer Book used by Charles Stuart on the scaffold, a lock of his hair, and a Bible in which John Evelyn has written his own marginal comments.

Evelyn and His Diary

JOHN EVELYN, lover of peace and good works, born at Wotton in 1620, shared a family fortune based on gunpowder, the manufacture of which was introduced into England by his grandfather.

His education, begun in the church porch and continued at Lewes and Oxford, led him to the Bar, but he never practised. During the Civil War he was for three days a Royalist soldier, and then, sending his black charger as a gift to Charles Stuart, he withdrew to the Continent, to travel and study, and to marry a bride of 12, daughter of an English ambassador. At home he had seen Strafford tried and executed; in exile he found a Europe still partly in the Dark Ages, with lepers begging in Dutch towns and men exposed for sale as slaves at Leghorn.

Returning to England, he settled at Deptford, where he let his home to Peter the Great, who ruined his flowerbeds and charged through his great holly hedges with a wheelbarrow. Not until he was 79 did he succeed his brother here, to continue as owner the improvements and plantings he had begun as a visitor.

From the Restoration he was high in favour, regularly in attendance, but shocked by the open vice at Court. He filled many public offices, including that of commissioner for the sick and wounded in the Dutch wars, of which he was writing a history when Charles, discovering that he was telling the truth, forbade him to proceed. He obtained the Arundel Marbles for Oxford University and the Arundel Library for the Royal Society. Author of works on architecture, painting, morals, education, agriculture, gardening, and commerce, he was the one man whom all scholars from the Continent made a point of visiting. He thought his Sylva, a Discourse on Forest Trees, was his greatest achievement, and in dedicating it to Charles the Second he reminded the king that millions of trees had been planted in the country as the result of this work. Of his Diary he apparently thought little, yet his immortality rests upon it. Begun in 1640, it was continued until within a month of his death in 1706. One of the most precious records of its kind in the world, it was lost for a century and found here in an old basket.

Like the Diary of Pepys (who refers to Evelyn several times and speaks of him as an extraordinary ingenious and knowing person), Evelyn's Diary was apparently never meant for publication. It extends over the long period from before the Commonwealth into the reign of Queen Anne, a run of 66 years. One of the most interesting things of which it tells us is his discovery of Grinling Gibbons, "that incomparable young man" whom he met with in an obscure spot in a poor solitary thatched house in a field. The saddest thing of which he tells is the death of his little son, after which he adds, "here ends the joy of my life and for which I go ever mourning to the grave." The Diary lay in its manuscript form for a hundred years after Evelyn's death, and a selection was first published soon after Waterloo.

SURREY TOWNS AND VILLAGES

In this key to our map of Surrey are all the towns and villages treated in this book. If a place is not on the map by name, its square is given here so that the way to it is easily found, each square being five miles. One or two hamlets are in the book with their neighbouring villages; for these see Index.

Abinger	E5	Dorking	E4	Leatherhead	E3	Shamley	
Abinger Hammer	E4	Dunsfold	D6	Leigh	F4	Green	D5
Addington	H2	Eashing	C5	Leith Hill	E5	Shere	D4
Addlestone	D2	East Clandon	D4	Limpsfield	H4	Shirley	H2
Albury	D4	East Horsley	E4	Lingfield	H5	Stoke	C4
Alfold	D6	East Molesey	E2	Little Bookham	E4	Stoke D'Abernon	E3
Ash	B4	Effingham	E4	Longcross	C2	Surbiton	F2
Ashtead	F3	Egham	D1	Long Ditton	E2	Sutton	G2
		Elstead	B5	Lower Kingswood	F4	Tandridge	H4
Bagshot	B2	Epsom	F3			Tatsfield	H3
Banstead	G3	Esher	E2	Malden	F2	Thames Ditton	E2
Barnes	F1	Ewell	F3	Merrow	D4	Thorpe	D2
Beddington	G2	Ewhurst	E5	Merstham	G4	Thursley	B5
Betchworth	F4			Merton	G2	Tilford	B5
Bisley	C3	Farleigh	H3	Mickleham	F4	Titsey	H3
Blechingley	G4	Farncombe	C5	Mitcham	G2	Tongham	B4
Box Hill	F4	Farnham	B4	Morden	F2		
Bramley	D5	Felbridge	H5	Mortlake	F1	Virginia Water	C2
Brockham Green	F4	Fetcham	E3				
Buckland	F4	Frensham	B5	Newdigate	F5	Wallington	G2
Burstow	G5	Friday Street	E5	Normandy	C4	Walton-on-Thames	E2
Busbridge	C5	Frimley	B3	Nutfield	G4	Walton-on-the-Hill	F3
Byfleet	D3	Gatton	G4			Wanborough	C4
		Godalming	C5	Oakwood	E6	Warlingham	H3
Camberley	B3	Godstone	H4	Ockham	D3	Waverley	B5
Capel	F5	Great Bookham	E4	Ockley	E5	West Clandon	D4
Carshalton	G2	Guildford	C4	Outwood	G5	Westcott	E4
Caterham	H3			Oxted	H4	West Horsley	D4
Chaldon	G3	Ham	F1			West Molesey	E2
Charlwood	F5	Hambledon	C5	Peper Harow	C5	Weybridge	D2
Cheam	F2	Hascombe	C5	Petersham	F1	Whiteley	E3
Chelsham	H3	Haslemere	B6	Pirbright	C3	Wimbledon	F1
Chertsey	D2	Headley	F3	Purley	G3	Windlesham	C2
Chessington	F2	Hersham	E2	Puttenham	C4	Wisley	D3
Chiddingfold	C6	Hindhead	B6	Pyrford	D3	Witley	C5
Chilworth	D4	Holmbury St Mary	E5	Ranmore	E4	Woking	D3
Chipstead	G3	Holmwood	F5	Redhill	G4	Woldingham	H3
Chobham	C3	Hook	F2	Reigate	G4	Wonersh	D5
Cobham	E3	Horley	G5	Richmond	F1	Woodmansterne	G3
Coldharbour	E5	Horne	H5	Ripley	D3	Worcester Pk	F2
Compton	C4	Horsell	C3			Worplesdon	C4
Copthorne	G5			Sanderstead	H3	Wotton	E4
Coulsdon	G3	Kew	F1	Seale	B4		
Cranleigh	D5	Kingston	F2	Send	D3		
Crowhurst	H4			Shalford	C4		
Croydon	G2						

341

INDEX

This index includes all notable subjects and people likely to be sought for. The special index of pictures is at the beginning of the volume.

Abbot, Archbishop, 147
Abbot's Hospital, 147
Abinger, 11
Abinger Hammer, 12
Aclea, Battle of, 235
Adam of Usk, 215
Adcock, St John, 265
Addington, 12
Addlestone, 14
Aiton, William, 177
Albany, Duke of, 116
Albury, 15
Aldershot, 4
Alfold, 18
Allnutt, Sidney (poem), 67
Anchorite's cells, 76, 195
Andrewes, Lancelot, 56
Anningsley, 15
Anstiebury Camp, 75
Argyll, Duke of, 161
Arnold, Matthew, 71
Arundel, Thomas, 92
Asgill House, 260
Ash, 19
Ashcombe, Lord, 251
Ashtead, 20
Aubertin, Peter, 68
Austen, Jane, 146

Baden-Powell, Major Baden, 199, 274
Bagshot, 21
Banks, Sir Edwd., 69, 215
Banks, Sir Joseph, 180
Banstead, 22
Barclay, Florence, 200
Barn Church, 267
Barnard, Sir John, 227
Barnes, 23
Barrow Hills, 208
Bate, George, 190
Bauer, Francis, 177
Baynards Park, 84, 120
Beale, Robert, 24
Beddington, 25
Bells, notable :
  Bisley, 31

Chaldon, 51
Chertsey, 59, 61
Chiddingfold, 64
East Clandon, 99
Fetcham, 130
Guildford, 154
Headley, 168
Merstham, 214
Wotton, 338
Bench-ends, notable :
  Beddington, 26
  Dunsfold, 96
  Gatton, 136
  Lingfield, 206
  Reigate, 255
  Woking, 330
Benson, Archbishop, 13
Bent, VC, Philip, 170
Berkeley, Cranfield, 313
Berners, Juliana, 312
Betchworth, 30
Betchworth Park, 37
Bethune, Colonel, 196
Bisley, 31
Blechingley, 32
Bogle, VC, Andrew, 102
Boisragon, 211
Boleyn, Anne, 49
Borrodaile, Edward, 162
Boscawen, Admiral, 99
Botanic Gardens, 179
Boucher, Jonathan, 112
Bourchier, Archbishop, 93
Bourne, 129
Bowthe, John, 100
Box Hill, 31
Braddon, Miss, 264
Bradshaw, John, 303
Brady, Nicholas, 264
Bramley, 36
Brasses, notable :
  Addington, 13
  Albury, 16
  Beddington, 26
  Blechingley, 33
  Byfleet, 43

Carshalton, 48
Charlwood, 55
Cheam, 57
Cobham, 73
Cranleigh, 83
Crowhurst, 85
Croydon, 89
East Horsley, 100
Farnham, 128
Great Bookham, 145
Guildford, 150, 151
Horley, 175
Horsell, 175
Kingston, 190
Leigh, 197
Lingfield, 205
Long Ditton, 208
Merstham, 214
Oakwood, 232
Ockham, 234
Oxted, 238
Peper Harrow, 240
Puttenham, 249
Sanderstead, 271
Shere, 278
Stoke D'Abernon, 286
Thames Ditton, 294
Thorpe, 295
Walton-on-Thames, 302
Weybridge, 315
Wonersh, 334
Bray family, 279
Bridges, notable :
  Chertsey, 58
  Clattern, 193
  Eashing, 97
  Elstead, 109
  Kingston, 193
  Leatherhead, 194
  Richmond, 262
  Tilford, 297
  Unstead, 36
Brock, Commander, 56
Brockham Green, 37
Brodie, Sir Benjamin, 31
Brodrick, Admiral, 240

343

INDEX

Brookwood Cemetery, 246, 331
Brunel, Isambard, 31
Buckland, 38
Bunyan, John, 275
Burford Bridge, 34
Burhill, 303
Burney, Fanny, 146, 222, 256
Burstow, 38
Burton, Dr John, 336
Burton, Sir Rich., 227, 228
Busbridge, 40
Byfleet, 42

Cabrera, Ramon, 300
Caesar, Sir Julius, 225
Camberley, 45
Canterbury, Viscount, 14
Capel, 47
Carew family, 25
Carillon, 70
Carlyle, Thomas, 17
Carré, Jean, 19
Carroll, Lewis, 156
Carshalton, 47
Catacombs, 103
Caterham, 49
Cates, VC, George, 322
Catholic Apostolic Church, 17
Cawarden, Thomas, 33
Cedar House, 73
Cedars, notable, 72, 79
Chadwick, Sir Edwin, 229
Chaldon, 50
Chantrey sculpture, 112, 190, 302, 315
Charles the First, 124
Charlotte, Princess, 114
Charlotte, Queen, 180
Charlwood, 55
Charterhouse School, 139
Chatley Heath, 73
Cheam, 56
Chelsham, 58
Cherkley Court, 196
Chertsey, 58
Chesney, Sir George, 104
Chessington, 62
Chesterfield, Lord, 203
Chests, notable:
  Albury, 16
  Betchworth, 30
  Burstow, 39
  Chobham, 69

Elstead, 110
Epsom, 111
Godalming, 138
Leatherhead, 195
Mortlake, 226
Newdigate, 230
Oxted, 239
Send, 273
Shere, 278
Stoke D'Abernon, 288
Thames Ditton, 294
West Horsley, 311
Wisley, 326
Wonersh, 334
Chiddingfold, 63
Chilworth, 65
Chipstead, 67
Chobham, 69
Christmaspie, 231
Church, Sir Arthur, 181
Clandon Park, 212
Claremont, 114
Clive, Lord, 114
Clocks, notable:
  Abinger Hammer, 12
  Compton, 77
  Esher, 115
  Guildford, 154
Clutton-Brock, Arthur, 141
Cobbett, William:
  at Albury, 15
  at Farnham, 124, 128
  at Godstone, 142
  at Hindhead, 170
  at Kew, 186
  at Normandy, 231
Cobham, 70
Cobham family, 204
Cock Crow Hill, 324
Coldharbour, 74
Cole, Frank, 221
Coleridge-Taylor S., 94
Colley, Sir George, 283
Colley Hill, 256
Collins, Mortimer, 242
Colwall, Daniel, 148
Compton, 75
Coneyhurst Hill, 120
Connaught, Duke of, 21
Cook, Captain, 217
Copley, John, 90
Copthorne, 81
Corbet, Richard, 119
Cornwallis family, 100
Cotmandene, 94

Cotton, Sir Arthur, 96
Coulsdon, 82
Courtenay, Colonel, 100
Cowley, Abraham, 24, 60
Cowper, Theodora, 242
Cranleigh, 82
Cranmer, 92, 307
Crisp, Samuel, 62
Croham Hurst, 87
Croker, John Wilson, 313
Crouch Oak, 14
Crowhurst, 84
Croydon, 3, 86
Cubitt, Thomas, 251
Cubitt, VC, William, 133
Cunliffe, Lord, 68
Curfew poem, 61
Cutmill Common, 110

D'Arblay, General, 146, 222
Darell, Sir Lionel, 266
Dartnell Park, 42
Day, Thomas, 15
Dee, John, 227, 228
Delius, Frederick, 202
Denham, John, 104, 126
Derby, The, 113
Devil's Jumps, 131
Devil's Punch Bowl, 169
Dickens, Charles, 241
Disraeli, 95
Dodd, John, 178
Dodgson, Charles, 156
Dolmetsch, Arnold, 166
Donne, John, 225, 251
Doors, notable:
  Albury, 16
  Alfold, 18
  Crowhurst, 85
  Dunsfold, 97
  Merstham, 214
  Merton, 216
  Oxted, 238
  Woking, 330
Doorways, notable:
  Ash, 20
  Cobham, 72
  Compton, 76
  Merstham, 214
  Mortlake, 226
  Pyrford, 250
  Stoke d'Abernon, 286
  Wotton, 337
Dorking, 94
Doughty House, 265

INDEX

Drake, Sir Richard, 116
Druids Grove, 223
Drummond, Henry, 17
Duck, Stephen, 43
Duckett, William, 116
Dudley, Robert, 180, 228
Dunsfold, 96
Durdans, 110
Dwyer, VC, Edward, 191
Dykes, Mrs W. R., 331

Eashing, 97
East Clandon, 99
East Horsley, 99
East Molesey, 101
East Sheen Common, 23
Eclipse, racehorse, 211
Edmonstone, George, 102
Edward the Sixth, 9, 63
Effingham, 101
Egham, 102
Egham Hythe, 105
Eliot, George, 164
Elizabeth, Queen :
  at Addlestone, 14
  at Barnes, 24
  at Beddington, 27
  at Croydon, 92
  at Farnham, 126
  at Kew, 180
  at Mitcham, 225
  at Richmond, 259
  at Sanderstead, 271
  at Sutton Place, 273
Elles, Sir Edmond, 213
Elphinstone, Lord, 201
Elphinstone, Howard, 22
Elstead, 109
Ember Farm, 294
Epsom, 110
Esher, 114
Esher, Lord, 117
Essex, Earl of, 24, 259
Evelyn family, 338
Evelyn, John :
  at Albury, 15
  at Ashtead, 21
  at Barnes, 24
  at Felbridge, 130
  at Ham House, 161
  at Mickleham, 221
  at Oakwood, 232
  at Wotton, 337
Evelyn, Sir John, 142, 208
Evelyn, Richard, 111

Ewell, 118
Ewhurst, 120

Falklands, Battle of, 133
Farley, 120
Farncombe, 121
Farnham, 6, 122
Felbridge, 130
Ferguson's Gang, 276
Fetcham, 130
Fielding, Henry, 24
Fielding, Sir John, 25
Firmin, Thomas, 143
Fitzwilliam, Lord, 264
Flagstaff, Kew, 182
Flamsteed, John, 39
Flaxman sculpture, 59, 116, 263
Fonts, notable :
  Alfold, 19
  Ash, 20
  Beddington, 26
  Byfleet, 43
  Chobham, 69
  Gatton, 136
  Great Bookham, 146
  Lingfield, 206
  Lower Kingswood, 209
  Mortlake, 227
  Petersham, 243
  Redhill, 252
  Reigate, 254
  Thursley, 296
  Tongham, 299
  Walton-on-the-Hill, 305
  Warlingham, 307
  Wonersh, 334
Foster, Birket, 328
Foster, Sir Robert, 103
Fox, Charles James, 59
Foxwarren, 44
Frampton, Reginald, 251
Francis, Sir Philip, 227
Freeman, John, 296
Frensham, 131
Freshfield, Edwin, 209
Friday Street, 132
Frimley, 132
Frith, John, 92
Furse, Charles W., 133

Garth, Samuel, 226
Garvice, Charles, 265
Gatton, 135

Gay, John, 241
George the Third, 180
Gilmour, Douglas, 222
Glass, old :
  Alfold, 19
  Ashtead, 21
  Blechingley, 33
  Buckland, 38
  Byfleet, 43
  Charlwood, 55
  Chiddingfold, 63, 64
  Chipstead, 68
  Compton, 78
  Cranleigh, 83
  Crowhurst, 85
  Dunsfold, 97
  Effingham, 102
  Elstead, 110
  Gatton, 136
  Godalming, 138
  Guildford, 148
  Haslemere, 165
  Lingfield, 206
  Little Bookham, 207
  Merstham, 214
  Mickleham, 221
  Morden, 226
  Newdigate, 230
  Nutfield, 232
  Oakwood, 232
  Ockham, 233
  Oxted, 239
  Pyrford, 250
  Shere, 278
  Stoke D'Abernon, 288
  Thorpe, 295
  Walton-on-Thames, 301
  Walton-on-the-Hill, 305
  Warlingham, 306
  West Clandon, 310
  West Horsley, 311
  Wimbledon, 321
  Witley, 328
  Woking, 330
  Woodmansterne, 335
  Worplesdon, 336
Glassmaking, 64
Glory Woods, 94
Godalming, 137
Godstone, 142
Godwin-Austen, Colonel, 275
Goodenough, Commodore, 283

345

INDEX

Gordon Boys Home, 31
Gossip's bridle, 301
Gothic House, 262
Goulburn, Henry, 37
Great Bookham, 144
Great Fosters, 105
Great Tangley Manor, 334
Gresham family, 298
Grieve, Mackenzie, 174
Grote, George, 239
Grindal, Edmond, 90
Guildford, 2, 146
Gumbrell, Daniel, 253

Hall, Anna, 15
Hall, Samuel, 15
Hallam, Anne, 225
Hallowell-Carew, Benjamin, 28
Ham, 160
Hambledon, 163
Hamilton, Lady, 34, 216
Hampton, VC, Harry, 265
Handel, 177, 195
Hansard, Thomas, 192
Harestone Valley, 49
Harrison, VC, Arthur, 322
Harte, Bret, 46, 133, 134
Hascombe, 163
Haslemere, 164
Hawker, Harry, 173
Hawtrey, Sir Charles, 265
Head, Sir Francis, 272
Headley, 168
Heath, Nicholas, 70
Heidegger, John, 24
Henley Park, 19
Heriot, Blanche, 61
Hersham, 168
Hervey, Sir Felton, 104
Heseltine, Philip, 141
Highwayman story, 7
Hill, Octavia, 163, 224
Hindhead, 1, 169
Hog's Back, 2, 122
Holland, Robert, 19
Holloway, Thomas, 105
Holloway College, 105
Holly Hedge, 22
Holmbury Hill, 1, 170
Holmbury St Mary, 170
Holmwood, 171
Hood, Thomas, 161
Hook, 173
Hooker, Joseph, 177, 184
Hooker, Sir William, 177

Hoole, John, 11, 95
Hopkins, John, 322
Hopsonn, Thomas, 316
Horley, 174
Horne, 175
Horsell, 175
Horticultural Society, 326
Hotham, Sir John, 59
Howard of Effingham, 253–257
Howitt, William, 117
Howley, Archbishop, 13
Howson, Major, 266
Hubert de Burgh, 22, 216
Hull, Richard, 198
Hunt, Holman, 118
Hydon Ball, 163

Innes, John, 218
Iron tombstone, 85
Irving, Edward, 17

Jeffreys, Judge, 195, 289
Jekyll, Gertrude, 36, 40, 164
Jekyll, Sir Herbert, 40
Jerrold, Douglas, 24
John, King, 108
Jonson, Ben, 197
Juniper Hall, 222
Juniper Hill, 22
Jupp, Henry, 94

Kean, Edmund, 263
Keats, John, 34
Kemble, Maria, 15
Kennard, Harriet, 200
Kew, 176
Kew Observatory, 262
King family, 234
King's House, The, 303
Kingston-on-Thames, 3, 186

Lambert, Sir Daniel, 22
Lawrence, Frederick, 237
Leatherhead, 194
Lectern, old brass, 88
Leigh, 196
Leith Hill, 1, 197
Leopold, King, 114, 116
Lewis, Frederick, 133
Lilly, William, 169, 304
Lime Avenue, 37
Limpsfield, 199

Linacre, Thomas, 215
Lingfield, 204
Little Bookham, 206
Longcross, 207
Long Ditton, 208
Longley, Archbishop, 13
Loseley House, 150
Loud is the Vale, 60
Lovekyn's Chapel, 192
Lovelace, Earl, 234
Lowe, James, 119
Lower Kingswood, 208
Ludlam, Mother, 131, 309
Lumley, Lord, 57
Lushington, Stephen, 234
Lynch, Sir Thomas, 115

Macdonald, George, 164
Maginn, William, 302
Magna Carta, 103–107
Malden, 209
Malthus, Thomas, 311
Mammoth tusk, 124
Mangles, VC, Ross, 246
Manners-Sutton, Archbishop, 13
Manning, Owen, 138
Manningham, Gen., 207
Marconi, 260
Marden Park, 143
Markland, Jeremiah, 95
May Games, 193
McAlpine, Sir Robert, 73
McNair, VC, Eric, 141
McNamara, VC, John, 191
Meredith, George, 35, 221
Merrow, 210
Merstham, 213
Merton, 215
Merton, Walter, 209, 220
Meyer, Jeremiah, 177
Mickleham, 220
Milbanke, Ralph, 235
Miles, Walker, 143, 199
Mill, John Stuart, 222
Mill Church, 256
Millais, Sir John, 118
Milles, Jeremiah, 215
Millmead, 36
Milton Court, 95
Mitcham, 223
Mohammedan Mosque, 239
Mole, River, 1, 101, 221
Molesworth, Caroline, 72
Monsell, J. S. B., 104, 151

346

INDEX

Monson, Lord, 136
Moon, Sir Francis, 131
Moor Park, 308
Moore, Arthur, 130
Morden, 225
More Place, 30
Mortlake, 226
Munstead Wood, 42
Murgatroid, Michael, 93
Muybridge, Eadweard, 193

Nagle, Sir Edmund, 101
National Trust, 8
Nelson, Lord, 34, 216
Newark Priory, 250
Newdigate, 230
Newlands Corner, 210
Newton, Gilbert, 323
Nightingales, 237
Nixon, Francis, 218
Nonsuch Palace, 56, 111, 120, 151
Nonsuch Park, 58, 119
Norbury Park, 222
Norman Woodwork :
　Compton, 76
　Farnham, 125
　Merton, 216
　Wisley, 326
　Woking, 330
Normandy, 231
North, Marianne, 181
Northcliffe, Lord, 274
Norwood Farm, 102
Nottingham, Earl of, 257
Nower, The, 94
Nurscombe Farm, 36
Nutfield, 231

Oaks, notable :
　Addlestone, 14
　Cobham, 73
　Dunsfold, 96
　Tilford, 297
Oaks, The, 335
Oakwood, 232
Oatlands Palace, 314
Ockham, 233
Ockley, 235
Oglethorpe, Theophilus, 139
Old Pickhurst, 63
Olpherts, VC, General, 265
Onslow family, 212, 310
Onslow, Arthur, 150, 155, 212, 294

Orange trees, first, 27
Oughtred, William, 18, 276
Outwood, 236
Owen, Sir Richard, 162
Oxted, 237

Pains Hill, 71
Palewell Common, 23
Partridge, John, 227, 228
Peacock, Thomas, 35
Pendhill Court, 32, 142
Peper Harow, 239
Perdita, 104
Perry, James, 322
Petersham, 241
Pewley Hill, 147
Phillips, Augustine, 227
Phillips, John, 121, 139
Pilgrim's Way, 2, 65, 210
Pirbright, 245
Pirbright, Lord, 20
Pitch Hill, 1
Plaistow Street, 206
Plane tree, biggest, 24
Polesden Lacy, 146
Pollen, George, 207
Poppy Factory, 266
Porter family, 115
Pulpits, notable :
　Abinger, 11
　Alfold, 19
　Beddington, 27
　Bisley, 31
　Blechingley, 33
　Compton, 79
　Ewhurst, 120
　Gatton, 136
　Godalming, 138
　Guildford, 149, 151
　Mickleham, 221
　Pyrford, 250
　Reigate, 255
　Richmond, 267
　Stoke D'Abernon, 287
　West Molesey, 313
　Woking, 329, 330
Purley, 248
Puttenham, 249
Pyle Hill, 331
Pyrford, 250

Quare, Daniel, 93
Queen's Regiment, 149

Rack's Close, 154
Raglan, Lord, 145

Raleigh, Sir Walter, 29, 312
Ranelagh, 24
Ranmore, 251
Ranyard, Arthur, 192
Ravis, Thomas, 215
Rawson, Rawson W., 47
Redhill, 252
Reigate, 253
Rennie, George, 171
Richards, Sir George, 131
Richmond, 257
Rifle Brigade, 207
Ripley, 270
Rivers, 1
Robinson, Commodore, 11
Robinson, Mary, 104
Robsart, Amy, 180, 228
Romans in Surrey :
　Abinger Hammer, 12
　Ashtead, 20
　Beddington, 26
　Byfleet, 42
　Camberley, 46
　Cheam, 56
　Chilworth, 66
　Cranleigh, 84
　Dorking, 95
　Ewell, 118
　Holmwood, 172
　Ockley, 235
　Shamley Green, 277
　Stoke D'Abernon, 286
　Titsey, 298
　Walton-on-the-Hill, 304
　Wisley, 324
Roofs, notable :
　Abinger, 11
　Beddington, 25
　Compton, 79
　Croydon, 92
　Farnham, 126
　Godstone, 142
　Horne, 175
　Kingston, 190
　Lingfield, 205
　Merton, 217
　Ockham, 233
　Richmond, 267
　Walton-on-Thames, 301
Rosebery, Lord, 111
Royal Female Orphanage, 25
Rubber romance, 184

INDEX

Runnymede, 102
Ruskin, John, 47, 279
Rutherwyke, Abbot, 58, 103, 144

St George's Hill, 317
St Helier estate, 225
St Martha's church, 65
Sander, Nicholas, 55
Sanderstead, 270
Sandown Park, 114
Saxons in Surrey :
  Albury, 16
  Betchworth, 30
  Busbridge, 40
  Chilworth, 66
  Compton, 75
  Coulsdon, 82
  Croydon, 86
  Eashing, 98
  East Horsley, 99
  Fetcham, 130
  Godalming, 137
  Guildford, 152
  Kingston, 188, 189
  Lingfield, 205
  Ockley, 235
  Shere, 278
  Stoke D'Abernon, 286
  Thursley, 295
  Walton-on-Thames, 301
  Witley, 327
  Wonersh, 334
  Wotton, 337
Scott, Sir Gilbert, 292
Screens, notable :
  Busbridge, 41
  Charlwood, 55
  Chelsham, 58
  Compton, 78
  Farnham, 127
  Gatton, 136
  Hascombe, 164
  Lingfield, 206
  Nutfield, 231
  Ockham, 233
  Send, 273
  West Horsley, 311
  Wonersh, 334
Seale, 272
Selsdon Court, 271
Semaphore stations, 8, 73
Send, 272
Shadwell, Sir Lancelot, 24
Shaftesbury Homes, 117

Shalford, 275
Shamley Green, 277
Sharp, Richard, 222
Shelbeare, VC, Robert, 290
Sheldon, Gilbert, 89
Shellwood Manor, 197
Shere, 277
Sheridan, Richard, 34
Shirley, 279
Shoelands, 250
Shove, Edmund, 136
Sidmouth, Viscount, 227
Silent Pool, 15
Slyfield, 145
Smallfield Place, 39
Smallpiece family, 155
Smith, George, 44
Smith, Isaac, 217
Snowden, Philip, 298
Speed, Samuel, 139
Spence, Joseph, 43, 44
Stag Hill, 146
Stane Street, 135, 172, 277
Stanhope, Eugenia, 203
Stanley, H. M., 245, 247
Star and Garter Home, 266
Starborough Castle, 204
Stevenson, R. L., 34
Stoke, 283
Stoke D'Abernon, 284
Stone of Scone, 188
Strachey, John St Loe, 67
Strachey, Sir John, 273
Strathmore, Earl of, 243
Street, George E., 83, 170
Stuart, Charles, 242, 244
Stuart, Leslie, 265
Sturdee, Admiral, 46, 133
Sullivan, Sir Arthur, 47
Sumner, Archbishop, 13
Surbiton, 289
Sutton, 290
Sutton, Thomas, 140
Sutton Place, 273
Swift and Stella, 262, 308

Tait, Archbishop, 13
Talbot, Gilbert, 126
Tandridge, 291
Tate, Nahum, 264
Tatsfield, 293
Telegraph Hill, 164
Temple, Sir William, 262, 308

Tennyson, Lord, 165
Thames Ditton, 293
Thomson, J. Arthur, 200
Thomson, James, 262, 269
Thorpe, 295
Thunderfield Castle, 175
Thursley, 295
Tighe, Robert, 64
Tilford, 297
Tillingbourne, 275
Titanic tragedy, 121
Titsey, 298
Tongham, 299
Tooke, John, 249
Toplady, Augustus, 128
Totem pole, 44
Towers, notable :
  Albury, 15
  Ash, 20
  Beddington, 26
  Blechingley, 32
  Burstow, 39
  Cobham, 72
  Compton, 76
  Crowhurst, 86
  East Horsley, 99
  Frensham, 131
  Godalming, 137
  Great Bookham, 144
  Guildford, 152
  Horley, 174
  Leatherhead, 195
  Mickleham, 221
  Newdigate, 230
  Oxted, 237
  Tandridge, 292
  Tongham, 299
  West Molesey, 313
Townsend, Isaac, 295
Treloar, William, 279
Trower, Arthur, 253
Tucker, Abraham, 95
Tulip tree, oldest, 117
Tumble Beacon, 22
Trumpeter's Hall, 260
Tyndall, John, 165, 167
Tytings, 65

Unstead Bridge, 36
Unstead Farm, 36

Vancouver, George, 243
Vanderbilt, Alfred, 172
Vaux, Frederick, 169
Victoria Cross, story, 246
View Point, 49

INDEX

Village hospital, first, 83
Virginia Water, 299

Waghorn, Henry, 129
Wall-paintings, notable :
  Albury, 16
  Byfleet, 43
  Chaldon, 51
  Charlwood, 55
  East Clandon, 99
  Godalming, 138
  Pyrford, 250
  Ranmore, 251
  Stoke D'Abernon, 286
  Warlingham, 306
  Witley, 327
Waller, Sir William, 126
Wallington, 300
Walsingham, Francis, 24
Walton, Izaak, 127
Walton-on-Thames, 301
Walton-on-the-Hill, 304
Wanborough, 305
Wardrobe Court, 260
Warlingham, 306
Warlock, Peter, 141
Warton, Joseph, 97
Watermeads, 224
Water Mills, 8
Watts, G. F., 75
Watts Chapel, 80
Watts Memorial Garden, 156
Waverley, 307
Wearne, VC, Frank, 336
Weller, Sam, 94
Wellingtonia trees, 45
Wesley, John, 72, 194, 267

West Clandon, 310
Westcott, 310
Westcroft Park, 70
West Horsley, 311
West Humble, 34, 223
West Molesey, 313
Weston, Richard, 273, 314
Wey, River, 1, 314
Weybridge, 314
Whitaker, Sir Edward, 49
White Lodge, 261
White, Sir Henry, 240
White, Maude Valerie, 274
Whiteley, William, 318
Whiteley Village, 318
Whitgift, John, 89, 93
Whitgift Hospital, 91
Whitgift Schools, 93
Whymper, Josiah, 164
Wickham, Henry, 184
Wiggie, 253
Wilberforce, Bishop, 12, 26, 95
Wilberforce, William, 143, 321
Wilks, William, 279
William of Ockham, 235
Williamson, Francis, 116
Wilson, Dr Edward, 81
Wimbledon, 320
Windlesham, 324
Windmills, 8
Wisley, 324
Wither, George, 126
Witley, 327
Woking, 329
Woldingham, 333

Wonersh, 333
Wood, Richard, 215
Woodlands, 72
Woodlarks, 297
Wolsey, Cardinal, 118
Woodmansterne, 334
Worcester Park, 335
Wormley Hill, 328
Worms, Baron de, 20
Worplesdon, 336
Wotton, 337
Wray Common, 256
Wycliffe, John, 14
Wyke, 20

Yates, Mary Anne, 264
Yates, Richard, 264
Yews, notable :
  Abinger Hammer, 12
  Alfold, 19
  Ashtead, 20
  Barnes, 23
  Charlwood, 55
  Chelsham, 58
  Chipstead, 69
  Crowhurst, 84
  Dunsfold, 97
  Farley, 121
  Hambledon, 163
  Leatherhead, 196
  Little Bookham, 207
  Merrow, 210
  Mickleham, 223
York Town, 46
Young, Edward, 19

Zoffany, Johann, 178
Zouch, Sir Edward, 330

SURREY
IN 5-MILE SQUARES

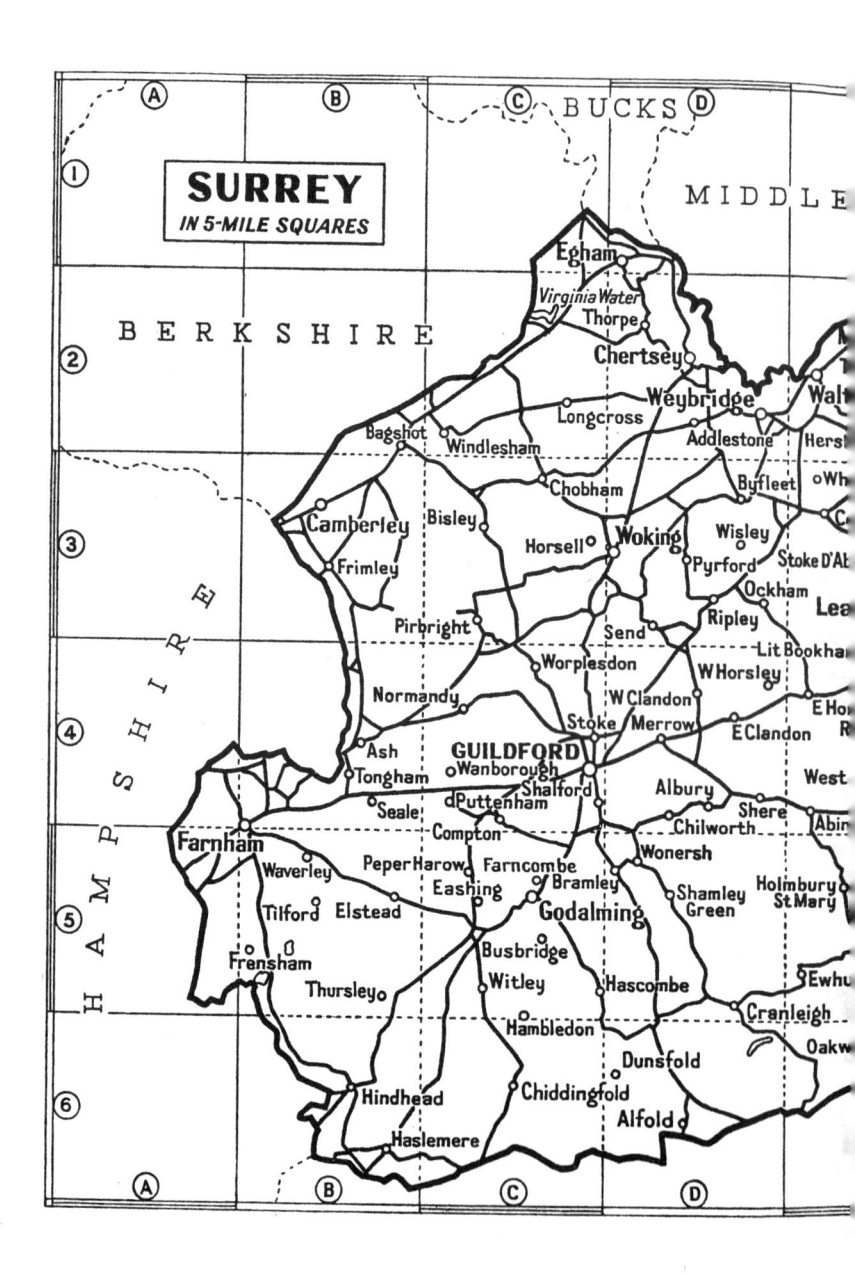